BARRON'S

PRACTICE EXERCISES

for the Test of English as a Foreign Language

TOEFL*

Second Edition

by
Pamela J. Sharpe, Ph.D.
The Ohio State University

BARRON'S

* TOEFL is a registered trademark of Educational Testing Service. Barron's Educational Series, Inc., bears sole responsibility for this book's contents, and is not connected in any way with Educational Testing Service.

Library of Congress Cataloging-in-Publication Data

Sharpe, Pamela J.
   Barron's practice exercises for the TOEFL
test of English as a foreign language.

   I. English language—Textbooks for foreign
speakers.   I. Title.   II. Title: Practice
exercises for the TOEFL test of English as a
foreign language.
PE1128.S524   1989   428.2'4'076   89-7010
ISBN 0-8120-4275-1

All inquiries should be addressed to:
Barron's Educational Series, Inc.
250 Wireless Boulevard
Hauppauge, New York 11788
ISBN No. 0-8120-4275-1

Library of Congress Catalog Card No. 89-7010

PRINTED IN THE UNITED STATES OF AMERICA
456   100   13 12 11 10

Contents

Acknowledgments

I gratefully acknowledge the cooperation of many friends and colleagues: Dr. Bill Leckie, Vice President for Academic Affairs, and Dr. Tom Clapp, Dean of the Division of Continuing Education, The University of Toledo, for their interest in the manuscript and for arranging the release time necessary to the completion of the first edition; Mr. Robert Sharpe, for patiently typing the manuscript from my handwritten notes; Mrs. Lillie Sharpe, for proofreading the manuscript, galleys, and page proofs; Mr. Manuel Barron, President of Barron's Educational Series, Inc., for expressing his confidence in the project by extending the date of completion to coincide with the dates of my sabbatical; Ms. Carolyn Horne, Editor, for skillfully managing the production of the second edition; and my students, past and present, for asking the thoughtful questions that inspired me to write the book.

Planning

chapter 1

Study Plan for the TOEFL

Many students do not prepare for the TOEFL. They do not even read the *Bulletin of Information* that they receive from Educational Testing Service along with their application forms. You have an advantage. You have a study plan.

BARRON'S TOEFL SERIES

There are three books in the Barron's TOEFL series to help you prepare for the Test of English as a Foreign Language. Each book has a different purpose.

Barron's Practice Exercises for the TOEFL. A book for intermediate learners who need preview and practice for the TOEFL. It includes a general preview of the TOEFL examination, a preview of the most frequently tested problems, and more than 1000 exercises. Separate cassette tapes are available to give you practice in listening comprehension. This is the book that you are using now.

Barron's How to Prepare for the TOEFL. A book for high intermediate and advanced learners who need review and practice for the TOEFL. It includes questions and answers about the TOEFL examination, a detailed review of each section of the examination, practice exercises, and seven model tests similar to the actual TOEFL examination. Separate cassette tapes are available to give you practice in listening comprehension. This is a book that you can use next (after this book) if you need more detailed preparation before taking the TOEFL.

Barron's Basic Tips on the TOEFL. A pocket-sized edition of *Barron's How to Prepare for the TOEFL.* It is for high intermediate and advanced learners who need review and practice for the TOEFL and want to be able to carry a book with them in a pocket or purse. It includes questions and answers about the TOEFL examination, 101 basic tips on how to prepare for the TOEFL, and two model tests from *Barron's How to Prepare for the TOEFL.* Separate tapes are available to give you practice in listening comprehension.

MORE ABOUT THIS BOOK

In preparing to take the TOEFL or any other examination, it is very important to preview the test and to have an opportunity to practice before you take it.

Previewing will help you become familiar with the test directions and will help you identify the types of problems that are frequently tested. Research has proven that when people know what to expect in an examination, they achieve higher scores.

Practicing will help you improve your skills in listening and reading and will help you increase your knowledge of structure and written expression.

The purpose of this book is to provide you with both preview and practice for a carefully selected series of problems. These are the problems that are most frequently tested on English proficiency examinations like the TOEFL.

By studying this book, you should know what to expect and you should improve your skills and increase your knowledge.

PLANNING TO TAKE THE TOEFL

Some learners take the TOEFL after they have finished studying this book, but others prefer to continue their preparation before taking it.

STUDY PLAN I

This plan is for intermediate learners.

First, use this book, *Barron's Practice Exercises for the TOEFL*. Then, use *Barron's How to Prepare for the TOEFL*.

STUDY PLAN II

This plan is for high intermediate learners.

Use this book, *Barron's Practice Exercises for the TOEFL*.

A Ten-Week Calendar for This Book

Week One
On Monday and Thursday, listen to Chapter Three, Exercises 1 and 2.
On Tuesday and Friday, study Chapter Four, Exercise 1.
On Wednesday and Saturday, read Chapter Five, Exercises 1 and 6.
On Sunday, review all the exercises that you have studied during the week and refer to the
    Answer Key in Chapter Six and the Explanatory Answers in Chapter Seven.

Week Two
On Monday and Thursday, listen to Chapter Three, Exercises 3 and 4.
On Tuesday and Friday, study Chapter Four, Exercises 2 and 3.
On Wednesday and Saturday, read Chapter Five, Exercise 7.
On Sunday, review all the exercises that you have studied during the week and refer to the
    Answer Key in Chapter Six and the Explanatory Answers in Chapter Seven.

Week Three
On Monday and Thursday, listen to Chapter Three, Exercises 5 and 6.
On Tuesday and Friday, study Chapter Four, Exercises 4 and 5.
On Wednesday and Saturday, read Chapter Five, Exercise 2.
On Sunday, review all the exercises that you have studied during the week and refer to the
    Answer Key in Chapter Six and the Explanatory Answers in Chapter Seven.

Week Four
On Monday and Thursday, listen to Chapter Three, Exercises 7 and 8.
On Tuesday and Friday, study Chapter Four, Exercises 6 and 7.
On Wednesday and Saturday, read Chapter Five, Exercise 8.
On Sunday, review all the exercises that you have studied during the week and refer to the
    Answer Key in Chapter Six and the Explanatory Answers in Chapter Seven.

Week Five
On Monday and Thursday, listen to Chapter Three, Exercises 9 and 10.
On Tuesday and Friday, study Chapter Four, Exercises 8 and 9.
On Wednesday and Saturday, read Chapter Five, Exercises 3 and 9.
On Sunday, review all the exercises that you have studied during the week and refer to the
    Answer Key in Chapter Six and the Explanatory Answers in Chapter Seven.

Week Six

On Monday and Thursday, listen to Chapter Three, Exercises 11 and 12.
On Tuesday and Friday, study Chapter Four, Exercises 10 and 11.
On Wednesday and Saturday, read Chapter Five, Exercise 10.
On Sunday, review all the exercises that you have studied during the week and refer to the
    Answer Key in Chapter Six and the Explanatory Answers in Chapter Seven.

Week Seven

On Monday and Thursday, listen to Chapter Three, Exercises 13 and 14.
On Tuesday and Friday, study Chapter Four, Exercises 12 and 13.
On Wednesday and Saturday, read Chapter Five, Exercise 4.
On Sunday, review all the exercises that you have studied during the week and refer to the
    Answer Key in Chapter Six and the Explanatory Answers in Chapter Seven.

Week Eight

On Monday and Thursday, listen to Chapter Three, Exercises 15 and 16.
On Tuesday and Friday, study Chapter Four, Exercises 14 and 15.
On Wednesday and Saturday, read Chapter Five, Exercise 11.
On Sunday, review all the exercises that you have studied during the week and refer to the
    Answer Key in Chapter Six and the Explanatory Answers in Chapter Seven.

Week Nine

On Monday and Thursday, listen to Chapter Three, Exercise 17.
On Tuesday and Friday, study Chapter Four, Exercises 16 and 17.
On Wednesday and Saturday, read Chapter Five, Exercises 5 and 12.
On Sunday, review all the exercises that you have studied during the week and refer to the
    Answer Key in Chapter Six and the Explanatory Answers in Chapter Seven.

Week Ten

On Monday and Thursday, listen to Chapter Three, Exercises 18 and 19.
On Tuesday and Friday, study Chapter Four, Exercise 18.
On Wednesday and Saturday, read Chapter Five, Exercise 13.
On Sunday, review all the exercises that you have studied during the week and refer to the
    Answer Key in Chapter Six and the Explanatory Answers in Chapter Seven.

Adjusting the Calendar

Ideally, you will have ten weeks to prepare for the TOEFL. But if you have a shorter time to prepare, follow the plan in the same order, adjusting the time to meet your needs.

If you have taken the TOEFL before, you already know which section or sections are difficult for you. Even if you have not taken the TOEFL, you probably know your strong and weak points. If you are weak in listening comprehension, then you should spend more time preparing for Section I. If you are weak in structure or reading, then you should spend more time preparing for Section II or III.

SUGGESTIONS FOR PREPARATION

To improve your scores most, follow three suggestions. First, concentrate on listening, structure, writing ability, and reading. Your scores will improve because when you are engaged in listening and reading, you are practicing skills that you can apply during the examination regardless of the content of the material. When you are reviewing structure, you are studying a system that is smaller and, like the skills of listening and reading, has the potential for application on the TOEFL that you take. Many of the structures that you study should appear on the examination.

But when you review lists of vocabulary, even very good lists, you may study hundreds of words but not find any of them on the examination. This is so because thousands of possible words may be tested.

Second, spend time preparing every day for at least an hour instead of sitting down to review once a week for seven hours. Even though you are studying the same amount of time, research shows that shorter sessions every day produce better results on the test.

Finally, do not try to memorize questions from this or any other book. The questions on the test that you take will be very similar to the questions in this book, but they will not be exactly the same.

What you should try to do as you use this and your other books is to learn how to apply your knowledge. Do not hurry through the Practice Exercises and the Model Tests. While you are checking your answers with the Answer Key, *think* about the correct answer. Why is it correct? Is it like other questions that you have seen before? Can you explain the answer to yourself before you check the Explanatory Answer?

SUGGESTIONS FOR ADDITIONAL PREPARATION

Although this book should provide you with enough preview and practice material, some of you will want to do more to prepare for the TOEFL. Some of you will want to review and test yourselves by using *Barron's How to Prepare for the TOEFL.*

Barron's How to Prepare for the TOEFL is written at a higher level than this book.

SUGGESTIONS FOR SUCCESS

Your attitude will influence your success on the TOEFL examination. You *must* develop patterns of positive thinking. To help you, memorize the following sentences and bring them to mind after each study session. Bring them to mind when you begin to have negative thoughts, also.

> I know more today than I did yesterday.
> I am preparing.
> I will succeed.

Remember, some tension is normal and good. Accept it. Use it constructively. It will motivate you to study. But don't panic or worry. Panic will cause loss of concentration and poor performance. Avoid people who panic or worry. Don't listen to them. They will encourage negative thoughts.

> You know more today than you did yesterday.
> You are preparing.
> You will succeed.

chapter 2

Preview of the
TOEFL Examination

Section I   Listening Comprehension
40 minutes   50 questions

In this section of the test, you will have an opportunity to demonstrate your ability to understand spoken English. There are three parts to this section, with special directions for each part.

PART A   20 STATEMENTS

Directions: For each question in Part A, you will hear a short statement. The statements will be spoken just one time. They will not be written out for you, and you must listen carefully to understand what the speaker says.

   After you hear a statement, read the four sentences in your test book, marked (A), (B), (C), and (D), and decide which *one* is closest in meaning to the statement you heard. Then, on your answer sheet, find the number of the question and blacken the space that corresponds to the letter of the answer you have chosen so that the letter inside the oval cannot be seen.

Example

Tape: "This ticket cost me two times as much as it did last year."

Test book:
(A)   I bought two tickets last year.
(B)   Last year there were twice as many tickets.
(C)   I bought the last two tickets.
(D)   Last year the ticket was half the price.

Answer sheet:
(A)   (B)   (C)   ●

PART B   15 CONVERSATIONS

Directions: In Part B you will hear short conversations between two speakers. At the end of each conversation, a third voice will ask a question about what was said. The question will be spoken just one time. After you hear a conversation and the question about it, read the four possible answers in your test book and decide which one is the best answer to the question you heard. Then, on your answer sheet, find the number of the question and blacken the space that corresponds to the letter of the answer you have chosen.

Example

Tape: First voice: "May I help you?"
          Second voice: "No thanks. I'm just looking."
          Third voice: "Where does this conversation probably take place?"

Test book:
(A)   At a store.
(B)   At the site of an accident.
(C)   At a bank.
(D)   At the front door of an apartment.

Answer sheet:
●   (B)   (C)   (D)

PART C   4–5 MINI TALKS
15 QUESTIONS

Directions: In this part of the test, you will hear several short mini talks. After each talk or conversation, you will be asked some questions. The talks and questions will be spoken just one time. They will not be written out for you, so you will have to listen carefully to understand what the speaker says.

After you hear a question, read the four possible answers in your test book and decide which one is the best answer to the question you heard. Then, on your answer sheet, find the number of the question and blacken the space that corresponds to the answer you have chosen.

Example

Tape: Questions 36–40 refer to the following announcement:

Have you seen the new AT&T Card Caller phones that are beginning to appear at airports, restaurants, hotels—almost anywhere you may need to make a call? If you haven't, you will. Because the Card Caller is turning up all over the country.

The AT&T Card Caller is a special public telephone that allows you to charge any kind of call simply by using your AT&T Card, a new charge card that you'll be receiving if you already have charge service. And, if you don't already have charge service, now is a good time to arrange for it. Just call your local telephone office.

The AT&T Card Caller is designed to read billing information directly from a magnetic strip attached to the back of the card so that there's no need to talk to an operator and no need to bother finding the correct change. But, best of all, there's no need to confirm billing to a third party at your telephone number. Because sometimes there's no one there when you're gone from your home or office. Now, just use your AT&T card at an AT&T Card Caller phone. Get one now.

AT&T. "Always there to serve you."

Tape: "**36.** What is the AT&T Card Caller?"

Test book:
(A)   A new telephone that uses a card instead of money.
(B)   A new telephone company.
(C)   A charge card for airline tickets, restaurants, and hotels.
(D)   A person who makes telephone calls for you.

Tape: "**37.** How can you use a Card Caller?"

Test book:
(A)   Call the operator.
(B)   Insert a card.
(C)   Use correct change.
(D)   Call your home or office.

Tape: "**38.** How is billing confirmed?"

Test book:
(A)   By a third party.
(B)   By a magnetic strip on the back of the card.
(C)   By the sound of the correct change in the phone.
(D)   By calling your telephone number.

Tape: "**39.** Who will receive cards?"

Test book:
(A)   Businesses.
(B)   Everyone.
(C)   People who travel.
(D)   People who have charge cards.

Tape: "**40.** What is the main purpose of the message?"

Test book:
(A)   To sell charge cards.
(B)   To sell telephones.
(C)   To compare different kinds of phone service.
(D)   To report news.

Answer sheet:
36.   (●)   (B)   (C)   (D)
37.   (A)   ●   (C)   (D)
38.   (A)   ●   (C)   (D)
39.   (A)   (B)   (C)   (●)
40.   (●)   (B)   (C)   (D)

Section II   Structure and Written Expression
25 minutes   40 questions

In this section of the test, you will be asked to demonstrate your ability to recognize language that is appropriate for standard written English. There are two types of questions in this section, with special directions for each type.

PART A   15 SENTENCES

Directions: Four words or phrases, marked (A), (B), (C), and (D), are given beneath each incomplete sentence. You are to choose the one word or phrase that best completes the sentence. Then, on your answer sheet, find the number of the question and blacken the space that corresponds to the letter of the answer you have chosen so that the letter inside the oval cannot be seen.

Example

Test Book:
At very high altitudes, _____ for conifers to survive.

(A)   the cold
(B)   very cold
(C)   it is too cold
(D)   so cold that

Answer sheet:
(A)   (B)   (●)   (D)

PART B   25 SENTENCES

Directions: Four words or phrases are underlined in each sentence and marked (A), (B), (C), and (D). You are to identify the one underlined word or phrase that should be corrected or rewritten. Then, on your answer sheet, find the number of the question and blacken the space that corresponds to the letter of the answer you have chosen.

Example

Test book:
Besides its usual song, a bird has a special call that warns other birds when an enemy
  (A)   (B)
such as a hawk or owl are near.
  (C)   (D)

Answer sheet:
(A)   (B)   (C)   (●)

Section III   Reading Comprehension and Vocabulary
45 minutes   60 questions

In this section of the test, you will have an opportunity to demonstrate your ability to understand various kinds of reading materials, as well as your ability to understand the meaning and use of the words. There are two types of questions in this section, with special directions for each type.

PART A   30 SENTENCES

Directions: One word or phrase is underlined in each sentence. Below each sentence are four other words or phrases, marked (A), (B), (C), and (D). You are to choose the one word or phrase that best keeps the meaning of the original sentence if it is substituted for the underlined word or phrase. Then, on your answer sheet, find the number of the question and blacken the space that corresponds to the letter you have chosen so that the letter inside the oval cannot be seen.

Example

Test Book:
Arizona has an <u>abundance</u> of cactus.
(A)   special area
(●)   large number
(C)   famous kind
(D)   organized plan

Answer sheet:
(A)   (B)   (C)   (D)

PART B   4–5 READING PASSAGES
2–5 RESTATEMENTS
30 QUESTIONS

Directions: In Part B, you will read a variety of passages (single sentences or paragraphs) followed by questions about the meaning of the material. You are to choose the one best answer, (A), (B), (C), or (D), to each question. Then, on your answer sheet, find the number of the question and blacken the space that corresponds to the letter of the answer you have chosen.

Answer all the questions based on what is stated or implied in the reading passage.

Example

Test book:
Questions 31–34
   Among the native North American animals that remain active during the winter are the Virginia deer and their western cousins the mule deer. When it begins to get cold, they shed their brown summer coats and replace them with heavier, gray ones. Some deer form herds. Like the American elk, the males drop their antlers and new ones start to grow.
   Being browsers as well as grazers, deer can eat the bark and twigs of trees and the foliage of evergreens as far up as they can reach. They may also paw through the snow to find grass, acorns, weeds, and moss on the ground.
   Another North American native, the American bison or buffalo, also remains active, foraging in the snow by sweeping its muzzle like a broom. In this way, it can dig down as far as four feet for food.

31.   What is another name for the American bison?
      (A)   Virginia deer
      (B)   Mule deer
      (C)   Buffalo
      (D)   Elk

32.   During the winter a deer would most likely eat
      (A)   grass buried four feet under the snow.
      (B)   large amounts of snow.
      (C)   other small animals.
      (D)   small branches on a pine tree.

33. What is the main subject of this passage?
  (A) Deer
  (B) The Virginia deer and relatives
  (C) North American animals that are active in winter
  (D) How animals eat during the winter time

34. The passage is probably taken from a book about
  (A) winter.
  (B) animals.
  (C) North America.
  (D) grass and trees.

Answer sheet:
31. (A) (B) (●) (D)
32. (A) (B) (C) (●)
33. (A) (B) (●) (D)
34. (A) (●) (C) (D)

Directions: At the end of Part B, you will read a few sentences. Below each sentence are four other sentences marked (A), (B), (C), and (D). You are to choose the one sentence that is closest in meaning to the original sentence. Remember that several of the sentences may be factually correct, but you must choose the one that is the closest restatement of the given sentence.

Example

Test book:
If programs of mass inoculation and chlorination of water sources are implemented, outbreaks of cholera can be controlled.

(A) When people are not inoculated and water is not chlorinated, outbreaks of cholera are more difficult to control.
(B) Outbreaks of cholera can be controlled by purifying the water.
(C) There are inoculations for cholera and purifications methods for water sources.
(D) The control of cholera is not possible without programs.

Answer sheet:
(●) (B) (C) (D)

Previewing and Practicing

Preview and Practice Exercises for the Listening Comprehension Section of the TOEFL

In this chapter, you will have an opportunity to practice your ability to understand spoken English. There are three different types of Practice Exercises with special directions for each type. *Note:* Practice Exercises One to Nineteen are available on cassette tapes. To order these cassettes, use the order form on page 332. *Note also:* The Transcript for *all* the Listening Comprehension Practice Exercises can be found on page 283.

Directions: For each question in Part A, you will hear a short statement. The statements will be spoken just one time. They will not be written out for you, and you must listen carefully to understand what the speaker says.

    After you hear a statement, read the four sentences in your test book, marked (A), (B), (C), and (D), and decide which *one* is closest in meaning to the statement you heard. Then, on your answer sheet, find the number of the question and blacken the space that corresponds to the letter of the answer you have chosen so that the letter inside the oval cannot be seen.

PREVIEW: IDENTIFYING TEENS AND TENS

In some statements in Part A of the Listening Comprehension Section, you will be asked to hear the difference between a teen number like 13, 14, or 15, and a ten number like 30, 40, or 50.

EXERCISE ONE: TEENS AND TENS

1.   (A)   I-19 is a busy highway.
     (B)   I-90 is the only busy highway.
     (C)   I-19 is not a busy highway.
     (D)   I-90 is a busy highway.

2.   (A)   The suitcase is not heavy.
     (B)   The suitcase weighs sixteen pounds too much.
     (C)   The weight of the suitcase is sixty pounds.
     (D)   You will not need to pay extra.

3.   (A)   The new address of the International Office is 70 South Speedway.
     (B)   The International Office used to be located at 70 South Speedway.
     (C)   Seventeen South Speedway is where the International Office has moved.
     (D)   The International Office has always been located at 17 South Speedway.

4.   (A)   A doctoral degree will be awarded to forty students this semester.
     (B)   Fourteen industrial engineers will receive their Ph.D.'s this semester.
     (C)   The Industrial Engineering Department does not award a doctoral degree.
     (D)   This semester fourteen students were enrolled in the Industrial Engineering Department.

5.   (A)   It costs eighteen dollars to go to Washington.
     (B)   Eighty dollars is the price of a ticket to Washington.
     (C)   A ticket to Washington costs eight dollars.
     (D)   One way to go to Washington is to buy a ticket.

6.   (A)   There are fifteen minutes left for this section of the test.
     (B)   It took fifteen minutes to finish this section of the test.
     (C)   In five minutes you must finish this section of the test.
     (D)   You have finished this section of the test in fifty minutes.

7.   (A)   Jane's room is on the fourteenth floor.
     (B)   Jane's room is the first one.
     (C)   Parks Tower has forty floors.
     (D)   Room fourteen is Jane's.

8. (A) A telephone call to Miami costs fifty cents after five o'clock.
   (B) Fifty cents is the price of a five-minute call to Miami.
   (C) After five o'clock a call to Miami costs fifteen cents.
   (D) Before five o'clock it costs fifteen cents to call Miami.

9. (A) This semester one of the English classes will meet in room 70.
   (B) English classes will all meet in room 170 this semester.
   (C) Room 117 is the meeting place for all English classes.
   (D) One English class in room 17 will meet this semester.

10. (A) The first fifty problems are assigned.
   (B) Your homework assignment can be found on page 60.
   (C) The problems on page 16 are assigned.
   (D) Page 15 is your first assignment.

11. (A) Thirteen degrees was the low temperature today.
   (B) Today's temperature was thirty degrees lower than it was yesterday.
   (C) Thirty degrees was today's low temperature.
   (D) The low temperature today was three degrees.

12. (A) Tomorrow morning I need eight copies.
   (B) I made eighty copies for my meeting.
   (C) I have eight meetings tomorrow.
   (D) At eight o'clock tomorrow morning I will need eighteen copies.

13. (A) Thirty-one is the rate of exchange.
   (B) Thirty-to-one is the rate of exchange.
   (C) Thirteen-to-one is the rate of exchange.
   (D) Three-to-one is the rate of exchange.

14. (A) A size large in this style would be a forty.
   (B) There are fourteen styles in size large.
   (C) There is a large selection in size forty.
   (D) In this style a size large is a fourteen.

15. (A) Channel three carries CBS news.
   (B) Channel six carries CBS news.
   (C) Channel thirteen carries CBS news.
   (D) Channel thirty carries CBS news.

16. (A) There are ninety answers in the textbooks.
   (B) All of the answers are on page 9.
   (C) The textbooks have only nineteen pages.
   (D) Page 90 has the answers on it.

17. (A) The package requires eighty cents postage.
   (B) It will cost eighteen cents to mail the package.
   (C) This package needs eight stamps.
   (D) One more eight-cent stamp is needed to mail this package.

18. (A) The flight at gate two is number fourteen.
(B) The flight to Dallas is number forty-two.
(C) The flight now boarding is number forty.
(D) The flight at gate two is new.

19. (A) The score achieved by half of the students tested was 450.
(B) Eighty-five percent of the students passed the examination.
(C) More than 415 points was the score that half of the students received.
(D) A score of 450 or more was achieved by 15 percent of the students tested.

20. (A) John will have his fortieth birthday in November.
(B) On November fourteenth John will celebrate his birthday.
(C) John is twelve years old now.
(D) John's birthday is on November thirtieth.

PREVIEW: SOLVING COMPUTATIONS

In some statements in Part A, you will be asked to perform simple mathematical computations, like adding, subtracting, multiplying, or dividing. In other statements, you will only need to listen for the answer.

EXERCISE TWO: COMPUTATIONS

1. (A) The dresses will cost $16.
    (B) The dresses will cost $30.
    (C) The dresses will cost $120.
    (D) The dresses will cost $60.

2. (A) The bus left at 8:45 A.M.
    (B) The bus left at 8:40 A.M.
    (C) The bus left at 8:35 A.M.
    (D) The bus left at 8:30 P.M.

3. (A) City College has 260 students now.
    (B) In 1960 City College had 520 students.
    (C) In 1960 City College had 1040 students.
    (D) City College was founded in 1960.

4. (A) The store opens at 9:00 A.M.
    (B) Miss Smith arrives at 9:30 A.M.
    (C) Miss Smith arrives at 10:00 A.M.
    (D) The store opens at 10:30 A.M.

5. (A) The speaker's salary is $250.
    (B) The speaker's salary is $750.
    (C) The speaker's salary is $500.
    (D) The speaker's salary is $125.

6. (A) The plane left at 11:30 A.M.
    (B) The plane left at 12:00 noon.
    (C) The plane left at 12:30 P.M.
    (D) The plane left at 1:00 P.M.

7. (A) The stadium has room for 100,000 people.
    (B) 7,500 people attended last night's game.
    (C) 25,000 people attended last night's game.
    (D) There were 50,000 people at the game last night.

8. (A) Sandy saved $165 when she bought the camera.
    (B) Sandy paid too much for the camera.
    (C) Sandy spent $200 for the camera.
    (D) Sandy paid $35 less than the regular price for the camera.

9. (A) Jane types half as fast as Judy.
    (B) Judy types as fast as Jane.
    (C) Both Jane and Judy type eighty words a minute.
    (D) Jane is a faster typist than Judy.

10. (A) One end table costs $85.
    (B) Each end table costs $75.
    (C) A pair of end tables cost $170.
    (D) A pair of end tables cost $300.

11. (A) Bill gets to class at eight o'clock.
    (B) Bill does not have a class in the morning.
    (C) Bill gets to class at eight-fifteen.
    (D) Bill gets to class fifteen minutes before it begins.

12. (A) We sold forty tickets.
    (B) We expected to sell twenty tickets.
    (C) We expected to sell eighty tickets.
    (D) We sold eighty tickets.

13. (A) Dr. Jones's taxi arrived at the airport on time.
    (B) Dr. Jones arrived at the airport at 11:30.
    (C) Dr. Jones's plane left at 11:00.
    (D) Dr. Jones's plane left at 10:30.

14. (A) Mr. Black must leave his house at 9:00.
    (B) Mr. Black must be at work at 8:30.
    (C) Mr. Black must spend an hour driving to work.
    (D) Mr. Black must spend a half-hour driving to work.

15. (A) Alice did not give the teller enough.
    (B) The teller charged Alice to cash her check.
    (C) Alice was ten dollars short.
    (D) The teller was shorter than Alice.

16. (A) I watched for ten minutes.
    (B) It was 9:30 when I set my watch.
    (C) The time is 9:20.
    (D) I set my watch ahead thirty minutes.

17. (A) We should make a double recipe.
    (B) We should make half a recipe.
    (C) We should make ten recipes.
    (D) We should make twenty recipes.

18. (A) Bob and Carole live half a mile from State University.
    (B) Bob and Carole walk one mile from married student housing to State University.
    (C) Bob and Carole live one mile from State University in married student housing.
    (D) Bob and Carole take the bus one mile to State University.

19. (A) John arrived for the twelve o'clock meal.
    (B) John was too late to eat.
    (C) John did not plan to arrive at noon.
    (D) John arrived at two o'clock.

20. (A) A used book is $6 cheaper than a new book.
    (B) A used book costs $2.50.
    (C) Mary saved $3.50.
    (D) A new book costs $8.50.

PREVIEW: MAKING REFERENCES

In some statements in Part A, you will be asked to separate and remember who each person is and what he or she is doing.

EXERCISE THREE: REFERENCE

1. (A)   Jeff and Nancy are happily married.
    (B)   Jeff is happy that he married Nancy.
    (C)   Nancy's family likes Jeff.
    (D)   Jeff's family approved of his marrying Nancy.

2. (A)   Mr. Johnson and his son are going into business together.
    (B)   Mr. Johnson's son and his nephew are in business together.
    (C)   Mr. Johnson's nephew owns a business.
    (D)   Mr. Johnson hopes that he and his nephew will go into business together.

3. (A)   Ann wants us to meet her.
    (B)   We met Ann at the bus station.
    (C)   Ann wants to meet us at the bus station.
    (D)   Ann met us at the bus station.

4. (A)   She bought him a suit.
    (B)   He bought himself a suit.
    (C)   He bought her a suit.
    (D)   She bought herself a suit.

5. (A)   The speaker does not remember Ellen's last name.
    (B)   Ellen does not remember her teacher's last name.
    (C)   The speaker does not remember the teacher's last name.
    (D)   The teacher does not remember Ellen's last name.

6. (A)   Pat went to the party with John.
    (B)   John was invited to Pat's party.
    (C)   John would not go to the party.
    (D)   Pat did not go to the party.

7. (A)   Nancy has Paul's scarf on.
    (B)   Nancy is wearing a knit scarf.
    (C)   Paul has a knit scarf.
    (D)   Paul never wears the knit scarf that Nancy made him.

8. (A)   It is Tom's birthday.
    (B)   Tom's roommate sent him a card.
    (C)   Tom's roommate wished him a happy birthday.
    (D)   Tom wished his roommate a happy birthday.

9. (A)   Bill's sister graduated.
    (B)   Bill was very proud when he graduated.
    (C)   Bill was very proud of his sister.
    (D)   When Bill graduated, his sister was very proud of him.

10. (A) James went to work while his mother stayed home.
    (B) James's mother works at home.
    (C) When James got home from work, his mother was there.
    (D) James's mother was at work when he got home.

11. (A) Charles's uncle was at the party last night.
    (B) We introduced Mary to Uncle Charles last night at the party.
    (C) Mary met us at Uncle Charles's party.
    (D) Last night we were introduced to Charles, Mary's uncle.

12. (A) Bob criticized his father's plans for a new office building.
    (B) Bob was unhappy when his father criticized his plans for a new office building.
    (C) Bob and his father criticized the plans for a new office building.
    (D) Bob's father criticized him in his new office.

13. (A) William was the woman's grandson.
    (B) Mrs. Williams's lawyer was the beneficiary.
    (C) Mrs. Williams was named in her lawyer's will.
    (D) The lawyer wrote the will for Mrs. Williams.

14. (A) Larry washed his brother's car.
    (B) Larry's brother washed the car.
    (C) Larry took the car to his brother's car wash.
    (D) Larry and his brother went to the car wash.

15. (A) Paul's wife would like him to finish his education.
    (B) Paul's wife would like to finish her education.
    (C) Paul would like to finish his education.
    (D) Paul would like his wife to finish her education.

16. (A) Mrs. Ayers is Dr. Smith's secretary.
    (B) Mrs. Ayers could not keep her appointment with Dr. Smith.
    (C) Dr. Smith instructed his secretary that she should cancel all of his appointments for the day.
    (D) Mrs. Ayers's secretary canceled her appointment.

17. (A) Alice studies at the University of Toledo.
    (B) Alice and her friends study at the University of Toledo.
    (C) Alice plans to transfer because none of her friends study at the University of Toledo.
    (D) Alice plans to study at the University of Toledo with her friends.

18. (A) Professor Baker gives the lecture every day.
    (B) Professor Baker would like to have a graduate assistant to give the lectures.
    (C) Professor Baker's graduate assistant was asked to give today's lecture.
    (D) Professor Baker's graduate assistant asked him how to give today's lecture.

19. (A) Mary called Bill.
    (B) Mary answered Bill's call.
    (C) Bill answered Mary's call.
    (D) Mary did not telephone Bill.

20. (A) Sally gave a bicycle to her sister.
    (B) Sally let her sister use her bicycle.
    (C) Sally's sister lent her a bicycle.
    (D) Sally borrowed a bicycle for her sister.

PREVIEW: UNDERSTANDING NEGATIVES

In some statements in Part A, you will be asked to understand negative words, such as *never* and *nothing* in phrases like *never better* and *nothing worse*.

EXERCISE FOUR: NEGATIVES

1. (A) She does not have many friends.
    (B) It is hard for her to have friends.
    (C) She tries hard to have friends.
    (D) It is hard for her friends to have any.

2. (A) Only one student is without insurance.
    (B) All students have insurance.
    (C) None of the students have insurance.
    (D) Some of the students have insurance.

3. (A) Business was better before.
    (B) Business is better now than ever before.
    (C) Business was never good.
    (D) Business is never slow.

4. (A) The tour was worth the time but not the money.
    (B) The tour was not worth the time or the money.
    (C) The tour was worth both the time and the money.
    (D) The tour was not worth the time.

5. (A) Tom is not as nice to his sister as she is to him.
    (B) Tom is nicer to his sister than most brothers are to their sisters.
    (C) Tom has a nicer sister than many brothers do.
    (D) Tom's sister is not nice to him.

6. (A) The students saw more snow before.
    (B) The students had never seen snow before.
    (C) This was the first time that the students had seen such a lot of snow.
    (D) Before the students saw the snow there had been much more.

7. (A) It is very dangerous to practice driving at the shopping center.
    (B) Some places are better to practice driving than the shopping center.
    (C) It is better not to practice driving at the shopping center.
    (D) The shopping center is the best place to practice driving.

8. (A) Nancy does not like to sleep late.
    (B) Nancy likes nothing.
    (C) Nancy likes to sleep late.
    (D) Nancy does not like anything.

9. (A) Mary likes to be unfriendly.
    (B) Mary waved when she saw you.
    (C) Mary did not wave because she did not see you.
    (D) You should have waved at Mary.

10. (A) The young man had some unusual problems.
    (B) The problem was common for young men.
    (C) It is not common for young men to leave home.
    (D) It was a problem for him when he left home.

11. (A) Professor Ayers speaks Arabic.
    (B) Professor Ayers speaks Farsi.
    (C) Professor Ayers speaks Arabic and Farsi.
    (D) Professor Ayers does not speak Arabic and Farsi.

12. (A) Bob is a friend of Jane's family.
    (B) Bob's family does not know Jane.
    (C) Bob does not know Jane's friend.
    (D) Bob and Jane's family have never met.

13. (A) There is doubt.
    (B) There is no doubt.
    (C) It is there.
    (D) There isn't any.

14. (A) The machine cannot be used.
    (B) The machine is used less.
    (C) The machine is used to make xerox copies.
    (D) The machine has been copied.

15. (A) The first apartment was more comfortable.
    (B) The new apartment was more comfortable.
    (C) Neither the first apartment nor the new one was comfortable.
    (D) Both apartments were very comfortable.

16. (A) English 190 is not difficult.
    (B) I hardly know anything about English 190.
    (C) Other courses are as difficult as English 190.
    (D) English 190 is the most difficult course.

17. (A) Betty had some extra work.
    (B) Betty does not have a job.
    (C) Betty is not required to work extra hours.
    (D) Betty does not need to work.

18. (A) He is always fair.
    (B) His students treat him unfairly.
    (C) He took his students to the fair.
    (D) He is a fairly good teacher.

19. (A) I will buy a Ford.
    (B) I am right to buy a car now.
    (C) I do not have enough money for a car.
    (D) I have bought a new car.

20. (A) He tried hard to eat the dessert.
    (B) The dessert was too hard.
    (C) John never eats dessert.
    (D) He ate the dessert with difficulty.

PREVIEW: UNDERSTANDING COMPARATIVES

In some statements in Part A, you will be asked to understand comparative words, such as *more, less,* or *same* in phrases like *more than, less than,* and *the same as.*

EXERCISE FIVE: COMPARATIVES

1. (A) There are more successful restaurants in the United States than any other small business.
   (B) The restaurant is a new successful business in the United States.
   (C) We have fewer successful restaurants in the United States now.
   (D) The United States has more successful restaurants now than other countries do.

2. (A) There was plenty of time to get there.
   (B) We needed more time to get there.
   (C) We had to get there in time.
   (D) We had a good time when we got there.

3. (A) The new students are not homesick.
   (B) The new students used to be homesick, but they are not homesick now.
   (C) The new students have not been here very long.
   (D) Since I have been here longer than the new students, I am not homesick.

4. (A) Kathy can see better than Ann.
   (B) Kathy is prettier than Ann.
   (C) Kathy has a better room than Ann.
   (D) Kathy is a better roommate than Ann.

5. (A) I think that the University is far away.
   (B) The University is nearer than I thought.
   (C) I think that I will go to the University.
   (D) The University is not as near as I thought.

6. (A) Bill should exercise more.
   (B) Bill gets more exercise than he used to.
   (C) Bill should not exercise so much.
   (D) Exercise should help Bill lose weight.

7. (A) Ellen does not like her husband.
   (B) Ellen and her husband are alike.
   (C) Tom does not like Ellen's husband.
   (D) Ellen and Tom are very different.

8. (A) Ann likes neither cold weather nor hot weather.
   (B) Ann likes hot weather better than cold weather.
   (C) Ann likes hot weather just as much as cold weather.
   (D) Ann likes cold weather better than hot weather.

9. (A) We have not lived here long, and neither have the Smiths.
   (B) We have lived here longer than the Smiths.
   (C) The Smiths have not lived here very long.
   (D) The Smiths have lived here longer than we have.

10. (A) Aspirin is good for colds but not for flu.
    (B) Anything is good for a cold.
    (C) Aspirin is not good for colds and flu.
    (D) One of the best remedies for colds and flu is aspirin.

11. (A) I thought that writing this term paper would be a big job.
    (B) I thought that I would write this term paper, but it was too big a job.
    (C) Writing this term paper is easier than I thought it would be.
    (D) Writing this term paper is not as easy as I thought it would be.

12. (A) I imagined that she would learn English quickly.
    (B) She has not been able to learn English very quickly.
    (C) I imagined that she would learn English more slowly than she did.
    (D) She learned English more quickly than I did.

13. (A) I like jogging because it is more fun.
    (B) I like to play tennis more than I like to jog.
    (C) Playing tennis is better for you than jogging according to some people.
    (D) In my opinion people should jog and play tennis.

14. (A) Both Jeff and Tom were surprised.
    (B) Neither Jeff nor I was surprised.
    (C) Jeff was more surprised than I was.
    (D) Tom surprised us.

15. (A) Government statistics show that it is not likely for older people to get married.
    (B) Older people like getting married.
    (C) People who get married young have a greater probability of getting a divorce.
    (D) Divorces are more common among older people who have gotten married.

16. (A) A steak dinner is more expensive than other dinners.
    (B) A steak dinner at City Steak House is cheaper than at most restaurants.
    (C) City Steak House has expensive dinners.
    (D) Most restaurants have steak dinners.

17. (A) Bill gets better grades on exams because he studies harder.
    (B) John's exams are harder than Bill's.
    (C) Bill does not study as hard as John.
    (D) John studies harder and gets better grades.

18. (A) Larry's son does not like him.
    (B) Larry and his son look very different.
    (C) Larry's son resembles him.
    (D) Larry and his son are alike.

19. (A) Betty would rather rent an apartment than live at home.
    (B) Betty likes neither living at home nor renting an apartment.
    (C) Betty likes living at home.
    (D) Betty's parents want her to live at home instead of renting an apartment.

20. (A) Mrs. Smith has traveled less than her husband has.
    (B) Mrs. Smith always travels with her husband.
    (C) Mrs. Smith's husband does not travel very far.
    (D) Neither Mrs. Smith nor her husband travel very much any more.

PREVIEW: UNDERSTANDING CONDITIONALS

In some statements in Part A, you will be asked to understand conditional words, such as *if, whether,* or *unless* in sentences of cause and result.

EXERCISE SIX: CONDITIONALS

1. (A) John weighs less now that he is playing tennis all of the time.
   (B) John wants to play tennis often.
   (C) John knows the way to play tennis.
   (D) John spends too much money on playing tennis.

2. (A) Mary got better grades when she studied.
   (B) Mary is getting better grades by studying.
   (C) Mary will get better grades.
   (D) Mary did not get better grades because she did not study.

3. (A) The project was not approved because the budget was high.
   (B) The project was approved in spite of the budget.
   (C) The budget for the project was approved.
   (D) The project was approved without a budget.

4. (A) We did not send a telegram because we did not need to get in touch with them.
   (B) We could not send a telegram although we needed to get in touch with them.
   (C) We sent a telegram to get in touch with them.
   (D) Since they needed to get in touch with us, they sent a telegram.

5. (A) You will need a smaller size in this style.
   (B) You will need a size six in this style.
   (C) This style runs a little smaller than usual.
   (D) Your usual size is a size seven.

6. (A) We got good seats although we were late.
   (B) We did not get good seats because we were late.
   (C) We were too late to get seats.
   (D) We got good seats because we arrived on time.

7. (A) She did not go with him because he did not ask her.
   (B) She went with him although he did not ask her.
   (C) He asked her to go with him.
   (D) She asked him to go with her.

8. (A) Fur coats should be cared for properly to last.
   (B) The woman does not care for fur coats.
   (C) A good fur coat does not need much care.
   (D) She lost her fur coat years ago.

9. (A) It is usually easy to get up early.
   (B) It is easier to get up early if you have an alarm clock.
   (C) It is hard to get up early.
   (D) Even with an alarm clock it may be difficult to get up early.

10. (A) We were sorry that Mr. Williams didn't teach the class.
    (B) We enjoyed attending Mr. Williams's class.
    (C) It was better that Mr. Williams did not teach the class.
    (D) The woman believes that Mr. Williams is not a good teacher.

11. (A) She will miss the bus unless she calls a cab soon.
    (B) She will call a cab if she misses the bus.
    (C) A cab takes longer than the bus.
    (D) She will take a cab instead of the bus.

12. (A) I will pick you up at your house at six o'clock.
    (B) I will meet you at the corner at six o'clock to give you a ride home.
    (C) I will drop you off at the corner at six o'clock.
    (D) I will wait at the corner at six o'clock for you to pick me up.

13. (A) Even with a good attitude it is difficult to live in another culture.
    (B) It is not difficult to have the right attitude in another culture.
    (C) A good attitude makes it easy to live in another culture.
    (D) You are the right person to live in another culture because you have a good attitude.

14. (A) Al is too sick to study.
    (B) Al will get sick from studying so much.
    (C) Al keeps getting sick.
    (D) In spite of being sick, Al studies.

15. (A) I am not ready to go to the party.
    (B) Everything is ready for the party.
    (C) The party is ready to start.
    (D) You and I will be able to go to the party as soon as you are ready.

16. (A) We got here last although we had planned to arrive sooner.
    (B) We could not hear them when we got lost.
    (C) We were not here sooner because we got lost.
    (D) We got lost soon after we left here.

17. (A) Orders that are placed on Wednesday should arrive on Saturday.
    (B) Orders arrive on either Wednesday or Saturday
    (C) Orders that are placed on Saturday should arrive by Wednesday.
    (D) Orders may be placed on either Wednesday or Saturday.

18. (A) The director is very busy this afternoon at two o'clock.
    (B) The director will see both of you this afternoon.
    (C) Two o'clock this afternoon is a good time to make an appointment with the director.
    (D) The director has no time for you this afternoon.

19. (A) John caught a cold while he was helping us.
    (B) John did not help us because of his cold.
    (C) John got cold helping us.
    (D) John did not help us because it was too cold.

20. (A) The secretary told you because you asked her.
    (B) The secretary did not tell you because you did not ask her.
    (C) The secretary did not tell you when you asked her.
    (D) The secretary told you although you did not ask her.

PREVIEW: UNDERSTANDING CONCESSIONS (PART 1)

In some statements in Part A, you will be asked to understand concession words, such as *but* in sentences of unexpected result.

EXERCISE SEVEN: CONCESSIONS (PART 1)

1. (A) Jane is frequently absent from tutoring.
   (B) Jane doesn't have tutoring on Monday.
   (C) Jane missed tutoring on Monday.
   (D) Jane has never missed tutoring.

2. (A) We made the invitations.
   (B) We could not go to the party.
   (C) We were not invited to the party.
   (D) We did not believe them.

3. (A) Both the hat and the coat are mine.
   (B) Neither the hat nor the coat is mine.
   (C) Only the hat is mine.
   (D) Only the coat is mine.

4. (A) The State University team won all of its games this year.
   (B) This year the State University team did not win as many games as usual.
   (C) This year the State University team won two games.
   (D) The State University team usually wins two games every year.

5. (A) I wrote you a letter.
   (B) I called you.
   (C) I let her call you.
   (D) I went to see you.

6. (A) Mike went to graduate school as he had planned.
   (B) Mike did not plan to go to graduate school.
   (C) Although Mike had planned to go to graduate school, he could not go.
   (D) It does not cost very much to go to graduate school.

7. (A) Mrs. Baker was not told about her incurable illness.
   (B) Mrs. Baker's illness was cured.
   (C) Mrs. Baker kept hoping that she would be cured.
   (D) Mrs. Baker gave the illness to her.

8. (A) She likes the dorm, but not her roommate.
   (B) She likes her roommate, but not the dorm.
   (C) She likes the dorm because she likes her roommate.
   (D) She only likes the dorm.

9. (A) The office is always open on Saturday.
   (B) The office is closed all day Saturday this week.
   (C) The secretary opens the office at noon on Saturdays.
   (D) This week the secretary will be at the office until twelve o'clock Saturday.

10. (A) We wanted a sandwich.
    (B) We wanted a tuna dinner.
    (C) We wanted fish.
    (D) We wanted a salad.

11. (A) The doctor is short.
    (B) The doctor is not there.
    (C) The doctor is not coming back.
    (D) The doctor is not right.

12. (A) His visa expires in February.
    (B) His visa expires in November.
    (C) His visa expires in August.
    (D) His visa expired three months ago.

13. (A) This year we are going to go camping.
    (B) We usually take a tour on vacation.
    (C) We never take tours on vacation.
    (D) We usually go camping on our vacation.

14. (A) Last night the food at the cafeteria was good.
    (B) The food at the cafeteria is always good.
    (C) The food at the cafeteria is usually bad.
    (D) The food at the cafeteria was bad last night.

15. (A) Forty-five of the students were supposed to take language lab.
    (B) Fifty of the booths in the language lab were scheduled for use by students.
    (C) Although there were only forty-five booths, fifty students wanted to take language lab.
    (D) Despite having fifty booths in the language lab, only forty-five were scheduled.

16. (A) Anne babysits on Friday more often than on any other day.
    (B) Anne only babysits on Friday.
    (C) On Friday Anne does not babysit.
    (D) Anne promised to babysit any Friday.

17. (A) Both of my children came.
    (B) Only my son came.
    (C) Only my daughter came.
    (D) Neither of my children came.

18. (A) Bill bought his wife some cologne.
    (B) Bill had planned to give his wife some cologne.
    (C) Bill's wife could not buy him any cologne.
    (D) Bill's wife bought him some cologne.

19. (A) Gas is not included in the rent for apartments near the University.
    (B) We did not rent an apartment near the University because they are so expensive.
    (C) Because we saved our money we were able to rent an apartment near the University.
    (D) Despite the expense, we rented an apartment near the University.

20. (A) It is usually a good idea to make an appointment to see the foreign student advisor.
    (B) The foreign student advisor does not make appointments with students.
    (C) One should make an appointment with the foreign student advisor during registration.
    (D) The foreign student advisor does not see students during registration.

PREVIEW: UNDERSTANDING CONCESSIONS (PART 2)

In some statements in Part A, you will be asked to understand concession words, such as *although, though, even though, despite,* or *in spite of* in sentences of unexpected result.

EXERCISE SEVEN: CONCESSIONS (PART 2)

1. (A) Students who turn in their final projects by the end of the week will be able to graduate this semester.
   (B) This semester no one in the College of Architecture can graduate.
   (C) Students must turn in their final projects at the graduation.
   (D) Students will graduate whether they turn in their final projects or not.

2. (A) The roads are bad because of the weather.
   (B) The weather has cleared, but the roads are still bad.
   (C) The weather is good now, and the roads are clear.
   (D) The roads are clear despite the bad weather.

3. (A) The speaker does not believe that Betty and Paul will get a divorce.
   (B) The speaker believes that Betty will divorce Paul because of their problems.
   (C) The speaker does not believe that Betty and Paul have any problems.
   (D) Betty and Paul doubt that they will get a divorce.

4. (A) The speaker thinks that the candidate is qualified.
   (B) The speaker thinks that the candidate should be hired.
   (C) The speaker thinks that the candidate's references are good.
   (D) The speaker thinks that he should check the candidate's letters of recommendation.

5. (A) The doctor thinks that you are better.
   (B) The speaker thinks that you should see a doctor.
   (C) The speaker thinks that he should see a doctor in spite of feeling better.
   (D) The doctor does not think that you should see him since you are feeling better.

6. (A) Mr. Brown will be there, but Miss Smith won't.
   (B) Neither Mr. Brown nor Miss Smith will be there.
   (C) Miss Smith will be there, but Mr. Brown won't.
   (D) Both Mr. Brown and Miss Smith will be there.

7. (A) Despite her telling me that she was not offended, I believe that she was.
   (B) She was afraid of offending me.
   (C) She insisted on offending me.
   (D) Although I was not offended, I was afraid.

8. (A) The rent includes all the utilities.
   (B) Only electricity is included in the rent.
   (C) Gas costs twenty dollars more than electricity.
   (D) You can expect to pay twenty dollars more than the rent for electricity.

9. (A) Ellen is not very well.
   (B) Ellen cannot read without her glasses.
   (C) Ellen does not need glasses.
   (D) Ellen uses her glasses to see far away.

10. (A) Despite its being rush hour, there was little traffic.
    (B) There was not much traffic because it was not rush hour.
    (C) There was a lot of traffic because it was rush hour.
    (D) Rush hour is before dark.

11. (A) I thought that the trip would be fun, and it was.
    (B) The trip was more fun than I thought it would be.
    (C) The trip was not as much fun as I thought it would be.
    (D) I did not think that the trip would be fun, and it was not fun.

12. (A) I bought tomatoes.
    (B) I bought soup.
    (C) I bought beef.
    (D) I bought stew.

13. (A) James was injured in the big game last Saturday.
    (B) James was able to play in the big game last Saturday even though he was injured.
    (C) James was not able to play in the big game last Saturday because of his injury.
    (D) James's injury prevented his playing football.

14. (A) My best friend is my roommate.
    (B) My roommate is not very nice, but my best friend is.
    (C) My roommate is very nice, but he is not my best friend.
    (D) If my roommate were nicer he would be my best friend.

15. (A) Although she has a scholarship, Ellen cannot attend the University.
    (B) If Ellen gets a scholarship, she can attend the University.
    (C) Ellen attends the University on a scholarship.
    (D) Ellen cannot get a scholarship until the University accepts her.

16. (A) You should go to Florida again this year.
    (B) Although you usually go to Florida, this year you should go to California instead.
    (C) This year you should go to Florida instead of to California.
    (D) You should return to California this year.

17. (A) Since Anna speaks English very well she will not study at the Institute.
    (B) Anna will study at the Institute until she speaks English well.
    (C) Anna will continue studying at the Institute in spite of speaking English well.
    (D) Although she does not speak English well, Anna does not want to study at the Institute.

18. (A) We will go to the movies because we could not get tickets for the concert.
    (B) We left our tickets for the movie at home.
    (C) Because there are no tickets available for the movie, we will go home.
    (D) We will go home because there are no tickets available for the concert.

19. (A) John always tells secrets.
    (B) John never tells a secret.
    (C) John is mean to tell secrets.
    (D) John keeps secrets.

20. (A) Mr. Smith stopped drinking when his doctor told him that he had to.
    (B) Mr. Smith's doctor did not stop drinking.
    (C) Mr. Smith agreed to follow his doctor's advice.
    (D) Mr. Smith drinks in spite of his doctor's advice.

PREVIEW: INTERPRETING HOMOPHONES AND HOMONYMS

Homophones are words that sound the same, but are spelled differently and have different meanings. Homonyms are words that sound the same and are spelled the same, but have different meanings.

In some statements in Part A, you will be asked to interpret homophones such as *fare*, which means a fee for transportation, and *fair*, which sounds the same but means a festival; and homonyms such as *fair*, which means a festival, and *fair*, which is spelled the same, but means impartial.

EXERCISE EIGHT: INTERPRETING HOMOPHONES AND HOMONYMS

1. (A) You can say good-bye before you go to court.
    (B) You can pay the fine now instead of appearing in court.
    (C) You are right to pay the fine.
    (D) You appeared fine when you waved.

2. (A) The flowers aren't very sweet.
    (B) Flour isn't used in the sweet recipe.
    (C) The recipe would be sweeter without so much flour.
    (D) There are too many flowers.

3. (A) The fair was reported in the newspaper.
    (B) The bus fare included a newspaper.
    (C) The newspaper reports impartially.
    (D) The story wasn't about the bus fare.

4. (A) The letter was in the mail.
    (B) There were three letters.
    (C) Three were little.
    (D) All but three were females.

5. (A) Pat passed the window.
    (B) Pat wanted to buy the windows.
    (C) I was saying good-bye to Pat.
    (D) I sold the window to Pat.

6. (A) If we lost weight, we would be more comfortable.
    (B) The other room is for the weights.
    (C) The other room is more comfortable for us to stay in.
    (D) We need to lose weight.

7. (A) They had decided to have meat.
    (B) They finished the meat at the cafeteria.
    (C) They went to the cafeteria.
    (D) They decided to finish taking their test.

8. (A) Doug became bored waiting.
    (B) Doug got on the plane after waiting for several hours.
    (C) Air travel is boring for Doug.
    (D) Doug waited to put wood on the plane.

9. (A) Most of the students did not see the sources.
    (B) Most of the students did not write down the sources.
    (C) There were very few quotations.
    (D) Few students knew the location of the sources.

10. (A) The hole made the place dangerous.
    (B) The entire area was dangerous.
    (C) The unsafe area had a hole.
    (D) The air was not safe.

11. (A) They were weak and they needed to rest up.
    (B) They were off work for seven days.
    (C) A few people who were not well had time off.
    (D) The rest of them took time off.

12. (A) Mary Anne learned a permanent lesson.
    (B) Therapy decreased the effects of Mary Anne's injury.
    (C) Mary Anne took therapy so that she could go to school.
    (D) Mary Anne was studying physical therapy.

13. (A) We needed wood for the camp fire.
    (B) The camp fire needed more wood.
    (C) We sat on the wood.
    (D) We used to sit around the camp fire.

14. (A) He is not using his time well.
    (B) There is more than enough money in his budget.
    (C) His waist is a lot bigger.
    (D) His budget is not very big.

15. (A) Sue is a seamstress.
    (B) Sue works at home.
    (C) Sue can sew for a living.
    (D) Sue's new job takes less time.

16. (A) He is seeing a doctor because he has a problem with his nose.
    (B) He can find Dr. Smith's office.
    (C) Dr. Smith's office is difficult to find.
    (D) Dr. Smith is a specialist in eyes, nose, ears, and throat.

17. (A) The material was harsh.
    (B) The course was difficult.
    (C) The professor didn't treat the students well.
    (D) The material was not treated in the course.

18. (A) They had the argument here.
    (B) We don't want to know about the argument.
    (C) Here is the other point of view.
    (D) We are willing to listen to both opinions.

19. (A) We want something sweet, but he doesn't.
    (B) He won't leave us.
    (C) He won't let us rest.
    (D) He isn't very loyal.

20. (A) The pavement was broken.
    (B) You should be careful because the car needs to be fixed.
    (C) You shouldn't stop abruptly when the street is wet.
    (D) If you slide, you will damage your car.

Directions: In Part B you will hear short conversations between two speakers. At the end of each conversation, a third voice will ask a question about what was said. The question will be spoken just one time. After you hear a conversation and the question about it, read the four possible answers in your test book and decide which one is the best answer to the question you heard. Then, on your answer sheet, find the number of the question and blacken the space that corresponds to the letter of the answer you have chosen.

PREVIEW: REMEMBERING DETAILS FROM DIRECT INFORMATION

In some conversations in Part B of the Listening Comprehension Section, you will be asked to remember details that are directly stated.

EXERCISE NINE: CONVERSATIONS/DIRECT INFORMATION

1. (A) She must begin writing a paper for her history class.
    (B) She must start writing up her laboratory assignments for her chemistry class.
    (C) She must begin studying for her English examination.
    (D) She must begin studying for her French examination.

2. (A) In New York.
    (B) In Boston.
    (C) In Michigan.
    (D) In Washington.

3. (A) First gear.
    (B) Second gear.
    (C) Reverse.
    (D) Drive.

4. (A) He relaxes.
    (B) He goes fishing.
    (C) He goes to work.
    (D) He works at home.

5. (A) He ordered chocolate cake.
    (B) He ordered apple pie.
    (C) He ordered vanilla ice cream.
    (D) He did not order dessert.

6. (A) From eight o'clock in the morning until noon.
    (B) From noon until six o'clock in the evening.
    (C) From eight o'clock in the morning until nine o'clock at night.
    (D) Twenty-four hours a day.

7. (A) Spanish.
    (B) Arabic.
    (C) Japanese.
    (D) Chinese.

8. (A) To a museum.
    (B) To a wedding.
    (C) To New Mexico.
    (D) To visit a friend in Arizona.

9. (A) She decided to buy a gold necklace.
    (B) She decided to buy a pair of gold earrings and a gold necklace to match them.
    (C) She decided to buy a pair of gold earrings to match a gold necklace that she already had.
    (D) She decided to buy a pair of silver earrings because they were cheaper than the gold ones.

10. (A) Two hours.
    (B) Four hours.
    (C) Six hours.
    (D) Eight hours.

11. (A) At home.
    (B) In the car.
    (C) On the counter.
    (D) In the auditorium.

12. (A) She has not bought him a gift yet.
    (B) She bought him a book.
    (C) She bought him a case for his coin collection.
    (D) She bought him a watch.

13. (A) To a dance.
    (B) To a party.
    (C) To a play.
    (D) To a concert.

14. (A) Because she does not like it.
    (B) Because it does not fit her very well.
    (C) Because it is too formal for the occasion.
    (D) Because the man likes the other dress better.

15. (A) For the woman.
    (B) An hour late.
    (C) Fifty minutes.
    (D) By drinking coffee.

PREVIEW: SOLVING COMPUTATIONS IN CONVERSATIONS

In some conversations in Part B, you will be asked to perform simple mathematical computations like adding, subtracting, multiplying, or dividing. In other conversations, you will only need to listen for the answer.

EXERCISE TEN: CONVERSATIONS/COMPUTATIONS

1. (A) The man's mileage is half that of the woman.
    (B) The woman's mileage is the same as that of the man.
    (C) The woman's mileage is twice that of the man.
    (D) The man's mileage is twice that of the woman.

2. (A) At 10:00.
    (B) At 9:00.
    (C) At 9:15.
    (D) At 9:30.

3. (A) The man will pay ten dollars.
    (B) The man will pay twenty dollars.
    (C) The man will pay thirty dollars.
    (D) The man will pay forty dollars.

4. (A) Twenty dollars.
    (B) Twenty-five dollars.
    (C) Forty dollars.
    (D) Fifty dollars.

5. (A) He will pay $65.
    (B) He will pay $1.00.
    (C) He will pay $1.25.
    (D) He will not pay for the call.

6. (A) He did not have time to talk to the woman.
    (B) He was not wearing his watch.
    (C) It is exactly 1:15.
    (D) It is a little before 1:15.

7. (A) He may write a check for ten dollars.
    (B) He may not pay by check.
    (C) He may write a check for the amount of purchase.
    (D) He may write a check for twenty-five dollars.

8. (A) $5.45.
    (B) $1.00.
    (C) $ .95.
    (D) $2.05.

9. (A) They cost $3.
    (B) They cost $3.15.
    (C) They cost $3.50.
    (D) They cost $2.50.

10. (A) At nine o'clock.
    (B) At eleven o'clock.
    (C) At twelve o'clock.
    (D) At four o'clock.

11. (A) $15.
    (B) $150.
    (C) $12.50.
    (D) $12.

12. (A) He will owe $160.
    (B) He will owe $150.
    (C) He will owe $120.
    (D) He will owe $50.

13. (A) Two zones.
    (B) Three dollars.
    (C) Fifty-five cents.
    (D) The fare.

14. (A) At eleven o'clock.
    (B) At one o'clock.
    (C) At twelve o'clock.
    (D) At two o'clock.

15. (A) She must walk five miles.
    (B) She must walk five or six blocks.
    (C) She must walk to the corner.
    (D) She must walk three blocks.

PREVIEW: DRAWING CONCLUSIONS ABOUT THE PLACE

In some conversations in Part B, you will be asked to draw conclusions about where the conversation is taking place. Words and phrases in the conversation will provide information for your conclusions.

EXERCISE ELEVEN: CONVERSATIONS/PLACE

1. (A) In a bakery.
    (B) In a restaurant.
    (C) In a bank.
    (D) On a farm.

2. (A) In a dentist's office.
    (B) In a drugstore.
    (C) In a dress shop.
    (D) In a restaurant.

3. (A) At a wedding.
    (B) On a honeymoon.
    (C) In Florida.
    (D) At an airport.

4. (A) In a laundry.
    (B) In an elevator.
    (C) In a library.
    (D) In a bakery.

5. (A) At a hospital.
    (B) At a political convention.
    (C) At a graduation.
    (D) At a funeral.

6. (A) In a bakery.
    (B) In a taxi.
    (C) In France.
    (D) In a post office.

7. (A) At a church.
    (B) At a library.
    (C) In England.
    (D) At a theater.

8. (A) In a doctor's office.
    (B) In a professor's office.
    (C) In a lawyer's office.
    (D) In a businessman's office.

9. (A) At a bookstore.
    (B) At a bank.
    (C) At a club.
    (D) At a grocery store.

10. (A) On an Indian reservation.
    (B) At a party.
    (C) At a restaurant.
    (D) On the telephone.

11. (A) At a gas station.
    (B) At a bank.
    (C) At a hospital.
    (D) At a school.

12. (A) At a laundry.
    (B) At a car wash.
    (C) At a beauty shop.
    (D) At a garage.

13. (A) At work.
    (B) At a bank.
    (C) At a restaurant.
    (D) At an apartment building.

14. (A) At a newspaper office.
    (B) At a dry cleaner.
    (C) At a dentist's office.
    (D) At a hospital.

15. (A) At a library.
    (B) At a university class.
    (C) At a bank.
    (D) At a store.

PREVIEW: DRAWING CONCLUSIONS FROM IMPLIED INFORMATION

In some conversations in Part B, you will be asked to draw conclusions about the speakers or the situation. Words and phrases and the tone of voice of speakers in the conversation will provide information for your conclusions.

EXERCISE TWELVE: CONVERSATIONS/IMPLIED

1. (A) He prefers staying at home because he doesn't like to travel.
    (B) He prefers taking a plane because the bus is too slow.
    (C) He prefers taking a bus because the plane makes him nervous.
    (D) He prefers traveling with the woman.

2. (A) He is being held against his will.
    (B) He doesn't want to talk on the telephone with Jan.
    (C) He is too busy to answer the telephone.
    (D) He wants Jan to buy a telephone.

3. (A) She will probably pay twenty-six dollars for the gloves.
    (B) She will probably buy the leather gloves.
    (C) She will probably buy both pairs of gloves.
    (D) She will probably buy the vinyl gloves.

4. (A) That Sally is serious about Bob.
    (B) That Bob is serious about Sally.
    (C) That Sally is not serious about Bob.
    (D) That Bob is not serious about Sally.

5. (A) Weights and measurements.
    (B) Political systems.
    (C) Employment.
    (D) Money.

6. (A) That she will go away.
    (B) That she will be sorry.
    (C) That she will not quit her job.
    (D) That she will not buy him a present.

7. (A) That she does not like plays.
    (B) That she went to see the play with the man and woman.
    (C) That she had not planned to attend the play.
    (D) That she was not at the play.

8. (A) He does not understand it.
    (B) He does not like it.
    (C) He is used to it.
    (D) He does not have to take it.

9. (A) They will buy a new house after they return from their vacation.
    (B) They will not buy a new house because they do not have enough money.
    (C) They will not buy a new house because they cannot find a smaller one.
    (D) They will buy a new house that they found while they were on vacation.

10. (A) She thinks that he should call to check his score.
    (B) She thinks that he should wait.
    (C) She thinks that he should take the test again.
    (D) She thinks that he should be more worried than he is.

11. (A) To a coach.
    (B) To an optometrist.
    (C) To a dentist.
    (D) To a waitress.

12. (A) He is sick.
    (B) He is worried.
    (C) He is confident.
    (D) He is angry.

13. (A) That both the man and the woman were in class Friday.
    (B) That the man was in class Friday but the woman was not.
    (C) That the woman was in class Friday but the man was not.
    (D) That neither the man nor the woman was in class Friday.

14. (A) He does not believe what the announcer says.
    (B) He thinks that the announcer is very good at his work.
    (C) He does not have an opinion of the announcer.
    (D) He thinks that they should do what the announcer says.

15. (A) The woman is helpful.
    (B) The woman is thankful.
    (C) The woman is offended.
    (D) The woman is sorry.

Directions: In this part of the test, you will hear several short mini-talks. After each talk or conversation, you will be asked some questions. The talks and questions will be spoken just one time. They will not be written out for you, so you will have to listen carefully to understand what the speaker says.

   After you hear a question, read the four possible answers in your test book and decide which one is the best answer to the question you heard. Then, on your answer sheet, find the number of the question and blacken the space that corresponds to the answer you have chosen.

PREVIEW: UNDERSTANDING OVERHEARD CONVERSATIONS

In some mini-talks in Part C of the Listening Comprehension Section, you will be asked to understand a long conversation between two or three speakers.

   Be sure to listen for the topic, the relationship between the speakers, and the individual opinions as well as details.

   It will help you to practice listening to movies and programs in English at the theater or on TV. It will help you even more if you don't watch the screen while you listen.

EXERCISE THIRTEEN:
MINI TALKS/OVERHEARD CONVERSATIONS

Mini Talk One

1. (A) In Pittsburgh.
   (B) At two o'clock.
   (C) At the bus station.
   (D) Because the woman needed a ticket.

2. (A) At 2:15 P.M.
   (B) At 11:00 A.M.
   (C) At 2:00 P.M.
   (D) At 1:45 P.M.

3. (A) One.
   (B) Two.
   (C) Three.
   (D) Four.

4. (A) That she has taken this trip before.
   (B) That she does not like to travel.
   (C) That she is traveling with a friend.
   (D) That she will take the bus again this month.

Mini Talk Two

1. (A) Pizza.
   (B) Fish.
   (C) Apple pie.
   (D) Cake.

2. (A) Because he has a test that night.
   (B) Because he plans to go home for the weekend.
   (C) Because he has not studied at all during the semester.
   (D) Because he is helping his friend.

3. (A) At six o'clock.
    (B) At six-thirty.
    (C) Over the weekend.
    (D) On Monday.

4. (A) Bill wants John to study with him.
    (B) Bill wants John to go home with him for the weekend.
    (C) Bill wants John to let him know if he orders a pizza.
    (D) Bill wants John to find out what is being served in the cafeteria.

Mini Talk Three

1. (A) With Master Charge.
    (B) With a check.
    (C) With money.
    (D) With a Sears credit card.

2. (A) Money.
    (B) Money or credit cards.
    (C) Credit cards or checks.
    (D) Checks or money.

3. (A) She used her student ID card and a charge card.
    (B) She used her Visa and Master Charge.
    (C) She used her driver's license and her student ID card.
    (D) She used her telephone number and her student ID card.

4. (A) At City College.
    (B) At Sears.
    (C) At the bank.
    (D) At the telephone company.

Mini Talk Four

1. (A) Two.
    (B) Five.
    (C) Three.
    (D) Seventeen.

2. (A) A driver's license.
    (B) A permission slip.
    (C) A registration card.
    (D) Nothing.

3. (A) Next quarter.
    (B) Friday at nine o'clock.
    (C) Friday afternoon.
    (D) Later the same day.

4. (A) That he is majoring in mathematics.
    (B) That he has never taken a chemistry course.
    (C) That he is a freshman.
    (D) That he does not like his advisor.

PREVIEW: UNDERSTANDING ANNOUNCEMENTS AND ADVERTISEMENTS

In some mini talks in Part C, you will be asked to understand announcements of services or events and advertisements of products or opinions.

Be sure to listen for the topic, date, time, and sponsor of the announcement or advertisement.

It will help you to practice listening to announcements and advertisements in English on radio and TV.

EXERCISE FOURTEEN:
MINI TALKS/ANNOUNCEMENTS AND ADVERTISEMENTS

Mini Talk One

1. (A) After five o'clock in the morning.
   (B) After eleven o'clock in the morning.
   (C) After five o'clock in the evening.
   (D) After eleven o'clock at night.

2. (A) $2.16.
   (B) $2.60.
   (C) $2.06.
   (D) $2.66.

3. (A) A collect call.
   (B) A direct dial call.
   (C) A person-to-person call.
   (D) A call from a pay phone.

4. (A) Dial the operator.
   (B) Check the phone book for the overseas operator's number so that he can help you.
   (C) Check the phone book for overseas area codes so that you can dial direct.
   (D) Call the Southern Bell Telephone Company.

Mini Talk Two

1. (A) Appalachian Airlines is very large.
   (B) Appalachian Airlines is comfortable.
   (C) Appalachian Airlines is faster.
   (D) Appalachian Airlines is new.

2. (A) In Washington, D.C.
   (B) In New York City.
   (C) In Boston, Massachusetts.
   (D) In Atlanta, Georgia.

3. (A) Only in the morning.
   (B) Only in the afternoon.
   (C) Only on Thursday.
   (D) Every morning and afternoon.

4. (A) 800-565-7000.
    (B) 800-575-7000.
    (C) 800-565-6000.
    (D) 800-575-6000.

Mini Talk Three

1. (A) One thousand.
    (B) Fifty percent of all fatal accidents.
    (C) Approximately five hundred.
    (D) Two thousand.

2. (A) Three days in jail and a thirty-dollar fine.
    (B) Six days in jail and a thirty-dollar fine.
    (C) Thirty days in jail and a thirty-day suspension of one's driver's license.
    (D) Three days in jail and a thirty-day suspension of one's driver's license.

3. (A) Three days.
    (B) Thirty days.
    (C) Sixty days.
    (D) Six months.

4. (A) If you drink, don't drive.
    (B) If you drink, drive carefully.
    (C) If you drink, don't invite your friends to ride with you.
    (D) If you drink, drive slowly.

Mini Talk Four

1. (A) The Colorado Court.
    (B) The Colorado Cornhuskers.
    (C) The Colorado Sooners.
    (D) The Colorado Buffaloes.

2. (A) By calling Walter Murphy.
    (B) By going to the box office at the Student Union.
    (C) By mailing ten dollars to the Student Union.
    (D) By going to the ticket office at the sports arena.

3. (A) For early paintings.
    (B) For rocks and minerals.
    (C) For exhibits of American Indian art.
    (D) For collections of pottery.

4. (A) Poor–fair.
    (B) Fair–good.
    (C) Good–very good.
    (D) Very good–excellent.

PREVIEW: UNDERSTANDING NEWS REPORTS

In some mini-talks in Part C, you will be asked to understand news reports.
   Be sure to listen for changes in topics. Three or four news stories may be reported.
   It will help you to practice listening to news reports in English on radio and TV.

EXERCISE FIFTEEN: MINI TALKS/NEWS REPORTS

Mini Talk One

1. (A) Because Dr. Scarsdale designed the diet.
    (B) Because the doctor who designed the diet was from Scarsdale, New York.
    (C) Because the book that outlined the diet was published by Scarsdale.
    (D) Because the diet leaves scars.

2. (A) Five pounds.
    (B) Ten pounds.
    (C) Twenty pounds.
    (D) Forty pounds.

3. (A) It is a limited-intake diet.
    (B) It is a new high-energy diet.
    (C) It is a restricted-menu diet.
    (D) It is a two-thousand-calorie diet.

4. (A) Two weeks ago.
    (B) Last year.
    (C) Two years ago.
    (D) Twenty years ago.

Mini Talk Two

1. (A) It is named for the city where it was developed.
    (B) It is named for its inventor.
    (C) It is named for the auto company where the inventor was working when he
         developed it.
    (D) It is named for the kind of engine that is used in it.

2. (A) 7.5 miles per gallon.
    (B) 11.1 miles per gallon.
    (C) 75 miles per gallon.
    (D) 85 miles per gallon.

3. (A) Because the car must pass some environmental tests.
    (B) Because General Motors has bought the rights to the patent.
    (C) Because few people are interested in buying one.
    (D) Because the car is difficult to drive.

4. (A) $2,000.
    (B) $3,500.
    (C) $7,000.
    (D) $20,000.

Mini Talk Three

1. (A) She has brown hair and blue eyes.
   (B) She has blonde hair and blue eyes.
   (C) She has blonde hair and brown eyes.
   (D) She has brown hair and brown eyes.

2. (A) First.
   (B) Second.
   (C) Third.
   (D) Fourth.

3. (A) $1,000.
   (B) $2,000.
   (C) $3,000.
   (D) $4,000.

4. (A) She is a choral director.
   (B) She is a secretary in the Speech and Drama Department.
   (C) She is a third-year student.
   (D) She is an instructor in the Theater Department.

Mini Talk Four

1. (A) Average tuition costs increased by 9 percent.
   (B) Average tuition costs increased by 15 percent.
   (C) Average tuition costs increased by 90 percent.
   (D) Average tuition costs increased by 150 percent.

2. (A) By $150.
   (B) By $2,150.
   (C) By $3,150.
   (D) By $5,300.

3. (A) That they must pay more than out-of-state students.
   (B) That only a few are accepted.
   (C) That they are not eligible for scholarships at state universities.
   (D) That their scholarships are very small.

4. (A) Better than it was last year.
   (B) Not as good as it was in 1960.
   (C) Especially good for graduates in liberal arts.
   (D) Not very good for recent graduates.

PREVIEW: UNDERSTANDING WEATHER REPORTS

In some mini-talks in Part C, you will be asked to understand weather reports.
  Be sure to listen for the weather today and for the weather prediction for the future.
  It will help you to practice listening to weather reports in English on radio and TV.

EXERCISE SIXTEEN: MINI TALKS/WEATHER REPORTS

Mini Talk One

1. (A) Spring.
   (B) Summer.
   (C) Fall.
   (D) Winter.

2. (A) They are below average.
   (B) They are average.
   (C) They are above average.
   (D) They are record high temperatures.

3. (A) Warm.
   (B) Cold.
   (C) Chilly.
   (D) Crisp.

4. (A) Cloudy and cool.
   (B) Clear and warm.
   (C) Cloudy and warm.
   (D) Clear and cold.

Mini Talk Two

1. (A) Twenty degrees.
   (B) Fifteen degrees.
   (C) Zero.
   (D) Ten degrees below zero.

2. (A) They have been used as emergency shelters.
   (B) They have been closed.
   (C) They have been destroyed.
   (D) They have been used as medical supply centers.

3. (A) Call the National Guard.
   (B) Stay at home.
   (C) Call 875-2000.
   (D) Call an area school.

4. (A) Today.
   (B) Friday.
   (C) Saturday.
   (D) Sunday.

Mini Talk Three

1. (A) Ten o'clock.
    (B) Two o'clock.
    (C) Twelve o'clock.
    (D) Five o'clock.

2. (A) Johnson.
    (B) Miami.
    (C) Jefferson.
    (D) Franklin.

3. (A) The formation of a funnel cloud.
    (B) The sighting of a funnel cloud.
    (C) The bulletin issued by the National Weather Service.
    (D) The convergence of favorable conditions for a funnel cloud to form.

4. (A) None.
    (B) Three.
    (C) Five.
    (D) Ten.

Mini Talk Four

1. (A) It is rainy and cool.
    (B) There are showers and thunderstorms.
    (C) It is cloudy and windy.
    (D) There are sunny skies and warm temperatures.

2. (A) Seventy degrees.
    (B) Eighty degrees.
    (C) Eighty-five degrees.
    (D) Ninety degrees.

3. (A) They were delayed until today.
    (B) They moved north of the area.
    (C) They ended overnight.
    (D) They moved south of the area.

4. (A) Today.
    (B) Tomorrow.
    (C) Thursday or Friday.
    (D) On the weekend.

PREVIEW: UNDERSTANDING INFORMATIVE SPEECHES

In some mini talks in Part C, you will be asked to understand informative speeches.

Be sure to listen for the topic of the speech, the speaker's viewpoint, and the name or qualifications of the speaker as well as the details of the speech.

It will help you to practice listening to editorials in English on radio and TV.

EXERCISE SEVENTEEN:
MINI TALKS/INFORMATIVE SPEECHES

Mini Talk One

1. (A) The president of the International Student Association.
   (B) Jim Johnson of WQAD radio.
   (C) The director of the Office of International Student Affairs.
   (D) The chairperson of the program committee.

2. (A) They are drinking coffee and tea.
   (B) They are serving themselves dinner.
   (C) They are dancing.
   (D) They are arriving at the dinner.

3. (A) To introduce the people who will participate in the program.
   (B) To explain the program to the people at the dinner.
   (C) To announce the winners of the annual international awards.
   (D) To welcome the people and thank those who participated in planning the dinner.

4. (A) The students will go to a party at the International Office.
   (B) The students will go to a disco downtown.
   (C) The students will listen to the radio.
   (D) The students will dance in the dining room at State University.

Mini Talk Two

1. (A) From Yale University.
   (B) From Cornell University.
   (C) From Illinois University.
   (D) From Washington University.

2. (A) At Illinois University.
   (B) At the Twin Towers office building.
   (C) At the Department of Housing and Urban Development.
   (D) At a journal for architects.

3. (A) Federal regulations for urban development.
   (B) Trends in urban design.
   (C) Functional architecture.
   (D) Urban planning.

4. (A) He does not want to introduce him.
   (B) He does not know him.
   (C) He respects him.
   (D) He does not believe that he is qualified.

Mini Talk Three

1. (A) Members of the Community Book Club.
    (B) A group of English teachers.
    (C) A club for historians.
    (D) A gathering of America's most celebrated inventors.

2. (A) Because Thomas Edison was a famous man.
    (B) Because Thomas Edison was a well-known literary figure.
    (C) Because Thomas Edison liked to read.
    (D) Because he chose to review a book about Thomas Edison.

3. (A) He used the money for travel.
    (B) He bought books and equipment for more experiments.
    (C) He donated the money to the public library.
    (D) He gave the money to his mother.

4. (A) It is the one-hundredth anniversary of Thomas Edison's birth.
    (B) It is the one-hundredth anniversary of the electric lamp.
    (C) It is the one-hundredth anniversary of Thomas Edison's death.
    (D) It is the one-hundredth anniversary of the Detroit public library.

Mini Talk Four

1. (A) A graduation.
    (B) A class reunion.
    (C) The dedication of a new building.
    (D) The groundbreaking ceremony for a pedestrian walkway on campus.

2. (A) The main campus looks the same.
    (B) The student population is the same.
    (C) The ideals are the same.
    (D) The Division of Continuing Education has the same programs.

3. (A) Because a bell tower was to be built on the site.
    (B) Because it was found unsafe.
    (C) Because a parking lot was to be constructed there.
    (D) Because no one wanted to preserve it.

4. (A) That everything at State University has changed in the past ten years.
    (B) That although the campus looks the same, some things have changed at State University.
    (C) That in spite of the changes on the campus, the commitments at State University are the same.
    (D) That everything has stayed the same at State University during the past ten years.

PREVIEW: UNDERSTANDING ACADEMIC STATEMENTS

In some mini talks in Part C, you will be asked to understand academic statements similar to short lectures that might be heard in a college classroom.

Be sure to listen for the topic of the lecture and the name or qualifications of the speaker as well as the details in the statement.

It will help you to practice listening to lectures in English on educational radio and TV networks or in lecture halls.

EXERCISE EIGHTEEN: MINI TALKS/ACADEMIC STATEMENTS (PART 1)

Mini Talk One

1. (A) To introduce the concept of inflation.
    (B) To discuss the causes of inflation.
    (C) To review yesterday's lecture on inflation.
    (D) To argue in favor of inflation.

2. (A) Rising prices.
    (B) Fixed income.
    (C) Real income.
    (D) Cost of living.

3. (A) Persons who have salaries agreed to in long-term contracts.
    (B) Persons who own businesses.
    (C) Persons with pensions.
    (D) Persons with slow-rising incomes.

4. (A) Inflation is controlled.
    (B) Real income decreases.
    (C) Purchasing power stays the same.
    (D) Dollar income increases.

Mini Talk Two

1. (A) The climax association.
    (B) Pioneer plants.
    (C) A forest fire.
    (D) A disturbance in the balance of nature.

2. (A) To demonstrate how man destroys his environment.
    (B) To show the process in establishing a climax association.
    (C) To prove that the balance of nature is not disturbed by local agitations.
    (D) To explain the "web of life."

3. (A) Because it prepares the environment for the forms that will replace it.
    (B) Because it is stable.
    (C) Because it assures that plants, animals and minerals are replaced by exactly the same flora and fauna.
    (D) Because it is the only life that will ever be able to grow in areas where the balance of nature has been disturbed.

4. (A) That the association can continue to withstand competition for the area by other flora and fauna.
   (B) That the same kind of plants and animals are in evidence as were in the area prior to the disturbance.
   (C) That only one more stage of transition will follow it.
   (D) That the balance of nature is in a state of disturbance.

Mini Talk Three

1. (A) The scientist exploited the laws of nature.
   (B) The engineer was more practical.
   (C) The engineer was an intellectual.
   (D) The scientist was deeply involved in the practical application of his or her work.

2. (A) A French chemist and bacteriologist.
   (B) A Dutch astronomer, mathematician, and physicist.
   (C) A British mathematician and philosopher.
   (D) A Dutch chemist and philosopher.

3. (A) As examples of pure scientists.
   (B) As examples of scientists who represented the best of each century.
   (C) As examples of scientists who made practical as well as theoretical contributions.
   (D) As examples of engineers who knew something about pure science.

4. (A) That it is detached from engineering.
   (B) That it is related to engineering.
   (C) That it is best explained by the historical distinctions made between science and engineering.
   (D) That it is a purely theoretical field.

Mini Talk Four

1. (A) A new way to take notes.
   (B) A short name for the survey reading method.
   (C) The five steps in the reading process.
   (D) Different ways to study for examinations.

2. (A) To take the first step.
   (B) To summarize.
   (C) To ask questions.
   (D) To look quickly.

3. (A) That one should think about the ideas while reading the words.
   (B) That one should always take notes.
   (C) That one should read only the titles and the important words, not the examples and details.
   (D) That one should read sequences of words.

4. (A) Read.
   (B) Recite.
   (C) Review.
   (D) Re-read.

EXERCISE EIGHTEEN: MINI TALKS/ACADEMIC STATEMENTS (PART 2)

Mini Talk One

1. (A) An English class.
   (B) A history class.
   (C) A chemistry class.
   (D) A foreign language class.

2. (A) To give an overview of the course.
   (B) To explain how to prepare for the test.
   (C) To cover the material from the textbooks.
   (D) To assist students with their lab assignments.

3. (A) Ten percent.
   (B) Twenty-five percent.
   (C) Forty percent.
   (D) Fifty percent.

4. (A) Ten percent.
   (B) Twenty-five percent.
   (C) Forty percent.
   (D) Fifty percent.

Mini Talk Two

1. (A) That birth order may influence personality.
   (B) That heredity and environment play a role in the development of the personality.
   (C) That there is research on birth order at the University of Texas at Arlington.
   (D) That firstborn children and only children have similar personalities.

2. (A) Heredity.
   (B) Environment.
   (C) Birth order.
   (D) Motivation.

3. (A) They are talkative.
   (B) They are ambitious.
   (C) They are truthful.
   (D) They are sociable.

4. (A) A man with younger sisters.
   (B) A man with older sisters.
   (C) A woman with younger sisters.
   (D) A woman with older sisters.

Mini Talk Three

1. (A) In a psychology class.
   (B) In a science class.
   (C) In a German class.
   (D) In a Greek class.

2. (A) The lecturer for this mini talk.
   (B) A friend of the lecturer at Duke University.
   (C) A professor who first used the term *parapsychology*.
   (D) A professor at Duke University who will give today's lecture.

3. (A) The study of the human mind.
   (B) The study of personality.
   (C) The history of psychology.
   (D) The phenomena that cannot be explained by ordinary means.

4. (A) The history of parapsychology.
   (B) The life of Professor Joseph Rhine.
   (C) ESP.
   (D) The term parapsychology.

Mini Talk Four

1. (A) Summarizing someone's ideas in your own words.
   (B) Using someone's ideas as your own.
   (C) Helping someone to clarify his or her ideas.
   (D) Changing someone's ideas.

2. (A) Using your own ideas.
   (B) Quoting someone's exact words and citing the source.
   (C) Enclosing someone's exact words in quotation marks.
   (D) Copying ideas without citing the source.

3. (A) Paraphrasing and plagiarizing.
   (B) Quoting and plagiarizing.
   (C) Paraphrasing and quoting.
   (D) Copying and paraphrasing.

4. (A) He will receive a lower grade.
   (B) He will be asked to repeat the course.
   (C) He will be asked to rewrite the paper.
   (D) He will fail the course.

PREVIEW: UNDERSTANDING CLASS DISCUSSIONS

In some mini talks in Part C, you will be asked to understand class discussions similar to the conversations that might be heard in a college classroom.

Be sure to listen for each person's opinion.

It will help you to practice listening to movies and programs in English at the theater or on TV. Remember, it will help you even more if you don't watch the screen while you listen.

EXERCISE NINETEEN: MINI TALKS/CLASS DISCUSSIONS

Mini Talk One

1.   (A)   By the water displacement method.
     (B)   By the limestone method.
     (C)   By the carbon dioxide method.
     (D)   By the hydrochloric acid method.

2.   (A)   Magnesium.
     (B)   Limestone.
     (C)   Carbon.
     (D)   Water.

3.   (A)   The hydrochloric acid broke the carbon bonds in the carbon dioxide.
     (B)   The magnesium oxide broke the carbon-oxygen bonds in the carbon dioxide.
     (C)   The burning magnesium broke the carbon-oxygen bonds in the carbon dioxide.
     (D)   The gas collection method broke the carbon-oxygen bonds in the carbon dioxide.

4.   (A)   They could not light the magnesium ribbon.
     (B)   They did not understand the result.
     (C)   They could not collect enough gas.
     (D)   They did not know how to explain the procedure.

Mini Talk Two

1.   (A)   He believes that the tests are good.
     (B)   He believes that the required test scores are too low.
     (C)   He believes that they are more important than academic preparation.
     (D)   He believes that the tests should not be used.

2.   (A)   That they don't always use the TOEFL and the Michigan Test scores correctly.
     (B)   That they look at transcripts instead of scores.
     (C)   That they should insist on a rigid cut-off score.
     (D)   That they are looking for an appropriate alternative.

3.   (A)   Standardized examinations.
     (B)   Alternatives to standardized examinations.
     (C)   Alternatives to scores on standardized examinations.
     (D)   Scores on standardized examinations.

4. (A) In a college classroom.
   (B) At the Office of International Student Services.
   (C) In the cafeteria.
   (D) At a party.

Mini Talk Three

1. (A) Both a final examination and a term paper.
   (B) Only a final examination.
   (C) Only a term paper
   (D) Either a final examination or a term paper.

2. (A) A report.
   (B) A book review.
   (C) A research study.
   (D) A five-page composition.

3. (A) An essay examination.
   (B) An objective examination.
   (C) An open-book examination.
   (D) A take-home examination.

4. (A) English 355.
   (B) Psychology 201.
   (C) Political Science 400.
   (D) Chemistry 370.

Mini Talk Four

1. (A) The language laboratory.
   (B) Travel.
   (C) Studying in high school.
   (D) Going to movies and watching TV.

2. (A) It is easy because the people are friendly.
   (B) It is difficult because the people are not friendly.
   (C) It is difficult in spite of friendly people.
   (D) It is easy even when the people are not friendly.

3. (A) He goes to movies, watches TV, and reads newspapers and magazines.
   (B) He makes friends who speak the language.
   (C) He goes to class.
   (D) He studies grammar and vocabulary.

4. (A) He believes that it is a good idea to do all of the things that Betty and Bill suggested.
   (B) He agrees with Betty.
   (C) He believes that going to class is the best way to learn.
   (D) He believes that it is ideal to live in a country where the language is spoken.

chapter 4

Preview and
Practice Exercises
for the Structure and
Written Expression
Section of the TOEFL

Directions: Four words or phrases, marked (A), (B), (C), and (D), are given beneath each incomplete sentence. You are to choose the one word or phrase that best completes the sentence. Then, on your answer sheet, find the number of the question and blacken the space that corresponds to the letter of the answer you have chosen so that the letter inside the oval cannot be seen.

PREVIEW: VERBS

In some sentences in Part A of the Structure and Written Expression Section, you will be asked to identify the correct verb. In fact, most of the sentences in this part are verb problems.

A verb is a word or phrase that expresses action or condition. A verb can be classified as transitive or intransitive according to whether it requires a complement; it can be classified further according to the kind of complement it requires, including not only nouns, pronouns, adjectives, and adverbs but also *-ing* forms or infinitives.

EXERCISE ONE: PROBLEMS WITH VERBS (PART 1)

1. Al's doctor insists _____ for a few days.
   - (A) that he is resting
   - (B) his resting
   - (C) him to rest
   - (D) that he rest

2. I don't like iced tea, and _____.
   - (A) she doesn't too
   - (B) either doesn't she
   - (C) neither does she
   - (D) she doesn't neither

3. We wish that you _____ such a lot of work, because we know that you would have enjoyed the party.
   - (A) hadn't had
   - (B) hadn't
   - (C) didn't have had
   - (D) hadn't have

4. Since your roommate is visiting her family this weekend, _____ you like to have dinner with us tonight?
   - (A) will
   - (B) won't
   - (C) do
   - (D) wouldn't

5. Please _____ photocopies of documents.
   - (A) not to submit
   - (B) do not submit
   - (C) no submit
   - (D) not submit

6. I _____ bacon and eggs every morning.
   - (A) am used to eat
   - (B) used to eating
   - (C) am used to eating
   - (D) use to eat

7. The team really looks good tonight because the coach had them _____ every night this week.
   - (A) practice
   - (B) to practice
   - (C) practiced
   - (D) the practice

8. Would you mind _____, please?
   - (A) to answer the telephone
   - (B) answering the telephone
   - (C) answer the telephone
   - (D) to the telephone answering

9. You _____ your seats today if you want to go to the game.
    (A) had better to reserve   (C) had better reserve
    (B) had to better reserve   (D) had to reserve better

10. If it _____ so late we could have coffee.
    (A) wasn't   (C) weren't
    (B) isn't   (D) not be

11. Your sister used to visit you quite often, _____?
    (A) didn't she   (C) wouldn't she
    (B) doesn't she   (D) hadn't she

12. If Bob _____ with us, he would have had a good time.
    (A) would come   (C) had come
    (B) would have come   (D) came

13. Frankly, I'd rather you _____ anything about it for the time being.
    (A) do   (C) don't
    (B) didn't do   (D) didn't

14. Since they aren't answering their telephone, they _____.
    (A) must have left   (C) need have left
    (B) should have left   (D) can have left

15. We were hurrying because we thought that the bell _____.
    (A) had already rang   (C) had already rung
    (B) has already rang   (D) have already ringing

EXERCISE TWO: PROBLEMS WITH VERBS (PART 2)

1. I hadn't expected James to apologize but I had hoped _____.
   - (A) him calling me
   - (B) that he would call me
   - (C) him to call me
   - (D) that he call me

2. My husband lived at home before we were married, and so _____.
   - (A) did I
   - (B) had I
   - (C) I had
   - (D) I did

3. Does your new secretary _____ shorthand?
   - (A) know to take
   - (B) know how to take
   - (C) know how take
   - (D) know how taking

4. Tommy had his big brother _____ his shoes for him.
   - (A) to tie
   - (B) tie
   - (C) tied
   - (D) tying

5. I wish that the weather _____ not so warm.
   - (A) was
   - (B) be
   - (C) were
   - (D) is

6. His English teacher recommends that he _____ a regular degree program.
   - (A) begin
   - (B) begins
   - (C) will begin
   - (D) is beginning

7. Let's go out for dinner, _____?
   - (A) will we
   - (B) don't we
   - (C) shall we
   - (D) are we

8. I'd _____ the operation unless it is absolutely necessary.
   - (A) rather not have
   - (B) not rather had
   - (C) rather not to have
   - (D) rather not having

9. Would you please _____ write on the test books?
   - (A) don't
   - (B) not to
   - (C) not
   - (D) to not

10. The old man asked her to move because he _____ in that chair.
    - (A) used to sit
    - (B) was used to sit
    - (C) used to sitting
    - (D) was used to sitting

11. After the way she treated you, if I _____ in your place, I wouldn't return the call.
    - (A) be
    - (B) am
    - (C) was
    - (D) were

12. If I _____ the flu I would have gone with you.
    - (A) hadn't
    - (B) hadn't had
    - (C) didn't have
    - (D) wouldn't have had

13. He's taken his medicine, _____?
    - (A) hasn't he
    - (B) didn't he
    - (C) doesn't he
    - (D) isn't he

14. Your mother and I are looking forward _____ you.
   (A) of seeing
   (B) for seeing
   (C) to see
   (D) to seeing

15. It is imperative that you _____ there in person.
   (A) be
   (B) will be
   (C) will
   (D) are

EXERCISE THREE: PROBLEMS WITH VERBS (PART 3)

1. The brakes need _____.
    (A) adjusted
    (B) to adjustment
    (C) to adjust
    (D) adjusting

2. I wish that we _____ with my brother when he flies to England next week.
    (A) could go
    (B) had gone
    (C) will go
    (D) are going

3. Are you sure Miss Smith _____ use the new equipment?
    (A) knows to
    (B) knows the
    (C) knows how to
    (D) knows how

4. Mary and John _____ to the parties at the Student Union every Friday.
    (A) used to go
    (B) use to go
    (C) are used to go
    (D) were used to go

5. You _____ me, because I didn't say that.
    (A) must misunderstand
    (B) must be misunderstanding
    (C) must have misunderstood
    (D) had to misunderstand

6. _____ you rather sit by the window?
    (A) Don't
    (B) Will
    (C) Wouldn't
    (D) Won't

7. His government insisted that he _____ until he finished his degree.
    (A) should stay
    (B) shall stay
    (C) stayed
    (D) stay

8. After he had researched and _____ his paper, he found some additional material that he should have included.
    (A) wrote
    (B) written
    (C) writing
    (D) have written

9. The man who was driving the truck would not admit that he had been at fault, and _____.
    (A) neither the other driver
    (B) neither would the other driver
    (C) neither had the other driver
    (D) the other driver neither

10. If it _____ rain, we'll have the party outside.
    (A) wouldn't
    (B) doesn't
    (C) didn't
    (D) won't

11. Excuse me, but it is time to have your temperature _____.
    (A) taking
    (B) to take
    (C) take
    (D) taken

12. Almost everyone fails _____ the driver's test on the first try.
    (A) passing
    (B) to have passed
    (C) to pass
    (D) in passing

13. Mike had hoped _____ his letter.
  (A) her to answer
  (B) that she answer
  (C) that she would answer
  (D) her answering

14. I think that you had better _____ earlier so that you can get to class on time.
  (A) to start to get up
  (B) started getting up
  (C) start getting up
  (D) to get up

15. Today's weather isn't as cold as it was yesterday, _____?
  (A) wasn't it
  (B) was it
  (C) isn't it
  (D) is it

PREVIEW: PRONOUNS

In some sentences in Part A, you will be asked to identify the correct pronoun.

A pronoun is a word that can be used instead of a noun, usually to avoid repeating the noun. A pronoun may be singular or plural; masculine, feminine, or neuter; and first, second, or third person to agree with the noun to which it refers. A pronoun may be used as the subject of a sentence or a clause or as the object of a sentence, a clause, or a preposition. In English, pronouns are also used to express possessives and reflexives.

EXERCISE FOUR: PROBLEMS WITH PRONOUNS

1. Tito was the only foreigner _____ I saw at the convention.
   (A) whom
   (B) which
   (C) who
   (D) what

2. They forgot about _____ them to join us for lunch.
   (A) us to ask
   (B) us asking
   (C) our asking
   (D) we asking

3. Our host family always invites my roommate and _____ to their house on Sundays.
   (A) me
   (B) my
   (C) I
   (D) mine

4. Because they usually receive the same score on standardized examinations, there is often disagreement as to _____ is the better student, Bob or Helen.
   (A) who
   (B) which
   (C) whom
   (D) whose

5. I really appreciate _____ to help me, but I am sure that I will be able to manage by myself.
   (A) you to offer
   (B) your offering
   (C) that you offer
   (D) that you are offering

6. Do you know the woman _____ was hurt in the accident?
   (A) which
   (B) whom
   (C) who
   (D) whose

7. I would like to leave a message for _____ if I may.
   (A) they
   (B) them
   (C) their
   (D) theirs

8. A few of _____ are planning to drive to Florida during spring break.
   (A) we girls
   (B) us girls
   (C) girls we
   (D) girls

9. This is the woman _____ the artist said posed as a model for the painting.
   (A) who
   (B) whom
   (C) which
   (D) whose

10. Of those who took the exam with Jane and _____, I am the only one who studied for it.
    (A) he
    (B) his
    (C) him
    (D) himself

11. Let you and _____ agree to settle our differences without involving any of the other students.
  (A) I
  (B) myself
  (C) me
  (D) my

12. If you had told us earlier _____ he was, we could have introduced him at the meeting.
  (A) who
  (B) which
  (C) whom
  (D) whoever

13. I always ask my sister and _____ for advice.
  (A) her
  (B) she
  (C) hers
  (D) herself

14. Two of the notebooks _____ Tom had lost on the bus were returned to the main desk at his dormitory.
  (A) what
  (B) who
  (C) which
  (D) whose

15. He didn't seem to mind _____ TV while he was trying to study.
  (A) their watching
  (B) that they watch
  (C) them watching
  (D) them to watch

PREVIEW: NOUNS

In some sentences in Part A, you will be asked to identify the correct noun.

A noun is a word that names persons, objects, and ideas. There are two basic classifications of nouns in English: count nouns and non-count nouns. Count nouns are those that can be made plural by -s, -es, or an irregular form. They are used in agreement with either singular or plural verbs. Non-count nouns are those that cannot be made plural in these ways. They are used in agreement with singular verbs.

It is necessary to know whether a noun is count or non-count to maintain verb agreement and to choose correct adjective modifiers.

EXERCISE FIVE: PROBLEMS WITH NOUNS

1. Please go to _____ to pick up your ID card.
    (A) third window
    (B) the window three
    (C) window third
    (D) the third window

2. May I have two _____ instead of beans, please?
    (A) corn's ear
    (B) ear of corns
    (C) corn ears
    (D) ears of corn

3. If you want to find good information about graduate programs in the United States, look in _____ of the *College Blue Books*.
    (A) volume two
    (B) volume second
    (C) the volume two
    (D) second volume

4. Let's buy our tickets while I still have _____ left.
    (A) a few money
    (B) a little moneys
    (C) a few dollars
    (D) a few dollar

5. The assignment for Monday was to read _____ in your textbooks.
    (A) chapter tenth
    (B) the chapter ten
    (C) chapter the tenth
    (D) the tenth chapter

6. I always put my best _____ in a safe-deposit box.
    (A) jewelries
    (B) jewelry's pieces
    (C) pieces of jewelry
    (D) piece of jewelries

7. It's a shame that you have _____ time in New York on the tour.
    (A) so few
    (B) so little
    (C) a few
    (D) a little

8. We haven't had _____ news from the disaster site since the earthquake.
    (A) many
    (B) quite a few
    (C) much
    (D) some

9. John Kennedy was _____ of the United States.
    (A) the thirty-five president
    (B) the thirty-fifth president
    (C) the president thirty-fifth
    (D) president the thirty-five

10. I'll have a cup of tea and _____.
    (A) two toasts
    (B) two piece of toasts
    (C) two pieces of toast
    (D) two pieces of toasts

11. The ticket agent said that the plane would be boarding at _____.
- (A) the gate six
- (B) sixth gate
- (C) gate six
- (D) the six gate

12. I will need _____ about the climate before I make a final decision.
- (A) a few informations
- (B) a few information
- (C) a little informations
- (D) a little information

13. Sending _____ "special delivery" costs about fifteen times as much as sending it "regular delivery."
- (A) mails
- (B) a mail
- (C) a piece of mail
- (D) pieces of a mail

14. The Chicago bus is parked at _____.
- (A) the lane two
- (B) the two lane
- (C) lane two
- (D) lane the two

15. We don't have _____ tonight.
- (A) many homeworks
- (B) much homeworks
- (C) many homework
- (D) much homework

PREVIEW: MODIFIERS

In some sentences in Part A, you will be asked to identify the correct modifier.

A modifier can be an adjective or an adjectival phrase that describes a noun or an -ing form. A modifier can also be an adverb or an adverbial phrase that adds information about the verb, adjective, or another verb.

Adjectives do not change form to agree with the nouns or -ing forms that they describe, but some adjectives are used only with count nouns and others are used only with non-count nouns.

EXERCISE SIX: PROBLEMS WITH MODIFIERS (PART 1)

1. She hasn't seen her family _____ three years ago.
   (A) since
   (B) for
   (C) from
   (D) before

2. Just put your coat in _____.
   (A) the hall closet
   (B) the closet of the hall
   (C) the hall's closet
   (D) hall closet

3. Bill came to work at the University thirty years _____ today.
   (A) since
   (B) before
   (C) from
   (D) ago

4. This drink tastes a little _____ to me.
   (A) strongly
   (B) so strong
   (C) strong
   (D) too much strong

5. I like these dishes but _____ is a little too small.
   (A) the tea cup
   (B) the cup of tea
   (C) the tea's cup
   (D) the cup for the tea

6. My sister has a _____ baby.
   (A) two-months-old
   (B) two-month-olds
   (C) two-months-olds
   (D) two-month-old

7. The one in the window was _____ expensive that I couldn't afford it.
   (A) so
   (B) too
   (C) too much
   (D) very

8. We used to go skiing in Michigan every winter, but _____ for the past five seasons.
   (A) I don't go
   (B) I haven't gone
   (C) I'm not going
   (D) I didn't go

9. It is _____ day that travel advisories have been issued for most of the major highways.
   (A) such snowy
   (B) so snowy
   (C) such a snowy
   (D) such snowy a

10. Our reservations are for _____.
    (A) sixth June
    (B) six June
    (C) the sixth of June
    (D) the six of June

11. They listened _____ while the examiner gave them the directions for Part I.
(A) attentive
(B) attentively
(C) attentiveness
(D) attention

12. The cookies that you sent over were _____ that I ate them all.
(A) very good
(B) too good
(C) so good
(D) good

13. Jacobson's is one of the most expensive _____ in the city.
(A) department store
(B) departments stores
(C) departments store
(D) department stores

14. I don't understand how John could have made _____ in judgment.
(A) such big mistake
(B) such a big mistake
(C) so a big mistake
(D) so big mistake

15. You can give me a receipt if you want to, but your word is _____ for me.
(A) enough good
(B) good as enough
(C) good enough
(D) good than enough

EXERCISE SEVEN: PROBLEMS WITH MODIFIERS (PART 2)

1. Sam usually does his work very _____ and well, but today he seemed a little preoccupied.
   - (A) careful
   - (B) careful manner
   - (C) carefully
   - (D) care

2. Besides being expensive, the food in the cafeteria tastes _____.
   - (A) badly
   - (B) too badly
   - (C) too much bad
   - (D) bad

3. _____ here since 1976 when her parents moved from New York.
   - (A) She's lived
   - (B) She's living
   - (C) She was living
   - (D) She'd live

4. We'll get _____ by train if we leave tonight.
   - (A) fast enough there
   - (B) there fast enough
   - (C) there enough fast
   - (D) enough fast there

5. If the cab arrives _____ you will miss your flight.
   - (A) lately
   - (B) lateness
   - (C) more later
   - (D) late

6. It was _____ that we went camping in the mountains last weekend.
   - (A) such nice weather
   - (B) so nice a weather
   - (C) too nice weather
   - (D) nice weather so

7. The homecoming football game will be played on _____.
   - (A) two September
   - (B) the second of September
   - (C) September two
   - (D) the two of September

8. Mary overslept and was _____ late that she missed her bus.
   - (A) so
   - (B) too
   - (C) much
   - (D) very

9. Could you please tell me the _____ for Biology 457 and Chemistry 610?
   - (A) rooms numbers
   - (B) rooms number
   - (C) room's number
   - (D) room numbers

10. I think it's _____ to take a few more pictures.
    - (A) enough light
    - (B) light as enough
    - (C) light enough
    - (D) enough as light

11. Last Sunday was _____ that we took a drive in the country.
    - (A) so beautiful day
    - (B) such a beautiful a day
    - (C) such a beautiful weather
    - (D) so beautiful a day

12. The conference was organized for all of the _____ in the state.
    - (A) mathematic teachers
    - (B) mathematics teachers
    - (C) mathematics teacher
    - (D) mathematic's teachers

13. It is difficult to find a _____ in the Washington area for less than $300 a month.
- (A) two-bedroom apartment
- (B) two-bedrooms apartment
- (C) two-bedrooms apartments
- (D) two-bedroom apartments

14. I am especially glad that Bob decided to come to the party because we hadn't seen him _____ several months.
- (A) since
- (B) until
- (C) before
- (D) for

15. John and I like to watch the games on TV because we can see more _____ than we could from a seat in the stadium.
- (A) clear
- (B) clearness
- (C) clearly
- (D) clearer

PREVIEW: COMPARATIVES

In some sentences in Part A, you will be asked to identify the correct comparative.

A comparative can be a word or phrase that expresses similarity or difference. A comparative can also be a word ending like -er or -est that expresses a degree of comparison with adjectives and adverbs.

EXERCISE EIGHT: PROBLEMS WITH COMPARATIVES

1. I will return your notes as soon as _____ copying them.
    (A) I will finish
    (B) I do finish
    (C) I finish
    (D) I be finished

2. _____ the worse I seem to feel.
    (A) When I take more medicine
    (B) The more medicine I take
    (C) Taking more of the medicine
    (D) More medicine taken

3. We will have to be careful not to get our suitcases mixed up because yours is almost the same _____ mine.
    (A) like
    (B) to
    (C) as
    (D) that

4. My new glasses cost me _____ the last pair that I bought.
    (A) times three
    (B) three times more than
    (C) three times as much as
    (D) as much three times as

5. Although she is very popular, she is not _____ her sister.
    (A) pretty as
    (B) as pretty
    (C) prettier than
    (D) more pretty than

6. We are going to Florida as soon as _____ taking our final exams.
    (A) we're finish
    (B) we'll finish
    (C) we'd finish
    (D) we finish

7. This new soap is not much _____ the others that I have tried
    (A) different
    (B) different than
    (C) different from
    (D) different that

8. Ms. Jones isn't as nice _____ Ms. Smith.
    (A) as
    (B) for
    (C) like
    (D) to

9. The rooms in Graduate Towers are _____ Patterson Hall.
    (A) larger than
    (B) larger than that of
    (C) larger than those in
    (D) larger than in

10. We'll be there as soon as we _____ a babysitter for our son.
    (A) will find
    (B) found
    (C) find
    (D) are finding

11. The final will be _____ the midterm.
    (A) alike
    (B) like
    (C) same
    (D) similar

12. They are _____ my other neighbors.
    (A) more friendlier than
    (B) friendly than
    (C) friendlier as
    (D) more friendly than

13. Tuition at an American university runs _____ one thousand dollars a semester.
    (A) so high as
    (B) as high to
    (C) as high as
    (D) as high than

14. _____ I get to know her, the more I like her.
    (A) For more
    (B) More
    (C) The more
    (D) The most

15. I would have paid _____ for my car if the salesman had insisted, because I really wanted it.
    (A) as much twice
    (B) much twice
    (C) twice as much
    (D) times two

PREVIEW: CONNECTORS

In some sentences in Part A, you will be asked to identify the correct connector.

A connector is a word or phrase that joins words, phrases, or clauses. A connector expresses relationships between the words, phrases, and clauses that it joins. Some common relationships are cause and result, contradiction, substitution, addition, exception, example, and purpose.

EXERCISE NINE: PROBLEMS WITH CONNECTORS

1. We are considering buying a house in Gainesville, but we want to find out _____ there first.
    (A) what the taxes are
    (B) what are the taxes
    (C) the taxes what are
    (D) the taxes are

2. Betty moved from the dormitory _____ the noise.
    (A) because
    (B) cause
    (C) because of
    (D) caused from

3. I didn't hear _____ when he gave us the assignment.
    (A) what the professor says
    (B) that the professor said
    (C) what the professor said
    (D) which the professor says

4. He had to borrow a little money from his brother _____ he could finish his education without working.
    (A) so
    (B) that
    (C) so that
    (D) in order so

5. I wonder where _____.
    (A) he did go
    (B) did he go
    (C) he went
    (D) went he

6. Both Mary and Ellen, _____ Jane, are studying nursing at the University of Toledo.
    (A) as well as
    (B) well
    (C) as well to
    (D) and well as

7. We had a disagreement _____ the bus was late.
    (A) because of
    (B) caused of
    (C) because
    (D) caused

8. _____ the light rain, the baseball game will not be cancelled unless the other team concedes.
    (A) Despite of
    (B) Despite in
    (C) In spite
    (D) Despite

9. I don't have any idea what _____ for graduation.
    (A) does she want
    (B) she wants
    (C) she want
    (D) is she wanting

10. We were both pleased _____ honored to be guests of the president.
    (A) also
    (B) and
    (C) alike
    (D) as

11. I wonder _____ on sale.
    (A) how much cost these shoes   (C) how much these shoes cost
    (B) how much do these shoes cost   (D) how much are these shoes cost

12. We moved to the front row _____ we could hear and see better.
    (A) so   (C) such
    (B) so that   (D) such that

13. James plays not only on the basketball squad _____.
    (A) but on the baseball team   (C) also on the baseball team
    (B) but on the baseball team also   (D) but also on the baseball team

14. _____ his wealth, he is not spoiled.
    (A) Despite of   (C) In spite of
    (B) In despite   (D) In spite

15. Could you please tell me where _____?
    (A) is the nearest bus stop located   (C) is located the nearest bus stop
    (B) the nearest bus stop is located   (D) located is the nearest bus stop

PREVIEW: CUMULATIVE PRACTICE WITH STRUCTURES

In the sentences in Part A, you will be asked to identify the correct answer for a variety of structures.

Remember, a structure can be a verb, pronoun, noun, modifier, comparative, or connector. These cumulative exercises include a variety of structures.

EXERCISE TEN: CUMULATIVE PRACTICE WITH STRUCTURES (PART 1)

1. Allen said that his trip was very _____.
   (A) interested
   (B) interest
   (C) interesting
   (D) of interest

2. The cost is _____ much for me.
   (A) so much
   (B) too much
   (C) very much
   (D) much too

3. Let's call to see if _____ an extra ticket at the box office.
   (A) is there
   (B) it may be
   (C) there is
   (D) it is

4. Please don't leave without _____ the lights.
   (A) you turn off
   (B) to turn off
   (C) turning off
   (D) you'll turn off

5. By the time he retires Professor Baker _____ for almost forty years.
   (A) will teach
   (B) has taught
   (C) will have taught
   (D) will has taught

6. At a *potluck* dinner, everyone who comes must _____ a dish.
   (A) take
   (B) get
   (C) carry
   (D) bring

7. I'm sorry, but there isn't _____.
   (A) any left
   (B) left any
   (C) leaving any
   (D) some left

8. If you still don't have an answer from the University of Iowa, why _____ call the admissions office?
   (A) you don't
   (B) not to
   (C) not
   (D) don't

9. How much snow _____ now?
   (A) it is
   (B) is it
   (C) there is
   (D) is there

10. My roommate lost a lot of weight _____ every day.
    (A) to exercise
    (B) for exercise
    (C) for exercising
    (D) by exercising

11. Something must be done quickly if endangered species _____ saved.
    (A) are to be
    (B) be
    (C) can be
    (D) will be

12. I thought I saw Professor Davis _____ in the library last night.
(A) working
(B) to work
(C) worked
(D) works

13. Mr. Jones got very sick _____ too hard.
(A) for working
(B) from working
(C) by working
(D) to work

14. I prefer writing a term paper _____ taking an examination.
(A) than
(B) to
(C) for
(D) that

15. I am going to take the bus _____ money.
(A) for to save
(B) saving
(C) to save
(D) by saving

EXERCISE ELEVEN: CUMULATIVE PRACTICE WITH STRUCTURES (PART 2)

1. I _____ to be ready by the time you get here.
   (A) must
   (B) ought
   (C) can
   (D) should

2. She told us _____ so impatient.
   (A) don't to be
   (B) not to be
   (C) we shouldn't been
   (D) not to been

3. Mr. Black's secretary has _____ appointments scheduled for him today.
   (A) none
   (B) not any
   (C) not
   (D) no

4. _____ of the students will be going on the trip.
   (A) Near all
   (B) Almost all
   (C) The all
   (D) The most all

5. Mother's Day is _____ May.
   (A) on
   (B) in
   (C) at
   (D) for

6. Thank you for inviting us, but my husband is not really interested _____.
   (A) in going dancing
   (B) for going dancing
   (C) going dancing
   (D) to go dancing

7. Could you _____ five dollars?
   (A) borrow me
   (B) borrowing me
   (C) to lend me
   (D) lend me

8. Please get me some milk when you _____ to the store.
   (A) will go
   (B) go
   (C) are going
   (D) went

9. I have finished typing all _____ the last page.
   (A) until
   (B) but
   (C) to
   (D) for

10. Some of these pants go with the jackets and _____ are sold separately.
    (A) anothers
    (B) the other
    (C) some other
    (D) others

11. Jane went home _____ her clothes.
    (A) to changing
    (B) for change
    (C) to change
    (D) for changing

12. Will her mother let her _____ with us to the party?
    (A) go
    (B) goes
    (C) going
    (D) to go

13. _____ an exciting city New Orleans is!

(A) So

(B) Very

(C) How

(D) What

14. It is a beautiful car, but it is not _____ the price that I paid for it.

(A) price

(B) worthy

(C) worth

(D) value

15. My pictures _____ until next week.

(A) won't develop

(B) aren't developing

(C) don't develop

(D) won't be developed

Directions: Four words or phrases are underlined in each sentence and marked (A), (B), (C), and (D). You are to identify the one underlined word or phrase that should be corrected or rewritten. Then, on your answer sheet, find the number of the question and blacken the space that corresponds to the letter of the answer you have chosen.

PREVIEW: POINT OF VIEW

In some sentences in Part B of the Structure and Written Expression Section, you will be asked to identify errors in point of view.

Point of view is the relationship between the verb in the main clause of a sentence and other verbs or between the verbs in a sentence and the adverbs that express time.

EXERCISE TWELVE: PROBLEMS WITH POINT OF VIEW

1. Although there are approximately 120 intensive language institutes in the United
              (A)   (B)   (C)
    States in 1970, there are more than twice as many now.
                                        (D)

2. Cartographers did not make an accurate map because the political situation in the

    area changes so rapidly that they were not able to draw the boundaries correctly.
         (A)   (B)   (C)   (D)

3. This year designers are showing very bright colors and styles that were worn closer to
                                       (A)   (B)
    the body than those shown last year.
              (C)   (D)

4. Everyone who saw *Star Wars* said that it is one of the best science fiction movies that
                 (A)   (B)   (C)
    has ever been released.
             (D)

5. If there were no alternative we will try to get enough people interested to charter a bus.
                  (A)   (B)   (C)   (D)

6. Before he retired last April, Mr. Thompson is working as foreign student advisor
                       (A)   (B)
    for thirty years at Community College.
          (C)   (D)

7. When he tried to make a reservation, he found that the hotel that he wants was
                    (A)   (B)
    completely filled because of a convention.
        (C)   (D)

8. The secretary thought that she <u>will</u> have to <u>wait</u> until tomorrow to send the letters
                                     (A)   (B)
because the mail had already <u>gone,</u> but her boss suggested that she <u>take</u> them to the
                           (C)   (D)
post office instead.

9. Although Emily Dickinson <u>publishes</u> <u>only</u> three of her verses before she died, today
                                 (A)   (B)
there <u>are</u> <u>more than</u> one thousand of her poems printed in many important collections.
      (C)   (D)

10. Between <u>one thing and another,</u> Anna <u>does</u> not get through <u>with</u> her <u>term paper</u> last
                (A)   (B)   (C)   (D)
Friday.

11. Dew <u>usually</u> <u>disappeared</u> by seven o'clock <u>in the morning</u> when the sun comes up.
      (A)   (B)   (C)   (D)

12. She was among <u>the few</u> <u>who</u> <u>want</u> to quit <u>smoking</u> instead of cutting down.
               (A)   (B) (C)   (D)

13. It is <u>an accepted custom</u> for guests <u>to take</u> their gifts to the wedding reception when
         (A)   (B)   (C)
the couple <u>invited</u> them to attend.
        (D)

14. I thought that they <u>are</u> arriving <u>at the airport</u> today, but so far no one from their embassy
             (A)   (B)
<u>has</u> called <u>to confirm</u> the time.
(C)   (D)

15. <u>On</u> October 19, 1781, Cornwallis <u>surrenders</u> his army <u>to</u> General Washington, a
(A)   (B)   (C)
gesture <u>that</u> signaled the end of the Revolutionary War.
      (D)

16. The price of coffee <u>is</u> low last month, but everyone <u>knows</u> that <u>it</u> is <u>going to</u> go
                (A)   (B)   (C)   (D)
up this month.

17. Until the day she died, the old lady <u>who</u> <u>lives</u> <u>by the</u> University was working <u>part time</u> at
                             (A) (B) (C)   (D)
the language lab.

18. On last night's news, Walter Cronkite said that the crime rate is increasing <u>in spite of</u>
                                                      (A)   (B)
community and government programs <u>aimed at</u> providing education and employ-
                                   (C)
ment opportunities <u>for</u> first offenders.
               (D)

19. *Public Opinion Magazine* reported that 57 percent of all Americans <u>strongly</u> <u>believe</u>
                                                                            (A)   (B)
    that mothers with young children <u>should not work</u> outside of the home unless <u>their</u>
                                          (C)   (D)
    families badly needed the extra income.

20. The instructor told us that <u>to remember</u> details, it <u>is</u> important <u>to take notes</u> while
                                     (A)   (B)   (C)
    <u>listening</u> to the lecture.
       (D)

21. The <u>fruit</u> and vegetables at the Shop Mart are always very fresh because <u>they</u> <u>were</u>
        (A)   (B)   (C)
    shipped in every day from the local <u>farm markets</u>.
                                              (D)

22. The maid <u>does</u> not finish <u>cleaning</u> the rooms at College Dormitory yesterday because
             (A)   (B)
    she had <u>to help</u> <u>scrub</u> the floors in the kitchen and the cafeteria.
               (C)   (D)

23. Since banks usually give gifts to customers <u>who</u> <u>deposited</u> large amounts to savings
                                                (A)   (B)
    accounts, it is a good idea <u>to ask</u> the bank officials whether you <u>are</u> entitled to receive
                                   (C)   (D)
    one.

24. The race driver accelerated to 190 <u>miles per hour</u> and <u>qualifies</u> for the Indianapolis
                                            (A)   (B)
    500, <u>America's</u> <u>most celebrated</u> auto racing competition.
            (C)   (D)

25. It is necessary <u>to put</u> a <u>return address</u> that <u>included</u> your name, street number, city,
                       (A)   (B)   (C)
    state, and zip code on <u>all</u> correspondence.
                              (D)

PREVIEW: AGREEMENT

In some sentences in Part B, you will be asked to identify errors in agreement.

Agreement is the relationship between a subject and verb or between a pronoun and noun, or between a pronoun and another pronoun.

To agree, a subject and verb must both be singular or both be plural. To agree, a pronoun and the noun or pronoun to which it refers must both be singular or plural and both be masculine or feminine or neuter.

EXERCISE THIRTEEN: PROBLEMS WITH AGREEMENT

1. If one does not have respect for himself, you cannot expect others to respect him.
                                        (A)   (B)   (C)   (D)

2. What happened at Kent State in 1970 were the result of the president's order to invade
                        (A)   (B)   (C)   (D)
    Cambodia.

3. The governor, with his wife and children, are at home watching the election returns
                          (A)   (B)   (C)
    on television.
        (D)

4. Those of us who belong to the National Association for Foreign Student Affairs
                    (A)
    should have their memberships renewed in September.
        (B)   (C)   (D)

5. Both a term paper and a final exam is required for Chemistry 320.
                          (A)   (B) (C)   (D)

6. Neither my traveler's checks nor the money that my father cabled me are sufficient
                                                                (A)   (B)
    to pay for the tickets.
        (C)   (D)

7. There have been little rain in the last twenty-four-hour period because of a high
            (A)   (B)   (C)   (D)
    pressure area over most of the state.

8. Everyone who takes the examination will receive their score reports in six weeks.
                (A)   (B)   (C)   (D)

9. The popularity of soccer in the United States were increased significantly by
                                                      (A)   (B)
    the signing of Pelé to play for the North American Soccer League.
        (C)   (D)

10. Not one in a hundred seeds develop into a healthy plant, even under laboratory
                (A)   (B)   (C)   (D)
    conditions.

11. Although the body has been reduced in size by eighteen inches, there have been
                      (A)   (B)   (C)
    little change in the engine of the new models.
    (D)

12. Benjamin Franklin strongly objected to the eagle being chosen as the national bird
                        (A)   (B)
    because of their predatory nature.
       (C)   (D)

13. In order to grow well, the Blue Spruce, like other pine trees, require a temperate
                     (A)   (B)   (C)   (D)
    climate.

14. Few airports in the United States is as modern as that of Atlanta.
                                   (A)   (B) (C) (D)

15. Work on improving industrial disposal methods were begun in the early 1970's,
            (A)   (B)
    shortly after the Clean Air bill was passed by Congress.
       (C)   (D)

16. The president, with his Secret Service staff and two White House aides, are en route
                   (A)   (B)
    to NBC studios to tape a special press conference.
    (C)   (D)

17. The officials of the Board of Elections asked that each voter present their registration
                                                                    (A)   (B)
    card and a valid Texas driver's license before receiving a ballot.
                           (C)   (D)

18. Those of us who move during the semester should have their addresses changed at
                   (A)   (B)   (C)   (D)
    the registrar's office.

19. Neither of the two alternatives that had been outlined at the last meeting were
                                        (A)   (B)   (C)
    acceptable to the executive committee.
               (D)

20. If one had considered the consequences carefully, you would not have agreed to
            (A)   (B)   (C)
    sign a two-year lease.
         (D)

21. Buenos Aires is one of the world capitals that are noted for its busy harbor.
                 (A)   (B)   (C)   (D)

22. In spite of his being a professor of chemical engineering, one of the people who know
                  (A)   (B) (C)
    the most about theoretical mathematics is Dr. Ayers.
                                            (D)

23. If one <u>has</u> a special medical condition such as diabetes, epilepsy, or allergy, it is
     (A)
    advisable that <u>they</u> <u>carry</u> some kind of identification in order to avoid <u>being</u> given
            (B) (C)   (D)
    improper medication in an emergency.

24. <u>It is</u> surprising that there <u>were</u> not a serious objection to <u>their changing</u> the regulations
    (A)   (B)   (C)
    for the chess tournament without <u>consulting</u> the officials.
                               (D)

25. A large percentage of the federal employees at the Denver government center
    <u>are participating</u> in an experimental <u>four-day</u> <u>work week</u> aimed at curbing gasoline
        (A)   (B)   (C)
    consumption and pollution, two of <u>the most urgent problems</u> facing cities today.
                                 (D)

PREVIEW: INTRODUCTORY VERBAL MODIFIERS

In some sentences in Part B, you will be asked to identify errors in introductory verbal modifiers and the subjects that they modify.

Introductory verbal modifiers are *-ing* forms, participles, and infinitives. A phrase with an introductory verbal modifier occurs at the beginning of a sentence and is followed by a comma. The subject modified by an introductory verbal modifier must follow the comma.

If the correct subject does not follow the comma, then the meaning of the sentence is changed. Often the changed meaning is not logical.

EXERCISE FOURTEEN: PROBLEMS WITH INTRODUCTORY VERBAL MODIFIERS

1. After finishing *Roots,* the one-hundred-year history of a black American family, the
     (A)   (B)
   Nobel Prize Committee awarded author Alex Haley a special citation for literary
                           (C)   (D)
   excellence.

2. A competitive sport, gymnasts perform before officials who must use their judgment
          (A)   (B)
   along with their knowledge of the rules to determine the relative skill of each
      (C)   (D)
   participant.

3. To remove stains from permanent press clothing, carefully soaking in cold water
                    (A)   (B)
   before washing with one's regular detergent.
        (C)   (D)

4. Found in Tanzania by Mary Leakey, some archeologists estimated that the
    (A)   (B)
   three-million-year-old fossils were the oldest human remains to be discovered.
            (C)   (D)

5. After fighting the blaze for three days, the supertanker was hauled toward open seas
       (A)   (B)
   in an effort to save the southern Caribbean from the worst oil spill in history.
                 (C)   (D)

6. According to the conditions of their scholarships, after finishing their degrees, the
      (A)   (B)
   University will employ them for three years.
                        (C)   (D)

7. Originally having been buried in Spain, and later moved to Santo Domingo in the
      (A)   (B)   (C)
   Dominican Republic, Columbus's final resting place is Havana, Cuba.
                                      (D)

8. Written by Neil Simon, New York audiences received the new play enthusiastically at
          (A)   (B)   (C)
the world premiere Saturday evening.
                        (D)

9. By migrating to a warmer climate every fall, survival is assured for another year.
                              (A)   (B)   (C)   (D)

10. Saddened by the actor's sudden death, a memorial fund will be established so that
                        (A)   (B)   (C)
family and friends can make donations in his name to The American Cancer Society.
                        (D)

11. To prevent cavities, dental floss should be used daily after brushing one's teeth.
                              (A)   (B)   (C)   (D)

12. While researching the problem of violent crime, the Senate committee's discovery that
                                                            (A)
handguns were used to commit 54 percent of all murders in large cities.
                  (B)   (C)   (D)

13. Trying to pay for a purchase with cash, salespersons often ask for credit cards
          (A)   (B)   (C)
instead.
(D)

14. After reviewing the curriculum, several significant changes were made in traditional
                  (A)   (B)   (C)   (D)
business programs at Harvard University.

15. Having hit more home runs than any other player in the history of baseball,
                  (A)   (B)   (C)
Hank Aaron's record is famous.
                  (D)

16. Banned in the U.S., the effect of fluorocarbons continues at a level that could
          (A)   (B)
eventually damage the ozone layer, and bring about such serious results as high risk
      (C)   (D)
of skin cancer and global climate changes.

17. To avoid jet lag, many doctors recommend that their patients begin adjusting one
          (A)   (B)
week before departure time by shifting one hour each day toward the new
                                      (C)
time schedule.
          (D)

18. After cooking in the microwave oven for five minutes, one should put most meat dishes
          (A)   (B)   (C)
on a platter to cool.
                  (D)

19. Traditionally named for women, but recently Bob was chosen as the first male name
        (A)   (B)   (C)   (D)
    for a hurricane.

20. While testifying, their answers were recorded by the court stenographer.
         (A)   (B)   (C)   (D)

21. By reading the instructions carefully, mistakes on the examination can be avoided.
      (A)   (B)   (C)   (D)

22. Having been divorced, her credit could not be established in spite of
          (A)   (B)   (C)   (D)
    her high income.

23. Attempting to smuggle drugs into the country, customs officials apprehended them,
      (A)   (B)
    and took them to police headquarters for questioning.
       (C)   (D)

24. While trying to build a tunnel through the Blue Ridge Mountains, coal was discovered
       (A)   (B)   (C)   (D)
    at the construction site.

25. Founded in 1919, students and teachers who are interested in spending several
          (A)   (B)
    months abroad may benefit from educational programs administered by the Institute
             (C)   (D)
    for International Education.

PREVIEW: PARALLEL STRUCTURE

In some sentences in Part B, you will be asked to identify errors in parallel structure.

Parallel structure is the use of the same grammatical structures for related ideas of equal importance. Related ideas of equal importance often occur in the form of a list. Sometimes related ideas of equal importance are connected by conjunctions, such as *and, but,* and *or.*

EXERCISE FIFTEEN: PROBLEMS WITH PARALLEL STRUCTURE

1. The committee decided to cancel its law suit, to approve the contract, and
   _____ _____ _____
   (A)   (B)   (C)
   that it would adjourn the meeting.
   _____
         (D)

2. Air travel is fast, safe, and it is convenient.
   _____ ____ ____   _____
     (A)   (B) (C)   (D)

3. Rock music is not only popular in the United States but also abroad.
   _____ _____   __ _____
       (A)   (B)   (C)(D)

4. Every day the watchman would lock the doors, turning on the spot lights, and walk
              ___   _____   _____   ____
              (A)   (B)   (C)   (D)
   around the building.

5. To control quality and making decisions about production are among the many
                         _____   _____   ___ _____
                          (A)   (B)   (C)   (D)
   responsibilities of an industrial engineer.

6. I suggest that the instructor react to the situation by changing the textbook instead
                                  _____
                                   (A)
   of to modify the objectives of the course.
   __ _____ _____
   (B)   (C)   (D)

7. Dr. Johnson, the first woman elected president of the University, was intelligent,
                                 _____   ___
                                  (A)   (B)
   capable, and awareness of the problems to be solved.
                _____   _____
                  (C)   (D)

8. The insurance program used to include not only employees but their families.
                         _____   ___ _____ _____
                              (A)   (B) (C)   (D)

9. The six main parts of a business letter are the address, the inside address, the
       _____   _____ ___
          (A)   (B)   (C)
   salutation, the body, the closing, and signing your name.
                                          _____
                                                 (D)

10. We solved the problem by using a computer rather than to do it all by hand.
                                                ____ ____ __ _____
                                                (A) (B) (C)   (D)

11. To read literature and being introduced to a different culture are two excellent
                          (A)   (B)   (C)
    reasons for studying a foreign language.
             (D)

12. The proposed increase in the utility rate was neither a fair request and not a practical
        (A)   (B)   (C)
    one.
    (D)

13. Tom is the best candidate for the position because he understands the project, knows
              (A)   (B)
    the University, and who works very hard.
                     (C)   (D)

14. Ice skating and to go skiing are popular winter sports in the Northern United
    (A)   (B)   (C)   (D)
    States.

15. The surgeon examined the patient quickly, and then the operation was begun.
                       (A)   (B)   (C)   (D)

16. Because we were not sure where the house was, and because of the time, we decided
                                   (A)   (B)
    to ask for directions.
    (C) (D)

17. To treat minor diarrhea, drink plenty of liquids, especially tea, water, and carbonated
    (A)
    beverages, eat soup, yogurt, salty crackers, and bananas, and avoiding milk, butter,
               (B)   (C)
    eggs, and meat for twenty-four hours.
                   (D)

18. The new electric typewriters are equipped not only with an element for foreign
                                               (A)
    languages but also a key for correcting errors automatically.
                       (B)   (C)   (D)

19. The examiner did not know whether to report the student for cheating or warning
                                                                (A)   (B) (C)
    him first.
    (D)

20. Jim had spent his vacation traveling in Arizona, visiting some of the Indian reservations,
                (A)   (B)   (C)
    and had finished several paintings that he had begun last year.
            (D)

21. The Smithsonian Institute is famous because it contains such interesting exhibits as

    the flag that was raised over Fort McHenry in 1812, the airplane that the Wright
                    (A)   (B)
    brothers built for their first flight at Kitty Hawk, and there are the gowns worn by every
            (C)   (D)
    first lady since Martha Washington.

22. Please send me the smallest, most recently published, and less expensive
         (A) (B)   (C)   (D)
    dictionary that you have available.

23. In order to become a law, a bill must be passed not only by the Senate but also
    (A)   (B)   (C)
    the House of Representatives.
         (D)

24. The cloverleaf is a common engineering design for expressways that permits traffic
                                                                        (A)
    between two intersecting highways to move more safely, efficiently, and with ease.
       (B)   (C)   (D)

25. A new product should be judged not by the promises made in commercials and
                       (A)   (B)
    advertisements, but also by the results demonstrated in actual use.
                     (C)   (D)

PREVIEW: REDUNDANCY

In some sentences in Part B, you will be asked to identify errors in redundancy.
Redundancy is the unnecessary repetition of words and phrases.

EXERCISE SIXTEEN: PROBLEMS WITH REDUNDANCY

1. Some international students use a cassette recorder to make tapes of their classes
                      (A)   (B)
   so that they can repeat the lectures again.
     (C)   (D)

2. Blood plasma it is the transportation system for all of the widely separated organs
           (A)   (B)   (C)
   in the human body.
      (D)

3. It is a good idea to be careful in buying or purchasing magazines from salespersons
   (A)   (B)   (C)
   who may come to your door.
   (D)

4. Appointed by the General Assembly for five years, the Secretary-General of the
     (A)   (B)
   United Nations must act in an impartial manner toward all members.
         (C)   (D)

5. Since there was not any clarity the farm workers refused to sign the new contract and
         (A)   (B)   (C)
   voted to go on strike instead.
        (D)

6. Men who lived thousands of years ago, long before alphabets were devised, they
    (A)   (B)   (C)
   used pictures to record events and to communicate ideas.
               (D)

7. If one does not pick up his drycleaning within thirty days, the management is not
           (A)   (B)
   obligated to return it back.
     (C)   (D)

8. Professor Baker is an authority who knows a great deal about the effects of a rapid
                    (A)   (B)
   rise in temperature on different metals and alloys.
   (C)   (D)

9. Homestays in an American family add a great deal in terms of the experience that
             (A)   (B)
   students have when they are learning to speak English.
     (C)   (D)

10. Mr. Williams he told us that he was planning to get married next June.
        (A) (B)   (C)   (D)

11. The Southern part of the United States has ideal conditions for raising cotton because
                                                                    (A)
the climate is sufficiently warm enough to allow a six-month growing period.
                              (B)   (C)   (D)

12. A person who is competitive in nature is more likely to suffer from the effects of stress
              (A)   (B)   (C)
on his health.
(D)

13. Charles Schulz he made the first drawing of the famous cartoon strip *Peanuts* twenty
                    (A) (B)   (C)
years ago.
      (D)

14. Translations must be done in a careful manner so that the accuracy of the original
                        (A)   (B)   (C)
manuscripts is preserved.
            (D)

15. International law is made up of the rules and customs that they deal with the
                      (A)   (B) (C)
relationships between different nations and the citizens of different nations.
              (D)

16. My mother she always says that if one burns himself in the kitchen, he should put an
                (A)   (B)   (C)
ice cube on the affected area immediately.
                            (D)

17. It was Isadora Duncan who was responsible for many of the new innovations that
(A)   (B)   (C)
have made modern dance different from classical ballet.
                        (D)

18. This entry is more perfect than that of the other contestant.
                    (A)   (B) (C)   (D)

19. *Little House on the Prairie,* now a successful television program, was adapted from a

series of books by a young pioneer woman whose life was similar to that of the
(A)   (B)   (C)
character called by name Laura.
              (D)

20. In recent years great advances forward have been made in the field of
        (A)   (B)   (C)
genetic research.
      (D)

21. Today the United States is one of the few countries in the Western Hemisphere
                          (A)
that it has laws providing for the death penalty.
    (B)(C)   (D)

22. According to recent geological research, the climate of the states along the Canadian
        (A)   (B)
    border is changing with rapidity.
        (C)   (D)

23. My friend she had the admissions officer send me an I-20 so that I could come to the
              (A)   (B)   (C)   (D)
    University.

24. The South is mostly Democrat in politics, while the North has both Democrats and
              (A)   (B)   (C)   (D)
    Republicans.

25. World hunger it is one of the most urgent problems that we face today.
                (A)(B)   (C)   (D)

PREVIEW: WORD CHOICE

In some sentences in Part B, you will be asked to identify errors in word choice.

Word choice is the selection of words that express the exact meaning of an idea. Sometimes it is necessary to make a choice between words that are very similar in appearance but very different in meaning.

EXERCISE SEVENTEEN: PROBLEMS WITH WORD CHOICE

1. According to the Pythagorean Theorem, the sum of the squares of the two sides
       (A)
    of a triangle is equal as the square of the hypotenuse.
       (B)   (C)   (D)

2. Although you must get off while the bus is being cleaned, you may leave your
                                            (A)   (B)
    suitcases and other belongings laying on your seats.
                     (C)   (D)

3. The flag over the White House is risen at dawn every day by a color guard from the
              (A)   (B)   (C)   (D)
    United States armed forces.

4. Mr. Davis had to sell his business because he made some unwise investments and
                 (A)   (B)   (C)
    went broke.
        (D)

5. Commercials on the educational television network are generally shorter comparing
                                                       (A)   (B)   (C)
    those on other networks.
         (D)

6. After trying without success to talk with them, Mr. Brown lost his patience and
                  (A)   (B)   (C)
    gave them their walking papers.
             (D)

7. The economy class on most airlines is similar as the first class, but there is usually
                          (A)   (B)   (C)   (D)
    less space assigned to each passenger.

8. Since everyone would like to find an apartment near to the University, there are
                              (A)   (B)   (C)
    very few vacancies in the area.
    (D)

9. The Food and Drug Administration has not declared the drug a carcinogen because

    it has not been proven conclusively that the effects in rats can be generalized
    (A)   (B)   (C)   (D)
    for human beings.

10. The <u>carefulness</u> with <u>which</u> she prepared <u>the</u> thesis was evident <u>to the committee</u>.
       (A)   (B)   (C)   (D)

11. Marian Anderson, recognized both in the U.S. <u>and</u> in Europe as a <u>real great</u> vocalist,
                                             (A)   (B)
<u>was</u> <u>the first</u> black singer to appear with the Metropolitan Opera Company.
(C)   (D)

12. <u>Formally,</u> when he lived in his country, he <u>was</u> a <u>university professor,</u> but now he
    (A)   (B)   (C)
<u>is working</u> toward a higher degree at an American university.
   (D)

13. In some states the law allows drivers <u>to turn</u> right at a red light, but in <u>other</u> states, the
                               (A)   (B)
law does not <u>leave</u> <u>them</u> do it.
        (C)   (D)

14. <u>Bored of</u> his job, <u>he</u> made an appointment <u>to see</u> an advisor <u>at</u> the counseling
    (A)   (B)   (C)   (D)
center.

15. The <u>effectiveness</u> of the project on the population will be difficult <u>to measure</u> unless we
       (A)   (B)
<u>employ</u> a statistician <u>to tabulate</u> the variables.
  (C)   (D)

16. <u>In spite</u> of their differences, Jane has always <u>been</u> <u>very</u> <u>considerable</u> to her roommate.
   (A)   (B) (C)   (D)

17. He <u>can't</u> hardly remember the accident because he was only a <u>four-year-old</u> boy
    (A)   (B)
<u>when</u> <u>it</u> occurred.
 (C) (D)

18. If the <u>water level</u> had <u>raised</u> any <u>higher</u> the dam would <u>probably</u> have broken.
       (A)   (B)   (C)   (D)

19. One should try <u>to reconcile</u> his views with <u>those</u> <u>of his company</u> when they are
             (A)   (B)   (C)
<u>on conflict</u>.
   (D)

20. When a person is arrested, <u>the cops</u> must <u>let</u> <u>him</u> make one <u>telephone call</u>.
                      (A)   (B) (C)   (D)

21. With regard <u>of</u> your letter dated May 1, I am canceling my subscription to *Time*
           (A)
magazine <u>because</u> I am leaving the United States <u>to return</u> <u>to</u> my country.
       (B)   (C)   (D)

22. Most therapists agree that it is <u>not</u> a good idea for patients <u>to lay</u> <u>in bed</u> without
                           (A)   (B)   (C)
exercising.
   (D)

23. Excepting for vending machines, there is no food service on campus during the
     (A)   (B)(C)
ten-day spring break.
   (D)

24. When the owner of the disco suspicioned that their identification was not valid, he
                                (A)   (B)
refused to serve them.
      (C)   (D)

25. The condition of menkind has been improved by recent technological advances.
               (A)   (B)   (C)   (D)

PREVIEW: STRUCTURE

In some sentences in Part B, you will be asked to identify errors in structure.

Remember, structure is the correct use of verbs, pronouns, nouns, modifiers, comparatives, and connectors.

EXERCISE EIGHTEEN: PROBLEMS WITH STRUCTURE

1. Of the two lectures, <u>the first</u> was by far <u>the best,</u> partly because the person <u>who</u>
    　　　　　　　　　　　　(A)　　　　　　　　　(B)　　　　　　　　　　　　　　　　　　　　　(C)

    delivered it had <u>such a</u> dynamic style.
    　　　　　　　　　　(D)

2. That modern science <u>knows to assist</u> women who are unable <u>to give birth</u> to babies
    　　　　　　　　　　　(A)　　　　　　　　　　　　　　　　　　　(B)

    <u>by normal means</u> <u>is</u> one of the miracles of the twentieth century.
    　　(C)　　　　　　　(D)

3. After he had researched his paper and <u>wrote</u> <u>it,</u> he found <u>some</u> additional data that
    　　　　　　　　　　　　　　　　　　　(A)　(B)　　　　　　　　　(C)

    he <u>should have included.</u>
    　　　(D)

4. <u>Because of</u> the light, the city seemed <u>differently from</u> the way that I <u>had remembered</u> it.
    　　(A)　　　　　　　　　　　　　　　　(B)　　(C)　　　　　　　　　　　(D)

5. The Federal Aviation Agency <u>has grounded</u> all DC-10 aircraft <u>so</u> they <u>can be checked</u>
    　　　　　　　　　　　　　　(A)　　　　　(B)　　　　　　　　(C)　　　　(D)

    for possible problems in the design of the under-wing jet systems.

6. The colonel wanted <u>to retreat,</u> but the general insisted that <u>he continue</u> <u>do</u> everything
    　　　　　　　　　　(A)　　　　　　　　　　　　　　　　　　　(B)　　　　(C)

    necessary in order <u>to win</u> the battle.
    　　　　　　　　　　(D)

7. There <u>are</u> not <u>many</u> people <u>which</u> adapt to a new culture without <u>feeling</u> some
    　　　(A)　　　(B)　　　　(C)　　　　　　　　　　　　　　　　　(D)

    disorientation at first.

8. Bob wishes that his wife <u>understands</u> <u>why</u> he has not had time to write <u>her</u> <u>lately.</u>
    　　　　　　　　　　　　(A)　　　　　(B)　　　　　　　　　　　　　(C)　(D)

9. Because of the accident, the judge forbade Joe and <u>me</u> <u>from</u> <u>driving</u> for <u>six</u> months.
    　　　　　　　　　　　　　　　　　　　　　　　　　(A)　(B)　　(C)　　　　(D)

10. After he had <u>ran</u> the program through the computer, he <u>noticed</u> that he had forgotten
    　　　　　　　(A)　　　　　　　　　　　　　　　　　　　(B)

    <u>to do</u> <u>the last</u> operation.
    　(C)　　(D)

11. <u>Most</u> small appliances have <u>ninety-days</u> guarantees that <u>entitle</u> the purchaser to free
    　(A)　　　　　　　　　　(B)　　　　　　　　　　　(C)

    repair or replacement if the item <u>breaks</u> before the expiration date.
    　　　　　　　　　　　　　　　　(D)

12. Although everyone in our group was pleased with <u>his</u> meal, Mrs. Brown insisted
$\qquad\qquad\qquad\qquad\qquad\qquad\qquad\qquad$ (A)

on <u>complaining</u> that the coffee <u>tasted badly</u>.
(B)$\quad$(C)$\qquad\qquad\qquad\qquad$(D)

13. Let you and <u>I</u> agree <u>to cancel</u> the last shipment unless the company <u>meets</u> the
$\qquad\qquad$(A)$\qquad\quad$(B)$\qquad\qquad\qquad\qquad\qquad\qquad\qquad\qquad$(C)

conditions of <u>our</u> original contract.
$\qquad\qquad$(D)

14. His recommendation that the Air Force <u>investigates</u> the UFO sighting <u>was</u> approved
$\qquad\qquad\qquad\qquad\qquad\qquad\qquad$(A)$\qquad\qquad\qquad\qquad$(B)

<u>by the commission</u> and referred <u>to</u> the appropriate committee.
$\quad$(C)$\qquad\qquad\qquad\qquad$(D)

15. Although she seems to be <u>very</u> mature, Ann is <u>much</u> younger <u>as</u> <u>the other girls</u> in her
$\qquad\qquad\qquad\qquad$(A)$\qquad\qquad\qquad$(B)$\qquad\qquad$(C)$\quad$(D)

class.

16. Nuclear power plants are <u>still</u> supported <u>by</u> the Society of Professional Engineers
$\qquad\qquad\qquad\qquad$(A)$\qquad\qquad$(B)

<u>in spite</u> the unfortunate accident <u>at</u> Three Mile Island.
$\quad$(C)$\qquad\qquad\qquad\qquad$(D)

17. Miss Smith returned home quite <u>lately</u> that night <u>to find</u> that someone had broken into
$\qquad\qquad\qquad\qquad\qquad$(A)$\quad$(B)$\qquad$(C)

her garage and <u>stolen</u> her car.
$\qquad\qquad$(D)

18. If Mary <u>would have been</u> <u>more careful</u> in <u>proofreading</u> her dissertation, she would not
$\qquad\quad$(A)$\qquad\qquad\qquad$(B)$\qquad\qquad$(C)

have had to get <u>it</u> typed again.
$\qquad\qquad$(D)

19. The more <u>that</u> she tried <u>to remove</u> the stain, <u>the worst</u> it <u>looked</u>.
$\qquad\quad$(A)$\qquad\qquad$(B)$\qquad\qquad$(C)$\qquad$(D)

20. The national television networks have been criticized <u>for</u> <u>not showing</u> <u>much</u> good
$\qquad\qquad\qquad\qquad\qquad\qquad\qquad\qquad\qquad$(A)$\qquad$(B)$\qquad$(C)

movies <u>during</u> prime time.
$\qquad$(D)

21. This is the athlete <u>whom</u> everyone <u>says</u> will win the gold medal at <u>the winter</u>
(A)$\qquad\qquad\qquad$(B)$\qquad\qquad$(C)$\qquad\qquad\qquad\qquad\qquad\qquad$(D)
<u>Olympic Games</u>.

22. If you <u>would have checked</u> your <u>answer sheet</u> <u>more carefully</u>, you would have
$\qquad\qquad$(A)$\qquad\qquad\qquad\qquad$(B)$\qquad\qquad$(C)

corrected these errors <u>yourself</u>.
$\qquad\qquad\qquad\qquad$(D)

23. It was <u>her</u> <u>who</u> suggested that <u>he go</u> to New York in order <u>to get</u> a direct flight.
      (A) (B)   (C)   (D)

24. <u>We</u> veterans often fail <u>taking</u> advantage <u>of</u> the scholarship programs at the
  (A)   (B)   (C)
<u>university level.</u>
    (D)

25. It is necessary that the directors <u>will sign</u> <u>all of the copies,</u> <u>not</u> just the top <u>one.</u>
                              (A)   (B)   (C)   (D)

chapter 5

Preview and
Practice Exercises
for the Vocabulary and
Reading Comprehension
Section of the TOEFL

Directions: In each sentence in the following Practice Exercises, a word or phrase is underlined. Below each sentence are four other words or phrases. You are to choose the one word or phrase which would *best keep the meaning* of the original sentence if it were substituted for the underlined word.

PREVIEW: RECOGNIZING VOCABULARY WORDS

In some sentences in Part A of the Vocabulary and Reading Comprehension Section, you will be asked to recognize vocabulary words. Most of the words that you see will be nouns, verbs, adjectives, and adverbs.

Some of the words will have more than one meaning, but you must recognize the meaning of the word as it is used in the sentence in which it is found.

In some tests, it is possible to guess the meaning from context, that is, from the general meaning of the sentence in which the word appears. In this section of the TOEFL, it is not possible to guess the meaning from context. All the words might be possible in the sentence, but only *one* will be a synonym for the underlined word. Only one choice will retain the same meaning of the sentence.

You should finish this part of the test as rapidly as you can. First, read the sentence quickly. Then, re-read the underlined word and find the synonym. If you finish this section quickly, you will have more time for the reading comprehension passages.

EXERCISE ONE: VOCABULARY REVIEW (PART 1)

1. The knife that is displayed in the museum is more than one thousand years old and was a gift to the president of the United States from the Kingdom of Saudi Arabia.
   (A) pillar
   (B) meteor
   (C) dagger
   (D) boulder

2. In the fall the weather is cool in the morning but warm by midday.
   (A) chilly
   (B) rusty
   (C) silly
   (D) fluffy

3. Doctors of medicine are among the most affluent members of American society.
   (A) clever
   (B) wealthy
   (C) careful
   (D) educated

4. After Senator Smith announced that he planned to run for president, the telephone at campaign headquarters rang continuously.
   (A) incessantly
   (B) ignorantly
   (C) incisively
   (D) impartially

5. In many states, when someone has an accident while driving a friend's car, both the driver and the owner of the car share the responsibility.
   (A) blame
   (B) wrath
   (C) hoax
   (D) chaos

6. Because he has been such a conscientious student, I know that he must have had a good reason for being absent today.
   (A) superior
   (B) careful
   (C) valuable
   (D) popular

7. Seeds are contained in the core of fleshy fruit, such as apples and pears.
   (A) center   (C) surface
   (B) nature   (D) top

8. Mrs. Palmer was offended by the clerk's mean remark.
   (A) casual   (C) inopportune
   (B) nasty   (D) amusing

9. The plane that crashed was carrying a group of entertainers en route to the State Fair.
   (A) troupe   (C) cage
   (B) hog   (D) donation

10. Strenuous activity should be avoided after an operation.
    (A) lengthy   (C) routine
    (B) arduous   (D) calculated

11. The food at the picnic attracted a large number of bees.
    (A) swarm   (C) pack
    (B) herd   (D) flock

12. Many apartments have doors with a security window so that one may peek outside and observe visitors without being seen.
    (A) reach   (C) look
    (B) stay   (D) walk

13. After the war of 1847, the United States took New Mexico and California.
    (A) purchased   (C) probed
    (B) avoided   (D) seized

14. A construction crew is usually paid to scrub the area.
    (A) wash   (C) fix
    (B) build   (D) change

15. Many designers have cut skirts several inches in the side, back, or front seams this year.
    (A) styled   (C) stretched
    (B) slit   (D) shrunk

16. Some of the little boys sneaked into the ball game without buying a ticket.
    (A) went secretly   (C) ran fast
    (B) earned their way   (D) entered several times

17. A few specks of paint splattered on the floor in spite of the care that we took to cover it.
    (A) spots   (C) colors
    (B) lines   (D) cuts

18. The party that we are planning for midterm will give students, instructors, conversation partners, host families, and friends an opportunity to mingle in a social setting.
    (A) mix   (C) enjoy
    (B) talk   (D) eat

19. A hot land covered with a dense growth of trees offers the best climate for the experiment.
    (A) plateau   (C) jungle
    (B) plain   (D) forest

20. A good supervisor gives <u>hints</u> to his or her employees without interfering with creativity.
    (A) freedom   (C) funds
    (B) assistance   (D) clues

21. The last week of classes is always <u>hectic</u> because students are taking examinations, making applications to the university, and extending their visas.
    (A) busy   (C) fast
    (B) sad   (D) difficult

22. <u>Sudden rushes of wind</u> up to one hundred miles per hour accompanied the hurricane.
    (A) damage   (C) floods
    (B) disease   (D) gusts

23. It is better to try to change things than to <u>grumble</u> about them.
    (A) accept   (C) complain about
    (B) continue   (D) contribute to

24. In spite of being tortured, a captured soldier often does not <u>tell</u> anything.
    (A) consume   (C) alter
    (B) neglect   (D) divulge

25. Psychologists make lists of the people their clients <u>adore</u>.
    (A) love   (C) hate
    (B) help   (D) do not trust

26. A shorter haircut can <u>enhance</u> one's appearance.
    (A) make freer   (C) make better
    (B) make younger   (D) make different

27. Members of an <u>intrigue</u> meet in secret so that their conspiracy will not be discovered.
    (A) team   (C) cabal
    (B) band   (D) mob

28. Feather pillows are <u>fluffier</u> than foam pillows.
    (A) softer   (C) harder to find
    (B) more expensive   (D) larger

29. Because of advances in technology in recent years, Americans are enjoying more <u>leisure</u>.
    (A) free time   (C) new things
    (B) business   (D) money

30. Having a <u>fair</u> attitude toward people with different ideas is an indication that one has been well educated.
    (A) generous   (C) confident
    (B) tolerant   (D) flexible

EXERCISE TWO: VOCABULARY REVIEW (PART 2)

1. A satire by Mark Twain, the story is about a prince and a <u>very poor person</u> who exchanged places for a time.
   - (A) pauper
   - (B) tyro
   - (C) recluse
   - (D) captive

2. Regular use of cream will help to <u>relieve</u> the rough, dry condition of your skin.
   - (A) alleviate
   - (B) reverse
   - (C) prolong
   - (D) aggravate

3. I have only the time to tell you the <u>gist</u>.
   - (A) reference
   - (B) main idea
   - (C) first part
   - (D) a few details

4. A <u>meticulous</u> typist must be very conscientious about correcting even the smallest error.
   - (A) careful
   - (B) fast
   - (C) new
   - (D) good

5. Only five hundred people live in this tiny <u>village</u>.
   - (A) hamlet
   - (B) resort
   - (C) ranch
   - (D) suburb

6. The choir sang as a <u>preliminary event</u> to the ceremony.
   - (A) benediction
   - (B) prelude
   - (C) dedication
   - (D) termination

7. When snow <u>collects</u> on top of a building during the winter, the weight sometimes weakens the construction and occasionally causes the roof to collapse.
   - (A) accumulates
   - (B) melts
   - (C) congeals
   - (D) scatters

8. The <u>room and meals</u> at the Campus Motel were not only adequate but also inexpensive.
   - (A) registrations
   - (B) reservations
   - (C) accommodations
   - (D) confirmations

9. Some people have such an <u>intense dislike for</u> flying that they must undergo therapy.
   - (A) addiction to
   - (B) aversion to
   - (C) affection for
   - (D) impartiality for

10. Because of the new <u>estimate of the value</u> of our homes, the taxes were much higher this year.
    - (A) sites
    - (B) appraisals
    - (C) improvements
    - (D) acquisitions

11. After <u>eating an excessive amount</u> at the dinner he became ill.
    - (A) surfeiting
    - (B) lamenting
    - (C) quarreling
    - (D) expounding

12. How the ancient builders were able to raise the <u>large rocks</u> that they used in constructing their pyramids and cities is still an unanswered question.
    - (A) minerals
    - (B) pebbles
    - (C) gems
    - (D) boulders

13. One of the responsibilities of a forest ranger is to <u>drive slowly</u> through the area in search of animals in distress.
    (A) cruise
    (B) race
    (C) stroll
    (D) stalk

14. Because she was a few minutes late, she <u>walked quietly</u> into class and sat in the back of the room.
    (A) rambled
    (B) tiptoed
    (C) stumbled
    (D) crawled

15. The little red colt shares the barn with that brown <u>female horse</u>.
    (A) hog
    (B) gander
    (C) rooster
    (D) mare

16. The candidates seemed more interested in <u>slandering</u> each other than in talking about the issues.
    (A) maligning
    (B) confining
    (C) avoiding
    (D) baiting

17. Giving children <u>jobs</u> teaches them what you expect them to do.
    (A) chores
    (B) pets
    (C) snacks
    (D) bribes

18. <u>Natural disturbances of wind</u> are most common during the spring.
    (A) Suicides
    (B) Storms
    (C) Explosions
    (D) Riots

19. In negotiating a treaty diplomats must be careful not to <u>incite</u> suspicion.
    (A) heed
    (B) promulgate
    (C) arouse
    (D) foresee

20. As a result of severe illness or treatments for illness, one may become temporarily <u>hairless</u>.
    (A) bald
    (B) hoarse
    (C) lame
    (D) stiff

21. During a long <u>period of dry weather</u> farmers have to make adjustments to save their crops.
    (A) drought
    (B) flood
    (C) frost
    (D) foreclosure

22. A patient who suffers a <u>light blow</u> on the head should remain quiet.
    (A) bruise
    (B) abrasion
    (C) bump
    (D) fracture

23. We will need to <u>leave out</u> some of the preliminary exercises at the graduation because of the large number of students receiving degrees.
    (A) revise
    (B) omit
    (C) amplify
    (D) exhibit

24. Sixteen-weight bond paper is too <u>lacking in strength</u> to be used in typing a manuscript.
    (A) flimsy
    (B) tiny
    (C) transparent
    (D) lustrous

25. According to federal regulations, it is required that all canned and packaged food have a list of the <u>ingredients</u> printed on the label.
    (A) dates prepared
    (B) places sold
    (C) calorie content
    (D) items used

26. Since you don't know them very well, it would be <u>suitable</u> for you to send a card.
    (A) outrageous
    (B) hilarious
    (C) appropriate
    (D) considerate

27. When Professor Baker suffered a <u>relapse</u> he was ordered to enter the hospital.
    (A) serious accident
    (B) severe shock
    (C) return of his illness
    (D) minor injury

28. People living along the coast <u>escaped</u>.
    (A) fled
    (B) remained
    (C) disbanded
    (D) perished

29. Many people stood outside the church during the funeral to <u>pay homage</u> to the president.
    (A) protest against
    (B) show respect for
    (C) celebrate with
    (D) surprise

30. It is difficult for a foreign student <u>to increase</u> the income from his scholarship.
    (A) budget
    (B) augment
    (C) retain
    (D) predict

EXERCISE THREE: VOCABULARY REVIEW (PART 3)

1. Married student housing is <u>adjacent to</u> the campus.
   (A) from
   (B) being added to
   (C) next to
   (D) from

2. This tapestry has a very <u>complicated</u> pattern.
   (A) appropriate
   (B) obsolete
   (C) expensive
   (D) intricate

3. Some psychologists insist that a child's <u>behavior</u> should be modified by imposing a system of rewards, whereas others believe that punishment is also necessary.
   (A) problems
   (B) actions
   (C) preferences
   (D) motivations

4. Many common <u>illnesses</u> are not serious enough for professional intervention.
   (A) accords
   (B) transactions
   (C) collisions
   (D) ailments

5. Those who <u>help</u> criminals must also face charges.
   (A) hire
   (B) emulate
   (C) abet
   (D) conceal

6. It is customary for the bride and groom to <u>practice</u> their wedding ceremony the evening before the occasion.
   (A) imagine
   (B) rehearse
   (C) recite
   (D) initiate

7. Most eyeglasses will not <u>break into many pieces</u> because they are made with either plastic or a special blend of glass.
   (A) shatter
   (B) crack
   (C) bend
   (D) melt

8. We watched as the plane <u>disappeared</u> behind the clouds.
   (A) exploded
   (B) escaped
   (C) vanished
   (D) plunged

9. Some seminars teach people how to <u>affirm opinions</u>.
   (A) assert themselves
   (B) modify themselves
   (C) accept themselves
   (D) value themselves

10. When dogs and cats go <u>astray</u>, they often end up in the city dog pound.
    (A) wandering
    (B) playing
    (C) hiding
    (D) hunting

11. In some cases of <u>lapse of memory,</u> the loss may be limited to a single incident, whereas in other cases it may be inclusive.
    (A) paralysis
    (B) aphasia
    (C) deafness
    (D) amnesia

12. During the electrical storm the lights <u>shined unsteadily.</u>
    (A) glowed
    (B) beamed
    (C) flickered
    (D) dimmed

13. The area is roped off because the water is <u>contaminated</u>.
    (A) polluted
    (B) sluggish
    (C) restricted
    (D) purified

14. She was <u>confused</u> by the new customs when she first arrived.
    (A) impressed
    (B) stunned
    (C) bewildered
    (D) intrigued

15. The bus driver left the door <u>ajar</u> so that returning passengers could reboard after the rest stop.
    (A) unlocked
    (B) well marked
    (C) well lit
    (D) slightly open

16. To treat skin that is <u>without sensation</u> from exposure to the cold, soak it in cool water.
    (A) numb
    (B) swollen
    (C) flushed
    (D) flaky

17. If we hadn't had a cat, the garage would have been <u>inhabited by</u> mice.
    (A) penetrated by
    (B) damaged by
    (C) infested with
    (D) abandoned to

18. The accident occurred because the driver was <u>negligent</u>.
    (A) asleep
    (B) careless
    (C) inexperienced
    (D) tired

19. The <u>margins</u> of the paper must be 1½ inches.
    (A) first try
    (B) extra measure
    (C) bottom part
    (D) blank space

20. Although there are many plastic <u>objects to sweep the floor</u>, most homemakers prefer the ones made from plants and bushes.
    (A) brims
    (B) brooms
    (C) bags
    (D) baskets

21. During a long trip, when one becomes <u>drowsy</u>, he should pull off the road to rest.
    (A) sleepy
    (B) sick
    (C) lost
    (D) bored

22. According to the newspaper this morning, the political situation remains <u>threatening</u>.
    (A) ominous
    (B) stable
    (C) vague
    (D) confidential

23. Bob Hope is an internationally <u>renowned</u> comedian.
    (A) loved
    (B) famous
    (C) professional
    (D) long-standing

24. In recent years many people have <u>sued</u> doctors.
    (A) checked references
    (B) brought to court
    (C) given gifts
    (D) failed to pay

25. There is a fierce <u>competition</u> between Ohio State University and the University of Michigan for the Big Ten Championships.
    (A) merger
    (B) reconciliation
    (C) rivalry
    (D) scrutiny

26. I have a <u>deep</u> respect for your opinion, although I do not agree with you.
(A) genuine   (C) profound
(B) comprehensive   (D) renewed

27. Committing a <u>deception</u> in obtaining car insurance is against the law.
(A) prank   (C) theft
(B) hoax   (D) fraud

28. Betty was offended because she thought that her friends had ignored her <u>in a planned way</u>.
(A) haphazardly   (C) deliberately
(B) arrogantly   (D) callously

29. The campfire <u>burned with little smoke and no flame</u>.
(A) blazed   (C) roared
(B) smoldered   (D) crackled

30. Poor nutrition in the early stages of infancy can <u>hold back</u> adult growth.
(A) influence   (C) predict
(B) retard   (D) deform

EXERCISE FOUR: VOCABULARY REVIEW (PART 4)

1. Enrollment in courses numbered 500 or above will be <u>limited</u> to seniors and graduate students.
    (A) required   (C) restricted
    (B) optional   (D) available

2. People with red hair often have <u>rosy-colored</u> complexions.
    (A) splotchy   (C) florid
    (B) freckled   (D) pallid

3. To treat <u>temporary discoloration of the skin caused by an injury,</u> press with a clean, cold cloth and follow with a gentle massage.
    (A) bruises   (C) sprains
    (B) breaks   (D) gashes

4. Since the money in the budget had been <u>spent wastefully</u>, the board was hesitant to allocate the additional funds.
    (A) dissipated   (C) misplaced
    (B) diverted   (D) audited

5. After a war there is often a huge <u>departure</u>.
    (A) exodus   (C) celebration
    (B) famine   (D) epidemic

6. <u>Adult</u> students require less supervision.
    (A) adolescent   (C) infantile
    (B) juvenile   (D) mature

7. A <u>thorough</u> person, she spent hours polishing the furniture and waxing the floors before the party.
    (A) fastidious   (C) gregarious
    (B) obsequious   (D) loquacious

8. The salesman had a <u>glib</u> answer when a customer asked him a question.
    (A) smooth   (C) long
    (B) correct   (D) new

9. If you continue to be absent from your classes, we will have to <u>notify</u> your sponsor.
    (A) visit   (C) inform
    (B) change   (D) cancel

10. Lawyers are often accused of <u>misleading by using ambiguous language</u>.
    (A) debating   (C) coercing
    (B) equivocating   (D) yelling

11. The United Nations was asked to mediate the <u>break</u> between the two governments.
    (A) grievance   (C) rift
    (B) treaty   (D) rivalry

12. The problem was not serious enough to elicit such a <u>long, vehement speech</u>.
    (A) ramification   (C) punishment
    (B) quarrel   (D) tirade

13. Some of the smaller canyons south of the Grand Canyon are also very colorful.
   (A) gorges   (C) buttes
   (B) meadows   (D) deserts

14. The basement was dank after being closed for such a long time.
   (A) damp   (C) dark
   (B) dusty   (D) cold

15. A smoke discovery system provides families with early warning of fire.
   (A) collection   (C) detection
   (B) replication   (D) fabrication

16. After the storm the lake returned to its usual calm state.
   (A) tepid   (C) placid
   (B) transparent   (D) choppy

17. The members of the congregation ignored him because he had married outside the church.
   (A) detested   (C) shamed
   (B) harmed   (D) shunned

18. John's abrupt manner often caused him to be misunderstood.
   (A) humorous   (C) brusque
   (B) peculiar   (D) consistent

19. A student may be expelled from school for using as his own the written work of another.
   (A) plagiarizing   (C) pilfering
   (B) disseminating   (D) defacing

20. Please detach the coupon and mail it with a check for two dollars to the Colgate-Palmolive Company.
   (A) locate   (C) identify
   (B) separate   (D) complete

21. Sally likes to tease her brother.
   (A) charm   (C) chide
   (B) chase   (D) cheat

22. Every year employees receive a salary increase to offset the high cost of living.
   (A) variation   (C) trend
   (B) increment   (D) petition

23. One of the slots at the post office is for local mail and the other one is for out-of-town mail.
   (A) rooms   (C) windows
   (B) openings   (D) boxes

24. Numbers are drawn by chance in the state lottery.
   (A) randomly   (C) annually
   (B) mechanically   (D) routinely

25. Bill taught his dog to recover sticks when he threw them.
   (A) retrieve   (C) conceal
   (B) substitute   (D) ignore

26. Natural food stores claim that their products are more <u>healthful</u> than those found in supermarkets.
    (A) convenient
    (B) wholesome
    (C) economical
    (D) secure

27. When the king <u>gave up</u> his throne, his brother succeeded him.
    (A) exploited
    (B) neglected
    (C) abused
    (D) abdicated

28. The <u>unlawful</u> possession of drugs is a serious crime.
    (A) excessive
    (B) prescribed
    (C) recent
    (D) illicit

29. Bob received many cards and letters from friends who wanted to offer their <u>sympathy</u>.
    (A) friendship
    (B) invitations
    (C) congratulations
    (D) condolences

30. Benjamin Franklin was famous for the many <u>proverbs</u> that he published in *Poor Richard's Almanac*.
    (A) maxims
    (B) poems
    (C) drawings
    (D) essays

PREVIEW: RECOGNIZING TWO- AND THREE-WORD VERBS

In some sentences in Part A, you will be asked to recognize two- and three-word verbs.

Some of the verbs have more than one meaning, but you must recognize the meaning of the word as it is used in the sentence in which it is found.

Remember that you should finish this part of the test as rapidly as you can. First, read the sentence quickly. Then, re-read the underlined two- or three-word verb and find the synonym.

EXERCISE FIVE: VOCABULARY REVIEW (TWO- AND THREE-WORD VERBS)

1. Although we always send a representative to the airport to welcome new international students, very often they don't <u>arrive</u> on the flights that we expect them to.
   - (A) show down
   - (B) show over
   - (C) show out
   - (D) show up

2. Mr. Taylor is still in the intensive care unit, but as long as he responds to the antibiotics, he has a good chance to <u>get well.</u>
   - (A) pull with
   - (B) pull through
   - (C) pull over
   - (D) pull along

3. How did John <u>get</u> so much money?
   - (A) come by
   - (B) come to
   - (C) come at
   - (D) come of

4. Many people enjoy <u>visiting</u> their friends at Christmastime.
   - (A) calling on
   - (B) calling up
   - (C) calling of
   - (D) calling to

5. Abdullah was the only one who knew how to cook because he had <u>aided</u> in the kitchen when he was a boy.
   - (A) helped about
   - (B) helped with
   - (C) helped up
   - (D) helped out

6. The advocates of the Equal Rights Amendment believe that it will <u>cause</u> many improvements in the employment of women.
   - (A) bring about
   - (B) bring along
   - (C) bring aside
   - (D) bring away

7. This year the company <u>manufactured</u> almost twice as many motors as it did last year.
   - (A) turned down
   - (B) turned in
   - (C) turned out
   - (D) turned to

8. If you plan to go to Venezuela next month, you had better <u>review</u> your Spanish.
   - (A) brush up over
   - (B) brush over on
   - (C) brush up on
   - (D) brush back on

9. In spite of her having lied to us before, we <u>were fooled by</u> her story.
   - (A) fell from
   - (B) fell of
   - (C) fell to
   - (D) fell for

10. Every director needs an assistant that he can <u>trust</u> to take care of problems that may occur in his absence.
    (A) count on   (C) count of
    (B) count for   (D) count to

11. The Immigration Service <u>refused</u> his request for transfer because he had not completed one term of instruction at the university that had issued his I-20.
    (A) turned back   (C) turned down
    (B) turned over   (D) turned off

12. If you <u>happen to meet</u> Bob, would you please tell him that I am looking for him?
    (A) run to   (C) run into
    (B) run down   (D) run over

13. Because all of the gas stations along the freeway were closed, we had to <u>continue</u> driving until we got to Detroit.
    (A) keep on   (C) keep off
    (B) keep out   (D) keep back

14. Some of the tapes in the language lab have <u>been made useless by wear</u> and should be replaced.
    (A) worn up   (C) worn out
    (B) worn off   (D) worn down

15. A simple rule for losing weight is to <u>reduce</u> the number of calories that one consumes daily.
    (A) cut out on   (C) cut down on
    (B) cut under on   (D) cut up on

16. Cowboys used to <u>capture</u> cattle in Texas and drive them to Missouri where they were put on trains and shipped to cities in the East.
    (A) round in   (C) round with
    (B) round up   (D) round about

17. I suggest that you <u>review</u> these figures before you submit them in your final report.
    (A) go across   (C) go up
    (B) go over   (D) go on

18. Since she was accustomed to having her own room, it was difficult for her to <u>tolerate</u> a roommate.
    (A) put up from   (C) put up to
    (B) put up by   (D) put up with

19. One who <u>jokes about</u> another person is usually not confident about himself.
    (A) makes fun of   (C) makes fun from
    (B) makes fun for   (D) makes fun to

20. The couple had to <u>postpone</u> their wedding because the bride's mother was very ill.
    (A) put off   (C) put out
    (B) put away   (D) put back

21. Mrs. Wilson works more slowly than the other secretaries because she has to be satisfied with everything that she does.

(A) takes pride in   (C) takes pride to
(B) takes pride of   (D) takes pride on

22. Before we move we should have a garage sale to discard some of this furniture.
(A) get rid for   (C) get rid from
(B) get rid of   (D) get rid to

23. Since Dr. Baker cannot be present, Ms. Smith will have charge of the staff meeting.
(A) preside about   (C) preside into
(B) preside from   (D) preside over

24. Ron looks like the men on his mother's side of the family.
(A) takes from   (C) takes after
(B) takes of   (D) takes about

25. Would you please distribute these invitations to the students in your class?
(A) hand in   (C) hand over
(B) hand out   (D) hand back

26. In order to avoid contracting serious illnesses, most travelers receive medical advice and innoculations prior to leaving their countries.
(A) coming through with   (C) coming after with
(B) coming out with   (D) coming down with

27. Some people insist on criticizing the results of other people's work, without ever making a constructive contribution to their efforts.
(A) finding fault on   (C) finding fault from
(B) finding fault with   (D) finding fault over

28. Before you establish a small business in your home, you must be sure that you are acting in compliance with the zoning laws.
(A) set down   (C) set up
(B) set about   (D) set aside

29. It is more difficult to save money now because the rate of inflation is so high.
(A) lay about   (C) lay along
(B) lay across   (D) lay aside

30. The public is beginning to cooperate by recycling bottles and cans instead of discarding them.
(A) throwing them off   (C) throwing them out
(B) throwing them over   (D) throwing them up

Directions: In Part B, you will read a variety of passages (single sentences or paragraphs) followed by questions about the meaning of the material. You are to choose the one best answer, (A), (B), (C), or (D), to each question. Then, on your answer sheet, find the number of the question and blacken the space that corresponds to the letter of the answer you have chosen.

Answer all the questions based on what is stated or implied in the reading passage.

PREVIEW: READING INDEXES AND CHARTS

In some passages in Part B of the Vocabulary and Reading Comprehension Section, you will be asked to read indexes and charts.

First, look at the title of the index or chart. Do *not* read the entire index or chart. Then, read the test questions and begin to locate answers on the index or chart.

It will help you to practice reading indexes and charts in English language newspapers, magazines, and books. Especially notice tables of contents.

EXERCISE SIX: PRACTICE IN READING INDEXES AND CHARTS

Questions 1–4 refer to Passage One:

INDEX

Business and Finance	21–25
Classified	34–39
Comics	50–51
Editorials	19–20
Entertainment and Leisure	47–49
Home	27–33
News	1–16
Obituaries	26
Sports	40–46

1. The word <u>comics</u> in line 3 most nearly means
   (A) advertisements
   (B) opinions
   (C) TV guide
   (D) cartoons

2. On which of the following pages would one look to find the current value of General Motors stock?
   (A) 42
   (B) 24
   (C) 34
   (D) 14

3. In which section would one find a list of death notices?
   (A) Finance
   (B) Comics
   (C) Obituaries
   (D) Editorials

4. This passage is most probably an index for a
   (A) newspaper
   (B) book
   (C) catalog
   (D) dissertation

Questions 1–4 refer to Passage Two:

AIRMAIL RATES

Mexico and Canada	$0.15 first ounce. $0.13 each additional ounce.
American Samoa, Bahamas, Bermuda, Caribbean Islands, Central America, Colombia, Guam, Miquelon, Philippines, St. Pierre, Venezuela, Western Samoa	$0.25 per half-ounce through 2 ounces. $0.21 each additional half-ounce.
All other countries	$0.31 per half-ounce through 2 ounces. $0.26 each additional half-ounce.

1. The word <u>rates</u> in the title most nearly means
   (A) prices
   (B) countries
   (C) charts
   (D) changes

2. How much does it cost to mail a half-ounce letter to the Philippines?
   (A) $.21
   (B) $.25
   (C) $.26
   (D) $.31

3. How much does it cost to airmail a six-ounce package to India?
   (A) $.57
   (B) $1.24
   (C) $1.56
   (D) $3.32

4. It may be concluded that the purpose of this passage is to
   (A) entertain
   (B) persuade
   (C) complain
   (D) inform

Questions 1–4 refer to Passage Three:

1. Another word which is often used in place of glossary is
   (A) survey
   (B) examination
   (C) dictionary
   (D) essay

2. To which page would one refer in order to learn about outlining research papers?
   (A) 67
   (B) 129
   (C) 162
   (D) 171

3. This passage would most probably be found in
   (A) a textbook on study skills
   (B) a textbook on composition
   (C) a textbook on reading
   (D) a dictionary

4. Which of the following would be the best heading for this passage?
   (A) Bibliography
   (B) Table of Contents
   (C) Title Page
   (D) Introduction

Questions 1–4 refer to Passage Four:

Date	Reference	Charges	Balance Due
May 7	Room 1006	$30.00	
May 7	Tax 1006	1.50	
May 7	Phone 1006	0.35	
			$31.85
May 8	Coffee Shop 1006	6.13	
May 8	Room 1006	30.00	
May 8	Tax 1006	1.50	
			$69.48
May 9	Coffee Shop 1006	2.36	
May 9	Room 1006	30.00	
May 9	Tax 1006	1.50	
May 9	Phone 1006	1.75	
			$105.09
May 10	Room 1006	30.00	
May 10	Tax 1006	1.50	
			$136.59
May 11	Coffee Shop 1006	3.94	
May 11	Room 1006	30.00	
May 11	Tax 1006	1.50	
	Phone	0.35	
			$172.38

1. The word <u>due</u> at the top of the right-hand column is closest in meaning to
   (A) money
   (B) today
   (C) owed
   (D) paid

2. What was the balance due on May 10?
   (A) $172.38
   (B) $136.59
   (C) $105.09
   (D) $31.50

3. How much were the charges for the day of May 8?
   (A) $31.50
   (B) $37.63
   (C) $37.85
   (D) $69.48

4. This passage is
   (A) A budget for a vacation
   (B) A hotel bill
   (C) A train ticket
   (D) A telephone bill

Questions 1– 4 refer to Passage Five:

National and World News————————————— 1–4
State News——————————————————— 6–11
Local News——————————————————— 11
Editorial————————————————————2
Financial News————————————————— 12–13
Sports————————————————————— 14–15
Features————————————————————5
Classified————————————————————16
Weather: Sunny, low in mid 60's

1. In line 7, the word <u>features</u> most nearly means
   (A) society news   (C) special articles
   (B) pictures   (D) letters

2. On which of the following pages would one look to find the score for a football game?
   (A) 2   (C) 13
   (B) 11   (D) 14

3. We can estimate from this passage that today's low temperature will be
   (A) 60 degrees   (C) 65 degrees
   (B) 61 degrees   (D) 69 degrees

4. Which of the following would be the best title for this magazine?
   (A) *U.S. Information*   (C) *Weather Magazine*
   (B) *The World*   (D) *News Report*

PREVIEW: READING INSTRUCTIONS

In some passages in Part B, you will be asked to read instructions.

First, read the instructions quickly. Then, read the questions. After you have answered questions for main idea, begin to answer the other questions by referring to the passage. Use underlining and larger type to help you locate the answers.

It will help you to practice reading instructions in English on medicine bottles, household products, and grocery store items.

EXERCISE SEVEN: PRACTICE IN READING INSTRUCTIONS

Questions 1– 4 refer to Passage One:

> For temporary relief of nasal congestion and to make breathing easier in head colds and hay fever. In most cases, the weaker solutions are fully satisfactory and are preferred, namely $\frac{1}{8}\%$ for infants, $\frac{1}{4}\%$ for children, and $\frac{1}{2}\%$ for adults. Keep tightly stoppered.

1. The word infants in line 4 most nearly means
   (A) teenagers   (C) babies
   (B) women   (D) the elderly

2. According to the instructions, weaker solutions
   (A) are usually less effective than stronger solutions
   (B) may not be used by adults
   (C) should be used instead of stronger solutions
   (D) are not recommended, but may be used

3. Where would this passage most probably be found?
   (A) On a bottle of medicine   (C) In a cookbook
   (B) In a newspaper   (D) On a receipt

4. What is the main purpose of this passage?
   (A) To recommend dosage for the medication
   (B) To warn against side effects
   (C) To explain storage procedures
   (D) To advise against using the medication

Questions 1– 4 refer to Passage Two:

For a hold that lasts all day without leaving your hair stiff or sticky, Cleanspray is recommended by professional hairdressers everywhere. To use, remove cap, hold can upright with valve 10–14 inches from hair. Spray evenly.

New formula contains no fluorocarbons. Improved propellant is safe to the ozone layer. Please note: Since the propellant is lighter, the weight of the can has been reduced, but you actually get 25 percent more applications than before. Saves you money!

Warning. Avoid spraying in eyes. Contents under pressure. Do not puncture or incinerate. Do not store at temperatures above 120 degrees F. Flammable. Do not use near fire or flame or while smoking. Keep out of the reach of children.

1. The word <u>flammable</u> in line 12 most nearly means
   (A) easily burned
   (B) easily evaporated
   (C) easily frozen
   (D) easily broken

2. Why are there more sprays in the can now?
   (A) Because the can is larger
   (B) Because the can is heavier
   (C) Because the propellant is lighter
   (D) Because the can is more expensive

3. What is Cleanspray?
   (A) Shampoo
   (B) Hairspray
   (C) Spray deodorant
   (D) Spray cleaner

4. What are the main points in this passage?
   (A) Suggestions for using the product correctly, warnings against dangerous new formulae, and comparisons of cost with other brands
   (B) Instructions on how to use the product and how to save money
   (C) Recommendations for use, information about the results of the new formula, and admonishments for safety
   (D) Directions for using the product safely

Questions 1– 4 refer to Passage Three:

FOR PAIN
USUAL ADULT DOSE: 2 or 3 tablets four times daily; for children under twelve, consult a physician. KEEP TIGHTLY CLOSED. AVOID EXPOSURE TO LIGHT.

1. In line 2, <u>tablets</u> is closest in meaning to
    (A) pills
    (B) tablespoonfuls
    (C) injections
    (D) drops

2. What recommendations are given for using the medication referred to in this passage?
    (A) That one should keep the lid on the bottle and store it in a dark place
    (B) That one should keep air out of the bottle but allow light to filter through the medicine
    (C) That one should always ask a doctor for his or her advice before taking the medication
    (D) That one should not take the medication every day

3. What is the maximum dosage for an adult?
    (A) Three tablets every twenty-four hours
    (B) Four tablets every day
    (C) Eight tablets every day
    (D) Twelve tablets every twenty-four hours

4. Why should you take this medication?
    (A) To soothe an upset stomach
    (B) To relieve a headache
    (C) To treat itching caused by sunburn
    (D) To suppress coughs

Questions 1– 4 refer to Passage Four:

Comfortact is an all-purpose solution for the care of hard contact lenses. Wets, soaks and cleans.

1. *Wetting.* Before inserting contact lenses in the eye, apply one drop of Comfortact and rinse with water.

2. *Soaking.* Fill contact case one-half full of Comfortact. Place lenses in case and add a few more drops to cover all surfaces.

3. *Cleaning.* Apply a few drops of Comfortact to lenses and rub gently for ten seconds. Rinse and repeat.

Note: Wash hands thoroughly before touching lenses. Do not let the tip of the bottle come into contact with any surface which may contaminate the solution. Do not use with soft contact lenses.

1. Another word which is often used in place of <u>contaminate</u> is
   (A) deplete   (C) pollute
   (B) eat   (D) dilute

2. How much Comfortact should be used in the case to soak lenses?
   (A) one drop   (C) one-half case full
   (B) a few drops   (D) a full case

3. Evidently, it is very important to
   (A) soak the lenses on one side only
   (B) apply plenty of Comfortact to hands before touching the lenses
   (C) use Comfortact with soft contact lenses only
   (D) keep the lenses very clean

4. What is the main idea in this passage?
   (A) That Comfortact is used to clean contact lenses
   (B) That Comfortact is not soft
   (C) That Comfortact solves problems
   (D) That Comfortact may be used for many purposes

Questions 1– 4 refer to Passage Five:

> Especially well-suited for those who should not take aspirin or aspirin-containing products. DOSAGE: Adults, 1 to 2 tablets 4 times daily. Consult a physician for use by children under 6 or for use longer than 10 days.

1. The phrase that is closest in meaning to the word <u>dosage</u> is
   (A) recommended amount
   (B) notice this
   (C) be careful
   (D) two ages of life

2. What should you do if you want to give this medication to a four-year-old child?
   (A) ask a doctor
   (B) wait for ten days before giving it to him
   (C) give him half of the adult dosage
   (D) be sure that it does not contain aspirin

3. According to the instructions, what is the maximum dosage per day for an adult?
   (A) 8 tablets
   (B) 4 tablets
   (C) 3 tablets
   (D) 2 tablets

4. What is this medication?
   (A) aspirin
   (B) a substitute for aspirin
   (C) a product containing aspirin
   (D) a product that should not be taken

PREVIEW: READING ANNOUNCEMENTS AND ADVERTISEMENTS

In some passages in Part B, you will be asked to read announcements and advertisements.

First, read the announcement or advertisement quickly. Then, read the questions. After you have answered questions for the main idea, begin to answer the other questions by referring to the passage. Use underlining and larger type to help you locate the answers.

It will help you to practice reading announcements and advertisements in the classified section of English language newspapers.

EXERCISE EIGHT: PRACTICE IN READING ANNOUNCEMENTS AND ADVERTISEMENTS

Questions 1– 4 refer to Passage One:

SOUTHGATE AREA

Brand new luxury 1 and 2 bedroom apts. at Heatherdowns and Green Streets. Convenient to Southgate Shopping Center. Close to bus route 22.

Rentals from $250 include heat, air, shag carpet, appliances, dishwasher. Patio, laundry room, pool. 1 year lease. Security deposit.

One pre-school-aged child considered in 2 bedroom. Absolutely no pets.

Model open weekdays 1–6. Sat., Sun. 1–5 or by appointment. 241–7721. Managed by Sands Corporation.

An equal housing opportunity.

1. The word <u>convenient</u> in line 2 most nearly means
   (A) close to
   (B) beside
   (C) across from
   (D) behind

2. Which of the following statements about the apartment complex is true?
   (A) There is no lease required
   (B) The bus route is no longer in service
   (C) The rent includes partial utilities
   (D) Only two-bedroom apartments are available

3. Which of the following families would be able to rent an apartment according to the ad?
   (A) A woman and her ten-year-old child
   (B) A husband, wife, and their baby
   (C) An elderly man with a small dog
   (D) A husband, wife, and two small children

4. The sentence below that best summarizes the main idea in this passage is
   (A) Model apartments are open for inspection every afternoon
   (B) The apartments available are equal housing opportunities
   (C) There are one- and two-bedroom apartments for rent from $250 near Southgate
   (D) Apartments for rent include heat, air, carpet, appliances, patio, laundry, and pool

Questions 1– 4 refer to Passage Two:

Visit Nashville, Tennessee, the capital of country music and the home of the Grand Ole Opry. Four-day motor coach tour escorted from Pittsburgh.

Departures August 23, September 13, September 27, October 11, October 25.

$185 per person based on double occupancy. Includes private motor coach from Pittsburgh, hotel accommodations, reserved tickets for the Grand Old Opry Country Festival Friday and Saturday nights, sightseeing tour of Nashville, admissions to points of interest.

For information, free brochures, and reservations, call 421-6060. Travel and Tours, 2245 Market Street, Pittsburgh, Pennsylvania 15219.

14-day advanced booking required. Visa and Master Charge welcome.

1. In line 7, <u>accommodations</u> is closest in meaning to
    (A)   entertainment   (C)   rooms
    (B)   reservations   (D)   transportation

2. Why is Nashville an interesting city to visit?
    (A)   Because it is a very old city
    (B)   Because it is in Tennessee
    (C)   Because it is famous for country music
    (D)   Because many famous Americans have their homes there

3. If one plans to join the tour on September 27, on what date should reservations be made?
    (A)   August 27   (C)   September 14
    (B)   September 13   (D)   September 26

4. The title that best expresses the main idea of this passage is
    (A)   Free Brochures   (C)   Bus Tour of Nashville
    (B)   Tour of Pittsburgh   (D)   Travel and Tours

Questions 1–4 refer to Passage Three:

FOR SALE
1977 Cutlass Supreme.
White w/light blue interior.
Low mileage. Like new.
Air, automatic, power steering, brakes.
AM/FM, cassette stereo.
$5000 or best offer.
By original owner.
241-3281 weekdays. 287-4479 weekends.
Ask for Jim Black.

---

1. The word <u>weekdays</u> in line 9 most nearly means
   (A) Every day from 9:00 A.M.–6:00 P.M.
   (B) Monday–Friday
   (C) Saturday and Sunday
   (D) Every day except Sunday

2. What color is the car?
   (A) blue   (C) red
   (B) white   (D) black

3. It may be concluded that Jim will
   (A) not sell his car for less than $5000
   (B) sell his car to a buyer who offers him $4500 if no one offers him more
   (C) sell his car to the original owner
   (D) sell his car for more than $5000

4. Which of the following best describes this passage?
   (A) A classified ad   (C) An editorial
   (B) A news item   (D) A feature

Questions 1– 4 refer to Passage Four:

> Professional Typing Service announces a new location in Westside Mall, 1400 University Avenue across from State University Student Union.
>
> We specialize in term papers, theses, and dissertations typed to the specifications of the Graduate School of State University.
>
> Twenty-four-hour service for fifty pages or less. Forty-eight-hour service for more than fifty pages.
>
> **Rates:** $1.00 per page on regular stock paper
> $1.25 per page on cotton bond paper
> $ .25 extra for each carbon copy
>
> **Hours:**   8:00 A.M.–10:00 P.M. Monday–Friday
> 8:00 A.M.– 4:00 P.M. Saturday
> Closed all day   Sunday

1. Another word which is often used in place of <u>specifications</u> is
  (A) calendars   (C) requirements
  (B) quality   (D) majors

2. When does Professional Typing Service close on Wednesday?
  (A) 10:00 P.M.   (C) 4:00 P.M.
  (B) 8:00 P.M.   (D) It is closed all day

3. How much would it cost to have a fifteen-page report typed on cotton bond paper?
  (A) $15.00   (C) $18.75
  (B) $18.25   (D) $22.00

4. The main purpose of this passage is
  (A) to inform   (C) to advertise
  (B) to describe   (D) to celebrate

Questions 1– 4 refer to Passage Five:

Leading multinational industrial corporation is seeking a qualified individual with a degree in industrial engineering and a minimum of five years experience in design of mechanical components.

The successful candidate will design, stress analyze, and select custom built air control equipment for nuclear power plants.

Excellent beginning salary and complete benefits package, including medical, dental, and life insurance plans.

Interested applicants should forward résumé listing qualifications, skills, employment and salary history, accompanied by a letter of interest to:

Box A 304 *Daily News*

Deadline for applications: July 16.

1. The word <u>deadline</u> in this ad most nearly means
   (A) the first day for applications to be submitted
   (B) the last day for applications to be submitted
   (C) the day that the ad appeared in the newspaper
   (D) the day that the applicants will be informed of the decision

2. What are the qualifications for a successful candidate?
   (A) A degree in industrial engineering or five years of experience working in nuclear power plants
   (B) A degree in industrial design
   (C) More than five years experience as an industrial engineer in a leading multinational corporation
   (D) Both a degree in industrial engineering and five or more years experience in design

3. We can infer from this passage that
   (A) the successful candidate will be employed by the *Daily News*
   (B) the *Daily News* will forward résumés to the corporation
   (C) the successful candidate will work for an insurance company
   (D) the corporation is small

4. Which of the following would be the best headline for this ad?
   (A) For Sale   (C) Help Wanted
   (B) Lost and Found   (D) Personal

PREVIEW: READING ACADEMIC INFORMATION

In some passages in Part B, you will be asked to read academic information, such as course descriptions and college regulations.

You will usually be reading this kind of information for details. First, read the passage quickly. Then, read the questions. After you have answered questions for the main idea, begin to answer the other questions by referring to the passage. Use key words in the questions to help you locate the place in the passage where the answer is found.

It will help you to practice reading catalogues and brochures distributed by American, Canadian, English, and Australian colleges and universities.

EXERCISE NINE: PRACTICE IN READING ACADEMIC INFORMATION

Questions 1– 4 refer to Passage One:

> **202. Computer Programming II.** Fall. Spring. 3 hours. Lecture.
> Prerequisites: 200 or 201. Computer programming in languages other than
> Fortran. Major emphasis will be given to PL-1 and Cobol. Computer
> projects in these languages will be assigned.
> Professor Baker.

1. The word <u>prerequisites</u> in line 2 most nearly means
   (A) courses that must be taken after finishing Computer Programming II
   (B) examinations that must be taken while enrolled in Computer Programming II
   (C) courses that must be completed before enrollment in Computer Programming II
   (D) alternative courses that may be taken instead of Computer Programming II

2. Which of the following computer languages will NOT be studied?
   (A) PL-1   (C) Fortran
   (B) Cobol   (D) Major

3. How many times per year will this course be offered?
   (A) One   (C) Three
   (B) Two   (D) Four

4. What is the main purpose of this passage?
   (A) To describe a course
   (B) To give an example of a computer language
   (C) To announce a lecture
   (D) To advertise a job opportunity in Computer Programming

Questions 1– 4 refer to Passage Two:

> To drop a course on the day of open registration, obtain a drop-add petition from your college office, complete it, and take it to your academic advisor for his or her signature. To add a course, go to the Student Union registration area, obtain a class card for the course you wish to add, and pay the additional fee at the registrar's desk.
>
> To drop or add a course after the second day of classes, obtain a drop-add petition from your college office, complete it, and take it to the instructor of the course in question for his or her signature.
>
> No drops or adds will be permitted after the first fifteen calendar days of each quarter without permission of the dean of your college.

1. The word <u>drop</u> in line 1 most nearly means
   - (A) enroll in
   - (B) withdraw from
   - (C) pay for
   - (D) stop offering

2. In order to add a course after the second day of classes it is necessary to obtain the permission of
   - (A) the dean of the college
   - (B) the academic advisor
   - (C) the instructor of the course
   - (D) the registrar

3. It may be concluded from this passage that
   - (A) everyone who wishes to add a course must do so during the first fifteen days of class
   - (B) the University is on a semester system
   - (C) all students are assigned to an academic advisor
   - (D) registration is held in the college office

4. This passage is a summary of how to
   - (A) register for classes
   - (B) drop a course
   - (C) apply for admission to the University
   - (D) change the classes on a student schedule

Questions 1– 4 refer to Passage Three:

> Candidates for the bachelor of business administration degree must complete 186 quarter hours of course work with a minimum of 372 quality points; that is, the equivalent of an average grade of C (2.0 on a 4.0 scale). Candidates must also maintain a cumulative grade point average of 2.0 or better in all required professional business courses, and must earn a minimum grade of C or better in each course in the area of specialization. For example, a student majoring in accounting must earn an average of C for all courses, including not only accounting courses but also history, English, math, and so on. He or she must earn a C or better in each accounting course. Accounting classes in which the student has received a D, F, or Incomplete must be repeated.

1. Another word which is often used in place of specialization is
   (A) importance
   (B) degree
   (C) administration
   (D) major

2. Which grade would be acceptable for a professional course?
   (A) I
   (B) C
   (C) D
   (D) F

3. We can infer that a student who had completed 170 quarter hours would be a
   (A) freshman
   (B) sophomore
   (C) junior
   (D) senior

4. The sentence below that best summarizes this passage is
   (A) Business majors must complete 186 hours with an average grade of C, and must earn a grade of C or better in each business course
   (B) Business majors must repeat all accounting courses in which they receive a grade of less than C
   (C) Business majors must earn at least 372 quality points in order to graduate
   (D) Business majors must earn a grade of C or better in every class that they take, and must earn at least 186 quality points

Questions 1– 4 refer to Passage Four:

CHEMICAL ENGINEERING

Freshman Year

Fall Quarter

100	General Chemistry I	3 hours
101	Calculus I	5 hours
110	Graphics I	3 hours
100	Orientation to Engineering	1 hour
	Humanities Elective	4 hours
		16 hours

Winter Quarter

101	General Chemistry II	3 hours
121	Chemistry Laboratory	1 hour
102	Calculus II	4 hours
200	Introduction to Computer Programming	3 hours
	Humanities Elective	5 hours
		16 hours

Spring Quarter

102	General Chemistry III	3 hours
122	Chemistry Laboratory	1 hour
103	Calculus III	4 hours
100	General Physics I	5 hours
100	Economics I	4 hours
		17 hours

1. The word <u>elective</u> most nearly means
   (A) a required course
   (B) an economics course
   (C) an alternative among courses
   (D) an introductory course

2. What is the course number for Graphics I?
   (A) 100
   (B) 101
   (C) 110
   (D) 200

3. How many hours of chemistry must be taken during the freshman year, including laboratory sessions?
   (A) 2 hours
   (B) 3 hours
   (C) 9 hours
   (D) 11 hours

4. This passage is
   (A) a grade report
   (B) a plan of study for a chemistry student
   (C) a plan of study for an engineering student
   (D) a list of all of the courses offered to freshmen

Questions 1– 4 refer to Passage Five:

Accreditation is a system for setting national standards of quality in education. The United States is unique in the world because its accreditation system is not administered by the government, but rather by committees of educators and private agencies like the Middle States Association of Colleges and Secondary Schools and the Society of Engineers.

Before registering to study in any educational institution in the United States, a student should make certain that the institution is accredited in order to assure that the school has a recognized standard of organization, instruction, and financial support. Foreign students should be particularly careful to check an institution's accreditation because other governments or future employers may not recognize a degree earned from a school that has not received accreditation.

If a college is accredited, catalogues and brochures will usually indicate the accreditation status. If you are not sure about a certain school, don't hesitate to check its reputation with an education officer at the nearest U.S. Embassy.

1.   The word <u>unique</u> in line 2 most nearly means
     (A) unusual   (C) standard
     (B) first   (D) large

2.   What should students do in order to check the accreditation of a school that may interest them?
     (A) Write to the school
     (B) Write to the U.S. Ministry of Education
     (C) Register to study at the school
     (D) Consult a U.S. Embassy official

3.   From this passage, it may be concluded that an unaccredited school
     (A) does not offer a degree
     (B) may close because of financial disorganization
     (C) is administered by the government
     (D) is better than an accredited school

4.   The title that best expresses the ideas in this passage is
     (A) Studying in the United States
     (B) Accreditation
     (C) How to Find the Best School
     (D) The Middle States Association of Colleges and Secondary Schools

PREVIEW: READING TEXTBOOKS

In some passages in Part B, you will be asked to read information contained in college textbooks, especially those used in courses like business, the natural sciences, the social sciences, and the arts.

The most frequently tested type of reading passage on the TOEFL is the textbook passage.

You will usually be reading this kind of information for details. First, read the passage quickly. Then, read the questions. After you have answered questions for the main idea, begin to answer the other questions by referring to the passage. Use key words in the questions to help you locate the place in the passage where the answer is found.

It will help you to practice reading textbooks written in English.

EXERCISE TEN: PRACTICE IN READING TEXTBOOKS

Questions 1– 4 refer to Passage One:

BIOGRAPHY

Universally acclaimed as America's greatest playwright, Eugene O'Neill was born in 1888 in the heart of the theater district in New York City. As the son of an actor he had early exposure to the world of the theater. He attended Princeton University briefly in 1906, but returned to New York to work in a variety of jobs before joining the crew of a freighter as a seaman. Upon returning from voyages to South Africa and South America, he was hospitalized for six months to recuperate from tuberculosis. While he was recovering, he determined to write a play about his adventures on the sea. He went to Harvard where he wrote the one-act *Bound East for Cardiff*. It was produced on Cape Cod by the Provincetown Players, an experimental theater group that was later to settle the famous Greenwich Village theater district in New York City. The Players produced several more of his one-acts in the years between 1916–1920. With the full-length play *Beyond the Horizon*, produced on Broadway in 1920, O'Neill's success was assured. The play won the Pulitzer prize for the best play of the year. O'Neill was to be awarded the prize again in 1922, 1928, and 1957 for *Anna Christie*, *Strange Interlude*, and *Long Day's Journey Into Night*. In 1936, he was awarded the Nobel prize for literature.

O'Neill's plays, forty-five in all, cover a wide range of dramatic subjects, but several themes emerge, including the ambivalence of family relationships, the struggle between the sexes, the conflict between spiritual and material desires, and the vision of modern man as a victim of uncontrollable circumstances. Most of O'Neill's characters are seeking for meaning in their lives. According to his biographers, most of the characters were portraits of himself and his family. In a sense, his work chronicled his life.

1. In line 4, <u>briefly</u> is closest in meaning to
(A) seriously
(B) for a short time
(C) on scholarship
(D) without enthusiasm

2. How many times was O'Neill awarded the Pulitzer prize?
(A) One
(B) Three
(C) Four
(D) Five

3. We can infer from information in the passage that O'Neill's plays were not
(A) controversial
(B) autobiographical
(C) optimistic
(D) popular

4. This passage is a summary of O'Neill's
(A) work
(B) life
(C) work and life
(D) family

Questions 1– 4 refer to Passage Two:

BUSINESS

Although the composition and role of the board of directors of a company will vary from one organization to the next, a few generalizations may be made. As regards the composition of the board, customarily some directors are prominent men and women selected to give prestige to the group. Others are usually chosen from among retired executives of the organization for their specialized knowledge of the company.

It is generally true that, as long as the top management maintains the confidence of the board of directors, the directors will not actively intervene to dictate specific policies. This is the same administrative procedure usually followed by the board of trustees of a college or university, and is similar in many respects to the parliamentary system of ministerial responsibility practiced in Great Britain.

1. The word <u>prominent</u> in line 4 most nearly means
(A) professional
(B) ethical
(C) important
(D) elderly

2. Who generally formulates policies for a company?
(A) top management
(B) a dictator
(C) the board of directors
(D) retired executives

3. According to this passage, who would not be a likely candidate to be chosen as a member of the board of directors of City Bank?
(A) a retired president of City Bank
(B) a respected lawyer
(C) a City Bank employee
(D) a state senator

4. The title below that best expresses the ideas in this passage is
(A) The Board of Directors
(B) The Board of Trustees
(C) The Parliamentary System
(D) Management

Questions 1– 4 refer to Passage Three:

ASTRONOMY

A popular theory explaining the evolution of the universe is known as the Big Bang Model. According to the model, at some time between ten and twenty billion years ago, all present matter and energy were compressed into a small ball only a few kilometers in diameter. It was, in effect, an atom that contained in the form of pure energy all of the components of the entire universe. Then, at a moment in time that astronomers refer to as $T = 0$, the ball exploded, hurling the energy into space. Expansion occurred. As the energy cooled, most of it became matter in the form of protons, neutrons, and electrons. These original particles combined to form hydrogen and helium, and continued to expand. Matter formed into galaxies with stars and planets.

1. Another word which is often used in place of <u>compressed</u> is
   (A) excited   (C) reduced
   (B) balanced   (D) controlled

2. According to this passage, when were the galaxies formed?
   (A) Ten billion years ago   (C) At $T = 0$
   (B) Fifteen billion years ago   (D) Twenty billion years ago

3. It may be inferred that
   (A) energy and matter are the same
   (B) protons, neutrons, and electrons are not matter
   (C) energy may be converted into matter
   (D) the galaxies stopped expanding as energy cooled

4. The sentence below that best summarizes this passage is
   (A) The Big Bang theory does not account for the evolution of the universe
   (B) According to the Big Bang Model, an explosion caused the formation of the universe
   (C) The universe is made of hydrogen and helium
   (D) The universe is more than ten billion years old

Questions 1– 4 refer to Passage Four:

PSYCHOLOGY

Although behavioral psychologists use many different kinds of equipment in operant conditioning experiments, one device that is frequently employed is the Skinner Box. The box, named for B. F. Skinner, the American psychologist who developed it, was used in Skinner's original operant conditioning experiment in 1932. It is a small, empty box except for a bar with a cup underneath it. In Skinner's experiment, a rat that had been deprived of food for twenty-four hours was placed in the box. As the hungry animal began to explore its new environment, it accidently hit the bar, and a food pellet dropped into the cup. The rat ate the pellet and continued exploring for more food. After hitting the bar three or four times with similar results, the animal learned that it could get food by pressing the bar. The food stimulus reinforced the bar pressing response. The rat had been conditioned.

1. In line 7, <u>deprived</u> is closest in meaning to
   (A) enticed   (C) denied
   (B) provided   (D) revealed

2. How did the rat obtain more food?
   (A) By exploring   (C) By making noise
   (B) By hitting a bar   (D) By eating pellets

3. It may be concluded that operant conditioning
   (A) always uses a Skinner Box
   (B) is no longer popular
   (C) involves a stimulus and a response
   (D) requires at least twenty-four hours

4. What is the main idea in this passage?
   (A) That learning is often accidental
   (B) That B. F. Skinner is a behavioral psychologist
   (C) That a Skinner Box may be used for operant conditioning
   (D) That rats are able to learn simple tasks

Questions 1–4 refer to Passage Five:

HISTORY

The first census of the American people in 1790 listed fewer than four million residents, most of whom had come from England. Ten years later, in 1800, although the English were still a majority, many Irish, Dutch, German, Swedish, Scottish, and French settlers had come to make their homes in the United States. Immigrants from all of these nations, along with an undocumented number of Africans who had been brought into the country as slaves, provided labor for the rapidly growing cities and the frontier farms. They built factories, roads, and canals, pushing West to settle towns on the edges of the American territory.

By 1880, large numbers of central and southern Europeans began to find their way to America. Italian, Greek, Russian, Austrian, Armenian, and Slavic immigrants settled in the cities where they supplied labor for hundreds of new industries. The census of 1910 listed almost one million immigrants.

After the Civil War, many Asians began to arrive, primarily to work on the railroads in the West. Chinese laborers by the thousands led the way, followed by Korean and Japanese immigrants.

In more recent years, hundreds of thousands of refugees have come to the United States, the largest numbers from Hungary, Cuba, Lebanon, Syria, and the West Indies. With the close of the Vietnam War, thousands of Indochinese relocated in the United States.

The United States is unique in the world because, with the notable exception of the Indians, all Americans are immigrants or the descendants of immigrants.

1. The word <u>majority</u> in line 3 most nearly means
   (A) the largest number
   (B) the smallest number
   (C) the average number
   (D) the correct number

2. When did many Italian immigrants enter the United States?
   (A) In 1790
   (B) In 1800
   (C) In 1880
   (D) in 1960

3. We can infer from the passage that the author's attitude toward immigrants is
   (A) discourteous
   (B) respectful
   (C) prejudiced
   (D) disinterested

4. Which of the following would be the best title for this passage?
   (A) A History of American Immigrants
   (B) A History of Immigration in the Nineteenth Century
   (C) A History of European Immigration to the United States
   (D) A History of Urban and Agricultural Development in the United States

PREVIEW: READING GENERAL INTEREST PASSAGES

In some passages in Part B, you will be asked to read general interest passages on consumer-related topics, such as banking, driving, housing, and shopping.

You will usually be reading this kind of information for details. First, read the passage quickly. Then, read the questions. After you have answered questions for the main idea, begin to answer the other questions by referring to the passage. Use key words in the questions to help you locate the place in the passage where the answer is found.

It will help you to practice reading pamphlets, magazines, and tourist information written in English.

EXERCISE ELEVEN: PRACTICE IN READING GENERAL INTEREST PASSAGES

Questions 1– 4 refer to Passage One:

A change in the federal regulations now requires that every international student admitted to the United States on an F-1 visa be assigned a social security number. The record will be marked to indicate that it is a non-work number and may not be used for off-campus employment purposes. If the number is ever used in a job, the Social Security Office will notify the Immigration and Naturalization Service, (INS). Unless prior work permission has been granted by INS, the student may be asked to depart the country. Students who wish to work on campus may do so without notifying INS.

1. In line 1, <u>regulations</u> is closest in meaning to
   (A) laws
   (B) government
   (C) employees
   (D) offices

2. Why are international students assigned social security numbers?
   (A) Because they need them in order to work off campus
   (B) Because they need them in order to depart the United States
   (C) Because they are required to have them in compliance with federal regulations
   (D) Because they need them in order to be granted F-1 status

3. Evidently, an international student can work without receiving permission from INS
   (A) at. the Social Security Office
   (B) at State University library
   (C) no where
   (D) at the city airport

4. The title below that best expresses the ideas in this passage is
   (A) Invitation
   (B) Notice
   (C) Questionnaire
   (D) Application

Questions 1– 4 refer to Passage Two:

RENTAL AGREEMENT

CAUTION: Your signature on this legal document indicates that you have read and understood its contents and agree to abide by its conditions.

For apartment number <u>109</u> of University Park Apartments located at 600 University Park.

1. Security deposit. The amount of the security deposit is $250, at no time to be applied as rent, and to be refunded upon termination of agreement less any amount retained in payment of damages to the apartment. Should damages to the premises exceed the amount of the deposit, the resident agrees to reimburse the management for such excess.

2. Termination of agreement. The security deposit shall be refunded less any retained amount specified upon the termination of this agreement at the end of the original rental period if notice in writing of termination has been given thirty (30) days in advance of such termination, the keys have been returned to the management, and the premises are found upon inspection to be clean and undamaged.

1. The word <u>premises</u> in line 8 and line 14 most nearly means
    (A) furniture
    (B) floors
    (C) property
    (D) utilities

2. Under what conditions could the manager refuse to return a security deposit?
    (A) If the keys were not returned 30 days before the resident planned to move
    (B) If the apartment were undamaged
    (C) If the resident did not give notice in writing
    (D) If the manager could not find another resident to take the apartment

3. If a resident plans to move from University Park Apartments on June 15, when should he notify the manager?
    (A) On May 15
    (B) On June 1
    (C) On July 15
    (D) On June 15

4. This passage is
    (A) a legal document
    (B) a caution
    (C) a termination of agreement
    (D) a security deposit

Questions 1- 4 refer to Passage Three:

FULL ONE YEAR WARRANTY

General Appliance Company guarantees the product to be free from manufacturing defects for one year after the original date of purchase. If the product should become defective within the warranty period, General Appliance will repair or replace it free of charge, provided that damage to the product has not resulted from accident or misuse. Deliver the product to any one of the authorized service facilities whose names and addresses are listed in the accompanying brochure. Direct any questions regarding the warranty to Consumer Service Division, General Appliance Company, 1621 Bergen Street, Newark, New Jersey 07102.

1. Another word which is often used in place of warranty is
   (A) purchase   (C) product
   (B) manufacturing   (D) guarantee

2. Where should a defective product be taken for repair or replacement?
   (A) To the store where it was purchased
   (B) To the Consumer Service Division of General Appliance Company
   (C) To an authorized service facility
   (D) To the manufacturer that made the product

3. We may assume that General Appliance Company would replace a product under the following circumstances
   (A) When the purchase was made fourteen months ago
   (B) When the product was recently purchased on sale
   (C) When the product was dropped and damaged after purchase
   (D) When the replacement was paid for by the customer

4. The sentence below that best summarizes this passage is
   (A) General Appliance Company is an honest manufacturer
   (B) If a General Appliance product is damaged in an accident, the company will replace it
   (C) If you have an accident while using a General Appliance product, the company will pay damages
   (D) If a General Appliance product is defective when purchased, the company will repair or replace it

Questions 1– 4 refer to Passage Four:

In order to request telephone service in the United States, either call or visit your local telephone store. A sales representative will be glad to show you samples of the designs and colors available. Simply choose the design and color that you prefer, and leave your name, address, and employer's name with the sales representative. Students on scholarship should provide their sponsor's name instead of an employer's name. A fifty-dollar security deposit must be paid prior to telephone installation, and may be made by check, cash, Master Charge or Visa. On the date that your telephone is to be installed, a responsible person, such as an apartment manager, must be at home to unlock the door for the serviceman.

1. The word <u>samples</u> in line 3 most nearly means
   (A) prices
   (B) examples
   (C) pictures
   (D) catalogues

2. According to this passage, who will install your telephone?
   (A) A sales representative
   (B) A serviceman
   (C) A manager
   (D) An employer

3. We can infer from this passage that
   (A) there is more than one kind of telephone
   (B) the person requesting telephone service must be at home when it is installed
   (C) students may not request telephone service
   (D) credit cards may not be used to pay for security deposits

4. The purpose of this passage is
   (A) to persuade
   (B) to correspond
   (C) to inform
   (D) to entertain

Questions 1– 4 refer to Passage Five:

> Please follow these procedures in order to make a machine withdrawal from your City Bank checking or savings accounts:
>
> 1. Insert your card face up into the card slot on the machine teller.
>
> 2. Enter your six-digit identification number on the numbered buttons.
>
> 3. Press the withdrawal button for *checking* or the button for *savings*.
>
> 4. Enter the amount of withdrawal, either fifty or one hundred dollars, on the numbered buttons, and wait for your receipt to be printed.
>
> 5. Remove your card from the slot. The drawer will open with receipt and your cash withdrawal in fifty-dollar packets.
>
> All customers are limited to two withdrawals in one twenty-four-hour period.

1. In line 3, <u>slot</u> is closest in meaning to
   (A) envelope
   (B) drawer
   (C) opening
   (D) box

2. What happens when you remove your card from the machine?
   (A) Your identification number appears on a screen
   (B) The drawer opens with your cash in it
   (C) The process stops immediately
   (D) Your receipt is printed

3. It may be concluded from this passage that
   (A) a fifty-dollar withdrawal would be received in two packets
   (B) a typical identification number would be 10227
   (C) the maximum amount of money that may be withdrawn in one day is $200
   (D) withdrawals may be made from checking accounts only

4. What is the main idea of this passage?
   (A) How to open an account at City Bank
   (B) How to use the City Bank machine teller
   (C) How to get a City Bank card
   (D) How to make deposits and withdrawals at City Bank

PREVIEW: READING SENTENCES

In some passages in Part B, you will be asked to read a very long and complicated sentence.

Because so much information is contained in one sentence, the grammar in the sentence is very complex.

First, read the sentence for meaning. Then, read the questions. You will often find the following types of questions: (1) vocabulary in context; (2) detail; (3) inference; and (4) main idea.

It will help you to practice reading complex sentences in grammar books.

EXERCISE TWELVE: PRACTICE IN READING SENTENCES

Questions 1– 4 refer to Passage One:

> The most serious problems surrounding the world hunger situation are (1) that food production gains in the developing world have been consumed by rapid population growth; (2) that efficient methods of distribution have not been developed to transport food to areas of greatest need; (3) that millions of people cannot afford subsistence food even when it is available.

1. In line 5, <u>afford</u> is closest in meaning to the word
(A) buy
(B) eat
(C) grow
(D) distribute

2. According to this passage, why does world hunger continue to be a serious problem?
(A) Because there has been a decrease in food production
(B) Because there are now more people to feed
(C) Because there is not enough subsistence food
(D) Because there are too many areas of need

3. We can infer from this passage that, in order to effect a solution to the world hunger situation, it will be necessary to
(A) improve methods for international transportation of food supplies
(B) grow more grain
(C) provide medical care for people in developing areas
(D) identify areas of greatest need

4. Which of the following would be the best title for this passage?
(A) The World Hunger Situation
(B) Problems in the World Today
(C) Food Production and Distribution
(D) World Population and Food

Questions 1– 4 refer to Passage Two:

According to the Department of Energy, by the year 2000, 1 percent of the nation's electricity will be generated from solar cells at the enormous cost of one billion dollars a year.

1. In line 3, <u>generated</u> most nearly means
    (A) replaced   (C) produced
    (B) improved   (D) purchased

2. How much solar electricity will be generated in the future?
    (A) 1 percent of the nation's total electricity
    (B) 2000 solar cells
    (C) 10 percent of the total electricity for the country
    (D) one billion solar cells per year

3. It may be inferred that
    (A) less than 1 percent of our energy sources today are from solar cells
    (B) solar energy is very popular today
    (C) the Department of Energy supports a complete solar electricity plan
    (D) the cost of solar energy is very cheap

4. This passage is
    (A) a statement by the Department of Energy
    (B) an ad for solar energy
    (C) an estimate by producers of solar energy
    (D) a report by the president's budget committee

Questions 1– 4 refer to Passage Three:

> The second leading cause of death in this country, cancer claims the lives of over 385,000 Americans every year.

1. The word <u>claims</u> in line 2 is closest in meaning to
   (A) terminates
   (B) changes
   (C) shortens
   (D) impairs

2. How many conditions rank above cancer as a cause of death?
   (A) One
   (B) Two
   (C) Three
   (D) None

3. Approximately how many Americans will die of cancer in the next five years?
   (A) 385,000
   (B) 1 million
   (C) 1.5 million
   (D) 2 million

4. What is the main idea in this passage?
   (A) That cancer can be fatal
   (B) That 385,000 Americans died this year
   (C) That cancer is one of the leading causes of death in the U.S.
   (D) That there is no cure for cancer

Questions 1– 4 refer to Passage Four:

> The principle of cultural relativism states that, as students of culture, we should try to attain as great a degree of objectivity as possible, seeking to understand patterns of behavior in terms of the established relationships within the new culture, rather than to judge them solely on the basis of our previous cultural experience.

1. Another word which is often used in place of <u>previous</u> is
   (A) limited
   (B) past
   (C) valuable
   (D) native

2. According to this passage, how should one begin to study culture?
   (A) By judging the relationships on the basis of experience
   (B) By objecting to new patterns of behavior
   (C) By trying to understand the new culture objectively
   (D) By relating the new culture to a familiar one

3. This passage would most likely be found in
   (A) a business text
   (B) an anthropology text
   (C) a history text
   (D) a fine arts text

4. Which of the following would be the best title for this passage?
   (A) Patterns of Behavior
   (B) New Cultures
   (C) Cultural Relativism
   (D) Students of Culture

Questions 1– 4 refer to Passage Five:

> UNESCO's activities in connection with the International Year of the Child in 1979 were part of a continuing effort on behalf of the world's children which began when UNESCO was formed over thirty years ago to help children whose lives had been disrupted by war.

1. The word <u>disrupted</u> in line 5 is closest in meaning to
   (A) sacrificed   (C) preserved
   (B) disturbed   (D) defended

2. Why was the International Year of the Child promoted?
   (A) To begin an effort to help the world's children
   (B) To celebrate the end of a war
   (C) To establish UNESCO
   (D) To continue the work of UNESCO in helping children

3. When was UNESCO founded?
   (A) 1979   (C) 1966
   (B) 1976   (D) 1949

4. The sentence below that best summarizes this passage is
   (A) UNESCO was established to help children
   (B) The Year of the Child is another effort by UNESCO to help children
   (C) Many children are innocent victims of war
   (D) UNESCO helps prevent wars that may involve innocent children

Directions: For each of these questions, choose the answer that is closest in meaning to the original sentence. Note that several of the choices may be factually correct, but you should choose the one that is the closest restatement of the given sentence.

PREVIEW: READING RESTATEMENTS

In some passages in Part B, you will be asked to read a sentence and identify a restatement.

Both the sentence and the restatement will have the same meaning. The sentence and the restatement will be expressed by different grammatical structures.

First, read the sentence for meaning. Then, read the four statements that follow it. Find the statement with the same meaning as the sentence.

It will help you to practice reading selected sentences in grammar books, especially passives, negatives, chronologies, comparatives, conditionals, and concessions.

EXERCISE THIRTEEN: PRACTICE IN READING RESTATEMENTS

PASSIVES

1. That Congress was slow to cooperate in drafting energy legislation bothered the president.
   (A) The president was slow to cooperate with the Congress in drafting the bothersome legislation.
   (B) The president did not have the energy to cooperate with the Congress in drafting legislation.
   (C) The Congress could not be bothered by drafting energy legislation.
   (D) The president was bothered by the fact that Congress was slow to cooperate in drafting energy legislation.

2. The manager can force them to leave the apartment.
   (A) The manager can be forced to leave.
   (B) They can leave because the manager is forced to.
   (C) They can be forced to leave by the manager.
   (D) Both the manager and they were forced to leave.

3. A Greek legend recorded that the Olympic Games were initiated by Hercules, son of Zeus.
   (A) Zeus initiated the Olympic Games.
   (B) Hercules and Zeus initiated the Olympic Games.
   (C) Hercules initiated the Olympic games.
   (D) Hercules's son initiated the Olympic Games.

4. According to the U.S. Department of Agriculture, it will be ten years before the African honey bee will have reached the borders of the United States.
   (A) In ten years the honey bee will reach the borders of Africa from the United States.
   (B) The African honey bee will have reached the United States ten years ago.
   (C) The U.S. borders will have been reached by the African honey bee in ten years.
   (D) It was years ago that the African honey bee reached the borders of the United States.

5. Studies show that first-born or only children are expected to be successful.
  (A) First-born or only children expect success according to studies.
  (B) Only children are first in their studies.
  (C) First-born children are only successful if they study.
  (D) Others expect that first-born and only children will be successful.

NEGATIVES

1. No less an authority than Senator Edward Kennedy spoke at the graduation exercises for the law school of The University of Virginia.
  (A) The authorities asked Senator Edward Kennedy to speak at the graduation exercises.
  (B) Senator Edward Kennedy was an authority on the University of Virginia.
  (C) Senator Edward Kennedy spoke at the graduation although he was not an authority.
  (D) Senator Edward Kennedy, a recognized authority, spoke at the graduation exercises.

2. Although American football is similar to European soccer in many respects, it is not illegal to catch the ball and run with it in the American version of the sport.
  (A) European soccer is not like American football at all.
  (B) American football permits the players to catch the ball and run with it whereas European soccer does not.
  (C) Catching the ball and running with it is not legal in either American football or European soccer.
  (D) It is legal to catch the ball and run with it in European soccer but not in American football.

3. According to NASA, not one of the fragments from Sky Lab fell over a densely populated area.
  (A) All but one of the fragments from Sky Lab fell over a densely populated area.
  (B) Of all the fragments that fell from Sky Lab, NASA reported only one that came down over a densely populated area.
  (C) When Sky Lab fell over a densely populated area, there was not one fragment.
  (D) None of the fragments from Sky Lab fell over a densely populated area.

4. It is unlikely that the city bus system will be able to continue its present level of service without a price increase.
  (A) The city bus system will probably have to increase its prices in order to continue similar service.
  (B) In order to increase the level of service, the city bus system will have to raise prices.
  (C) The level of service will probably not increase because of the prices.
  (D) The city bus system will probably not continue.

5. The tourists had never seen a more beautifully landscaped park than the one at Cypress Gardens, Florida.
  (A) Cypress Gardens impressed the tourists as being a beautiful park.
  (B) Other gardens that the tourists had seen were not as beautiful as Cypress Gardens.
  (C) The tourists were not able to see the beautiful Cypress Gardens.
  (D) The tourists had seen many parks that were as beautiful as Cypress Gardens.

CHRONOLOGY

1. Seventy million years ago, long before man appeared on the earth, dinosaurs became extinct.
   (A) Before man appeared years ago, seventy million dinosaurs were on the earth.
   (B) Seventy million years after dinosaurs became extinct, man appeared on the earth.
   (C) Dinosaurs had become extinct before man appeared on earth.
   (D) Man appeared on the earth seventy million years ago, just when dinosaurs were becoming extinct.

2. Water should be added to the mixture before adding the sodium solution.
   (A) After adding water to the mixture, add the sodium solution.
   (B) Mix the sodium with the solution before the water is added.
   (C) Add water to the sodium solution before mixing it.
   (D) Mix water with the sodium solution.

3. Before creating the puppets for the world-famous *Muppet Show,* Jim Henson worked with the team of writers and artists who produced the children's program *Sesame Street.*
   (A) Jim Henson worked on *Sesame Street* after he made the puppets for the *Muppet Show.*
   (B) The *Muppet Show* was famous before *Sesame Street* because Jim Henson made the puppets.
   (C) *Sesame Street* and the *Muppet Show* had puppets before other children's programs.
   (D) Jim Henson made puppets first for *Sesame Street,* and then for the *Muppet Show.*

4. After removing clothing from the dryer, please empty the lint filter.
   (A) One should empty the lint filter before putting clothes in the dryer.
   (B) The clothes should be dry before removing them from the lint filter.
   (C) The lint filter should be emptied before removing clothes from the dryer.
   (D) One should empty the lint filter after removing clothes from the dryer.

5. Students transferring from other colleges or universities must make individual counseling appointments with academic advisors prior to registering for classes.
   (A) Before making an appointment with an academic advisor, a transfer student must register.
   (B) Transfer students should make an appointment with an academic advisor in order to register for classes.
   (C) Before registering for classes at other colleges and universities, students should make an appointment with a counselor.
   (D) After an appointment with an academic counselor, a transfer student may register for classes.

COMPARATIVES

1. Only a few years ago there were twice as many whales as there are today.
    (A)   During the past few years, the number of whales has doubled.
    (B)   There are only half as many whales now as there were a few years ago.
    (C)   There are now two times as many whales as there were a few years ago.
    (D)   Years ago there were only a few whales.

2. The famous R. H. Macy and Company, which has a floor space of more than fifty acres, is larger than any other store in the world.
    (A)   Other stores in the world are smaller than R. H. Macy, but many have more floor space.
    (B)   R. H. Macy is not as large as other stores in the world, but it is very famous.
    (C)   R. H. Macy is larger than one of the famous stores in the world.
    (D)   Other stores in the world are not as large as the famous R. H. Macy.

3. The average size of all rough diamonds mined today is less than one carat, or 1/142 of an ounce.
    (A)   None of the rough diamonds mined today is more than one carat.
    (B)   Most of the rough diamonds that are less than one carat have already been mined.
    (C)   All of the rough diamonds mined today are less than one carat.
    (D)   Most of the rough diamonds mined today are less than one carat.

4. Soybeans produce more cash receipts for area farmers than any other product.
    (A)   It costs more to produce soybeans than another product.
    (B)   Producing other products is more profitable than growing soybeans.
    (C)   Farmers prefer growing soybeans in spite of the low return when compared with other products.
    (D)   Other products are not as profitable to farmers in this area as soybeans.

5. One of the problems that managers face when they become supervisors is the fact that explaining a task to an employee may be more difficult than performing it themselves.
    (A)   Supervisors cause employees problems by performing their work while they are explaining it.
    (B)   It is easy for a manager to supervise an employee who is performing a difficult task.
    (C)   The fact that doing a job may be easier than explaining how to do it is a problem for supervisors.
    (D)   Managers should face employees while explaining their tasks to them.

CONDITIONALS

1. If so many of the players on the Cincinnati Reds had not suffered injuries, they probably would have won the World Championship again.
    (A) Because few players on the Cincinnati Reds suffered injuries, they won the World Championship again.
    (B) In spite of the injured players, the Cincinnati Reds won the World Championship again.
    (C) The Cincinnati Reds did not win the World Championship again because there were many injured players on the team.
    (D) The World Championship was won by players on the Cincinnati Reds who had not suffered injuries.

2. If a hardback book is very popular, it is usually published in a paperback edition too.
    (A) Popular books are usually published in paperback, whereas unpopular books are published in hardback editions.
    (B) Paperback books are very popular in hardback editions too.
    (C) Hardback books are published in paperback editions when they become popular.
    (D) Both hardback and paperback books are very popular.

3. Had the British not insisted on collecting such heavy taxes, the Colonies might not have rebelled, and the United States might never have become an independent nation.
    (A) The Colonies rebelled and the United States became an independent nation because the British imposed heavy taxes.
    (B) The British had not insisted on heavy taxes because the Colonies had not rebelled.
    (C) The United States became an independent nation because of the Colonies' rebellion.
    (D) The British imposed heavy taxes so that the Colonies would rebel and the United States would become an independent nation.

4. If State University had had a degree program in criminal justice, the students could have stayed here.
    (A) The students could not stay here.
    (B) The students stayed at State University.
    (C) The students studied criminal justice at State University.
    (D) The students could study criminal justice at State University.

5. It would have been a good picture if the camera hadn't been so far away.
    (A) It was not a good picture because the camera was not far enough away.
    (B) Because the camera was far away, it was a good picture.
    (C) The picture was not good because the camera was too far away.
    (D) The camera was close enough for it to be a good picture.

CONCESSIONS

1. In spite of his efforts, Chief Tecumseh was not able to unite the American Indians in the Northwest Territory.
    (A)   Tecumseh did not make an effort to unite the American Indians.
    (B)   The American Indians were united as a result of Tecumseh's efforts.
    (C)   Tecumseh tried to unite the American Indians, but he was unable to do so.
    (D)   Because he did not try to unite the American Indians, Tecumseh was not able to be chief.

2. Unless the entire balance is paid within thirty days of the billing date, a finance charge of 1.5 percent per month must also be paid.
    (A)   You must pay a finance charge if you pay your balance every month.
    (B)   After you are billed, you have one month to pay the entire amount of the finance charge.
    (C)   There is no finance charge when you pay the entire balance every month.
    (D)   By paying a finance charge of 1.5 percent of the balance, you do not have to pay any more unless you continue to use your charge.

3. It would have been an ideal location for a nuclear energy plant except for the opposition of the people in a nearby town.
    (A)   The location was ideal in spite of the attitude of the people.
    (B)   The people interfered with the building of a nuclear power plant.
    (C)   There are always objections to a nuclear power plant even in ideal locations.
    (D)   The opposition of the people did not prevent the building of a nuclear power plant.

4. Because CD's pay higher interest, many people are now investing in Certificates of Deposit (CD's) instead of putting their money in regular savings accounts.
    (A)   Many people now prefer to put their money in both regular savings accounts and CD's.
    (B)   People who have a lot of money are interested in Certificates of Deposit as well as regular savings accounts.
    (C)   Regular savings accounts are popular because they pay higher interest.
    (D)   Many people have stopped putting their money in savings accounts in order to invest in Certificates of Deposit.

5. Although some jokes are funny in any language, many cannot be translated very well.
    (A)   When jokes are translated they are funny.
    (B)   Some jokes can be translated very well, but many cannot.
    (C)   Jokes that are funny cannot be translated.
    (D)   Every language has some funny jokes.

OTHER

1. We were surprised that the game of marbles had been popular for thousands of years.
    (A) It was surprising to us that marbles had been a popular game since thousands of years ago.
    (B) The game of marbles is surprisingly popular after so many thousands of years.
    (C) The surprising popularity of marbles thousands of years ago was not known to us.
    (D) That the game of marbles surprised people thousands of years ago is popular.

2. Chan asked his roommate what to wear to a wedding in the United States.
    (A) Chan asked his roommate what he should wear.
    (B) Chan should ask his roommate what to wear.
    (C) Chan asked him what his roommate should wear.
    (D) Chan should ask him what his roommate wore.

3. In an open-book examination the instructor does not mind if his students use their notes in answering the questions.
    (A) Students ought to stop using their notes in open-book examinations.
    (B) Students are instructed to use their minds instead of their notes in answering the questions on the examination.
    (C) Students may use their notes to answer the questions on an open-book examination.
    (D) The questions in an open-book examination do not come from a student's notes.

4. When the supply exceeds the demand for a good, then the market price of the good usually falls.
    (A) The price of a good decreases when the demand is greater than the supply.
    (B) When the demand for a good is less than the supply, the price usually goes down.
    (C) The greater the demand, the greater the supply of a good on the market.
    (D) If the demand is less than the supply, the price is usually good.

5. The travel agent suggested that we go camping in the Canadian woods this year because the weather was very hot at the beach.
    (A) The travel agent told us to go to the beach because of the hot weather.
    (B) We were told to go camping instead of to the beach.
    (C) We went to the beach because the travel agent suggested it.
    (D) Since the weather was so hot, we went to talk to a travel agent.

chapter 6

Answer Key
for the TOEFL
Practice Exercises

ANSWERS FOR CHAPTER THREE

EXERCISE ONE: TEENS AND TENS

1. (D)	**5.** (B)	**9.** (B)	**13.** (C)	**17.** (B)
2. (C)	**6.** (A)	**10.** (C)	**14.** (D)	**18.** (C)
3. (A)	**7.** (D)	**11.** (C)	**15.** (C)	**19.** (D)
4. (A)	**8.** (C)	**12.** (D)	**16.** (D)	**20.** (B)

EXERCISE TWO: COMPUTATIONS

1. (B)	**5.** (C)	**9.** (A)	**13.** (D)	**17.** (A)
2. (C)	**6.** (C)	**10.** (A)	**14.** (D)	**18.** (C)
3. (B)	**7.** (C)	**11.** (C)	**15.** (C)	**19.** (D)
4. (B)	**8.** (D)	**12.** (D)	**16.** (C)	**20.** (D)

EXERCISE THREE: REFERENCE

1. (D)	**5.** (C)	**9.** (D)	**13.** (D)	**17.** (D)
2. (D)	**6.** (D)	**10.** (D)	**14.** (A)	**18.** (C)
3. (A)	**7.** (C)	**11.** (D)	**15.** (D)	**19.** (D)
4. (C)	**8.** (D)	**12.** (B)	**16.** (B)	**20.** (C)

EXERCISE FOUR: NEGATIVES

1. (A)	**5.** (B)	**9.** (C)	**13.** (B)	**17.** (C)
2. (B)	**6.** (C)	**10.** (B)	**14.** (A)	**18.** (A)
3. (A)	**7.** (D)	**11.** (D)	**15.** (C)	**19.** (C)
4. (B)	**8.** (C)	**12.** (D)	**16.** (D)	**20.** (D)

EXERCISE FIVE: COMPARATIVES

1. (A)	**5.** (D)	**9.** (D)	**13.** (B)	**17.** (C)
2. (A)	**6.** (A)	**10.** (D)	**14.** (B)	**18.** (B)
3. (C)	**7.** (D)	**11.** (D)	**15.** (C)	**19.** (C)
4. (B)	**8.** (D)	**12.** (C)	**16.** (B)	**20.** (A)

EXERCISE SIX: CONDITIONALS

1. (B)	**5.** (C)	**9.** (B)	**13.** (C)	**17.** (A)
2. (D)	**6.** (B)	**10.** (A)	**14.** (B)	**18.** (C)
3. (A)	**7.** (A)	**11.** (A)	**15.** (D)	**19.** (B)
4. (A)	**8.** (A)	**12.** (B)	**16.** (C)	**20.** (B)

EXERCISE SEVEN: CONCESSIONS (PART 1)

1. (C)	**5.** (B)	**9.** (D)	**13.** (D)	**17.** (A)
2. (B)	**6.** (C)	**10.** (A)	**14.** (D)	**18.** (B)
3. (D)	**7.** (C)	**11.** (B)	**15.** (C)	**19.** (D)
4. (B)	**8.** (B)	**12.** (B)	**16.** (C)	**20.** (C)

EXERCISE SEVEN: CONCESSIONS (PART 2)

1. (A)	**5.** (B)	**9.** (D)	**13.** (B)	**17.** (C)
2. (D)	**6.** (C)	**10.** (A)	**14.** (C)	**18.** (A)
3. (A)	**7.** (A)	**11.** (B)	**15.** (B)	**19.** (A)
4. (D)	**8.** (D)	**12.** (D)	**16.** (B)	**20.** (D)

EXERCISE EIGHT: INTERPRETING HOMOPHONES AND HOMONYMS

1. (B)	**5.** (A)	**9.** (B)	**13.** (D)	**17.** (A)
2. (C)	**6.** (C)	**10.** (B)	**14.** (B)	**18.** (D)
3. (C)	**7.** (C)	**11.** (B)	**15.** (D)	**19.** (B)
4. (D)	**8.** (B)	**12.** (B)	**16.** (B)	**20.** (C)

EXERCISE NINE: CONVERSATIONS/DIRECT INFORMATION

1. (A)	**4.** (D)	**7.** (A)	**10.** (C)	**13.** (D)
2. (D)	**5.** (B)	**8.** (B)	**11.** (C)	**14.** (C)
3. (B)	**6.** (C)	**9.** (C)	**12.** (D)	**15.** (C)

EXERCISE TEN: CONVERSATIONS/COMPUTATIONS

1. (D)	**4.** (B)	**7.** (D)	**10.** (D)	**13.** (C)
2. (C)	**5.** (C)	**8.** (B)	**11.** (A)	**14.** (C)
3. (C)	**6.** (D)	**9.** (C)	**12.** (B)	**15.** (B)

EXERCISE ELEVEN: CONVERSATIONS/PLACE

1. (B)	**4.** (B)	**7.** (B)	**10.** (C)	**13.** (D)
2. (B)	**5.** (C)	**8.** (A)	**11.** (C)	**14.** (C)
3. (A)	**6.** (A)	**9.** (B)	**12.** (C)	**15.** (C)

EXERCISE TWELVE: CONVERSATIONS/IMPLIED

1. (C)	**4.** (B)	**7.** (D)	**10.** (B)	**13.** (D)
2. (C)	**5.** (A)	**8.** (B)	**11.** (B)	**14.** (A)
3. (D)	**6.** (C)	**9.** (B)	**12.** (C)	**15.** (C)

EXERCISE THIRTEEN: MINI TALKS/OVERHEARD CONVERSATIONS

Mini Talk One	Mini Talk Two	Mini Talk Three	Mini Talk Four
1. (C)	**1.** (B)	**1.** (B)	**1.** (C)
2. (A)	**2.** (B)	**2.** (D)	**2.** (A)
3. (B)	**3.** (B)	**3.** (C)	**3.** (C)
4. (A)	**4.** (C)	**4.** (B)	**4.** (C)

EXERCISE FOURTEEN: MINI TALKS/ANNOUNCEMENTS AND ADVERTISEMENTS

Mini Talk One	Mini Talk Two	Mini Talk Three	Mini Talk Four
1. (D)	**1.** (B)	**1.** (B)	**1.** (D)
2. (B)	**2.** (A)	**2.** (D)	**2.** (B)
3. (B)	**3.** (D)	**3.** (D)	**3.** (B)
4. (C)	**4.** (A)	**4.** (A)	**4.** (C)

EXERCISE FIFTEEN: MINI TALKS/NEWS REPORTS

Mini Talk One	Mini Talk Two	Mini Talk Three	Mini Talk Four
1. (B)	1. (B)	1. (B)	1. (A)
2. (C)	2. (C)	2. (C)	2. (C)
3. (C)	3. (A)	3. (B)	3. (C)
4. (D)	4. (C)	4. (C)	4. (A)

EXERCISE SIXTEEN: MINI TALKS/WEATHER REPORTS

Mini Talk One	Mini Talk Two	Mini Talk Three	Mini Talk Four
1. (C)	1. (C)	1. (A)	1. (D)
2. (A)	2. (B)	2. (B)	2. (C)
3. (A)	3. (C)	3. (B)	3. (B)
4. (B)	4. (C)	4. (C)	4. (C)

EXERCISE SEVENTEEN: MINI TALKS/INFORMATIVE SPEECHES

Mini Talk One	Mini Talk Two	Mini Talk Three	Mini Talk Four
1. (C)	1. (B)	1. (A)	1. (B)
2. (A)	2. (C)	2. (C)	2. (C)
3. (D)	3. (A)	3. (B)	3. (B)
4. (D)	4. (C)	4. (B)	4. (C)

EXERCISE EIGHTEEN: MINI TALKS/ACADEMIC STATEMENTS (PART 1)

Mini Talk One	Mini Talk Two	Mini Talk Three	Mini Talk Four
1. (C)	1. (D)	1. (B)	1. (C)
2. (A)	2. (B)	2. (B)	2. (D)
3. (B)	3. (A)	3. (C)	3. (A)
4. (B)	4. (A)	4. (B)	4. (B)

EXERCISE EIGHTEEN: MINI TALKS/ACADEMIC STATEMENTS (PART 2)

Mini Talk One	Mini Talk Two	Mini Talk Three	Mini Talk Four
1. (C)	1. (B)	1. (A)	1. (A)
2. (B)	2. (C)	2. (C)	2. (D)
3. (D)	3. (B)	3. (D)	3. (C)
4. (B)	4. (B)	4. (A)	4. (D)

EXERCISE NINETEEN: MINI TALKS/CLASS DISCUSSIONS

Mini Talk One	Mini Talk Two	Mini Talk Three	Mini Talk Four
1. (A)	1. (D)	1. (D)	1. (B)
2. (C)	2. (A)	2. (A)	2. (C)
3. (C)	3. (A)	3. (B)	3. (A)
4. (B)	4. (A)	4. (C)	4. (A)

ANSWERS FOR CHAPTER FOUR

EXERCISE ONE: PROBLEMS WITH VERBS (PART 1)

1. (D)	**4.** (D)	**7.** (A)	**10.** (C)	**13.** (B)
2. (C)	**5.** (B)	**8.** (B)	**11.** (A)	**14.** (A)
3. (A)	**6.** (C)	**9.** (C)	**12.** (C)	**15.** (C)

EXERCISE TWO: PROBLEMS WITH VERBS (PART 2)

1. (B)	**4.** (B)	**7.** (C)	**10.** (D)	**13.** (A)
2. (A)	**5.** (C)	**8.** (A)	**11.** (D)	**14.** (D)
3. (B)	**6.** (A)	**9.** (C)	**12.** (B)	**15.** (A)

EXERCISE THREE: PROBLEMS WITH VERBS (PART 3)

1. (D)	**4.** (A)	**7.** (D)	**10.** (B)	**13.** (C)
2. (A)	**5.** (C)	**8.** (B)	**11.** (D)	**14.** (C)
3. (C)	**6.** (C)	**9.** (B)	**12.** (C)	**15.** (D)

EXERCISE FOUR: PROBLEMS WITH PRONOUNS

1. (A)	**4.** (A)	**7.** (B)	**10.** (C)	**13.** (A)
2. (C)	**5.** (B)	**8.** (B)	**11.** (C)	**14.** (C)
3. (A)	**6.** (C)	**9.** (A)	**12.** (A)	**15.** (A)

EXERCISE FIVE: PROBLEMS WITH NOUNS

1. (D)	**4.** (C)	**7.** (B)	**10.** (C)	**13.** (C)
2. (D)	**5.** (D)	**8.** (C)	**11.** (C)	**14.** (C)
3. (A)	**6.** (C)	**9.** (B)	**12.** (D)	**15.** (D)

EXERCISE SIX: PROBLEMS WITH MODIFIERS (PART 1)

1. (A)	**4.** (C)	**7.** (A)	**10.** (C)	**13.** (D)
2. (A)	**5.** (A)	**8.** (B)	**11.** (B)	**14.** (B)
3. (D)	**6.** (D)	**9.** (C)	**12.** (C)	**15.** (C)

EXERCISE SEVEN: PROBLEMS WITH MODIFIERS (PART 2)

1. (C)	**4.** (B)	**7.** (B)	**10.** (C)	**13.** (A)
2. (D)	**5.** (D)	**8.** (A)	**11.** (D)	**14.** (D)
3. (A)	**6.** (A)	**9.** (D)	**12.** (B)	**15.** (C)

EXERCISE EIGHT: PROBLEMS WITH COMPARATIVES

1. (C)	**4.** (C)	**7.** (C)	**10.** (C)	**13.** (C)
2. (B)	**5.** (C)	**8.** (A)	**11.** (B)	**14.** (C)
3. (C)	**6.** (D)	**9.** (C)	**12.** (D)	**15.** (C)

EXERCISE NINE: PROBLEMS WITH CONNECTORS

1. (A)	**4.** (C)	**7.** (C)	**10.** (B)	**13.** (D)
2. (C)	**5.** (C)	**8.** (D)	**11.** (C)	**14.** (C)
3. (C)	**6.** (A)	**9.** (B)	**12.** (B)	**15.** (B)

EXERCISE TEN: CUMULATIVE PRACTICE WITH STRUCTURES (PART 1)

1. (C)	**4.** (C)	**7.** (A)	**10.** (D)	**13.** (B)
2. (D)	**5.** (C)	**8.** (C)	**11.** (A)	**14.** (B)
3. (C)	**6.** (D)	**9.** (D)	**12.** (A)	**15.** (C)

EXERCISE ELEVEN: CUMULATIVE PRACTICE WITH STRUCTURES (PART 2)

1. (B)	**4.** (B)	**7.** (D)	**10.** (D)	**13.** (D)
2. (B)	**5.** (B)	**8.** (B)	**11.** (C)	**14.** (C)
3. (D)	**6.** (A)	**9.** (B)	**12.** (A)	**15.** (D)

EXERCISE TWELVE: PROBLEMS WITH POINT OF VIEW

1. (A)	**6.** (B)	**11.** (B)	**16.** (A)	**21.** (C)
2. (A)	**7.** (B)	**12.** (C)	**17.** (B)	**22.** (A)
3. (B)	**8.** (A)	**13.** (D)	**18.** (A)	**23.** (B)
4. (B)	**9.** (A)	**14.** (A)	**19.** (B)	**24.** (B)
5. (B)	**10.** (B)	**15.** (B)	**20.** (B)	**25.** (C)

EXERCISE THIRTEEN: PROBLEMS WITH AGREEMENT

1. (B)	**6.** (B)	**11.** (C)	**16.** (B)	**21.** (C)
2. (C)	**7.** (A)	**12.** (D)	**17.** (B)	**22.** (C)
3. (B)	**8.** (C)	**13.** (D)	**18.** (C)	**23.** (B)
4. (C)	**9.** (A)	**14.** (A)	**19.** (C)	**24.** (B)
5. (B)	**10.** (B)	**15.** (B)	**20.** (C)	**25.** (A)

EXERCISE FOURTEEN: PROBLEMS WITH INTRODUCTORY VERBAL MODIFIERS

1. (A)	**6.** (B)	**11.** (A)	**16.** (A)	**21.** (A)
2. (A)	**7.** (D)	**12.** (A)	**17.** (A)	**22.** (B)
3. (B)	**8.** (B)	**13.** (A)	**18.** (A)	**23.** (A)
4. (A)	**9.** (C)	**14.** (A)	**19.** (B)	**24.** (A)
5. (A)	**10.** (B)	**15.** (D)	**20.** (A)	**25.** (A)

EXERCISE FIFTEEN: PROBLEMS WITH PARALLEL STRUCTURE

1. (D)	**6.** (C)	**11.** (A)	**16.** (B)	**21.** (D)
2. (D)	**7.** (C)	**12.** (C)	**17.** (C)	**22.** (D)
3. (B)	**8.** (B)	**13.** (C)	**18.** (B)	**23.** (D)
4. (B)	**9.** (D)	**14.** (A)	**19.** (C)	**24.** (D)
5. (A)	**10.** (B)	**15.** (D)	**20.** (D)	**25.** (C)

EXERCISE SIXTEEN: PROBLEMS WITH REDUNDANCY

1. (D)	6. (C)	11. (B)	16. (A)	21. (B)
2. (A)	7. (D)	12. (B)	17. (C)	22. (D)
3. (C)	8. (A)	13. (A)	18. (A)	23. (A)
4. (D)	9. (B)	14. (B)	19. (D)	24. (B)
5. (A)	10. (A)	15. (C)	20. (B)	25. (A)

EXERCISE SEVENTEEN: PROBLEMS WITH WORD CHOICE

1. (D)	6. (D)	11. (B)	16. (D)	21. (A)
2. (D)	7. (C)	12. (A)	17. (A)	22. (B)
3. (B)	8. (B)	13. (C)	18. (B)	23. (A)
4. (D)	9. (C)	14. (A)	19. (D)	24. (A)
5. (C)	10. (A)	15. (A)	20. (A)	25. (A)

EXERCISE EIGHTEEN: PROBLEMS WITH STRUCTURE

1. (B)	6. (C)	11. (B)	16. (C)	21. (B)
2. (A)	7. (C)	12. (D)	17. (A)	22. (A)
3. (A)	8. (A)	13. (A)	18. (A)	23. (A)
4. (B)	9. (B)	14. (A)	19. (C)	24. (B)
5. (C)	10. (A)	15. (C)	20. (C)	25. (A)

ANSWERS FOR CHAPTER FIVE

EXERCISE ONE: VOCABULARY REVIEW (PART 1)

1.	(C)	7.	(A)	13.	(D)	19.	(C)	25.	(A)
2.	(A)	8.	(B)	14.	(A)	20.	(D)	26.	(C)
3.	(B)	9.	(A)	15.	(B)	21.	(A)	27.	(C)
4.	(A)	10.	(B)	16.	(A)	22.	(D)	28.	(A)
5.	(A)	11.	(A)	17.	(A)	23.	(C)	29.	(A)
6.	(B)	12.	(C)	18.	(A)	24.	(D)	30.	(B)

EXERCISE TWO: VOCABULARY REVIEW (PART 2)

1.	(A)	7.	(A)	13.	(A)	19.	(C)	25.	(D)
2.	(A)	8.	(C)	14.	(B)	20.	(A)	26.	(C)
3.	(B)	9.	(B)	15.	(D)	21.	(A)	27.	(C)
4.	(A)	10.	(B)	16.	(A)	22.	(C)	28.	(A)
5.	(A)	11.	(A)	17.	(A)	23.	(B)	29.	(B)
6.	(B)	12.	(D)	18.	(B)	24.	(A)	30.	(B)

EXERCISE THREE: VOCABULARY REVIEW (PART 3)

1.	(C)	7.	(A)	13.	(A)	19.	(D)	25.	(C)
2.	(D)	8.	(C)	14.	(C)	20.	(B)	26.	(C)
3.	(B)	9.	(A)	15.	(D)	21.	(A)	27.	(D)
4.	(D)	10.	(A)	16.	(A)	22.	(A)	28.	(C)
5.	(C)	11.	(D)	17.	(C)	23.	(B)	29.	(B)
6.	(B)	12.	(C)	18.	(B)	24.	(B)	30.	(B)

EXERCISE FOUR: VOCABULARY REVIEW (PART 4)

1.	(C)	7.	(A)	13.	(A)	19.	(A)	25.	(A)
2.	(C)	8.	(A)	14.	(A)	20.	(B)	26.	(B)
3.	(A)	9.	(C)	15.	(C)	21.	(C)	27.	(D)
4.	(A)	10.	(B)	16.	(C)	22.	(B)	28.	(D)
5.	(A)	11.	(C)	17.	(D)	23.	(B)	29.	(D)
6.	(D)	12.	(D)	18.	(C)	24.	(A)	30.	(A)

EXERCISE FIVE: VOCABULARY REVIEW (TWO- AND THREE-WORD VERBS)

1.	(D)	7.	(C)	13.	(A)	19.	(A)	25.	(B)
2.	(B)	8.	(C)	14.	(C)	20.	(A)	26.	(D)
3.	(A)	9.	(D)	15.	(C)	21.	(A)	27.	(B)
4.	(A)	10.	(A)	16.	(B)	22.	(B)	28.	(C)
5.	(D)	11.	(C)	17.	(B)	23.	(D)	29.	(D)
6.	(A)	12.	(C)	18.	(D)	24.	(C)	30.	(C)

EXERCISE SIX: PRACTICE IN READING INDEXES AND CHARTS

Passage One	Passage Two	Passage Three	Passage Four	Passage Five
1. (D)	1. (A)	1. (C)	1. (C)	1. (C)
2. (B)	2. (B)	2. (D)	2. (B)	2. (D)
3. (C)	3. (D)	3. (A)	3. (B)	3. (C)
4. (A)	4. (D)	4. (B)	4. (B)	4. (D)

EXERCISE SEVEN: PRACTICE IN READING INSTRUCTIONS

Passage One	Passage Two	Passage Three	Passage Four	Passage Five
1. (C)	1. (A)	1. (A)	1. (C)	1. (A)
2. (C)	2. (C)	2. (A)	2. (C)	2. (A)
3. (A)	3. (B)	3. (D)	3. (D)	3. (A)
4. (A)	4. (C)	4. (B)	4. (D)	4. (B)

EXERCISE EIGHT: PRACTICE IN READING ANNOUNCEMENTS AND ADVERTISEMENTS

Passage One	Passage Two	Passage Three	Passage Four	Passage Five
1. (A)	1. (C)	1. (B)	1. (C)	1. (B)
2. (C)	2. (C)	2. (B)	2. (A)	2. (D)
3. (B)	3. (B)	3. (B)	3. (C)	3. (B)
4. (C)	4. (C)	4. (A)	4. (C)	4. (C)

EXERCISE NINE: PRACTICE IN READING ACADEMIC INFORMATION

Passage One	Passage Two	Passage Three	Passage Four	Passage Five
1. (C)	1. (B)	1. (D)	1. (C)	1. (A)
2. (C)	2. (C)	2. (B)	2. (C)	2. (D)
3. (B)	3. (C)	3. (D)	3. (D)	3. (B)
4. (A)	4. (D)	4. (A)	4. (C)	4. (B)

EXERCISE TEN: PRACTICE IN READING TEXTBOOKS

Passage One	Passage Two	Passage Three	Passage Four	Passage Five
1. (B)	1. (C)	1. (C)	1. (C)	1. (A)
2. (C)	2. (A)	2. (C)	2. (B)	2. (C)
3. (C)	3. (C)	3. (C)	3. (C)	3. (B)
4. (C)	4. (A)	4. (B)	4. (C)	4. (A)

EXERCISE ELEVEN: PRACTICE IN READING GENERAL INTEREST PASSAGES

Passage One	Passage Two	Passage Three	Passage Four	Passage Five
1. (A)	1. (C)	1. (D)	1. (B)	1. (C)
2. (C)	2. (C)	2. (C)	2. (B)	2. (B)
3. (B)	3. (A)	3. (B)	3. (A)	3. (C)
4. (B)	4. (A)	4. (D)	4. (C)	4. (B)

EXERCISE TWELVE: PRACTICE IN READING SENTENCES

Passage One	Passage Two	Passage Three	Passage Four	Passage Five
1. (A)	1. (C)	1. (A)	1. (B)	1. (B)
2. (B)	2. (A)	2. (A)	2. (C)	2. (D)
3. (A)	3. (A)	3. (D)	3. (B)	3. (D)
4. (A)	4. (A)	4. (C)	4. (C)	4. (B)

EXERCISE THIRTEEN: PRACTICE IN READING RESTATEMENTS

Passives	Negatives	Chronology	Comparatives	Conditionals
1. (D)	1. (D)	1. (C)	1. (B)	1. (C)
2. (C)	2. (B)	2. (A)	2. (D)	2. (C)
3. (C)	3. (D)	3. (D)	3. (D)	3. (A)
4. (C)	4. (A)	4. (D)	4. (D)	4. (A)
5. (D)	5. (B)	5. (D)	5. (C)	5. (C)

Concessions	Other
1. (C)	1. (A)
2. (C)	2. (A)
3. (B)	3. (C)
4. (D)	4. (B)
5. (B)	5. (B)

Explanatory Answers for the TOEFL Practice Exercises Chapter 3

PART ONE
LISTENING COMPREHENSION

Exercise One: Teens and Tens

1. **(D)** Because I-90 is one of the busiest highways, it must be concluded that I-90 is a busy highway. Choices (A) and (C) refer to I-19, not to I-90. Choice (B) contradicts the fact that I-90 is *one* of the busiest highways.

2. **(C)** The speaker says that the suitcase weighs sixty pounds. Choice (A) contradicts the fact that the suitcase is overweight. Choice (D) contradicts the fact that you will have to pay overweight. The number sixteen sounds like sixty, but Choice (B) is not mentioned and may not be concluded from information in the statement.

3. **(A)** Because the International Office has been moved to 70 South Speedway, it must be concluded that the new address of the International Office is 70 South Speedway. Choice (B) contradicts the fact that 70 South Speedway is the new, not the old, address. Choice (C) contradicts the fact that the office has moved to 70, not 17 South Speedway. Choice (D) is not mentioned and may not be concluded from information in the statement.

4. **(A)** Because forty students will receive their Ph.D. degrees, it must be concluded that a doctoral degree will be awarded to forty students. Choice (B) contradicts the fact that forty, not fourteen, students will receive their Ph.D.'s. Choice (C) contradicts the fact that forty students will receive their Ph.D. degrees in industrial engineering. Choice (D) contradicts the fact that more than fourteen students graduated this semester.

5. **(B)** The speaker says that a one-way ticket to Washington costs eighty dollars. Choices (A) and (C) contradict the fact that it costs eighty, not eighteen or eight dollars, to go to Washington. Choice (D) is true but does not have the same meaning as the statement.

6. **(A)** Because you have fifteen minutes to finish this section of the test, it must be concluded that there are fifteen minutes left. Choices (B) and (D) refer to the past, not to the time remaining to finish this section. Choice (C) contradicts the fact that you have fifteen, not five, minutes to finish.

7. **(D)** The speaker says that Jane lives in room fourteen. Choice (A) contradicts the fact that Jane's room is on the first, not the fourteenth floor. Choices (B) and (C) are not mentioned and may not be concluded from information in the statement.

8. **(C)** The speaker says that it costs fifteen cents to call Miami after five o'clock. Choice (A) contradicts the fact that it costs fifteen, not fifty, cents to call Miami. Choice (D) contradicts the fact that it costs fifteen cents to call after, not before, five o'clock. Choice (B) is not mentioned and may not be concluded from information in the statement.

9. **(B)** The speaker says that all the English classes will meet in room 170. The numbers 70, 117, and 17 in Choices (A), (C), and (D) sound like 170, but they are not mentioned and may not be concluded from information in the statement.

10. **(C)** Because the speaker says to turn to page 16 and do the first fifteen problems, it must be concluded that the homework assignment can be found on page 16. Choice (A) contradicts the fact that the first fifteen, not fifty, problems are assigned. Choice (B) contradicts the fact that the problems are on page 16, not 60. The number *fifteen* in Choice (D) refers to the problems, not to the page.

11. **(C)** The speaker says that today's low temperature was thirty degrees. Choice (A) contradicts the fact that today's low temperature was thirty, not thirteen degrees. Choice (D) contradicts the fact that today's low was thirty, not three degrees. The number in Choice (B) refers to the low temperature today, not to the number of degrees lower than yesterday.

12. **(D)** The speaker says that he needs eighteen copies before his eight o'clock meeting tomorrow. Choice (A) contradicts the fact that he needs eighteen, not eight, copies. Choice (B) contradicts the fact that he needs, not made, copies and the fact that eighteen, not eighty, are needed. Choice (C) contradicts the fact that the speaker has one, not eight, meetings tomorrow at eight o'clock.

13. **(C)** The speaker says that the rate of exchange is thirteen-to-one. Choice (A) contradicts the fact that the rate is thirteen-to-one, not thirty-one. Choice (B) contradicts the fact that the rate is thirteen-to-one, not thirty-to-one. Choice (D) contradicts the fact that the rate is thirteen-to-one, not three-to-one.

14. **(D)** The speaker says that a fourteen is a size large. Choice (A) contradicts the fact that a fourteen, not a forty, is a size large. Choices (B) and (C) are not mentioned and may not be concluded from information in the statement.

15. **(C)** Because the speaker says that CBS news is on channel thirteen at six o'clock, it must be concluded that channel thirteen carries CBS news. Choice (A) contradicts the fact that channel thirteen, not channel three, carries CBS news. The number in Choice (B) refers to the hour, not the channel. Choice (D) contradicts the fact that CBS news is on channel thirteen, not thirty.

16. **(D)** The speaker says that the answers may be found on page 90. Choice (B) contradicts the fact that the answers may be found on page 90, not page 9. Choice (C) contradicts the fact that the answers are on page 90. The number in Choice (A) refers to the page number, not to the answers.

17. **(B)** Because the speaker says that you need an eighteen-cent stamp for the package, it must be concluded that it will cost eighteen cents to mail the package. Choice (A) contradicts the fact that you need eighteen, not eighty, cents. Choice (C) contradicts the fact that you need an [one] eighteen-cent stamp. Choice (D) contradicts the fact that you need eighteen, not eight, cents.

18. **(C)** The speaker says that flight forty is now boarding. Choice (A) contradicts the fact that the flight number is forty, not fourteen. Choice (B) contradicts the fact that the flight number is forty, not forty two, and that it leaves from gate two. Choice (D) is not mentioned and may not be concluded from information in the statement.

19. **(D)** The speaker says that 15 percent of the students scored above 450. Choice (A) contradicts the fact that 15, not 50 percent of the students scored above 450. Choice (C) contradicts the fact that 15, not 50 percent of the students scored above 450, not 415. Choice (B) is not mentioned and may not be concluded from information in the statement.

20. **(B)** Because the speaker says that John will be thirty on November 14, it must be concluded that on November fourteenth, John will celebrate his birthday. Choice (A) contradicts the fact that John will be thirty, not forty. Choice (C) contradicts the fact that John is twenty nine, not twelve, now. The number in Choice (D) refers to John's age on his next birthday, not the date.

Exercise Two: Computations

1. **(B)** If the $60 dresses are half-price, then they are 60 divided by 2, or $30. The number in Choice (A) sounds like 60. The number in Choice (C) is twice the cost, not half-price. The number in Choice (D) refers to the regular price of the dresses.

2. **(C)** If Dr. Baker arrived at 8:40 A.M., missing the bus by five minutes, then the bus left five minutes before he arrived, or 8:35 A.M. The time in Choice (A) is five minutes after, not before, Dr. Baker arrived. The time in Choice (B) refers to the time Dr. Baker arrived. The time in Choice (D) is ten, not five, minutes before Dr. Baker arrived.

3. **(B)** If City College had 520 students and doubled its enrollment, then it now has 2 times 520, or 1040 students. The number in Choice (A) is half, not double the enrollment. The number in Choice (C) refers to the enrollment now, not in 1969. The date in Choice (D) is the year that the school enrolled 520 students, not the year the college was founded.

4. **(B)** If Miss Smith arrived half an hour early and the store opens at 10:00 A.M., then she arrived at half an hour before 10, or 9:30 A.M. The time in Choice (A) is one hour before the store opens, not when the store opens. The time in Choice (C) refers to the time the store opens, not the time she arrives. The time in Choice (D) is half an hour after the store opens.

5. **(C)** If I pay $250 rent and I only have half my salary left, then my salary is 2 times $250, or $500. The amount in Choice (A) refers to the rent payment, or half the speaker's salary. The amount in Choice (B) is 3 times, not 2 times, the rent payment. The amount in Choice (D) is half, not two times the rent payment.

6. **(C)** If the flight was supposed to depart at 12:00 noon, but the plane was delayed for half an hour, then the plane left half an hour after noon, or 12:30 P.M. The time in Choice (A) is half an hour before the plane was supposed to depart. The time in Choice (B) refers to when the plane was supposed to depart. The time in Choice (D) is one hour, not half an hour after the plane was supposed to depart.

7. **(C)** If the stadium seats 50,000 people, but it was half empty, then 50,000 divided by 2, or 25,000 people attended. The number in Choice (A) is 2 times or double the number of seats in the stadium. The number in Choice (B) is 15,000, not 50,000, divided by 2. The number in Choice (D) refers to the total, not half of, the stadium seats.

8. **(D)** If Sandy bought a $200 camera for $165, then she saved $200 minus $165, or $35. The number in Choice (A) is the price of the camera, not the amount saved. Choice (B) contradicts the fact that she saved money. The number in Choice (C) is the original price, not the sale price, of the camera.

9. **(A)** If Jane types forty words a minute, and Judy types eighty words, then Jane types one to Judy's two, or Jane types half as fast as Judy, and Judy types twice as fast as Jane. Choice (B) contradicts the fact that Judy types twice as fast as Jane. Choice (C) contradicts the fact that Jane types forty, not eighty, words a minute. Choice (D) contradicts the fact that Judy types twice as fast as Jane.

10. **(A)** "These end tables are on sale for $85 each…" The amount in Choice (B) is half the cost of two tables at the sale price. The amount in Choice (C) is twice the regular cost of one end table, not the sale price for two. The amount in Choice (D) is twice the sale price for two end tables, or the cost of four, not two, end tables on sale.

11. **(C)** If the class begins at eight o'clock, and Bill is always fifteen minutes late, then Bill gets to class fifteen minutes after eight, or eight-fifteen. The time in Choice (A) refers to when class begins, not when Bill gets there. Choice (B) contradicts the fact that Bill goes to class at eight-fifteen. Choice (D) contradicts the fact that Bill is always late, not early.

12. **(D)** If we expected to sell forty tickets, but we sold twice as many, then we sold two times forty, or eighty tickets. The number in Choice (A) refers to how many tickets we expected to sell, not to how many we sold. The number in Choice (B) is half, not twice as many tickets as we expected to sell. The number in Choice (C) is how many tickets we actually sold, not how many we expected to sell.

13. **(D)** If Dr. Jones didn't get to the airport until 11:00 and he missed his flight by half an hour, then his flight left half an hour before 11:00, or 10:30. Choice (A) contradicts the fact that his taxi was late. The time in Choice (B) is half an hour after, not before, he arrived. The time in Choice (C) is when Dr. Jones arrived, not when the plane left.

14. **(D)** If Mr. Black has to leave his house at 8:30 to get to work by 9:00, then it takes him 9:00 minus 8:30, or thirty minutes to drive there. Choice (A) contradicts the fact that Mr. Black has to leave his house at 8:30, not 9:00. Choice (B) contradicts the fact that Mr. Black has to be at work at 9:00, not 8:30. Choice (C) is not mentioned and may not be computed from information in the statement.

15. **(C)** If Alice was shortchanged $10 from a $300 check, then Alice received $300 minus $10, or $290. She had $10 less, or she was short $10. Choice (A) contradicts the fact that Alice was shortchanged. Choices (B) and (D) are not mentioned and may not be concluded from information in the statement.

16. **(C)** If my watch says 9:30, but I set it ten minutes ahead, then it is ten minutes before 9:30, or 9:20. Choice (D) contradicts the fact that I set my watch ten minutes, not thirty minutes ahead. Choices (A) and (B) are not mentioned and may not be concluded from information in the statement.

17. **(A)** If this recipe serves ten, and we expect twenty, then we expect twice as many as the recipe will serve. We should make the recipe twice, or double the recipe. Choice (B) would serve half of ten, or five, not twenty. Choice (C) would serve ten times ten, or one hundred. Choice (D) would serve twenty times ten, or two hundred.

18. **(C)** If the bus goes halfway and they have to walk half a mile, then they live two times half a mile, or one mile from State University. The distance in Choice (A) is how far Bob and Carol walk, not how far they live. Choice (B) contradicts the fact that they walk half a mile, not one mile. Choice (D) contradicts the fact that the bus goes halfway, not all the way.

19. **(D)** If John was supposed to arrive for the noon meal but he was two hours late, then he arrived two hours after noon, or two o'clock. Choice (A) contradicts the fact that John was two hours late. Choice (C) contradicts the fact that John was supposed to arrive for the noon meal. Choice (B) is not mentioned and may not be concluded from information in the statement.

20. **(D)** If Mary bought a book for $6 and saved $2.50, then the book usually costs $6 plus $2.50, or $8.50. The amount in Choice (A) is the cost of a used book, not the amount saved. The amount in Choice (B) is the amount saved, not the cost of a used book. The amount in Choice (C) is not mentioned and may not be computed from information in the statement.

Exercise Three: Reference

1. **(D)** Because Jeff's family was happy when he married Nancy, it must be concluded that Jeff's family approved. Choice (C) contradicts the fact that it is Jeff's family, not Nancy's family, that approves of the marriage. Choices (A) and (B) are not mentioned and may not be concluded from information in the statement.

2. **(D)** Because Mr. Johnson wants his nephew to go into business with him, it must be concluded that Mr. Johnson hopes his nephew will do it. Choices (A) and (B) contradict the fact that Mr. Johnson does not have a son of his own. Choice (C) is not mentioned and may not be concluded from information in the statement.

3. **(A)** Because Ann would like us to pick her up, it must be concluded that she wants us to meet her. Choice (B) contradicts the fact that she would like us to pick her up in the future. Choices (C) and (D) contradict the fact that it is we who will meet Ann, not she who will meet us.

4. **(C)** Because Bill bought his wife a suit, it must be concluded that he bought her a suit. Choices (A) and (D) contradict the fact that it is Bill, not Ann, who bought the suit. Choice (B) contradicts the fact that he bought the suit for Ann, not for himself.

5. **(C)** Because I don't remember the last name of Ellen's teacher, it must be concluded that I don't remember the teacher's last name. Choice (A) contradicts the fact that it is the teacher's, not Ellen's name. Choice (B) contradicts the fact that it is I [the speaker] not Ellen, who cannot remember. Choice (D) contradicts the fact that it is I, not the teacher, who cannot remember.

6. **(D)** Because Pat refused John's invitation, it must be concluded that she did not go. Choice (A) contradicts the fact that Pat did not go. Choice (B) contradicts the fact that it was John who invited Pat. Choice (C) is not mentioned and may not be concluded from information in the statement.

7. **(C)** Because Nancy made Paul the scarf, it must be concluded that Paul has a scarf. Choices (A), (B), and (D) are not mentioned and may not be concluded from information in the statement.

8. **(D)** Because Tom sent his roommate a birthday card, it must be concluded that Tom wished his roommate a happy birthday. Choices (A), (B), and (C) contradict the fact that it is Tom's roommate, not Tom, who has a birthday.

9. **(D)** Because Bill's sister was very proud when he graduated, it must be concluded that when Bill graduated, his sister was very proud. Choice (A) contradicts the fact that it was Bill, not his sister, who graduated. Choices (B) and (C) contradict the fact that it was Bill's sister, not Bill, who was very proud.

10. **(D)** Because James's mother had already gone to work when he got home, it must be concluded that James's mother was at work when he got home. Choice (A) contradicts the fact that it was James's mother, not James, who went to work. Choice (B) contradicts the fact that James's mother had gone. Choice (C) contradicts the fact that James's mother had already gone.

11. **(D)** Because last night at the party we finally met Mary's Uncle Charles, it must be concluded that last night we were introduced to Charles, Mary's uncle. Choice (A) contradicts the fact that it was Mary's uncle, not Charles's uncle, whom we met. Choice (B) contradicts the fact that we, not Mary, met her Uncle Charles. Choice (C) is not mentioned and may not be concluded from information in the statement.

12. **(B)** Because Bob resented his father's criticizing the plans for his new office building, it must be concluded that Bob was unhappy when his father criticized. Choice (A) contradicts the fact that it was Bob's father, not Bob, who criticized the plans. Choice (C) contradicts the fact that it was Bob's father, not Bob and his father, who criticized the plans. Choice (D) contradicts the fact that it was the plans for his new office building, not Bob, that his father criticized.

13. **(D)** Because Mrs. Williams asked her lawyer to draw up a will naming her grandson as the sole beneficiary, it must be concluded that the lawyer wrote the will for Mrs. Williams. Choice (A) contradicts the fact that Williams is Mrs. Williams last name, not her grandson's first name. Choice (B) contradicts the fact that her grandson, not her lawyer, was sole beneficiary. Choice (C) contradicts the fact that the will belongs to Mrs. Williams, not her lawyer.

14. **(A)** Because Larry took his brother's car to the car wash, it must be concluded that Larry washed his brother's car. Choice (B) contradicts the fact that Larry, not Larry's brother, took the car to the car wash. Choice (C) contradicts the fact that it was his brother's car, not his brother's car wash. Choice (D) contradicts the fact that it was Larry, not Larry and his brother, who took the car to the car wash.

15. **(D)** Because Paul wants his wife to go back to school, it must be concluded that Paul would like his wife to finish her education. Choices (A) and (C) contradict the fact that it is Paul's wife, not Paul, who needs to finish her education. Choice (B) contradicts the fact that Paul, not his wife, wants her to go back to school.

16. **(B)** Because Mrs. Ayers told Dr. Smith's secretary to cancel her appointment, it must be concluded that Mrs. Ayers could not keep her appointment with Dr. Smith. Choice (A) contradicts the fact that Mrs. Ayers talked to Dr. Smith's secretary. Choice (D) contradicts the fact that the secretary is Dr. Smith's, not Mrs. Ayers's secretary. Choice (C) is not mentioned and may not be concluded from information in the statement.

17. **(D)** Because Alice wants to transfer to the University of Toledo because she has many friends studying there, it must be concluded that Alice plans to study at the University of Toledo with her friends. Choice (A) contradicts the fact that Alice wants to transfer [from another school] to the University of Toledo. Choice (B) contradicts the fact that Alice's friends, not Alice and her friends, now study at the University of Toledo. Choice (C) contradicts the fact that Alice has many friends studying at the University of Toledo.

18. **(C)** Because Professor Baker asked his graduate assistant to give the lecture today, it must be concluded that Professor Baker's graduate assistant was asked to give today's lecture. Choice (A) contradicts the fact that Professor Baker's graduate assistant will give the lecture today. Choice (B) contradicts the fact that Professor Baker has a graduate assistant now. Choice (D) is not mentioned and may not be concluded from information in the statement.

19. **(D)** Because Mary refused to return Bill's telephone call, it must be concluded that Mary did not telephone Bill. Choices (A) and (B) contradict the fact that Mary refused to call Bill. Choice (C) contradicts the fact that Bill, not Mary, made the first telephone call, and Mary, not Bill, would be the one to answer it.

20. **(C)** Because Sally borrowed her sister's bicycle, it must be concluded that Sally's sister lent her a bicycle. Choice (B) contradicts the fact that it is Sally's sister, not Sally, who has a bicycle. Choice (D) contradicts the fact that Sally borrowed the bicycle from, not for, her sister. Choice (A) is not mentioned and may not be concluded from information in the statement.

Exercise Four: Negatives

1. **(A)** *Hardly any* means *not many*. Choices (B), (C), and (D) refer to *hard* or difficult, not hardly.

2. **(B)** *No* who are *not* means *all*. Choices (A), C, and (D) contradict the fact that all students have insurance.

3. **(A)** *Never slower* means *slower than ever* or *better before*. Choice (B) contradicts the fact that business is slower now. Choice (D) contradicts the fact that business was slow and is slow now. Choice (C) is not mentioned and may not be concluded from information in the statement.

4. **(B)** *Neither...nor* means *not...or*. Choice (A) contradicts the fact that the tour was not worth the time. Choice (C) contradicts the fact that the tour was not worth the time, and the fact that the tour was not worth the money. Choice (D) is correct but does not include the fact that the tour was not worth the money.

5. **(B)** *Not many...as nice* means *nicer*. Choices (A), C, and (D) are not mentioned and may not be concluded from information in the statement.

6. **(C)** *Never...so much* means *the first time ever*. Choice (A) contradicts the fact that the students have never seen so much before. Choice (B) contradicts the fact that they had never seen so much snow [when they had seen snow] before. Choice (D) is not mentioned and may not be concluded from information in the statement.

7. **(D)** *No better place* means *the best place*. Choice (B) contradicts the fact that there is no better place than the shopping center. Choices (A) and (C) are not mentioned, but it may be concluded that because there is no better place, the shopping center is not dangerous and it is better to practice there.

8. **(C)** *To like nothing better* means *to like better than anything* or *to like very much*. Choices (A), (B), and (D) misinterpret the phrase *like nothing better* as a negative.

9. **(C)** *Not unfriendly* means *friendly*. Because Mary is friendly, it must be concluded that she did not wave because she did not see you. Choice (A) contradicts the fact that Mary is friendly. Choice (B) contradicts the fact that you, not Mary, waved. Choice (D) contradicts the fact that you waved.

10. **(B)** *Not uncommon* means *common*. Choice (A) contradicts the fact that the problems were common, not unusual. Choices (C) and (D) are not mentioned and may not be concluded from information in the statement.

11. **(D)** *Neither...nor* means *not...and not*. Choice (A) contradicts the fact that Professor Ayers does not speak Arabic. Choice (B) contradicts the fact that Professor Ayers does not speak Farsi. Choice (C) contradicts the fact that Professor Ayers does not speak Arabic and the fact that he does not speak Farsi.

12. **(D)** *Hasn't ever* means *never*. Choice (A) contradicts the fact that Jane's family hasn't met Bob. The word *family* in Choice (B) refers to Jane's, not Bob's family. The word *friend* in Choice (C) refers to Bob, not to another person Bob does not know.

13. **(B)** *Not any* means *no*. Choice (A) contradicts the fact that there is not any doubt. Choices (C) and (D) do not refer specifically to doubt.

14. **(A)** *Useless* means something that *cannot be used.* The phrase *used less* in Choice (B) sounds like useless but is not mentioned and may not be concluded from information in the statement. Choice (C) contradicts the fact that the machine cannot be used. The word *copied* in Choice (D) refers to the kind of machine it is, not to what happened to the machine.

15. **(C)** *No more comfortable* means *neither* was *comfortable.* Choice (A) contradicts the fact that the first apartment was not comfortable. Choice (B) contradicts the fact that the new apartment was not more comfortable. Choice (D) contradicts the fact that the first apartment was not comfortable and the fact that the new apartment was not more comfortable.

16. **(D)** *No harder course* means the *hardest* or *the most difficult.* Choices (A) and C contradict the fact that there is no harder course. Choice (B) is not mentioned and may not be concluded from information in the statement.

17. **(C)** *To not have to* means *to not be required to.* Choice (A) is true, but it does not have the same meaning as the statement. Choice (B) contradicts the fact that Betty has work but does not have to work overtime [on a job]. Choice (D) is not mentioned and may not be concluded from information in the statement. It is overtime, not work, that Betty does not have to do.

18. **(A)** *Never unfair* means *always fair.* The word *fair* in Choice (C) means a festival, not a just manner of treating people. Choices (B) and (D) are not mentioned and may not be concluded from information in the statement.

19. **(C)** *Can't afford* means *to not have enough money.* The word *Ford* in Choice (A) sounds like afford. Choice (B) contradicts the fact that I do not have enough money to buy a car now. Choice (D) contradicts the fact that I am considering buying a new car now, not in the past.

20. **(D)** *Could hardly* means *with difficulty.* Choice (A) contradicts the fact that he ate, not tried to eat, the dessert. The word *hard* in Choice (B) refers to the dessert, not to how John was able to eat it. Choice (C) contradicts the fact that John ate the dessert with difficulty.

Exercise Five: Comparatives

1. **(A)** Because the most successful small business is the restaurant business, it must be concluded that there are more successful restaurants than any other small business. Choice (B) contradicts the fact that traditionally the restaurant is the most successful small business. Choices (C) and (D) are not mentioned and may not be concluded from information in the statement.

2. **(A)** Because we had more than enough time, it must be concluded that there was plenty of time. Choice (B) contradicts the fact that we had enough time. Choices (C) and (D) are not mentioned and may not be concluded from information in the statement.

3. **(C)** Because the speaker says that the new students will feel less homesick when they have been there a little longer, it must be concluded that the new students have not been there very long. Choices (A) and (B) contradict the fact that the students will feel less homesick. Choice (D) is not mentioned and may not be concluded from information in the statement.

4. **(B)** Because Kathy is better looking, it must be concluded that she is prettier. In Choice (A), the word *better* refers to Kathy's sight, not to her looks. In Choice (C) *better* refers to her room. In Choice D, *better* refers to her roommate.

5. **(D)** Because the university is farther away than I thought, it must be concluded that the university is not as near as I thought. Choices (A) and (B) contradict the fact that the university is farther away than I thought. Choice (C) is not mentioned and may not be concluded from information in the statement.

6. **(A)** Because Bill gets less exercise than he should, it must be concluded that Bill should exercise more. Choice (C) contradicts the fact that Bill gets less, not more exercise than he should. Choices (B) and (D) are not mentioned and may not be concluded from information in the statement.

7. **(D)** Because Ellen isn't a bit like her husband Tom, it must be concluded that Ellen and Tom are very different. Choice (B) contradicts the fact that Ellen isn't like her husband. Choice (C) contradicts the fact that Tom is Ellen's husband. Choice (A) is not mentioned and may not be concluded from information in the statement.

8. **(D)** Because Ann prefers cold weather to hot, it must be concluded that Ann likes cold weather better. Choice (A) contradicts the fact that Ann prefers cold weather. Choices (B) and (C) contradict the fact that Ann prefers cold, not hot, weather.

9. **(D)** Because we haven't lived here as long as the Smiths, it must be concluded that the Smiths have lived here longer. Choice (B) contradicts the fact that the Smiths, not we, have lived here longer. The length of time that the Smiths have lived here is not mentioned in Choices (A) and (C) and may not be concluded from information in the statement.

10. **(D)** Because aspirin is as good as anything, it must be concluded that it is one of the best remedies. Choice (A) contradicts the fact that aspirin is good for colds and flu. Choice (B) contradicts the fact that aspirin, not anything, is good. Choice (C) contradicts the fact that aspirin is as good as anything.

11. **(D)** Because writing the term paper was a bigger job than I thought, it must be concluded that it is not as easy as I thought. Choice (A) contradicts the fact that it was a bigger job than I thought. Choice (B) contradicts the fact that I am writing the paper. Choice (C) contradicts the fact that writing the paper is a bigger job.

12. **(C)** Because she has been able to learn English more quickly than I had imagined, it must be concluded that I imagined she would learn English more slowly. Choice (A) contradicts the fact that I imagined she would learn English more slowly. Choice (B) contradicts the fact that she has been able to learn English more quickly. Choice (D) is not mentioned and may not be concluded from information in the statement.

13. **(B)** Because, in my opinion, tennis is more fun [than jogging], it must be concluded that I like to play tennis more than I like to jog. Choice (A) contradicts the fact that some people, not I, like jogging, and the fact that I think tennis, not jogging, is more fun. Choice (C) contradicts the fact that some people think jogging, not tennis, is better for your health. Choice (D) is not mentioned and may not be concluded from information in the statement.

14. **(B)** Because Jeff was no more surprised than I was, it must be concluded that neither Jeff nor I was surprised. Choice (A) contradicts the fact that it was Jeff and I, not Jeff and Tom, who were surprised. Choice (C) contradicts the fact that Jeff was no more surprised than I. Choice (D) contradicts the fact that Jeff was no more surprised than I, or that we were not surprised.

15. **(C)** Because the older one is when he gets married, the less likely it is that he'll get a divorce, it must be concluded that people who get married young have a greater probability of getting a divorce. Choice (D) contradicts the fact that it is less likely for an older person who marries to get a divorce. Choices (A) and (B) are not mentioned and may not be concluded from information in the statement.

16. **(B)** Because a steak dinner costs $10 at most restaurants but $3 at City Steak House, it must be concluded that a steak dinner at City Steak House is cheaper than at most restaurants. Choice (C) contradicts the fact that a steak dinner is cheaper at City Steak House. Choices (A) and (D) are true, but they are not mentioned and may not be concluded from information in the statement.

17. **(C)** Because John studies harder than Bill, it must be concluded that Bill does not study as hard as John. Choice (A) contradicts the fact that John studies harder than Bill. Choice (D) contradicts the fact that Bill gets better grades. Choice (B) is not mentioned and may not be concluded from information in the statement.

18. **(B)** Because Larry's son does not look like him at all, it must be concluded that Larry and his son look very different. Choice (C) contradicts the fact that Larry's son does not look like him. Choices (A) and (D) are not mentioned and may not be concluded from information in the statement.

19. **(C)** Because Betty prefers living at home with her parents, it must be concluded that Betty likes living at home. Choice (A) contradicts the fact that Betty prefers living at home to renting an apartment. Choice (B) contradicts the fact that Betty prefers living at home. Choice (D) is not mentioned and may not be concluded from information in the statement.

20. **(A)** Because Mrs. Smith hasn't traveled nearly as much as her husband has, it must be concluded that she has traveled less. Choices (B), (C), and (D) are not mentioned and may not be concluded from information in the statement.

Exercise Six: Conditionals

1. **(B)** This statement implies the two facts enclosed in parentheses: If John had his way (but he does not have his way), he would spend all of his time playing tennis (but he does not spend his time playing tennis). The word *weigh* in Choice (A) sounds like *way* but is not mentioned and may not be concluded from information in the statement. Choice (C) may be concluded from information in the statement, but it does not have the same meaning as the statement. Choice (D) is not mentioned and may not be concluded from information in the statement. It is time, not money, that John is spending.

2. **(D)** This statement implies the two facts enclosed in parentheses: Mary could have gotten better grades (but she did not get better grades) if she had studied more (but she did not study). Choice (A) contradicts the fact that Mary did not get better grades and the fact that she did not study. Choices (B) and (C) refer to the present and the future, not the past.

3. **(A)** This statement implies the two facts enclosed in parentheses: The project would have been approved (but it was not approved) if it hadn't been for the budget (but the budget was a problem). Choices (B) and (D) contradict the fact that the project was not approved. Choice (C) contradicts the fact that the budget was a problem and the fact that the project, not the budget, was being considered for approval.

4. **(A)** This statement implies the two facts enclosed in parentheses: If we had needed to get in touch with them (but we did not need to), we could have sent a telegram (but we did not send a telegram). Choice (B) contradicts the fact that we could have sent a telegram and the fact that we did not need to get in touch with them. Choice (C) contradicts the fact that we did not send a telegram. Choice (D) contradicts the fact that we, not they, could have sent a telegram if we, not they, needed to get in touch with them.

5. **(C)** This statement implies the facts enclosed in parentheses: If you usually take a size six, you'll need a size seven in this style (because this style is smaller than usual). Choice (A) contradicts the fact that a size seven is larger, not smaller, than a size six. The size in Choice (B) refers to the size you usually take, not to the size you need in this style. Choice (D) contradicts the fact that you usually take a size six, not seven.

6. **(B)** This statement implies the two facts enclosed in parentheses: If we had arrived on time (but we did not arrive on time), we would have gotten good seats (but we did not get good seats). Choice (A) contradicts the fact that we did not get good seats. Choice (C) contradicts the fact that we got seats, but not good seats. Choice (D) contradicts the fact that we did not arrive on time and the fact that we did not get good seats.

7. **(A)** This statement implies the two facts enclosed in parentheses: If he had asked her (but he did not ask her), she would have gone with him (but she did not go). Choice (B) contradicts the fact that she did not go with him. Choice (C) contradicts the fact that he did not ask her to go with him. Choice (D) contradicts the fact that he, not she, would have asked.

8. **(A)** This statement implies the facts enclosed in parentheses: A fur coat like this will last for years if it's cared for properly (but if it is not cared for, it will not last long). Choice (C) contradicts the fact that if a fur coat is not cared for, it will not last long. Choices (B) and (D) are not mentioned and may not be concluded from information in the statement.

9. **(B)** This statement implies the facts enclosed in parentheses: Getting up early isn't difficult if you have an alarm clock (but it is difficult if you do not have an alarm clock). Choice (A) contradicts the fact that it is difficult to get up if you do not have an alarm clock. Choice (C) contradicts the fact that getting up early isn't difficult if you have an alarm clock. Choice (D) contradicts the fact that if you have an alarm clock, getting up early isn't difficult.

10. **(A)** This statement implies the two facts enclosed in parentheses: We would have had a better class (but we did not have a better class) if Mr. Williams had taught it (but Mr. Williams did not teach it). Choice (B) contradicts the fact that Mr. Williams did not teach the class. Choice (C) contradicts the fact that we would have had a better class if Mr. Williams had taught it. Choice (D) contradicts the fact that the woman says we would have had a better class with Mr. Williams.

11. **(A)** This statement implies the facts enclosed in parentheses: If she waits much longer to call a cab, she's going to miss the bus (but if she calls now, she will catch the bus). In Choices (B) and (D) she is taking a cab to get to the bus station, not instead of taking a bus. Choice (C) is not mentioned and may not be concluded from information in the statement.

12. **(B)** This statement implies the facts enclosed in parentheses: If you are at the corner by six o'clock, I'll pick you up and take you home (but if you are not at the corner by six o'clock, I will not pick you up and take you home). The time in Choice (A) refers to when I will pick you up at the corner, not at your house. The time in Choice (C) refers to when I will pick you up, not to when I will drop you off. In Choice (D), I will pick you up, not the opposite.

13. **(C)** This statement implies the facts enclosed in parentheses: Living in another culture isn't difficult if you have the right attitude (but living in another culture is difficult if you do not have the right attitude). Choice (A) contradicts the fact that living in another culture isn't difficult with the right attitude. Choices (B) and (C) are not mentioned and may not be concluded from information in the statement.

14. **(B)** This statement implies the facts enclosed in parentheses: If Al keeps studying like he has been, he's going to make himself sick (but if Al does not keep studying, he's not going to make himself sick). Choices (A), (C), and (D) contradict the fact that Al might get sick in the future, not in the present.

15. **(D)** This statement implies the facts enclosed in parentheses: If you are ready we can go to the party together (but if you are not ready we can't go to the party together). Choice (A) contradicts the fact that we can go when you, not I, are ready. Choices (B) and (C) are not mentioned and may not be concluded from information in the statement.

16. **(C)** This statement implies the two facts enclosed in parentheses: We would have been here sooner (but we were not here sooner) if we hadn't got lost (but we did get lost). The word *last* in Choice (A) sounds like *lost*, but it is not mentioned and may not be concluded from information in the statement. The word *hear* in Choice (B) sounds like *here*, but it is not mentioned and may not be concluded from information in the statement. We are trying to arrive, not leave here, in Choice (D).

17. **(A)** This statement implies the facts enclosed in parentheses: Your order will arrive on Saturday if placed by Wednesday (but your order will not arrive on Saturday if not placed by Wednesday). Choice (C) contradicts the fact that orders are placed on, not arriving, on Wednesday and the fact that orders arrive, not are placed, on Saturday. Choices (B) and (D) are not mentioned and may not be concluded from information in the statement.

18. **(C)** This statement implies the facts enclosed in parentheses: If you want to see the director, he has time this afternoon at two o'clock (but if you can't see him at two o'clock, you can't see him at all). Choices (A) and (D) contradict the fact that the director has time this afternoon at two o'clock. The other person in Choice (B) is not mentioned and may not be concluded from information in the statement.

19. **(B)** This statement implies the two facts enclosed in parentheses: John would have helped us (but he did not help us) if he hadn't had such a bad cold (but he did have a bad cold). Choices (A) and (B) contradict the fact that John did not help us. Choice (C) contradicts the fact that John did not help us and the fact that he already had a cold.

20. **(B)** This statement implies the two facts enclosed in parentheses: If you had asked the secretary (but you did not ask the secretary), she would have told you (but she did not tell you). Choice (A) contradicts the fact that you did not ask the secretary and the fact that she did not tell you. Choice (C) contradicts the fact that you did not ask the secretary. Choice (D) contradicts the fact that the secretary did not tell you.

Exercise Seven: Concessions (Part 1)

1. **(C)** Choice (C) has the same meaning as the last part of the statement, but it is expressed by a different grammatical structure. Choice (A) contradicts the fact that she comes. Choice (B) contradicts the fact that she was absent from tutoring on Monday. Choice (D) contradicts the fact that Jane was absent.

2. **(B)** *To not be able to make it* means *could not go.* Choice (C) contradicts the fact that we thank you for inviting us. Choices (A) and (D) are not mentioned and may not be concluded from information in the statement.

3. **(D)** Choice (D) has the same meaning as the statement but it is expressed by a different grammatical structure. Choices (A) and (B) contradict the fact that the hat isn't mine. Choice (C) contradicts the fact that the coat, not the hat, is mine.

4. **(B)** Because State University usually wins all its games, but this year lost two, it must be concluded that the State University team did not win as many games as usual. The number of games won in Choice (A) refers to how many State usually wins, not to how many it won this year. The number in Choice (C) refers to how many games State lost, not won. Choice (D) refers to how many games State lost this year, not to how many it wins every year.

5. **(B)** Choice (B) has the same meaning as the last part of the statement, but it is expressed by a different grammatical structure. Choice (A) refers to what I was going to do, not to what I did. Choices (C) and (D) are not mentioned and may not be concluded from information in the statement.

6. **(C)** Because Mike did not have enough money, it must be concluded that he did not go to graduate school. Choice (A) contradicts the fact that Mike did not have enough money to go. Choice (B) contradicts the fact that Mike was planning to go to graduate school. Choice (D) is not mentioned and may not be concluded from information in the statement.

7. **(C)** *To not give up* means *to keep hoping.* Choice (A) contradicts the fact that Mrs. Baker was told that her illness was incurable. Choice (B) contradicts the fact that her illness was incurable. Choice (D) is not mentioned and may not be concluded from information in the statement.

8. **(B)** Choice (B) has the same meaning as the statement, but it is expressed by a different grammatical structure. Choice (A) contradicts the fact that she doesn't like the dorm and the fact that she likes her roommate. Choices (C) and (D) contradict the fact that she doesn't like the dorm.

9. **(D)** Choice (D) has the same meaning as the last part of the statement, but it is expressed by a different grammatical structure. Choice (A) contradicts the fact that the office is usually closed on Saturday. Choice (B) contradicts the fact that this week the secretary will be there until noon. The time in Choice (C) refers to when the secretary will close, not open, the office this Saturday.

10. **(A)** Because we ordered an egg salad sandwich, it must be concluded that we wanted a sandwich. The dish in Choice (B) refers to the kind of sandwich we were brought, not to a dinner. The dish in Choice (C) refers to the kind of sandwich we were brought. The word *salad* in Choice (D) refers to egg salad, the kind of sandwich that we wanted.

11. **(B)** Choice (B) has the same meaning as the first part of the statement, but it is expressed by a different grammatical structure. The word *short* in Choice (A) refers to the time for the doctor to return, not to the size of the doctor. Choice (C) contradicts the fact that he should be back shortly. The word *right* in Choice (D) refers to the phrase *right now,* not to the accuracy of the doctor.

12. **(B)** Choice (B) is a direct quotation from the statement. The time *three months* in Choice (D) refers to the length of the extension, not to when the visa expired. Choices (A) and (C) contradict the fact that the visa expires in November, not February or August.

13. **(D)** *Ordinarily* means *usually.* Choice (A) contradicts the fact that this year we are going to take a tour. Choice (B) contradicts the fact that we usually go camping. Choice (C) contradicts the fact that we are going to take a tour.

14. **(D)** *Awful* means *bad.* Choice (A) contradicts the fact that last night the food was awful. Choice (B) contradicts the fact that last night the food was not good. Choice (C) contradicts the fact that the food is usually good.

15. **(C)** Choice (C) has the same meaning as the statement, but it is expressed by a different grammatical structure. Choice (A) contradicts the fact that fifty, not forty-five are scheduled for language lab. Choice (B) contradicts the fact that there are only forty-five, not fifty booths. Choice (D) contradicts the fact that there are forty-five, not fifty booths, and the fact that fifty students, not forty-five booths, were scheduled.

16. **(C)** *But* means *except.* Choice (A) contradicts the fact that Ann babysits every day except Friday. Choice (B) contradicts the fact that Ann only babysits on other days, not Friday. Choice (D) contradicts the fact that Ann does not babysit on Fridays.

17. **(A)** Because I expected my daughter, and my son showed up, too, it must be concluded that both of my children came. Choice (B) contradicts the fact that my daughter came as expected. Choice (C) contradicts the fact that my son came, too. Choice (D) contradicts the fact that my daughter came and the fact that my son came, too.

18. **(B)** Choice (B) has the same meaning as the first part of the statement, but it is expressed by a different grammatical structure. Choice (A) contradicts the fact that the store didn't carry the brand his wife uses. Choices (C) and (D) are not mentioned and may not be concluded from information in the statement.

19. **(D)** Choice (D) has the same meaning as the statement, but it is expressed by a different grammatical structure. The word *gas* in Choice (A) refers to heating fuel, not to gas for cars. Choice (B) contradicts the fact that we decided to rent an apartment anyway. The word *saving* in Choice (C) refers to the money that will be saved on gas, not to the money that we saved to rent an apartment.

20. **(C)** Choice (C) has the same meaning as the last part of the statement, but it is expressed by a different grammatical structure. Choice (A) contradicts the fact that it isn't normally necessary to have an appointment. Choice (B) contradicts the fact that during registration it is a good idea to make an appointment with the foreign student advisor. Choice (D) contradicts the fact that in order to see the foreign student advisor during registration, it is a good idea to make an appointment.

Exercise Seven: Concessions (Part 2)

1. **(A)** Choice (A) has the same meaning as the statement, but it is expressed by a different grammatical structure. Choice (B) contradicts the fact that students who turn in their final projects by the end of the week can graduate. Choice (C) contradicts the fact that students turn in their projects by the end of the week, not at graduation. Choice (D) contradicts the fact that students who do not turn in their projects will not graduate.

2. **(D)** Choice (D) has the same meaning as the statement, but it is expressed by a different grammatical structure. Choice (A) contradicts the fact that the roads are clear. Choice (B) contradicts the fact that the weather is bad and the fact that the roads are clear. Choice (C) contradicts the fact that the weather is bad.

3. **(A)** Choice (A) has the same meaning as the last part of the statement, but it is expressed by a different grammatical structure. Choice (B) contradicts the fact that the speaker doubts Betty and Paul will get a divorce. Choice (C) contradicts the fact that the speaker refers to problems. Choice (D) is not mentioned and may not be concluded from information in the conversation.

4. **(D)** Choice (D) has the same meaning as the last part of the statement, but it is expressed by a different grammatical structure. Choices (A), (B), and (C) contradict the fact that the speaker thinks we should check the candidate's references.

5. **(B)** Choice (B) has the same meaning as the statement, but it is expressed by a different grammatical structure. Choice (A) contradicts the fact that the speaker thinks you should see a doctor. Choice (C) contradicts the fact that you, not he, should see a doctor. Choice (D) is not mentioned and may not be concluded from information in the statement.

6. **(C)** Choice (C) has the same meaning as the statement, but it is expressed by a different grammatical structure. Choice (A) contradicts the fact that Mr. Brown won't be able to work today and the fact that Miss Smith will be there. Choice (B) contradicts the fact that Miss Smith will be there. Choice (D) contradicts the fact that Mr. Brown won't be able to work today.

7. **(A)** Choice (A) has the same meaning as the statement, but it is expressed by a different grammatical structure. Choices (B), (C), and (D) contradict the fact that it was she, not I, who might be offended.

8. **(D)** *Extra* means *additional* or *more*. Choice (A) contradicts the fact that electricity costs about twenty dollars extra. Choice (B) contradicts the fact that the rent includes water and gas and the fact that the rent does not include electricity. The amount in Choice (C) refers to the cost of electricity, not to how much more than electricity gas costs.

9. **(D)** Choice (D) has the same meaning as the last part of the statement, but it is expressed by a different grammatical structure. Choice (B) contradicts the fact that Ellen can read quite well without her glasses. Choice (C) contradicts the fact that Ellen needs her glasses to see at a distance. Choice (A) is not mentioned and may not be concluded from information in the statement.

10. **(A)** *Light* means *little*. Choice (B) contradicts the fact that it was rush hour. Choice (C) contradicts the fact that traffic was light. Choice (D) is not mentioned and may not be concluded from information in the statement.

11. **(B)** Choice (B) has the same meaning as the statement, but it is expressed by a different grammatical structure. Choice (A) contradicts the fact that I thought the trip would not be fun. Choice (C) contradicts the fact that the trip turned out to be fun and the fact that I thought the trip would not be fun. Choice (D) contradicts the fact that the trip turned out to be fun.

12. **(D)** Choice (D) has the same meaning as the last part of the statement, but it is expressed by a different grammatical structure. Choice (A) refers to the kind of soup I wanted, not to what I bought. Choice (B) refers to the food I looked for on the shelf, not to what I bought. Choice (C) refers to the kind of stew I bought.

13. **(B)** Choice (B) has the same meaning as the statement, but it is expressed by a different grammatical structure. Choices (C) and (D) contradict the fact that James was able to play football in the big game last Saturday. Choice (A) is not mentioned and may not be concluded from information in the statement. He could have been injured before the game or during the game.

14. **(C)** Choice (C) has the same meaning as the statement, but it is expressed by a different grammatical structure. Choice (A) contradicts the fact that he's [my roommate's] not my best friend. Choice (B) contradicts the fact that my roommate is a very nice person. Choice (D) is not mentioned and may not be concluded from information in the statement.

15. **(B)** Choice (B) has the same meaning as the statement, but it is expressed by a different grammatical structure. Choices (A) and (C) contradict the fact that Ellen needs a scholarship to attend the university. Choice (D) is not mentioned and may not be concluded from information in the statement.

16. **(B)** Choice (B) has the same meaning as the statement, but it is expressed by a different grammatical structure. Choice (A) contradicts the fact that you ought to go to California this year. Choice (C) contradicts the fact that you go back to Florida every year and the fact that you ought to go to California this year. Choice (D) contradicts the fact that you go back to Florida every year.

17. **(C)** Choice (C) has the same meaning as the statement, but it is expressed by a different grammatical structure. Choice (A) contradicts the fact that Anna wants to continue studying at the Institute. Choice (B) contradicts the fact that Anna already speaks English very well. Choice (D) contradicts the fact that Anna already speaks English very well and the fact that she wants to continue studying at the Institute.

18. **(A)** Choice (A) has the same meaning as the statement, but it is expressed by a different grammatical structure. The word *left* in Choice (B) refers to the fact that there aren't any tickets left for the concert. Choice (C) contradicts the fact that the tickets were for the concert, not the movie, and the fact that we are going to a movie, not back home. Choice (D) contradicts the suggestion that we go to the movies instead of going back home.

19. **(A)** Choice (A) has the same meaning as the last part of the statement, but it is expressed by a different grammatical structure. Choices (B) and (D) contradict the fact that John can't keep a secret. Choice (C) contradicts the fact that John doesn't mean to tell.

20. **(D)** Choice (D) has the same meaning as the statement, but it is expressed by a different grammatical structure. Choice (A) contradicts the fact that Mr. Smith would not stop drinking. Choice (B) contradicts the fact that Mr. Smith, not his doctor, did not stop drinking. Choice (C) contradicts the fact that his doctor advised him to stop drinking and the fact that he didn't stop.

Exercise Eight: Homophones and Homonyms

1. **(B)** To *waive* means to give up; to surrender. A fine is a penalty. Choices (A) and (D) refer to the homophone *wave,* which means to gesture hello or good-bye with the hand. Choice (C) refers to the homonym *fine,* which means well.

2. **(C)** *Flour* is powdered grain. Choices (A) and (D) refer to the homophone *flower,* which is a blossom. Choice (B) contradicts the fact that the recipe isn't sweet.

3. **(C)** *Fair* means impartial. Choice (A) refers to the homonym *fair,* which means a festival. Choices (B) and (D) refer to the homophone *fare,* which means a transportation fee.

4. **(D)** *Males* are the masculine sex. Choices (A) and (B) refer to the homophone *mail,* which means letters. Choice (C) is not mentioned and may not be concluded from information in the statement.

5. **(A)** To *pass* means to go by. Choices (B) and (D) refer to the homophone *buy,* which means to purchase. Choice (C) refers to the homophone *bye,* which means good-bye.

6. **(C)** To *wait* means to stay. Choices (A) and (D) refer to the homophone *weight,* which means a measure of pounds, kilograms, and so on. Choice (B) refers to the homophone *weights,* which means athletic equipment used for body building.

7. **(C)** To *meet* means to go to a certain place. Choices (A) and (B) refer to the homophone *meat,* which means animal flesh that is prepared for food. Choice (D) is not mentioned and may not be concluded from information in the statement.

8. **(B)** To *board* means to get on a bus, train, plane. Choices (A) and (C) refer to the homophone *bored,* which means disinterested. Choice (D) refers to the homonym *board,* which means wood.

9. **(B)** To *cite* means to quote in written form. Choice (A) refers to the homophone *sight,* which means to see. Choices (C) and (D) are not mentioned and may not be concluded from information in the statement.

10. **(B)** *Whole* means entire. Choices (A) and (C) refer to the homophone *hole,* which means an opening. Choice (D) is not mentioned and may not be concluded from information in the statement.

11. **(B)** A *week* is seven days. To *rest* means to relax. Choices (A) and (C) refer to the homophone *weak,* which means not strong; not well. Choice (D) refers to the homonym the *rest* which means the others.

12. **(B)** To *lessen* means to decrease. Choices (A), (C), and (D) refer to the homophone *lesson,* which means a class.

13. **(D)** *Would* means *used to.* Choices (A), (B), and (C) refer to the homophone *wood,* which means the bark and fiber of trees and shrubs.

14. **(B)** *Waste* means unnecessary items, especially in a budget. Choice (C) refers to the homophone *waist,* which means the middle section of the human torso. Choices (A) and (D) are not mentioned and may not be concluded from information in the statement.

15. **(D)** *So* means *therefore.* Choices (A) and (C) refer to the homophone *sew,* which means to work as a seamstress. Choice (B) is not mentioned and may not be concluded from information in the statement.

16. **(B)** To *know* (he *knows*) means to be certain. Because he is certain where the office is, it must be concluded that he can find it. Choices (A) and (D) refer to the homophone *nose,* which is the organ that controls smell and appears on the face as the beginning of the respiratory tract. Choice (C) contradicts the fact that he knows where the office is.

17. **(A)** *Coarse* means *harsh.* Choices (B), (C), and (D) refer to the homophone *course,* which is a class.

18. **(D)** To *hear* means to listen. Choices (A) and (C) refer to the homophone *here,* which means in this place. Choice (B) contradicts the fact that we want to hear the other side of the argument.

19. **(B)** To *desert* means to leave. The *rest* means the others. Choice (A) refers to the homophone *dessert,* which is something sweet that is usually served at the end of a meal. Choice (C) refers to the homonym *rest,* which means to relax. Choice (D) contradicts the fact that he won't leave.

20. **(C)** To *brake* means to use the brake to stop abruptly. Choices (A) and (B) refer to the homophone *break,* which means to separate into pieces or to become unusable. Choice (D) is not mentioned as a result and may not be concluded from information in the statement.

Exercise Nine: Conversations/Direct Information

1. **(A)** "Have you started writing your paper for history?" "Not yet." Choices (B), (C), and (D) refer to assignments that she is doing now, not to an assignment she must begin.

2. **(D)** "Are you glad that you came to Washington?" "Yes, indeed." Choices (A) and (B) refer to places the man considered before coming to Washington. Choice (C) is not mentioned and may not be concluded from information in the conversation.

3. **(B)** "Something is wrong with second gear." Choices (C) and (D) refer to gears that run fine. Choice (A) is not mentioned and may not be concluded from information in the conversation.

4. **(D)** "You're always working around the house on Saturday…" Choices (A) and (B) refer to what the man would rather do, not to what he does. Choice (C) refers to what he does during the week, not on Saturday.

5. **(B)** "I'll have apple pie with vanilla ice cream on top." Choice (A) refers to the dessert that the waitress suggests, not to the dessert that the man orders. Choice (C) refers to the topping, not to the dessert that the man orders. Choice (D) contradicts the fact that the man ordered apple pie.

6. **(C)** "The main library is open from eight A.M. until nine P.M. Monday through Friday…" Choice (B) refers to the hours that the library is open on weekends, not weekdays. Choice (D) refers to the hours that the library is open during finals week, not weekdays. Choice (A) is not mentioned and may not be concluded from information in the conversation.

7. **(A)** "Mr. Black is fluent in Spanish." Choice (B) refers to the language he is beginning to study, not to the language he speaks well. Choices (C) and (D) refer to the languages in which he knows a few words.

8. **(B)** "…my best friend is getting married on Sunday and I wouldn't miss it…" Choice (A) refers to where the man, not the woman is going. The places in Choices (C) and (D) refer to the location of the art exhibit, not to where the woman is going on Sunday.

9. **(C)** "…give me the gold ones [earrings]. I have a gold necklace that would look very nice with them." Choices (A) and (B) contradict the fact that she already has a gold necklace. Choice (D) contradicts the fact that she decides to buy the gold, not the silver, earrings.

10. **(C)** "…you'll have a six-hour layover…" Choice (A) refers to the number of hours that it takes to get to New York, not to the number of hours she will be there. Choices (B) and (D) are not mentioned and may not be concluded from information in the conversation.

11. **(C)** "Maybe I put it down on the counter…" Choice (A) refers to the place where the man, not the woman, believes she left her purse. Choice (B) refers to the place where she originally thought she left her purse, not to where she now believes she has left it. Choice (D) refers to the place near where she checked her coat.

12. **(D)** "I got a watch for my husband." Choice (A) refers to her dad, not to her husband. The gifts in Choices (B) and (C) refer to ideas the woman has for her dad, not for her husband.

13.   **(D)** Because the man says he'd rather go with the woman to the concert, it must be concluded that the woman is going to the concert. Choice (B) refers to the place where the man, not the woman, is going. The word *play* in Choice (C) refers to playing music, not to a place where the woman is going. Choice (A) is not mentioned and may not be concluded from information in the conversation.

14.   **(C)** "...it's [the black one] probably too dressy." Choice (A) contradicts the fact that she likes it. Choice (B) contradicts the fact that the black one fits her better than the red one. Choice (D) is not mentioned and may not be concluded from information in the conversation.

15.   **(C)** "I've only been here fifty minutes." Choice (A) answers the question *for whom* has the man been waiting, not *how long* has the man been waiting? Choice (B) answers the question, *how late* is the woman? Choice (D) answers the question, *how* did the man pass the time?

Exercise Ten: Conversations/Computations

1. **(D)** If the man's car gets forty miles per gallon and the woman's car gets twenty, then the man's mileage is two times or twice that of the woman. The woman's mileage is half that of the man. Choices (A), (B), and (C) cannot be computed from information in the conversation.

2. **(C)** If the appointment is for 9:00 and the man has to be fifteen minutes late, he will probably arrive at fifteen minutes after nine, or 9:15. Choice (A) refers to a time one hour, not fifteen minutes, later. Choice (B) refers to the original time of the appointment, not to the time when the man will actually arrive. Choice (D) refers to a time thirty, not fifteen, minutes later.

3. **(C)** If general-public tickets are ten dollars each and student tickets are half-price or five dollars, then two general and two student tickets would cost ten times two or twenty dollars, plus five times two or ten dollars, for a total of thirty dollars. Choice (A) refers to the price of one general-public or two student tickets. Choice (B) refers to the price of two general-public or four student tickets. Choice (D) refers to the price of four general-public tickets.

4. **(B)** "Twenty-five dollars each..." Choice (A) refers to half the sale price of two sweaters. Choice (C) refers to the sale price of two, not one, sweaters. Choice (D) refers to the regular, not the sale price, of two sweaters. It was not necessary to make a computation in order to answer this question.

5. **(C)** If it costs 55¢ for the first three minutes, and 10¢ for each additional minute, then a ten-minute call would cost 55¢ plus 10¢ times 7 or 70¢ for a total of $1.25. Choice (B) refers to the price of a ten-minute call if the first three minutes as well as additional minutes cost 10¢ each. Choices (A) and (D) are not mentioned and may not be computed or concluded from information in the conversation.

6. **(D)** If his watch says 1:15, but it is a little fast, it must be before 1:15. Choice (A) contradicts the fact that he told the woman what time it was. Choice (B) contradicts the fact that he told the woman what time it was and the fact that he said that his watch was a little fast. Choice (C) contradicts the fact that his watch was fast.

7. **(D)** If he owes fifteen dollars, and he may write the check for ten dollars over the amount of purchase, he may write the check for fifteen plus ten, or a total of twenty-five dollars. Choice (A) refers to the amount over the purchase, not to the total. Choice (B) contradicts the fact that the woman agrees to his paying by check. Choice (C) contradicts the fact that he may write the check for ten dollars over the amount, not just the amount of purchase.

8. **(B)** If the man has three 15¢ stamps or 45¢ plus two 25¢ stamps, or 50¢ for a total of 95¢, and he needs one more 5¢ stamp, the total postage is $1.00. Choice (C) refers to the amount of postage he has on the package, not to the amount required. Choices (A) and (D) cannot be computed from information in the conversation.

9. **(C)** If the typewriter ribbons used to cost $3 and the price has gone up 50¢, the ribbons now cost $3 plus 50¢ or $3.50. Choice (A) refers to the price of the ribbons before, not now. The word *fifteen* in Choice (B) sounds like *fifty*. Choice (D) refers to the price of ribbons if the price has gone down, instead of up, 50¢.

10. **(D)** If the woman arrives in Chicago at eleven A.M. and she must wait for five hours, she will leave Chicago at five hours after eleven A.M. or four o'clock P.M. Choice (A) refers to the time she will leave to go to Chicago, not depart from Chicago. Choice (B) refers to the time she will arrive in, not depart from, Chicago. The number in Choice (C) refers to the flight number, not to the time.

11. **(A)** "They're $15 apiece…" Choice (B) refers to the cost of a dozen glasses, not one glass. Choice (C) refers to the price of one glass when one dozen are purchased at the same time, not to the purchase price of one glass. Choice (D) may not be computed from information in the conversation.

12. **(B)** If the room rents for $50 per week and he stays for three weeks, he will owe $50 times 3 or $150. Choice (A) refers to the rent per month. Choice (C) refers to the rent for three weeks if paid at the monthly rate. Choice (D) refers to the rent for one, not three, weeks.

13. **(C)** If the fare is $2.45 and the woman gives the driver three dollars, then his tip is three minus $2.45 or 55¢. Choice (A) refers to the length of the ride, not to the amount of the tip. Choice (B) refers to the total amount, not the tip, that the woman gave the driver. Choice (D) refers to the $2.45 for two zones.

14. **(C)** If the man agreed to call someone in Houston at ten o'clock their time and their time is two hours earlier, then the man should call two hours after ten o'clock his time, or twelve o'clock. Choice (A) refers to the time he should call if Houston is one hour, not two hours, earlier. Choice (B) refers to the time he should call if Houston is three hours, not two hours, earlier. Choice (D) refers to the time he should call if Houston is four hours, not two hours, earlier.

15. **(B)** If she must walk to the corner, then three more blocks, then two blocks, she must walk a total of five or six blocks. The number in Choice (A) refers to miles, not blocks. Choice (C) refers to the first, not all the directions. Choice (D) refers to the second, not all the directions.

Exercise Eleven: Conversations/Place

1. **(B)** From the references to the *special, baked chicken, coffee,* and the *check,* it must be concluded that this conversation takes place at a restaurant. Baked pastries, not chicken, may be found in a bakery in Choice (A). Checks, but not chicken and coffee, may be found in a bank in Choice (C). Chickens, but not checks, may be found on a farm in Choice (D).

2. **(B)** From the references to a *prescription* and *refilled,* it must be concluded that this conversation takes place in a drugstore. A prescription may be written, but not refilled, in a dentist's office in Choice (A). It is not customary to get a prescription refilled at the places referred to in Choices (C) and (D).

3. **(A)** From the reference to *bride,* it must be concluded that this conversation takes place at a wedding. The words *Florida* and *honeymoon* in Choices (B) and (C) refer to where the couple is going, not to where they are now. It is not customary for a bride to be recognized at an airport in Choice (D).

4. **(B)** From the references to *press, twelve,* and *where* [he is] *going,* it must be concluded that this conversation takes place in an elevator. It is not customary to press a number in order to go somewhere in the places referred to in Choices (A), (C), and (D).

5. **(C)** From the references to *doctoral candidates* and *black robes,* it must be concluded that this conversation takes place at a graduation. It is customary to wear black colors or black clothing, not black robes, at a funeral in Choice (D). It is not customary to wear black robes at the places referred to in Choices (A) and (B).

6. **(A)** From the references to *glazed doughnuts,* a *loaf,* and French *bread,* it must be concluded that this conversation takes place at a bakery. The word *French* in Choice (C) refers to a kind of bread, not to a place. It is not customary to find baked goods in the places referred to in Choices (B) and (D).

7. **(B)** From the references to *title* and a *book,* it must be concluded that this conversation takes place at a library. The words *God* and *England* in Choices (A) and (C) refer to the title of the book, not to places. It is not customary to be looking for a book in a theater in Choice (D).

8. **(A)** From the reference to *treatments,* it must be concluded that this conversation takes place in a doctor's office. It is not customary to discuss treatments in the places referred to in Choices (B), (C), and (D).

9. **(B)** From the references to *accounts, interest rate,* and *monthly balance,* it must be concluded that this conversation takes place in a bank. The word *club* in Choice (C) refers to a kind of account, not a place. Accounts, but not interest rates, might be found in the places referred to in Choices (A) and (D).

10. **(C)** From the references to *reservation, party of two,* and *table,* it must be concluded that this conversation takes place in a restaurant. The word *reservation* in Choice (A) refers to a place saved, not to an Indian reservation. The word *party* in Choice (B) refers to a group, not to an occasion. In choice (D) the woman says that she will call the man, but a telephone is not mentioned and may not be concluded from information in the conversation.

11. **(C)** From the references to the *room, intensive care,* and *nurse's station,* it must be concluded that this conversation takes place in a hospital. It is not customary to find intensive care units and nurse's stations in the places in Choices (A), (B), and (D).

12. **(C)** From the references to a *wash and set, blow dry, put it up,* and *rollers,* it must be concluded that this conversation takes place at a beauty shop. It is customary to wash and dry clothing at a laundry in Choice (A) and cars at a car wash in Choice (B), but it is not customary to use rollers to put it [hair] up at any of the places referred to in Choice (A), (B), or (D).

13. **(D)** From the references to *check* and *rent,* it must be concluded that this conversation takes place at an apartment building. The word *work* in Choice (A) refers to the place where the woman is going, not to where she is now. Checks, but not checks for rent, may be found in the places referred to in Choices (A), (B), and (C).

14. **(C)** From the references to *cavities, x-rays,* and getting *teeth cleaned,* it must be concluded that this conversation takes place at a dentist's office. The phrase *good news* refers to the fact that the woman has no cavities, not to a newspaper in Choice (A). It is customary to clean clothing, not teeth, at a dry cleaner in Choice (B). It is customary to x-ray the body, not teeth, at a hospital in Choice (D).

15. **(C)** From the references to a *passbook, deposit, savings account, receipt,* and *balance,* it must be concluded that this conversation takes place at a bank. It is not customary to make a deposit to a savings account at any of the places referred to in Choices (A), (B), and (D).

Exercise Twelve: Conversations/Implied

1. **(C)** Because the man offers an argument against taking a plane, it must be concluded that he prefers to take a bus. Choice (B) refers to the way that the woman, not the man prefers to travel. Choices (A) and (D) are not mentioned and may not be concluded from information in the conversation.

2. **(C)** Because the man says that he is *all tied up,* it must be concluded that he is busy. From the request that Jan *get* the phone, it must also be concluded that the phone is ringing. Choice (A) misinterprets the idiom, *tied up,* which means busy, not held. Choice (B) contradicts the fact that Jan will answer his phone, not call him by phone. Choice (D) misinterprets the man's request that Jan *get* the phone, which means answer, not buy, in this context.

3. **(D)** Because she can't pay twenty-six dollars for the leather gloves, it must be concluded that she will buy the vinyl ones. Choices (A), (B), and (C) contradict the fact that she can't pay twenty-six dollars for the leather gloves.

4. **(B)** Because the man has never seen Bob go out so often with the same person, it must be concluded that Bob is serious about Sally. Choice (D) contradicts the fact that Bob has never gone out so often with the same person. Choices (A) and (C) are not mentioned and may not be concluded from information in the conversation.

5. **(A)** From the references to *metric units, meters, grams, feet,* and *pounds,* it must be concluded that the people are discussing weights and measures. The phrase *European nations* refers to the countries using the metric system, not to politics, in Choice (B). The word *employ* refers to use, not employment, in Choice (C). The word *pounds* refers to weight, not money, in Choice (D).

6. **(C)** Because the man says that Jane always says she is going to quit her job, it must be concluded that he does not take her seriously. Choice (A) contradicts the fact that the man does not believe Jane will quit. Choice (B) refers to the way that the woman, not Jane, feels. The word *present* in Choice (D) refers to a going-away present for Jane, not for the man.

7. **(D)** Because they do not see her there, it must be concluded that Betty was not at the play. Choices (A) and (C) contradict the fact that she told the man she would be at the play. Choice (B) contradicts the fact that the man and woman don't see her at the play.

8. **(B)** Because the man says that he *can't stand* the class, it must be concluded that he does not like it. To *can't stand* means to *not like.* Choice (C) contradicts the fact that the woman tells him he must get used to the class. Choice (D) contradicts the fact that the class is required. Choice (A) is not mentioned and may not be concluded from information in the conversation.

9. **(B)** Because the man does not see how they can afford a new house, it must be concluded that they will not buy one because they do not have enough money. Choice (C) contradicts the fact that they need a bigger, not a smaller, house. The word *vacation* in Choices (A) and (D) refers to the fact that they spend so much money on vacations that they don't have enough for a house, not to what they will do during or after their vacation.

10. **(B)** Because the woman tells the man not to worry because it usually takes six weeks, it must be concluded that she thinks he should wait. Choice (A) refers to what the man, not the woman, thinks. Choice (D) contradicts the fact that she tells him not to worry. Choice (C) is not mentioned and may not be concluded from information in the conversation.

11. **(B)** From the references to *glasses, frames,* and *contact lenses,* it must be concluded that the woman is speaking with an optometrist. It is not customary to discuss eye problems with the professionals referred to in Choices (A), (C), and (D).

12. **(C)** Because the man says he *couldn't feel better* about it, it must be concluded that he is confident. *Could not feel better* means to feel *the best* possible. Choices (A), (B), and (D) contradict the fact that he could not feel better.

13. **(D)** Because the man says *either* when he asks the question, we know that he was not in class. The woman answers that she was not in class. Choice (A) contradicts the fact that the man was not in class, and the woman wasn't either. Choice (B) contradicts the fact that the man was not in class. Choice (C) contradicts the fact that the woman was not in class.

14. **(A)** Because the man contradicts the radio announcer, it must be concluded that he does not believe what the announcer says. Choices (B) and (C) contradict the fact that he does not believe the announcer. Choice (D) contradicts the fact that he suggests doing the opposite by going the other way.

15. **(C)** The woman's tone is sarcastic. By using a sarcastic tone, the speaker means the opposite of what she says, that is, that she does *not* thank the man and she does *not* think he is helpful. Choice (A) refers to what is said but not meant about the man, not the woman. Choice (B) refers to what the woman says, not to what she means. Choice (D) refers to the way the man, not the woman, says he feels.

Exercise Thirteen: Mini Talks/Overheard Conversations

Mini Talk One

1. **(C)** From the references to *this bus, gate eleven,* and *these baggage checks,* it must be concluded that this conversation takes place at a bus station. Choice (A) refers to the place where the woman is going, not to where she is now. Choice (B) refers to the time that the passengers should be at the door. Choice (D) refers to the purpose of the conversation, not the place.

2. **(A)** "Two-fifteen at gate eleven." The number in Choice (B) refers to the gate, not the time. Choice (C) refers to the time that the passengers should be at the door. Choice (D) refers to a time fifteen minutes before the passengers should be at the door and half an hour before the bus leaves.

3. **(B)** "Just two. I'll carry the other one with me." Choice (A) refers to the number of suitcases she will carry, not to the number she will check. Choice (C) refers to the total number of suitcases she has to check and to carry. Choice (D) refers to twice the number of suitcases she will check.

4. **(A)** Because the woman says that the fare was only twenty dollars the last time she took the bus, it must be concluded that she has taken this trip before. Choices (B), (C), and (D) are not mentioned and may not be concluded from the conversation.

Mini Talk Two

1. **(B)** "They're serving fish cakes and baked potatoes." Choice (A) refers to what the boys might eat later for a snack. Choices (C) and (D) are not mentioned and may not be concluded from information in the conversation.

2. **(B)** "It's [the test is] not until Monday but I want to go home this weekend." Choice (A) contradicts the fact that the test is on Monday, not that night. Choices (C) and (D) are not mentioned and may not be concluded from information in the conversation.

3. **(B)** Because the cafeteria is going to close in half an hour and it is six o'clock now, it must be concluded that the cafeteria closes thirty minutes later, or at six-thirty. Choice (A) refers to the time it is now, not to the time the cafeteria closes. Choice (C) refers to when John is going to go home. Choice (D) refers to when John has a test.

4. **(C)** "Well, knock on my door if you decide to get that pizza later." Choice (D) contradicts the fact that Bill tells John what is being served in the cafeteria. Choices (A) and (B) are not mentioned and may not be concluded from information in the conversation.

Mini Talk Three

1. **(B)** "I want to pay by check if I may." Choice (A) refers to identification that can be used to verify the check. Choice (C) refers to one method of payment that is considered cash. Choice (D) refers to the store where the woman is shopping, but not to the method of payment she uses.

2. **(D)** "Both money and checks are considered cash." Choice (A) is considered correct, but incomplete. Choices (B) and (C) contradict the fact that money and checks, not charge cards, are considered cash.

3. **(C)** "Well, here's my driver's license. I don't have any charge cards, but I do have my student ID card from City College." Choice (A) contradicts the fact that the woman doesn't have any charge cards. Choice (B) refers to identification that can be used, not to the identification that the woman actually uses. Choice (D) refers to the fact that she must put her telephone number on the front of the check, but it is not a piece of identification.

4. **(B)** "And thank you for shopping at Sears." Because the woman makes out the check to Sears, it must be concluded that she is shopping there. Choice (A) refers to where she has her student ID card, not to where she is shopping. Choices (C) and (D) are not mentioned and may not be concluded from information in the conversation.

Mini Talk Four

1. **(C)** "That's only three classes." Choice (A) refers to the number of hours that the two-hour laboratory meets per week. Choice (B) refers to the number of hours that each five-hour class meets per week. Choice (D) refers to the total number of hours that the classes meet per week.

2. **(A)** "A driver's license will be fine." Choice (B) refers to the man's suggestion, not to what he needs. Choice (D) contradicts the fact that the man needs identification to be admitted to the examination. Choice (C) is not mentioned and may not be concluded from information in the conversation.

3. **(C)** "Come back Friday afternoon." Choice (B) refers to the time and date of the placement test, not to the time and date when the man will see his advisor again. Choices (A) and (D) are not mentioned and may not be concluded from information in the conversation.

4. **(C)** Because the woman says that she advises first-year students, it must be concluded that the student is a first-year student, or a freshman. Choice (A) contradicts the fact that he is an engineering student. Choice (B) contradicts the fact that he has had two courses in chemistry. Choice (D) is not mentioned and may not be concluded from information in the conversation.

Exercise Fourteen: Mini Talks/Announcements and Advertisements

Mini Talk One

1. **(D)** "Rates on direct calls are…lowest after eleven o'clock at night." Choice (C) refers to a time when rates are cheaper, but not the cheapest. Choices (A) and (B) are not mentioned and may not be concluded from information in the advertisement.

2. **(B)** "In fact, you can make a ten-minute call anywhere in the Continental United States for just $2.60." Choices (A), (C), and (D) are not mentioned and may not be concluded from information in the advertisement.

3. **(B)** "For even greater savings, always dial direct, that is, without an operator's assistance." Choices (A), (C), and (D) contradict the fact that collect, credit card, person-to-person, and pay phone calls require the services of an operator.

4. **(C)** "Now calls to many overseas locations may be dialed direct. Check your telephone directory for overseas area codes." Choice (A) refers to what you should do in order to make a collect, credit card, person-to-person, or pay phone call. Choice (B) contradicts the fact that you should check the phone book for overseas area codes, not for the overseas operator's number. Choice (D) refers to the sponsor of the message, not to what you should do to call overseas.

Mini Talk Two

1. **(B)** "Appalachian Airlines will use comfortable Boeing 737 twin jets….Fly comfortably." Choice (A) contradicts the fact that unlike large airplanes, Appalachian seats 106 passengers. Choice (D) contradicts the fact that Appalachian Airlines will begin passenger service at Charlotte Airport Thursday. Choice (C) is not mentioned and may not be concluded from information in the advertisement.

2. **(A)** "…with connections in Washington for Cleveland…" Choices (B) and (C) refer to other cities for which connecting flights originate from Washington. Choice (D) refers to the city for which there is an afternoon departure daily from Charlotte.

3. **(D)** "…morning and afternoon departures daily to Atlanta." Choices (A) and (B) are correct but incomplete. Choice (C) contradicts the fact that departures leave daily. Service begins on Thursday.

4. **(A)** "…the Appalachian Airlines toll-free number: 800-565-7000." Choices (B), (C), and (D) are not mentioned and may not be concluded from information in the advertisement.

Mini Talk Three

1. **(B)** Because one-half of all fatal traffic accidents involve alcohol, it must be concluded that fifty percent of all fatal accidents resulting in death are caused by drunk driving. The number in Choice (C) refers to the amount of the fine, not to the number of accidents resulting in death. Thousands of people are killed, but the numbers in Choices (A) and (D) are not mentioned and may not be concluded from information in the announcements.

2. **(D)** "If you are convicted of drunk driving you will be sentenced to at least three days in jail, and your license will be suspended for thirty days." The jail sentence in Choice (A) is correct, but the thirty-dollar fine is not mentioned and may not be concluded from information in the announcement. The jail sentence in Choice (B) refers to the amount of time that the court can sentence, not to the minimum required sentence, and the thirty-dollar fine is not mentioned and may not be concluded from information in the announcement. Choice (C) contradicts the fact that the minimum required sentence is three, not thirty days.

3. **(D)** "…the court can sentence you to as much as six months in jail." Choice (A) refers to the minimum sentence, not to the length of time that the court can sentence. Choice (B) refers to the length of time that a license can be suspended. Choice (C) is not mentioned and may not be concluded from information in the announcement.

4. **(A)** "If you drink, don't drive." Choices (B), (C), and (D) are not mentioned and may not be concluded from information in the announcement.

Mini Talk Four

1. **(D)** "The Colorado Buffaloes will play the Oklahoma Sooners…" Choice (A) refers to the place where the game is played, not to the name of the team. Choice (B) refers to the name of the Nebraska, not the Colorado, team. Choice (C) refers to the name of the Oklahoma team.

2. **(B)** "To reserve seats, call the Student Union…or drop by the box office." Choice (A) refers to the name of the performer, not the way to get a ticket to the concert. Choices (C) and (D) are not mentioned and may not be concluded from information in the announcement.

3. **(B)** "In addition to the famous rock and mineral collection and the exhibits of early people, there will be a special exhibit of American Indian pottery and sand paintings." Choices (A), (C), and (D) are mentioned but not referred to as famous.

4. **(C)** "Snow Valley is reporting good conditions.…Pine Mountain is reporting very good conditions.…Oak Creek Canyon Resort is reporting very good conditions…" Choices (A), (B), and (D) contradict the fact that good and very good conditions only were mentioned.

Exercise Fifteen: Mini Talks/News Reports

Mini Talk One

1. **(B)** "...the Scarsdale diet...was originally outlined twenty years ago by Dr. Herman Tarnower, a cardiologist and internist from Scarsdale, New York." Choice (A) contradicts the fact that the doctor's name was Tarnower, not Scarsdale. Choices (C) and (D) are not mentioned and may not be concluded from information in the report.

2. **(C)** "...a dieter who follows his plan will be able to lose up to twenty pounds in two weeks." Choices (A), (B), and (D) are not mentioned and may not be concluded from information in the report.

3. **(C)** "For two weeks at a time the dieter must follow a strict menu....Although the amount of food that the dieter may eat is not limited, most dieters average less than one thousand calories a day." Choice (A) contradicts the fact that the amount of food that the dieter may eat is not limited. Choice (B) contradicts the fact that many [dieters] complain that their energy levels are low. Choice (D) contradicts the fact that most dieters average less than one thousand calories a day.

4. **(D)** "...the Scarsdale diet...was originally outlined twenty years ago..." The time in Choice (A) refers to the amount of time it takes dieters to lose twenty pounds. Choice (B) refers to when the book was published, not when the diet was developed. Choice (C) is not mentioned and may not be concluded from information in the report.

Mini Talk Two

1. **(B)** "It is called the Moodymobile, named for its inventor Ralph Moody." Choice (D) contradicts the fact that the car has a diesel engine, not a Moodymobile engine. Choices (A) and (C) are not mentioned and may not be concluded from information in the report.

2. **(C)** "...it gets 75 miles per gallon of fuel." The number in Choice (A) sounds like 75, but it is not mentioned and may not be concluded from information in the report. Choice (B) refers to the number of gallons of fuel to make the trip from Oak Hill, Florida, to Washington, D.C. The number in Choice (D) sounds like 850, the number of miles from Oak Hill, Florida, to Washington, D.C.

3. **(A)** "Before the car can be commercially sold, it must pass a series of environmental tests." Choice (B) contradicts the fact that Ford, Chrysler, and General Motors have expressed interest, not bought, the rights. Choice (C) contradicts the fact that Moody is filing the names of persons who have written him in hopes of purchasing a Moodymobile. Choice (D) is not mentioned and may not be concluded from information in the report.

4. **(C)** "He says that he hopes to market 2,000 of the cars late this year for about $7,000 each." Choice (A) refers to the number of cars he plans to market, not to how much the car will cost. Choices (B) and (D) are not mentioned and may not be concluded from information in the report.

Mini Talk Three

1. **(B)** "A blue-eyed blonde from Los Angeles, Miss Brown is 5 feet 10 inches tall and weighs 120 pounds." The word *brown* in Choices (A), (C), and (D) refers to the last name of the new Miss State University, not the color of her hair or eyes.

2. **(C)** "She placed...third in the talent competition." Choice (A) refers to her place in the swimming suit and evening gown competitions, her place in the beauty category, and her overall place. Choice (B) refers to her place in the intelligence competition. Choice (D) is not mentioned and may not be concluded from information in the report.

3. **(B)** "Miss Brown received a check for $1,000 and a scholarship award for $2,000." Choice (A) refers to the amount of the check, not the scholarship. Choice (C) refers to the total amount of the check and the scholarship. Choice (D) is not mentioned and may not be concluded from information in the report.

4. **(C)** Because Miss Brown is a junior majoring in speech and drama, it must be concluded that she is in the third year. Choice (B) contradicts the fact that she is a student majoring in speech and drama, not a secretary. Choice (D) refers to what she may do after she graduates, not to what she is doing now. Choice (A) is not mentioned and may not be concluded from information in the report.

Mini Talk Four

1. **(A)** "...tuition at most American universities will be on an average of 9 percent higher this year than last." The number 90 in Choice (C) sounds like 9, but it is not mentioned and may not be concluded from information in the report. Choice (D) refers to the percentage increase in the last decade, not in the last year. The number in Choice (B) sounds like 150, but it is not mentioned and may not be concluded from information in the report.

2. **(C)** "...$5,300 for tuition....Ten years ago the tuition was $2,150." If the tuition is $5,300 today and was $2,150 ten years ago, then the cost has increased by $5,300 minus $2,150, or $3,150. The number in Choice (A) refers to the percentage increase, not to the dollar increase. Choice (B) refers to the cost of tuition ten years ago, not to the increase in cost. Choice (D) refers to the cost of tuition today.

3. **(C)** "...foreign students who are not eligible for scholarships." Choice (D) contradicts the fact that they are not eligible for scholarships. Choices (A) and (B) are not mentioned and may not be concluded from information in the report.

4. **(A)** "...college graduates are entering the best job market since the middle 1960s. Job offers are up 16 percent from last year." Choice (C) contradicts the fact that a student with a liberal arts degree might expect to make about half the salary of a student with a technical degree. Choice (D) contradicts the fact that the job market is the best since the middle 1960s and the fact that job offers are up from last year. Choice (B) contradicts the fact that the middle 1960s or 1965, not 1960, is mentioned as the year of a good job market.

Exercise Sixteen: Mini Talks/Weather Reports

Mini Talk One

1. **(C)** "And it promises to be a beautiful weekend." Choices (A), (B), and (D) were not mentioned and may not be concluded from information in the report.

2. **(A)** "...temperatures to average a little below seasonal norms." Choices (B), (C), and (D) contradict the fact that temperatures are below norm, or below average.

3. **(A)** "Tomorrow morning will be chilly under partly cloudy skies, with temperatures in the low forties warming to about sixty degrees by noon." Choice (C) refers to the temperatures tomorrow morning, not at noon. Choice (D) refers to morning temperatures generally. Choice (B) is not mentioned and may not be concluded from information in the report.

4. **(B)** "...temperatures to rise by midday on both Saturday and Sunday...under bright, sunny skies." Choice (A) contradicts the fact that temperatures will rise and the fact that the skies will be bright and sunny, not cloudy. Choice (C) contradicts the fact that the skies will be bright and sunny. Choice (D) contradicts the fact that temperatures will rise.

Mini Talk Two

1. **(C)** "Lows from zero to ten degrees above zero." Choices (A) and (B) refer to high temperatures, not low temperatures. The number in Choice (B) refers to the speed of the wind, not the temperatures. The number in Choice (D) refers to degrees above, not below, zero.

2. **(B)** "Area schools and factories will remain closed." Choices (A), (C), and (D) are not mentioned and may not be concluded from information in the report.

3. **(C)** "If you have need of emergency transportation, call 875-2000." Choice (A) refers to the group providing transportation, not to what you should do to obtain it. Choice (B) refers to what people should do if they do not require emergency transportation. Choice (D) contradicts the fact that area schools will be closed.

4. **(C)** "Light snow flurries will continue Friday, clearing by Saturday, with cold but mostly fair weather predicted for Sunday....Otherwise, stay at home until it clears on Saturday." Choices (A) and (B) contradict the fact that light snow flurries are falling and will continue Friday. Choice (D) contradicts the fact that the weather is clearing on Saturday and remains clear and fair Sunday.

Mini Talk Three

1. **(A)** "The watch will be in effect until ten o'clock tonight or until cancellation by the Weather Service." The number in Choice (D) refers to the number of counties affected, not to the time. Choices (B) and (C) are not mentioned and may not be concluded from information in the report.

2. **(B)** "The National Weather Service has issued a tornado watch for the following five counties: Douglas, Johnson, Jefferson, Leavenworth, and Franklin." Choices (A), (C), and (D) are all mentioned as being included in the tornado watch.

3. **(B)** "A *tornado warning* means that a funnel cloud has been sighted." Choice (D) refers to the definition of a tornado watch, not warning. Choices (A) and (C) are not mentioned and may not be defined from information in the report.

4. **(C)** "...a tornado watch for the following five counties..." The number in Choice (D) refers to the time that the watch will be canceled, not to the number of counties affected. Choice (A) contradicts the fact that five counties are included in the watch. Choice (B) is not mentioned and may not be concluded from information in the report.

Mini Talk Four

1. **(D)** "The showers and thunderstorms moved north of us leaving all stations in the Tri-State Area with reports of sunny skies and warm temperatures." Choice (B) refers to the weather that moved north, not to the weather in the Tri-State Area. Choices (A) and (C) are not mentioned and may not be concluded from information in the report.

2. **(C)** "The current temperature reading here at Philadelphia is eighty-five degrees..." Choice (D) refers to the temperature expected tomorrow, not now. Choices (A) and (B) are not mentioned and may not be concluded from information in the report.

3. **(B)** "The showers and thunderstorms moved north of us..." Choice (D) contradicts the fact that the rain moved north, not south of us. Choices (A) and (C) are not mentioned and may not be concluded from information in the report.

4. **(C)** "...no rain in sight until Thursday or Friday." Choice (A) contradicts the fact that today there are reports of sunny skies and warm temperatures. Choice (B) contradicts the fact that fair weather is predicted for tomorrow. Choice (D) is not mentioned and may not be concluded from information in the report.

Exercise Seventeen: Mini Talks/Informative Speeches

Mini Talk One

1. **(C)** "As director of the Office of International Student Affairs…" Choice (A) refers to one of the people the speaker thanks, not to the speaker. Choice (B) refers to the person who is providing music, not to the speaker. Choice (D) refers to Mr. Sim Lee, not to the speaker.

2. **(A)** "Right now coffee from Brazil and Colombia is being served at the tables, and for those of you who prefer tea, there is a selection…" Choice (B) refers to what people did before, not now. Choice (C) refers to what people will do later, not now. Choice (D) is not mentioned and may not be concluded from information in the speech.

3. **(D)** "…it is one of my more pleasant duties to welcome you on behalf of State University. …In the meantime, I would like to take a few moments to thank some of the people who have worked so hard to make this evening possible." Choices (A), (B), and (C) are not mentioned and may not be concluded from information in the speech.

4. **(D)** "After the program, may I invite you to stay to dance to disco music…" Choices (A) and (B) contradict the fact that they are invited to stay, not to go somewhere else. Choice (C) contradicts the fact that the students will dance to disco music, not listen to it.

Mini Talk Two

1. **(B)** "Dr. Taylor received his B.A. degree…at Yale….a masters degree…and a Ph.D. … from Cornell University." Choice (A) refers to the university where Dr. Taylor received his B.A., not his Ph.D. Choice (C) refers to the university where he taught. The place in Choice (D) refers to the city where Dr. Taylor worked, not to the university where he received his Ph.D.

2. **(C)** "Last year Dr. Taylor resigned from the university in order to accept a research position with the Department of Housing and Urban Development…" Choice (A) refers to the place where Dr. Taylor was employed after he received his Ph.D., not to where he is employed now. Choice (B) refers to a building that Dr. Taylor designed, not to the place where he works. Choice (D) refers to the place where Dr. Taylor's articles are published.

3. **(A)** "Today Dr. Taylor will speak to us about federal regulations for urban development…" Choices (B), (C), and (D) refer to areas of Dr. Taylor's expertise, but not to the topic of the lecture.

4. **(C)** Because the speaker says that he can think of no one more qualified to speak than Dr. Taylor, it must be concluded that he respects him. Choice (A) contradicts the fact that the speaker says it is a great honor to introduce Dr. Taylor. Choice (B) contradicts the fact that Dr. Taylor is well known to all of us. Choice (D) contradicts the fact that the speaker can think of no one more qualified.

Mini Talk Three

1. **(A)** "…when I was asked to speak at the Book Club luncheon, I thought about several topics that might be of interest to a group of avid readers…" The word *inventor* in Choice (D) refers to the topic, not to the audience. Choices (B) and (C) are not mentioned and may not be concluded from information in the speech.

2. **(C)** "…with reference to Mr. Edison's great love for books and reading." Choice (A) is true, but it is not the reason that the speaker chose to talk about Edison. Choices (B) and (D) are not mentioned and may not be concluded from information in the speech.

3. **(B)** "Whenever he was paid for an invention, he used the money for his two loves— more experiments and more books." Choices (A), (C), and (D) are not mentioned and may not be concluded from information in the speech.

4. **(B)** "…in October, 1979, we observed the one-hundredth anniversary of the electric lamp…" Choices (A), (C), and (D) are not mentioned and may not be concluded from information in the speech.

Mini Talk Four

1. **(B)** "It is a great privilege for me to be invited to speak at the tenth-year reunion of State University's graduating class." Choice (A) contradicts the fact that the occasion is the reunion of a graduating class, not a graduation. Choices (C) and (D) are not mentioned and may not be concluded from information in the speech.

2. **(C)** "We are still committed to the same age-old ideals of quality education…" Choice (A) contradicts the facts that University Tower was torn down, a bell tower was built, and parking lots were replaced by grass, trees, and pedestrian walkways. Choice (B) contradicts the fact that many young people from abroad have been added to the student population. Choice (D) contradicts the fact that the Division of Continuing Education has been expanded, including a Saturday and summer enrichment program for children, and an afternoon and evening special interest program for adults.

3. **(B)** "Two years ago University Tower was inspected and found to be unsafe." Choice (A) contradicts the fact that the belltower was constructed after the tower was found to be unsafe and had to be torn down. Choice (C) contradicts the fact that the parking lots were replaced by grass, trees, and pedestrian walkways, and the fact that a belltower, not a parking lot, was constructed over the site. Choice (D) contradicts the fact that there were efforts to restore it.

4. **(C)** "And so, State is a different place, but like University Tower, it is built of the same brick." Choice (A) contradicts the fact that it is built of the same brick, or that we are still committed to the same age-old ideals. Choice (B) contradicts the fact that University Tower has been torn down, a belltower has been built, and parking lots have been replaced by grass, trees, and pedestrian walkways. Choice (D) contradicts the fact that State is a different place.

Exercise Eighteen: Mini Talks/Academic Statements (Part 1)

Mini Talk One

1. **(C)** "Yesterday we discussed…inflation….We concluded….We also talked about…" Choice (A) contradicts the fact that yesterday we discussed inflation. Choices (B) and (D) are not mentioned and may not be concluded from information in the statement.

2. **(A)** "…rising prices, or in the economist's terms, inflation." Choice (B) refers to pensions, not to inflation. Choice (C) refers to the ability to purchase goods and services. Choice (D) refers to how much it costs to maintain a standard of living.

3. **(B)** "…stockholders and persons with business interests and investments would probably benefit most from inflation…" Choice (A) contradicts the fact that an employee with a salary agreed to in a long-term contract will be most seriously affected by inflation. Choice (C) contradicts the fact that persons with fixed incomes, for example, the elderly who depend on pensions, will be most seriously affected by inflation. Choice (D) contradicts the fact that persons with slow-rising incomes will be most seriously affected by inflation.

4. **(B)** "…while their dollar incomes stay the same, the cost of goods and services rises, and in effect, real income decreases; that is, they are able to purchase less with the same amount of money." Choice (A) contradicts the fact that inflation is rising prices. Choice (C) contradicts the fact that they are able to purchase less with the same amount of money. Choice (D) contradicts the fact that dollar incomes stay the same.

Mini Talk Two

1. **(D)** "Today we will discuss what occurs when the balance of nature is disturbed, either by a geological change such as a change of climate, or a local agitation such as a fire." Choices (A), (B), and (C) are secondary ideas that are used to develop the main idea.

2. **(B)** "…a local agitation such as a fire….After the balance of nature has been disturbed, a period of rehabilitation must occur….The final stage…is called a climax association." Choice (C) contradicts the fact that the balance of nature is disturbed, either by a geologic change such as a change of climate, or a local agitation such as a fire. Choice (D) refers to the total complex of relationships in ecology, not to the forest fire example. Choice (A) is not mentioned and may not be concluded from information in the statement.

3. **(A)** "The pioneer life is temporary and soon replaced by other forms of life…preparing the environment for the forms that will replace them." Choice (B) contradicts the fact that it is temporary and soon replaced by other forms of life. Choices (C) and (D) contradict the fact that pioneer plants are replaced by shrubs and shrubs are replaced by trees.

4. **(A)** "What is essential is that the balance of nature permits the association to continue in spite of other organic competition…" Choice (B) contradicts the fact that the climax association may not have the same kinds of plants and animals as the association that was prevalent before the fire. Choice (C) contradicts the fact that a climax association is the final stage, not the stage before the final stage. Choice (D) contradicts the fact that a climax association is stable, not a state of disturbance.

Mini Talk Three

1. **(B)** "Whereas the scientist was thought of as an intellectual…the engineer was thought of as a busy, practical person….The scientist might discover the laws of nature, but the engineer would be the one to exploit them…" Choice (A) contradicts the fact that the engineer, not the scientist, would be the one to exploit the laws of nature. Choice (C) contradicts the fact that the scientist, not the engineer, was thought of as an intellectual. Choice (D) contradicts the fact that the engineer, not the scientist, would be the one to exploit nature for use, that is, to apply science.

2. **(B)** "Christian Huygens, a Dutch astronomer, mathematician, and physicist who developed theorems on centrifugal force and wave motion also developed the first accurate timepiece." Choice (A) refers to Louis Pasteur, not to Christian Huygens. Choice (C) refers to Sir Isaac Newton. Choice (D) is not mentioned and may not be concluded from information in the statement.

3. **(C)** "In every century, noted theoretical scholars were deeply involved in the practical application of their own work." Choice (A) contradicts the fact that they made practical application of their own work. Choice (B) contradicts the fact that the scientists were identified as noted theoretical scholars, not the best of each century. Choice (D) contradicts the fact that they were theoretical scholars, not engineers.

4. **(B)** "I propose that the popular detachment of science from engineering has not provided us with a useful model for comparison, and perhaps not even an historically correct one." Choices (A), (C), and (D) contradict the fact that the detachment has not provided us with a useful model.

Mini Talk Four

1. **(C)** "…SQ3R. The letters stand for five steps in the reading process…" Choices (A), (B), and (D) are not mentioned and may not be concluded from information in the statement.

2. **(D)** "*Survey* means to look quickly." The first step in Choice (A) refers to the order in the five steps that surveying occupies, not to the meaning of survey. Choice (B) refers to the last step *recite,* not survey. Choice (C) refers to the second step, *question*.

3. **(A)** "Think about what you are reading as a series of ideas, not just a sequence of words." Choice (B) contradicts the fact that some students prefer to underline important points, and that seems to be just as useful as note taking. Choice (C) refers to step one, *survey,* not to step three, *read.* Choice (D) contradicts the fact that readers should think about what they are reading as a series of ideas, not just a sequence of words.

4. **(B)** "The last step is recite." Choice (A) refers to the third, not the last step. Choice (C) refers to the fourth step. Choice (D) is not included in the five steps and may not be concluded from information in the statement.

Exercise Eighteen: Mini Talks/Academic Statements (Part 2)

Mini Talk One

1. **(C)** "Your test on Friday will cover material from both of your textbooks, my lecture notes, and your lab assignments….there won't be any math problems, but that doesn't mean that you shouldn't review the formulas…" Choices (A), (B), and (D) would be less likely to have *lab assignments* and *formulas.*

2. **(B)** "Your test on Friday will cover material from both of your textbooks, my lecture notes and your lab assignments." Choice (A) refers to the first lecture, not to this lecture. Choice (C) refers to the test on Friday. Choice (D) refers to the material to be tested, not to the purpose of the lecture.

3. **(D)** "The multiple-choice will count half of your grade [on the test]." Choice (A) refers to the credit toward the final grade for attendance, not to the credit on the test for multiple-choice questions. Choice (B) refers to the credit toward the final grade for the test and for the lab report, not to the credit for the multiple-choice questions. Choice (C) refers to the credit toward the final grade for the final exam.

4. **(B)** "Oh yes, this test represents twenty-five percent of your total grade for the semester." Choice (A) refers to the credit toward the final grade for attendance, not for the test. Choice (C) refers to the credit toward the final grade for the final exam. Choice (D) refers to the credit on the test for the multiple-choice questions and for the essay questions.

Mini Talk Two

1. **(B)** "As you know from your text, both heredity and environment play a role in the development of the personality." Choice (A) refers to the topic of the lecture, not to what students should know before the lecture. Choices (C) and (D) refer to information in the lecture.

2. **(C)** "…research at the University of Texas at Arlington has shown that the order of one's birth in relationship to brothers and sisters may be a significant factor." Choices (A), (B), and (D) are secondary themes that are used to develop the main theme of the lecture.

3. **(B)** "Those born first tend to develop personality traits that make them domineering, ambitious, and highly motivated to achieve." Choices (A) and (D) refer to traits exhibited by children born later, not by firstborn children. Choice (C) is not mentioned and may not be concluded from information in the lecture.

4. **(B)** "…a woman with older brothers and a man with older sisters seem to be able to interact more easily with the opposite sex." Choice (A) contradicts the fact that a man with older sisters is able to interact more easily. Choices (C) and (D) contradict the fact that a woman with older brothers is able to interact more easily.

Mini Talk Three

1. **(A)** "The term *parapsychology* was coined by Professor Joseph Rhine of Duke University because he felt that a word was needed to identify the kinds of phenomena that did not fit into the conventional framework of psychology..." The classes mentioned in Choices (B), (C), and (D) would be less likely to hear a lecture on a branch of psychology.

2. **(C)** "The term *parapsychology* was coined by Professor Joseph Rhine of Duke University..." Choices (A) and (D) contradict the fact that the lecturer is talking about Professor Rhine. Choice (B) is not mentioned and may not be concluded from information in the lecture.

3. **(D)** "Parapsychology...deals with those phenomena of the human mind...that can't be explained on the basis of ordinary psychology." Choice (C) refers to the topic of today's lecture, not to the definition of parapsychology. Choices (A) and (B) are secondary themes that are used to develop the main theme of the introduction.

4. **(A)** "With these two terms in mind, let us turn to the topic of today's lecture—the history of parapsychology." Choices (C) and (D) refer to terms presented in the introduction to the lecture. Choice (B) is not mentioned and may not be concluded from information in the lecture.

Mini Talk Four

1. **(A)** "...I expect you to paraphrase, that is, to summarize someone else's ideas in your own words." Choice (B) refers to plagiarizing, not to paraphrasing. Choices (C) and (D) are not mentioned and may not be concluded from information in the lecture.

2. **(D)** "If you do not cite the source, then you are plagiarizing." Choices (B) and (C) refer to quoting, not to plagiarizing. Choice (A) is not mentioned and may not be concluded from information in the lecture.

3. **(C)** "...whereas paraphrasing and quoting are legitimate writing strategies..." Choices (A) and (B) contradict the fact that plagiarizing is not a legitimate writing strategy. Choice (D) contradicts the fact that copying [without citing the source] is not a legitimate writing strategy.

4. **(D)** "If I discover that you have plagiarized on your term paper, you will receive a zero for the paper and an F for the course." Choices (A), (B), and (C) are not mentioned as alternatives, and may not be concluded from information in the lecture.

Exercise Nineteen: Mini Talks/Class Discussions

Mini Talk One

1. **(A)** "What was the method of collection?" "Water displacement." Choice (B) refers to the substance that was put in the bottle, not to the method. Choice (C) refers to the gas collected, not to the method of collection. Choice (D) refers to the acid added to the limestone during collection.

2. **(C)** "And carbon deposits began to form on the bottom of the bottle." Choice (A) refers to the ribbon that was lit, not to the deposits. Choice (B) refers to the material that was put in the bottle at the beginning of the experiment, not to what was deposited at the end. Choice (D) refers to the method of collection, water displacement.

3. **(C)** "The burning magnesium broke the carbon-oxygen bonds in the carbon dioxide, and then the oxygen combined with the magnesium to produce magnesium oxide." Choices (A), (B), and (D) contradict the fact that burning magnesium broke the carbon-oxygen bonds.

4. **(B)** "…we didn't have any problem with procedure….The big problem was that we didn't understand what happened." Choice (A) contradicts the fact that they lit the ribbon after some difficulty. Choice (C) contradicts the fact that they collected a bottle of carbon dioxide. Choice (D) contradicts the fact that they were able to answer all of Professor Smith's questions about the procedure.

Mini Talk Two

1. **(D)** "I don't agree with having the tests, Professor Ayers, and that's my position." Choice (A) refers to Sally's, not Paul's opinion. Choices (B) and (C) are not mentioned and may not be concluded from information in the discussion.

2. **(A)** "…Sally believes that the tests are good, but that many people don't use them for their intended purpose." Choice (C) refers to what the admissions officers do, not to what Sally believes they should do. Choices (B) and (D) refer to what Paul believes admissions officers should do, not to what they actually do.

3. **(A)** "…standardized tests like the TOEFL, the SAT, GMAT, and GRE." Choices (B), (C), and (D) contradict the fact that the TOEFL, SAT, GMAT, and GRE are named as examples of standardized tests.

4. **(A)** "Okay, class." From the reference to *class*, it must be concluded that this conversation took place in a classroom. Choices (B), (C), and (D) are not mentioned and may not be concluded from information in the discussion.

Mini Talk Three

1. **(D)** "You can either take a final examination or you can write a research paper instead." Choice (A) contradicts the fact that you can write a research paper instead of taking an examination. Choice (B) contradicts the fact that you can write a term paper. Choice (C) contradicts the fact that you can take a final examination.

2. **(A)** "What kind of research paper did you have in mind? A study? A report? A book review, perhaps?" "A report." Choices (B) and (C) refer to options that the student, not the professor, mentions. Choice (D) is not mentioned and may not be concluded from information in the discussion.

3. **(B)** "One hundred multiple-choice questions covering both the lectures and the outside readings." From the reference to *multiple-choice* questions, it must be concluded that it is an objective test. Choices (A), (C), and (D) are not mentioned and may not be concluded from information in the discussion.

4. **(C)** From the reference to current trends in *U.S. foreign policy,* it must be concluded that Dr. Anderson teaches political science. Choices (A), (B), and (D) are not mentioned and may not be concluded from information in the discussion.

Mini Talk Four

1. **(B)** "…I think that travel has probably been the most helpful to me." Choice (C) refers to what Betty did before traveling. Choice (D) refers to what helped Bill, not Betty. Choice (A) is not mentioned and may not be concluded from information in the discussion.

2. **(C)** "…it's difficult to make friends in a new place, even when the people are very friendly." Choice (A) contradicts the fact that it is difficult to make friends. Choice (B) contradicts the fact that people are friendly. Choice (D) contradicts the fact that it is difficult to make friends, and the fact that people are friendly.

3. **(A)** "…whether or not I'm living in a country where the language is spoken I always go to the movies, and whenever I can, I watch TV or listen to the radio in the language I'm trying to learn." Choice (B) refers to what Betty, not Bill, does to learn. Choices (C) and (D) refer to what students should do before taking advantage of practice opportunities.

4. **(A)** "Probably the best way to learn is to combine all of these ideas: traveling, talking with people, going to movies, watching TV, listening to the radio, and reading books, newspapers and magazines." Choice (B) is true, but incomplete. Choice (D) refers to Betty's opinion, not to Professor Baker's opinion. Choice (C) is not mentioned and may not be concluded from information in the discussion.

CHAPTER 4
PART TWO
STRUCTURE AND WRITTEN EXPRESSION

Exercise One: Problems With Verbs (Part 1)

1. **(D)** *That* is used before the subject *he* and the verb word *rest* in the clause after the verb *insists.*

2. **(C)** *Neither* is used before the auxiliary *does* followed by the subject *she. She doesn't either* would also be correct.

3. **(A)** *Hadn't* and the participle *had* are used after the verb *wish* in the main clause.

4. **(D)** *Wouldn't* is used before the subject *you* and the verb *like* in an invitation.

5. **(B)** *Do not* is used before the verb word *submit* to express a negative command.

6. **(C)** *Am* is used before the verb phrase *used to* followed by the *-ing* form *eating* to express habit.

7. **(A)** *Had* is used before the person *them* followed by the verb word *practice* to express an activity caused by *the coach.*

8. **(B)** The *-ing* form *answering* is used after the verb phrase *not mind.*

9. **(C)** *Had better* is used before the verb word *reserve* to express advice.

10. **(C)** *Weren't* is used after *if* to express a condition contrary to fact.

11. **(A)** *Didn't she* is used to agree with *your sister* and *used to visit* in the main clause.

12. **(C)** *Had* is used before the participle *come* in the conditional clause.

13. **(B)** *Would rather* is used before the subject *you* and the past verb *didn't* followed by the verb word *do* to express preference.

14. **(A)** *Must have* is used before the participle *left* to express a logical conclusion.

15. **(C)** *Had* is used before the participle *rung* to refer to an activity *already* in the past.

Exercise Two: Problems With Verbs (Part 2)

1. **(B)** *That* is used before the subject *he* followed by *would* and the verb word *call* after the verb phrase *had hoped.*

2. **(A)** *Did* is used before the subject *I* to agree with *lived* in the main clause. *And I did too* would also be correct.

3. **(B)** *Know how* is used before the infinitive *to take* to express ability or skill. *Does your new secretary know shorthand* would also be correct.

4. **(B)** *Had* is used before the person *his big brother* followed by the verb word *tie* to express an activity caused by *Tommy.*

5. **(C)** *Were* is used after the verb *wish* in the main clause.

6. **(A)** The verb word *begin* is used in the clause after the verb *recommends.*

7. **(C)** *Shall we* is used to agree with *let's* in the main clause.

8. **(A)** *Would ['d] rather* is used before *not* and the verb word *have* to express preference.

9. **(C)** *Would you please* is used before *not* followed by the verb word *write* to express a negative command.

10. **(D)** *Was* is used before the verb phrase *used to* followed by the *-ing* form *sitting* to express a habit.

11. **(D)** *Were* is used after *if* to express a condition contrary to fact.

12. **(B)** *Hadn't* is used before the participle *had* in the conditional clause.

13. **(A)** *Hasn't he* is used to agree with *he's [he has]* in the main clause.

14. **(D)** The *-ing* form *seeing* is used after the verb phrase *looking forward to.*

15. **(A)** The verb word *be* is used in the clause after the impersonal expression *it is imperative.*

Exercise Three: Problems With Verbs (Part 3)

1. **(D)** *Need* is used before the *-ing* form *adjusting* to express necessity for repair. *The brakes need to be adjusted* would also be correct.

2. **(A)** *Could* is used before the verb word *go* after the verb *wish* in the main clause.

3. **(C)** *Knows how* is used before the infinitive *to use* to express ability or skill. *Miss Smith knows the equipment* would also be correct.

4. **(A)** *Used to* is used before the verb word *go* to express a habit in the past.

5. **(C)** *Must have* is used before the participle *understood* to express a logical conclusion.

6. **(C)** *Wouldn't* is used before the subject *you* followed by *rather* and the verb word *sit* to express preference.

7. **(D)** *That* is used before the subject *he* and the verb word *stay* in the clause after the verb *insisted*.

8. **(B)** The participle *written* is used after *had* to refer to an activity in the past.

9. **(B)** *Neither* is used before the auxiliary *would* followed by the subject *the other driver*. *The other driver wouldn't either* would also be correct.

10. **(B)** *Doesn't* is used in the clause of condition to agree with *we'll [we will]* in the clause of result.

11. **(D)** *Have* is used before the thing *your temperature* followed by the participle *taken* to express an activity caused by someone else.

12. **(C)** The infinitive *to pass* is used after the verb *fails*.

13. **(C)** *That* is used before the subject *she* followed by *would* and the verb word *answer* after the verb phrase *had hoped*.

14. **(C)** The verb word *start* is used after the verb phrase *had better* and the *-ing* form *getting up* is used after the verb *start*.

15. **(D)** *Is it* is used to agree with the subject *today's weather* and the verb *is* in the main clause.

Exercise Four: Problems With Pronouns

1. **(A)** *Whom* is used to refer to the person *foreigner* as the complement of the verb *saw.*

2. **(C)** The *-ing* form *asking* is used after the verb phrase *forgot about,* and the possessive pronoun *our* is used to modify the *-ing* form *asking.*

3. **(A)** The object pronoun *me* is used as the complement of the verb *invites.*

4. **(A)** *Who* is used to refer to the person *student* as the subject of the verb *is.*

5. **(B)** The *-ing* form *offering* is used after the verb *appreciate,* and the possessive pronoun *your* is used to modify the *-ing* form *offering.*

6. **(C)** *Who* is used to refer to the person *woman* as the subject of the verb *was hurt.*

7. **(B)** The object pronoun *them* is used after the preposition *for.*

8. **(B)** The object pronoun *us* is used after the preposition *of.*

9. **(A)** *Who* is used to refer to the person *woman* as the subject of the verb *posed.*

10. **(C)** The object pronoun *him* is used after the preposition *with.*

11. **(C)** The object pronoun *me* is used as the complement of the verb *let.*

12. **(A)** The subject pronoun *who* is used to refer to the person *he,* the subject of the verb *was.*

13. **(A)** The object pronoun *her* is used as the complement of the verb *asks.*

14. **(C)** *Which* is used to refer to the thing *notebooks.*

15. **(A)** The *-ing* form *watching* is used after the verb phrase *not mind,* and the possessive pronoun *their* is used to modify the *-ing* form *watching.*

Exercise Five: Problems With Nouns

1. **(D)** *The* is used with the ordinal number *third* before the noun *window. Window three* would also be correct.

2. **(D)** *Ears* to express a plural number with the noun *corn* is idiomatic.

3. **(A)** The cardinal number *two* is used after the noun *volume. The second volume* would also be correct.

4. **(C)** *A few* is used before the plural count noun *dollars. A little money* would also be correct.

5. **(D)** *The* is used with the ordinal number *tenth* before the noun *chapter. Chapter ten* would also be correct.

6. **(C)** *Pieces of* is used before the non-count noun *jewelry* to express a plural number.

7. **(B)** *So little* is used before the non-count noun *time. So little* has a negative meaning. *It is good that you have a little time* would also be correct. *A little* has a positive meaning.

8. **(C)** *Much* is used before the non-count noun *news. We have had some news* would also be correct.

9. **(B)** *The* is used with the ordinal number *thirty-fifth* before the noun *president. President thirty-five* would also be correct.

10. **(C)** *Two pieces of* is used before the non-count noun *toast* to express a plural number.

11. **(C)** The cardinal number *six* is used after the noun *gate. The sixth gate* would also be correct.

12. **(D)** *A little* is used before the non-count noun *information.*

13. **(C)** *A piece of* is used before the non-count noun *mail* to express a singular number.

14. **(C)** The cardinal number *two* is used after the noun *lane. The second lane* would also be correct.

15. **(D)** *Much* is used before the non-count noun *homework.*

Exercise Six: Problems With Modifiers (Part 1)

1. **(A)** *Since* is used before the duration of time *three years* followed by *ago.* *She hasn't seen her family for three years* would also be correct.

2. **(A)** *The* is used before the noun *hall,* which is used as an adjective to describe the second count noun *closet.* Adjectives do not have plural endings in English.

3. **(D)** *Ago* is used after the duration of time *thirty years.* *Bill has worked at the University for thirty years* would also be correct.

4. **(C)** The adjective *strong* is used after the verb of the senses *tastes.*

5. **(A)** *The* is used before the noun *tea,* which is used as an adjective to describe the second count noun *cup.* Adjectives do not have plural endings in English.

6. **(D)** The hyphenated adjective *two-month-old* is used before the noun *baby.* Adjectives do not have plural endings in English.

7. **(A)** *So* is used before the adjective *expensive* followed by *that* and the clause of result *I couldn't afford it.*

8. **(B)** *I haven't gone* is used before *for* and the duration of time *the past five seasons.*

9. **(C)** *Such a* is used before the adjective *snowy* and the noun *day* followed by *that* and the clause of result *travel advisories have been issued.*

10. **(C)** *The* is used before the ordinal number *sixth* followed by *of* and the month *June* to identify a date.

11. **(B)** The adverb of manner *attentively* is used to describe how *they listened.*

12. **(C)** *So* is used before the adjective *good* followed by *that* and the clause of result *I ate them all.*

13. **(D)** The noun *department* is used as an adjective to describe the second noun *store.* Adjectives do not have plural endings in English.

14. **(B)** *Such a* is used before the adjective *big* and the noun *mistake.*

15. **(C)** The adjective *good* is used before *enough* to express sufficiency.

Exercise Seven: Problems With Modifiers (Part 2)

1. **(C)** The adverb of manner *carefully* is used to describe how *Sam does his work.*

2. **(D)** The adjective *bad* is used after the verb of the senses *tastes.*

3. **(A)** *She's [has] lived here* is used before *since* and the specific point in time *1976.*

4. **(B)** *There* is used before the adjective *fast* followed by *enough* to express sufficiency.

5. **(D)** The adverb *late* does not have an *-ly* form.

6. **(A)** *Such* is used before the adjective *nice* and the non-count noun *weather* followed by *that* and the clause of result *we went camping.*

7. **(B)** *The* is used with the ordinal number *second* followed by *of* and the month *September* to identify a date.

8. **(A)** *So* is used before the adjective *late* followed by *that* and the clause of result *she missed her bus.*

9. **(D)** The noun *room* is used as an adjective to describe the second noun *numbers.* Adjectives do not have plural endings in English.

10. **(C)** The adjective *light* is used before *enough* to express sufficiency.

11. **(D)** *So* is used before the adjective *beautiful* followed by the determiner *a* and the noun *day. Such a beautiful day* would also be correct.

12. **(B)** The noun *mathematics,* which always has an *-s* ending, is used as an adjective to describe the second noun *teachers.* Adjectives do not have plural endings in English.

13. **(A)** The hyphenated adjective *two-bedroom* is used before the noun *apartment.* Adjectives do not have plural endings in English.

14. **(D)** *For* is used before the duration of time *several months. Since several months ago* would also be correct.

15. **(C)** The adverb of manner *clearly* is used to describe how *we can see.*

Exercise Eight: Problems With Comparatives

1. **(C)** *As soon as* is used before the subject *I* and the present tense verb *finish* to express a future activity.

2. **(B)** *The* is used before the comparative *more* in the clause of condition followed by *the* before the comparative *worse* in the clause of result.

3. **(C)** *The same* is used before *as* followed by the pronoun *mine* in a comparison. *Yours and mine are almost the same* would also be correct.

4. **(C)** The cardinal number *three* is used before *times* followed by *as much as* in a multiple number.

5. **(C)** The adjective *pretty* is used with *-er* followed by *than* in a comparison. *As pretty as her sister* would also be correct.

6. **(D)** *As soon as* is used before the subject *we* and the present verb *finish* to express a future activity.

7. **(C)** *Different* is used before *from* followed by the noun *the others* in a comparison. *This new soap and the others are not much different* would also be correct.

8. **(A)** *As* is used before the adjective *nice* followed by *as* in a comparison.

9. **(C)** The comparative adjective *larger* is used before *than* followed by *those* to refer to the *rooms*.

10. **(C)** *As soon as* is used before the subject *we* and the present verb *find* to express a future activity.

11. **(B)** *Like* is used before the noun *the midterm* in a comparison. *The final and the midterm will be alike* would also be correct.

12. **(D)** *More* is used before the adjective *friendly* followed by *than* in a comparison.

13. **(C)** *As high as* is used before the amount of money *one thousand dollars* to establish a limit.

14. **(C)** *The* is used before the comparative *more* in the clause of condition followed by *the* before the comparative *more* in the clause of result.

15. **(C)** *Twice* is used before *as much* in a multiple number.

Exercise Nine: Problems With Connectors

1. **(A)** *What* is used before the subject *the taxes* and the verb *are* to maintain word order.

2. **(C)** *Because of* is used before the noun *the noise* to express cause. *Because it was noisy* would also be correct.

3. **(C)** *What* is used before the subject *the professor* and the verb *said* to maintain word order.

4. **(C)** *So that* is used before the clause of purpose *he could finish.*

5. **(C)** The subject *he* and the verb *went* are used after the connector *where* to maintain word order.

6. **(A)** *As well as* is used before the third name *Jane.*

7. **(C)** *Because* is used before the subject *the bus* and the verb *was* to express cause. *Because of the bus* would also be correct.

8. **(D)** *Despite* is used before the noun *the light rain* in the clause of concession. *In spite of the light rain* would also be correct.

9. **(B)** The subject *she* and the verb *wants* are used after the connector *what* to maintain word order.

10. **(B)** *And* is used before the adjective *honored* in coordination with *both* and the adjective *pleased.*

11. **(C)** *How much* is used before the subject *these shoes* and the verb *cost* to maintain word order.

12. **(B)** *So that* is used before the clause of purpose *we could hear.*

13. **(D)** *But also* is used before the phrase *on the baseball team* in coordination with *not only* and the phrase *on the basketball squad.*

14. **(C)** *In spite of* is used before the noun *his wealth* in the clause of concession. *Despite his wealth* would also be correct.

15. **(B)** The subject *the nearest bus stop* and the verb *is located* are used after the connector *where* to maintain word order.

Exercise Ten: Cumulative Practice With Structures (Part 1)

1. **(C)** The *-ing* form adjective *interesting* is used to describe the noun *trip. Allen was interested* would also be correct.

2. **(D)** *Much too much* is a phrase that is used to express excess. *The cost is too much for me* would also be correct.

3. **(C)** *There* is used before *is* to refer to the noun *an extra ticket* at the specific place *the box office.*

4. **(C)** The *-ing* form *turning off* is used after the preposition *without.*

5. **(C)** *Will have* is used before the participle *taught* to express the future viewpoint *by the time he retires* of a past event *Professor Baker taught.*

6. **(D)** *Bring* is used to agree with the verb *come. Bring* means *to come with someone or something.*

7. **(A)** The negative *isn't* is used with *any* followed by *left* to express the amount remaining. *There are some left* would also be correct.

8. **(C)** *Why not* is a phrase that is used to express a suggestion. *Why don't you call* would also be correct.

9. **(D)** *Is* is used before *there* to refer to the noun *snow* at the specific place implied *[outside]* and to maintain word order for questions.

10. **(D)** *By* is used before the *-ing* form *exercising* to express method.

11. **(A)** *If* is used before the noun *endangered species* and the verb *are* followed by the infinitive *to be* to express the result of a condition with *must.*

12. **(A)** The *-ing* form *working* is used after the noun *Professor Davis* to describe him.

13. **(B)** *From* is used before the *-ing* form *working* to express cause.

14. **(B)** The preposition *to* is used after the verb *prefer.*

15. **(C)** The infinitive *to save* is used to express purpose.

Exercise Eleven: Cumulative Practice With Structures (Part 2)

1. **(B)** *Ought* is used before *to* to express obligation. *I should be ready* would also be correct.

2. **(B)** *Not* is used before the infinitive *to be* in the clause after the verb *told*. *She told us that we shouldn't be so impatient* would also be correct.

3. **(D)** *No* is used before the noun *appointments*. *Mr. Black's secretary has not scheduled any appointments* would also be correct.

4. **(B)** *Almost* is used before *all* to express approximation. *Nearly all* would also be correct.

5. **(B)** *In* is used before the month *May*.

6. **(A)** *In* is used after *interested*. The *-ing* form *going* is used after the preposition *in*.

7. **(D)** The verb word *lend* is used after the modal *could*. *Could I borrow five dollars* would also be correct.

8. **(B)** *When* is used before the subject *you* and the present verb *go* to express a future activity.

9. **(B)** *But* is used before the noun *the last page* to express exception.

10. **(D)** *Others* is used consecutively with *some*. *One pair of pants goes with the jackets, another is not yet marked, and the other [others] are sold separately* would also be correct.

11. **(C)** The infinitive *to change* is used to express purpose.

12. **(A)** *Let* is used before the complement *her* followed by the verb word *go* to express permission.

13. **(D)** *What* is used before the determiner *an* and the adjective *exciting* followed by the noun *city* in an exclamatory sentence. *How exciting New Orleans is* would also be correct.

14. **(C)** The subject *it* is used before the verb *is not* followed by *worth* and the indefinite amount *the price* to express value.

15. **(D)** *Won't* is used before *be* followed by the participle *developed* in a passive to express the importance of *the pictures*. *The photographer won't develop my pictures until next week* would also be correct to express the importance of *the photographer*.

Exercise Twelve: Problems With Point Of View

1. **(A)** The adverbial phrase *in 1970* establishes a point of view in the past. *Are* should be *were* to maintain the point of view.

2. **(A)** The verb *did not make* establishes a point of view in the past. *Changes* should be *changed* to maintain the point of view.

3. **(B)** The adverbial phrase *this year* establishes a point of view in the present. *Were* should be *are* to maintain the point of view.

4. **(B)** The verb *said* establishes a point of view in the past. *Is* should be *was* to maintain the point of view.

5. **(B)** The verb *were* establishes a point of view in the past. *Will* should be *would* to maintain the point of view.

6. **(B)** The adverbial phrase *last April* establishes a point of view in the past. *Is* should be *was* to maintain the point of view.

7. **(B)** The verb *found* establishes a point of view in the past. *Wants* should be *wanted* to maintain the point of view.

8. **(A)** The verb *thought* establishes a point of view in the past. *Will* should be *would* to maintain the point of view.

9. **(A)** The reference to an activity before the subject's death establishes a point of view in the past. *Publishes* should be *published* to maintain the point of view.

10. **(B)** The adverbial phrase *last Friday* establishes a point of view in the past. *Does* should be *did* to maintain the point of view.

11. **(B)** The adverbial phrase *seven o'clock in the morning when the sun comes up* establishes a point of view in the present. *Disappeared* should be *disappears* to maintain the point of view.

12. **(C)** The verb *was* establishes a point of view in the past. *Want* should be *wanted* to maintain the point of view.

13. **(D)** The verb *is* establishes a point of view in the present. *Invited* should be *invites* to maintain the point of view.

14. **(A)** The verb *thought* establishes a point of view in the past. *Are* should be *were* to maintain the point of view.

15. **(B)** The adverbial phrase *October 19, 1781* establishes a point of view in the past. *Surrenders* should be *surrendered* to maintain the point of view.

16. **(A)** The adverbial phrase *last month* establishes a point of view in the past. *Is* should be *was* to maintain the point of view.

17. **(B)** The reference to an activity before the subject's death establishes a point of view in the past. *Lives* should be *lived* to maintain the point of view.

18. **(A)** The verb *said* establishes a point of view in the past. *Is* should be *was* to maintain the point of view.

19. **(B)** The verb *reported* establishes a point of view in the past. *Believe* should be *believed* to maintain the point of view.

20. **(B)** The verb *told* establishes a point of view in the past. *Is* should be *was* to maintain the point of view.

21. **(C)** The verb *are* establishes a point of view in the present. *Were* should be *are* to maintain the point of view.

22. **(A)** The adverb *yesterday* establishes a point of view in the past. *Does* should be *did* to maintain the point of view.

23. **(B)** The verb *give* establishes a point of view in the present. *Deposited* should be *deposit* to maintain the point of view.

24. **(B)** The verb *accelerated* establishes a point of view in the past. *Qualifies* should be *qualified* to maintain the point of view.

25. **(C)** The verb *is* establishes a point of view in the present. *Included* should be *includes* to maintain the point of view.

Exercise Thirteen: Problems With Agreement

1. **(B)** There must be agreement between pronoun and antecedent. *You* should be *one* or *his* to agree with the impersonal antecedent *one*.

2. **(C)** There must be agreement between subject and verb. *Were* should be *was* to agree with the singular subject *what happened*.

3. **(B)** There must be agreement between subject and verb. *Are* should be *is* to agree with the third person singular subject *the governor*.

4. **(C)** There must be agreement between pronoun and antecedent. *Their* should be *our* to agree with the second person antecedent *those of us*.

5. **(B)** There must be agreement between subject and verb. *Is* should be *are* to agree with the plural subject *both*.

6. **(B)** There must be agreement between subject and verb. *Are* should be *is* to agree with the singular subject *neither...nor*.

7. **(A)** There must be agreement between subject and verb. *Have* should be *has* to agree with the inverted singular subject *little rain*.

8. **(C)** There must be agreement between pronoun and antecedent. *Their* should be *his* to agree with the singular subject *everyone*.

9. **(A)** There must be agreement between subject and verb. *Were* should be *was* to agree with the singular subject *the popularity*.

10. **(B)** There must be agreement between subject and verb. *Develop* should be *develops* to agree with the singular subject *not one*.

11. **(C)** There must be agreement between subject and verb. *Have* should be *has* to agree with the inverted singular subject *little change*.

12. **(D)** There must be agreement between pronoun and antecedent. *Their* should be *its* to agree with the third person singular neuter subject *the eagle*.

13. **(D)** There must be agreement between subject and verb. *Require* should be *requires* to agree with the singular subject *the Blue Spruce*.

14. **(A)** There must be agreement between subject and verb. *Is* should be *are* to agree with the plural subject *few airports*.

15. **(B)** There must be agreement between subject and verb. *Were* should be *was* to agree with the singular subject *work*.

16. **(B)** There must be agreement between subject and verb. *Are* should be *is* to agree with the singular subject *the president.*

17. **(B)** There must be agreement between pronoun and antecedent. *Their* should be *his* to agree with the singular subject *each voter.*

18. **(C)** There must be agreement between pronoun and antecedent. *Their* should be *our* to agree with the second person antecedent *those of us.*

19. **(C)** There must be agreement between subject and verb. *Were* should be *was* to agree with the singular subject *neither.*

20. **(C)** There must be agreement between pronoun and antecedent. *You* should be *one* or *he* to agree with the impersonal antecedent *one.*

21. **(C)** There must be agreement between subject and verb. *Are* should be *is* to agree with the singular subject *one.*

22. **(C)** There must be agreement between subject and verb. *Know* should be *knows* to agree with the singular subject *one.*

23. **(B)** There must be agreement between pronoun and antecedent. *They* should be *one* or *he* to agree with the impersonal antecedent *one.*

24. **(B)** There must be agreement between subject and verb. *Were* should be *was* to agree with the inverted singular subject *a serious objection.*

25. **(A)** There must be agreement between subject and verb. *Are* should be *is* to agree with the singular subject *a large percentage.*

Exercise Fourteen: Problems With Introductory Verbal Modifiers

1. **(A)** An introductory verbal phrase followed by a comma should immediately precede the noun that it modifies. *After finishing Roots* is misplaced because it does not precede the noun it modifies, *author Alex Haley.*

2. **(A)** An introductory verbal phrase followed by a comma should immediately precede the noun that it modifies. *A competitive sport* is misplaced because it does not precede the noun it modifies, *gymnastics.*

3. **(B)** An introductory verbal phrase followed by a comma should immediately precede the noun that it modifies. *Carefully soaking* should be *(you) carefully soak* to provide a noun for the introductory verbal phrase *to remove stains from permanent press clothing.*

4. **(A)** An introductory verbal phrase followed by a comma should immediately precede the noun that it modifies. *Found in Tanzania by Mary Leakey* is misplaced because it does not precede the noun it modifies, *the three-million-year-old fossils.*

5. **(A)** An introductory verbal phrase followed by a comma should immediately precede the noun that it modifies. *After fighting the blaze for three days* is misplaced because it does not precede the noun it modifies, *the fire-fighters.*

6. **(B)** An introductory verbal phrase followed by a comma should immediately precede the noun that it modifies. *After finishing their degrees* is misplaced because it does not precede the noun it modifies, *the students.*

7. **(D)** An introductory verbal phrase followed by a comma should immediately precede the noun that it modifies. *Columbus's final resting place* should be *Columbus* because the man, not the place, is modified by the verbal phrase *Originally having been buried in Spain.*

8. **(B)** An introductory verbal phrase followed by a comma should immediately precede the noun that it modifies. *New York audiences received the new play* should be *the new play was received by New York audiences* because the play, not the audiences, is modified by the verbal phrase *written by Neil Simon.*

9. **(C)** An introductory verbal phrase followed by a comma should immediately precede the noun that it modifies. *Survival is assured* should be *animals assure survival* because the animals, not the survival, is modified by the verbal phrase *by migrating to a warmer climate every fall.*

10. **(B)** An introductory verbal phrase followed by a comma should immediately precede the noun that it modifies. *A memorial fund will be established* should be *family and friends will establish a memorial fund* because the family and friends, not the memorial fund, are modified by the verbal phrase *saddened by the actor's sudden death.*

11. **(A)** An introductory verbal phrase followed by a comma should immediately precede the noun that it modifies. *Dental floss should be used* should be *(you) use dental floss* to provide a noun for the introductory verbal phrase *to prevent cavities.*

12. **(A)** An introductory verbal phrase followed by a comma should immediately precede the noun that it modifies. *The Senate committee's discovery* should be *The Senate committee discovered* because the committee, not the discovery, is modified by the verbal phrase *while researching the problem of violent crime.*

13. **(A)** An introductory verbal phrase followed by a comma should immediately precede the noun that it modifies. *Trying to pay for a purchase with cash* is misplaced because it does not precede the noun it modifies, *customers.*

14. **(A)** An introductory verbal phrase followed by a comma should immediately precede the noun that it modifies. *After reviewing the curriculum* is misplaced because it does not precede the noun it modifies, *faculty.*

15. **(D)** An introductory verbal phrase followed by a comma should immediately precede the noun that it modifies. *Hank Aaron's record* should be *Hank Aaron* because the man, not the record, is modified by the verbal phrase *having hit more home runs than any other player in the history of baseball.*

16. **(A)** An introductory verbal phrase followed by a comma should immediately precede the noun that it modifies. *Banned in the U.S.* is misplaced because it does not precede the noun it modifies, *fluorocarbons.*

17. **(A)** An introductory verbal phrase followed by a comma should immediately precede the noun that it modifies. *To avoid jet lag* is misplaced because it does not precede the noun it modifies, *patients.*

18. **(A)** An introductory verbal phrase followed by a comma should immediately precede the noun that it modifies. *After cooking in the microwave oven for five minutes* is misplaced because it does not precede the noun it modifies, *most meat dishes.*

19. **(B)** An introductory verbal phrase followed by a comma should immediately precede the noun that it modifies. *Traditionally named for women* is misplaced because it does not precede the noun it modifies, *a hurricane.*

20. **(A)** An introductory verbal phrase followed by a comma should immediately precede the noun that it modifies. *While testifying* is misplaced because it does not precede the noun it modifies, *witnesses.*

21. **(A)** An introductory verbal phrase followed by a comma should immediately precede the noun that it modifies. *By reading the instructions carefully* is misplaced because it does not precede the noun it modifies, *students.*

22. **(B)** An introductory verbal phrase followed by a comma should immediately precede the noun that it modifies. *Her credit* should be *the woman* because she, not the credit, is modified by the phrase, *having been divorced.*

23. **(A)** An introductory verbal phrase followed by a comma should immediately precede the noun that it modifies. *Attempting to smuggle drugs into the country* is misplaced because it does not precede the noun it modifies, *criminals.*

24. **(A)** An introductory verbal phrase followed by a comma should immediately precede the noun that it modifies. *While trying to build a tunnel through the Blue Ridge Mountains* is misplaced because it does not precede the noun it modifies, *workmen.*

25. **(A)** An introductory verbal phrase followed by a comma should immediately precede the noun that it modifies. *Founded in 1919* is misplaced because it does not precede the noun it modifies, *the Institute for International Education.*

Exercise Fifteen: Problems With Parallel Structure

1. **(D)** Ideas in a series should be expressed by parallel structures. *That it would adjourn* should be *to adjourn* to provide parallelism with the infinitives *to cancel* and *to approve*.

2. **(D)** Ideas in a series should be expressed by parallel structures. *It is* should be deleted to provide parallelism among the adjectives *fast, safe,* and *convenient*.

3. **(B)** Ideas after inclusives should be expressed by parallel structures. *Not only popular* should be *popular not only* to provide parallelism between the adverbial phrases *in the United States* and *abroad*.

4. **(B)** Ideas in a series should be expressed by parallel structures. *Turning* should be *turn* to provide parallelism with the verb words *lock* and *walk*.

5. **(A)** Ideas in a series should be expressed by parallel structures. *Making* should be *to make* to provide parallelism with the infinitive *to control*.

6. **(C)** Ideas in a series should be expressed by parallel structures. *To modify* should be *by modifying* to provide parallelism with the phrase *by changing*.

7. **(C)** Ideas in a series should be expressed by parallel structures. *Awareness* should be *aware* to provide parallelism with the adjectives *intelligent* and *capable*.

8. **(B)** Ideas after inclusives should be expressed by parallel structures, and inclusives should be used in coordinating pairs. *But* should be *but also* to coordinate with *not only*.

9. **(D)** Ideas in a series should be expressed by parallel structures. *Signing your name* should be *the signature* to provide parallelism with the nouns *the address, the inside address, the salutation, the body,* and *the closing*.

10. **(B)** Ideas in a series should be expressed by parallel structures. *To do* should be *by doing* to provide parallelism with the phrase *by using*.

11. **(A)** Ideas in a series should be expressed by parallel structures. *Being introduced* should be *to be introduced* to provide parallelism with the infinitive *to read*.

12. **(C)** Ideas after exclusives should be expressed by parallel structures, and exclusives should be used in coordinating pairs. *And not* should be *nor* to coordinate with *neither*.

13. **(C)** Ideas in a series should be expressed by parallel structures. *Who* should be deleted to provide parallelism among the verbs *understands, knows,* and *works*.

14. **(A)** Ideas in a series should be expressed by parallel structures. *Ice skating* should be *to go ice skating* to provide parallelism with the infinitive *to go skiing*.

15. **(D)** Ideas in a series should be expressed by parallel structures. *The operation was begun* should be *began the operation* to provide parallelism with the past, active verb *examined*.

16. **(B)** Ideas in a series should be expressed by parallel structures. *Because of the time* should be *because there was little time* to provide parallelism with the clause *because we were not sure*.

17. **(C)** Ideas in a series should be expressed by parallel structures. *Avoiding* should be *avoid* to provide parallelism with the verb words *drink* and *eat.*

18. **(B)** Ideas after inclusives should be expressed by parallel structures. *A key* should be *with a key* to provide parallelism with the phrase *with an element.*

19. **(C)** Ideas in a series should be expressed by parallel structures. *Warning* should be *to warn* to provide parallelism with the infinitive *to report.*

20. **(D)** Ideas in a series should be expressed by parallel structures. *Had finished* should be *finishing* to provide parallelism with the *-ing* forms *traveling* and *visiting.*

21. **(D)** Ideas in a series should be expressed by parallel structures. *There are* should be deleted to provide parallelism among the nouns *the flag, the airplane,* and *the gowns.*

22. **(D)** Ideas in a series should be expressed by parallel structures. *Less* should be *least* to provide parallelism with the superlative adjectives *the smallest* and *most recently published.*

23. **(D)** Ideas after inclusives should be expressed by parallel structures. *The House of Representatives* should be *by the House of Representatives* to provide parallelism with the phrase *by the Senate.*

24. **(D)** Ideas in a series should be expressed by parallel structures. *With ease* should be *easily* to provide parallelism with the adverbs *safely* and *efficiently.*

25. **(C)** Ideas after exclusives should be expressed by parallel structures and exclusives should be used in coordinating pairs. *But also* should be *but* to coordinate with *not.*

Exercise Sixteen: Problems With Redundancy

1. **(D)** Repetition of a word by another word with the same meaning is redundant. *Again* should be deleted because it means *repeat*.

2. **(A)** Repetition of the subject by a subject pronoun is redundant. *It* should be deleted.

3. **(C)** Repetition of a word by another word with the same meaning is redundant. *Or purchasing* should be deleted because it means *buying*.

4. **(D)** Indirect phrases instead of adverbs are redundant. *In an impartial manner* should be *impartially*.

5. **(A)** Indirect phrases are redundant. *There was not any clarity* should be *it was not clear*.

6. **(C)** Repetition of the subject by the subject pronoun is redundant. *They* should be deleted.

7. **(D)** Repetition of a word by another word with the same meaning is redundant. *Back* should be deleted because it means *return*.

8. **(A)** Repetition of a word by another word with the same meaning is redundant. *Who knows a great deal* should be deleted because it means *an authority*.

9. **(B)** Words or phrases that do not add information are redundant. *In terms of* should be *to*.

10. **(A)** Repetition of the subject by a subject pronoun is redundant. *He* should be deleted.

11. **(B)** Repetition of a word by another word with the same meaning is redundant. *Enough* should be deleted because it means *sufficiently*.

12. **(B)** Words or phrases that do not add information are redundant. *In nature* should be deleted.

13. **(A)** Repetition of the subject by a subject pronoun is redundant. *He* should be deleted.

14. **(B)** Indirect phrases instead of adverbs are redundant. *In a careful manner* should be *carefully*.

15. **(C)** Repetition of the subject by a subject pronoun is redundant. *They* should be deleted.

16. **(A)** Repetition of the subject by a subject pronoun is redundant. *She* should be deleted.

17. **(C)** Repetition of a word by another word with the same meaning is redundant. *New* should be deleted because it means *innovations*.

18. **(A)** Words or phrases that do not add information are redundant. *More* should be deleted.

19. **(D)** Repetition of a word by another word with the same meaning is redundant. *By name* should be deleted because it means *called*.

20. **(B)** Repetition of a word by another word with the same meaning is redundant. *Forward* should be deleted because it means *advances.*

21. **(B)** Repetition of the subject by a subject pronoun is redundant. *It* should be deleted.

22. **(D)** Indirect phrases instead of adverbs are redundant. *With rapidity* should be *rapidly.*

23. **(A)** Repetition of the subject by a subject pronoun is redundant. *She* should be deleted.

24. **(B)** Words or phrases that do not add information are redundant. *In politics* should be deleted.

25. **(A)** Repetition of the subject by a subject pronoun is redundant. *It* should be deleted.

Exercise Seventeen: Problems With Word Choice

1. **(D)** *Equal to* is a prepositional idiom. *As* should be *to*.

2. **(D)** *Lie* means *to occupy a place. Laying* should be *lying*.

3. **(B)** *Raise* means *to move to a higher place. Is risen* should be *is raised*.

4. **(D)** *Broke* is a colloquial expression. *Broke* should be *bankrupt*.

5. **(C)** *Compare with* is a prepositional idiom. *Comparing* should be *compared with*.

6. **(D)** *To give someone their walking papers* is a colloquial expression. *Gave them their walking papers* should be *dismissed them*.

7. **(C)** *Similar to* is a prepositional idiom. *As* should be *to*.

8. **(B)** *Near to* is not idiomatic. *To* should be *deleted*.

9. **(C)** *Effects on* is a prepositional idiom. *In* should be *on*.

10. **(A)** *Carefulness* is not idiomatic. *Carefulness* should be *care*.

11. **(B)** *Real* is a colloquial expression. *Real great* should be *very great*.

12. **(A)** *Formerly* means *in the past. Formally* should be *formerly*.

13. **(C)** *Let* means *allow. Leave* should be *let*.

14. **(A)** *Bored with* is a prepositional idiom. *Of* should be *with*.

15. **(A)** *Effectiveness* is not idiomatic. *Effectiveness* should be *effect*.

16. **(D)** *Considerate* means polite. *Considerable* should be *considerate*.

17. **(A)** *Can't hardly* is not idiomatic. *Can't hardly* should be *can hardly*.

18. **(B)** *Rise* means *to go up. Raised* should be *risen*.

19. **(D)** *In conflict* is a prepositional idiom. *On* should be *in*.

20. **(A)** *The cops* is a colloquial expression. *The cops* should be *the police*.

21. **(A)** *With regard to* is a prepositional idiom. *Of* should be *to*.

22. **(B)** *Lie* means *to occupy a place. To lay* should be *to lie*.

23. **(A)** *Except for* is a prepositional idiom. *Excepting* should be *except for*.

24. **(A)** *To suspicion* is not idiomatic. *Suspicioned* should be *suspected*.

25. **(A)** *Menkind* is not idiomatic. *Menkind* should be *mankind*.

Exercise Eighteen: Problems With Structure

1. **(B)** *The best* should be *the better* because two, not three lectures, are being compared.

2. **(A)** *Knows to assist* should be *knows how to assist* because *knows how* is used before the infinitive *to assist.*

3. **(A)** *Wrote* should be *written* because a participle, not a past form, is used with *had.*

4. **(B)** *Differently* should be *different* because an adjective, not an adverb, is used after the verb of the senses *seem.*

5. **(C)** *So* should be *so that* because it introduces a clause of purpose.

6. **(C)** *Do* should be *doing* because an *-ing* form, not a verb word, is used after the verb *continue.*

7. **(C)** *Which* should be *who* because it refers to people, not things.

8. **(A)** *Understands* should be *understood* because a past form, not a present form, is used after the verb *wishes.*

9. **(B)** *From* should be deleted because a preposition is not used after the verb *forbid.*

10. **(A)** *Ran* should be *run* because a participle, not a past form, is used with *had.*

11. **(B)** *Ninety-days* should be *ninety-day* because an adjective does not have a plural form.

12. **(D)** *Badly* should be *bad* because an adjective, not an adverb, is used after the verb of the senses *taste.*

13. **(A)** *I* should be *me* because an objective pronoun is used after *let.*

14. **(A)** *Investigates* should be *investigate* because the word *recommendation* requires a verb word.

15. **(C)** *As* should be *than* because *than* is used after the comparative *younger.*

16. **(C)** *In spite* should be *in spite of* because *in spite of* introduces a condition with an unexpected result. *Despite* would also be correct.

17. **(A)** *Lately* should be *late* because the adverb form of *late* does not have an *-ly* ending.

18. **(A)** *Would have been* should be *had been* because *had* and a participle are used in the condition and *would have* and a participle are used in the result.

19. **(C)** *The worst* should be *the worse* because comparative forms are used with *the* in double comparisons that express cause and result.

20. **(C)** *Much* should be *many* because *many* is used with the count noun *movies.*

21. **(B)** *Whom* should be *who* because it is the subject of the verb *will win.*

22. **(A)** *Would have checked* should be *had checked* because *had* and a participle are used in the condition and *would have* and a participle are used in the result.

23. **(A)** *Her* should be *she* because a subject pronoun is used after *it was.*

24. **(B)** *Taking* should be *to take* because an infinitive, not an *-ing* form, is used after the verb *fail.*

25. **(A)** *Will sign* should be *sign* because a verb word is used after the impersonal expression *is it necessary.*

CHAPTER 5
PART THREE
READING COMPREHENSION AND VOCABULARY

Exercise One: Vocabulary Review (Part 1)

1. **(C)** A *dagger* is a knife. Choice (A) is a column (of a building). Choice (B) is a celestial body smaller than one mile in diameter. Choice (D) is a large rock.

2. **(A)** *Chilly* means cool. Choice (B) means oxidized. Choice (C) means foolish. Choice (D) means soft.

3. **(B)** *Affluent* means wealthy or rich. Choices (A), (C), and (D) are not accepted meanings of the word *affluent*.

4. **(A)** *Incessantly* means continuously. Choice (B) means without knowledge or information. Choice (C) means sharply or trenchantly. Choice (D) means without favoring one more than another or justly.

5. **(A)** *Blame* means responsibility. Choice (B) means great anger. Choice (C) means a trick. Choice (D) means confusion.

6. **(B)** *Conscientious* means careful. Choices (A), (C), and (D) are not accepted meanings of the word *conscientious*.

7. **(A)** A *core* is the center of something. Choices (B), (C), and (D) are not accepted meanings of the word *core*.

8. **(B)** *Nasty* means mean. Choice (A) means informal. Choice (C) means inappropriate. Choice (D) means humorous.

9. **(A)** A *troupe* is a group, especially in reference to singers or actors. Choice (B) is a pig. Choice (C) is an enclosure for animals or prisoners. Choice (D) is a gift.

10. **(B)** *Strenuous* means arduous. Choice (A) means long. Choice (C) means the usual way of doing things. Choice (D) means planned.

11. **(A)** A *swarm* is a large number of insects. Choice (B) is a large number of cattle. Choice (C) is a large number of dogs or wolves. Choice (D) is a large number of birds or sheep.

12. **(C)** To *peek* means to take a look. Choices (A), (B), and (D) are not accepted meanings of the word *peek*.

13. **(D)** To *seize* means to take. Choice (A) means to buy. Choice (B) means to stay away. Choice (C) means to examine.

14. **(A)** To *scrub* means to wash vigorously. Choices (B), (C), and (D) are not accepted meanings of the word *scrub*.

15. **(B)** To *slit* means to cut. Choice (A) means to design. Choice (C) means to make larger. Choice (D) means to make smaller.

16. **(A)** To *sneak* means to go secretly. Choices (B), (C), and (D) are not accepted meanings of the word *sneak*.

17. **(A)** *Specks* are spots. Choices (B), (C), and (D) are not accepted meanings of the word *specks.*

18. **(A)** To *mingle* means to mix. Choices (B), (C), and (D) are not accepted meanings of the word *mingle.*

19. **(C)** A *jungle* is a hot land covered with a dense growth of trees. Choice (A) is an elevated, level expanse of land. Choice (B) is a flat expanse of land with few trees. Choice (D) is a dense growth of trees covering a large area.

20. **(D)** *Hints* are clues. Choice (A) is liberty. Choice (B) is help. Choice (C) is money.

21. **(A)** *Hectic* means very busy. Choices (B), (C), and (D) are not accepted meanings of the word *hectic.*

22. **(D)** *Gusts* are sudden rushes of wind. Choice (A) is destruction. Choice (B) is sickness. Choice (C) is an overflowing of water.

23. **(C)** To *grumble* means to complain. Choices (A), (B), and (D) are not accepted meanings of the word *grumble.*

24. **(D)** To *divulge* means to tell. Choice (A) means to use. Choice (B) means to pay little attention. Choice (C) means to change.

25. **(A)** To *adore* means to greatly love. Choices (B), (C), and (D) are not accepted meanings of the word *adore.*

26. **(C)** To *enhance* means to make better or to improve. Choices (A), (B), and (D) are not accepted meanings of the word *enhance.*

27. **(C)** A *cabal* is an intrigue. Choice (A) is a group, usually of players or workers. Choice (B) is a group of musicians. Choice (D) is a crowd without a leader.

28. **(A)** *Fluffier* means softer. Choices (B), (C), and (D) are not accepted meanings of the word *fluffier.*

29. **(A)** *Leisure* means free. Choices (B), (C), and (D) are not accepted meanings of the word *leisure.*

30. **(B)** *Tolerant* means fair. Choice (A) means willing to share. Choice (C) means sure of oneself. Choice (D) means able to change.

Exercise Two: Vocabulary Review (Part 2)

1. **(A)** A *pauper* is a very poor person. Choice (B) is a beginner. Choice (C) is a person who chooses to live apart from society. Choice (D) is a prisoner or a person who is confined.

2. **(A)** To *alleviate* means to relieve. Choice (B) means to change directions or to turn around. Choice (C) means to lengthen or to extend. Choice (D) means to make worse.

3. **(B)** A *gist* is the main idea. Choices (A), (C), and (D) are not accepted meanings of the word *gist*.

4. **(A)** *Meticulous* means careful. Choices (B), (C), and (D) are not accepted meanings of the word *meticulous*.

5. **(A)** A *hamlet* is a tiny village. Choice (B) is a popular vacation place. Choice (C) is a farm on which herds of animals are raised. Choice (D) is a residential area near a city.

6. **(B)** A *prelude* is a preliminary event. Choice (A) is a blessing. Choice (C) is an inscription on a literary work or artistic performance honoring someone. Choice (D) is an ending.

7. **(A)** To *accumulate* means to collect. Choice (B) means to change from a solid to a liquid. Choice (C) means to change from a liquid to a solid. Choice (D) means to throw out.

8. **(C)** *Accommodations* are rooms and meals. Choice (A) is enrollments. Choice (B) is an arrangement in advance for accommodations. Choice (D) is a verification.

9. **(B)** An *aversion* is an intense dislike. Choice (A) is a habit. Choice (C) is a liking or fondness. Choice (D) is fairness or justice.

10. **(B)** *Appraisals* are estimates of value. Choice (A) is a location or place. Choice (C) is a benefit. Choice (D) is an addition.

11. **(A)** To *surfeit* means to eat an excessive amount. Choice (B) means to express sorrow. Choice (C) means to disagree or to argue. Choice (D) means to explain in detail.

12. **(D)** *Boulders* are large rocks. Choice (A) is an inorganic substance. Choice (B) is a small stone. Choice (C) is a precious stone or a jewel.

13. **(A)** To *cruise* means to drive slowly. Choice (B) means to move rapidly. Choice (C) means to walk slowly. Choice (D) means to hunt or to track.

14. **(B)** To *tiptoe* means to walk quietly. Choice (A) means to wander idly, without purpose. Choice (C) means to move unsteadily. Choice (D) means to move on the hands and knees.

15. **(D)** A *female horse* is a mare. Choice (A) is a large pig. Choice (B) is a male goose. Choice (C) is a male chicken.

16. **(A)** To *slander* means to malign. Choice (B) means to limit or to imprison. Choice (C) means to keep away from or to shun. Choice (D) means to tease or to torment.

17. **(A)** *Chores* are jobs. Choice (B) is an animal kept for companionship. Choice (C) is a small meal. Choice (D) is money or a gift used to influence someone.

18. **(B)** *Storms* are natural disturbances of wind. Choice (A) is intentionally killing oneself. Choice (C) is a violent release of energy. Choice (D) is a disturbance by a large number of people.

19. **(C)** To *arouse* means to incite. Choice (A) means to pay attention to. Choice (B) means to make known. Choice (D) means to anticipate.

20. **(A)** *Bald* is hairless. Choice (B) is rough, particularly in reference to a voice. Choice (C) is disabled in a leg or foot so as to hinder walking. Choice (D) is difficult to bend or not flexible.

21. **(A)** A *drought* is a long period of dry weather. Choice (B) is an overflowing of water onto the land. Choice (C) is a light covering of ice. Choice (D) is the possession of property because the owner could not pay.

22. **(C)** A *bump* is a light blow. Choice (A) is a discoloration of the skin. Choice (B) is a cut. Choice (D) is a break.

23. **(B)** To *omit* means to leave out. Choice (A) means to change. Choice (C) means to make larger or more powerful. Choice (D) means to display or to show.

24. **(A)** *Flimsy* means lacking in strength. Choice (B) means small. Choice (C) means able to be seen through. Choice (D) means bright or shining.

25. **(D)** *Ingredients* are items used, especially in a recipe for food. Choices (A), (B), and (C) are not accepted meanings of the word *ingredients.*

26. **(C)** *Appropriate* means suitable. Choice (A) means very offensive or shocking. Choice (B) means very funny. Choice (D) means polite or thoughtful.

27. **(C)** A *relapse* is the return of an illness. Choices (A), (B), and (D) are not accepted meanings of the word *relapse.*

28. **(A)** To *flee* (fled is the past tense) means to escape. Choice (B) means to stay. Choice (C) means to discontinue association. Choice (D) means to die.

29. **(B)** To pay *homage* means to respect. Choice (A) means to object. Choice (C) means to observe a holiday or special occasion. Choice (D) means to take unaware or to act unexpectedly.

30. **(B)** To *augment* means to increase. Choice (A) means to plan finances. Choice (C) means to keep or to hold. Choice (D) means to tell what will happen in the future or to foretell.

Exercise Three: Vocabulary Review (Part 3)

1. **(C)** *Adjacent to* means next to. Choices (A), (B), and (D) are not accepted meanings of the phrase *adjacent to.*

2. **(D)** *Complicated* means intricate. Choice (A) means suitable. Choice (B) means no longer useful or outdated. Choice (C) means costly.

3. **(B)** *Behavior* is actions. Choices (A), (C), and (D) are not accepted meanings of the word *behavior.*

4. **(D)** *Ailments* are illnesses. Choice (A) is an agreement. Choice (B) is a business exchange. Choice (C) is a clash or a crash.

5. **(C)** To *abet* means to help or to aid. Choice (A) means to employ. Choice (B) means to copy or to try to equal or excel. Choice (D) means to hide.

6. **(B)** To *rehearse* means to practice. Choice (A) means to create in the mind. Choice (C) means to say aloud. Choice (D) means to begin.

7. **(A)** To *shatter* means to break into many pieces. Choice (B) means to break without dividing into parts. Choice (C) means to cause to curve without breaking. Choice (D) means to change from a solid to a liquid form.

8. **(C)** To *vanish* means to disappear. Choice (A) means to blow apart. Choice (B) means to get free. Choice (D) means to dive.

9. **(A)** To *assert oneself* means to affirm opinions. Choices (B), (C), and (D) are not accepted meanings of the phrase *assert oneself.*

10. **(A)** To *go astray* means to wander. Choices (B), (C), and (D) are not accepted meanings of the phrase *go astray.*

11. **(D)** *Amnesia* is a lapse of memory. Choice (A) is loss of movement. Choice (B) is loss of speech. Choice (C) is loss of hearing.

12. **(C)** To *flicker* means to shine unsteadily. Choices (A) and (B) mean to shine steadily and brightly. Choice (D) means to shine steadily but less brightly.

13. **(A)** *Polluted* means contaminated. Choice (B) means moving slowly. Choice (C) means not open to the general public. Choice (D) means clean.

14. **(C)** *Bewildered* means confused. Choice (A) means influenced. Choice (B) means shocked. Choice (D) means very interested.

15. **(D)** *Ajar* means slightly open. Choices (A), (B), and (C) are not accepted meanings of the word *ajar.*

16. **(A)** *Numb* means without sensation. Choice (B) means enlarged. Choice (C) means red. Choice (D) means dry and peeling.

17. **(C)** *Infested with* means inhabited by. Choice (A) means entered. Choice (B) means to cause harm or to destroy. Choice (D) means deserted.

18. **(B)** *Negligent* means careless. Choices (A), (C), and (D) are not accepted meanings of the word *negligent*.

19. **(D)** *Margins* are blank spaces. Choices (A), (B), and (C) are not accepted meanings of the word *margins*.

20. **(B)** *Brooms* are objects to sweep the floor. Choice (A) is the edge of a cup or hat. Choice (C) is a soft container of paper, cloth, plastic, or leather. Choice (D) is a woven container.

21. **(A)** *Drowsy* means sleepy. Choices (B), (C), and (D) are not accepted meanings of the word *drowsy*.

22. **(A)** *Ominous* means threatening. Choice (B) means unchanged. Choice (C) means not clear. Choice (D) means secret.

23. **(B)** *Renowned* means famous. Choices (A), (C), and (D) are not accepted meanings of the word *renowned*.

24. **(B)** To *sue* means to bring to court. Choices (A), (C), and (D) are not accepted meanings of the word to *sue*.

25. **(C)** A *rivalry* is a competition. Choice (A) is a legal combination of two businesses. Choice (B) is the settlement of a disagreement. Choice (D) is close, careful examination.

26. **(C)** *Profound* means deep. Choice (A) means sincere or true. Choice (B) means general or inclusive. Choice (D) means reaffirmed.

27. **(D)** A *fraud* is a deception. Choices (A) and (B) are jokes or tricks. Choice (C) is the act of stealing.

28. **(C)** *Deliberately* means in a planned way. Choice (A) means without a fixed or regular course or disorganized. Choice (B) means self-importantly. Choice (D) means insensitively.

29. **(B)** To *smolder* means to burn with little smoke and no flame. Choices (A) and (C) mean to burn with a bright, hot flame. Choice (D) means to burn with snapping noises.

30. **(B)** To *retard* means to hold back. Choice (A) means to affect. Choice (C) means to foretell the future. Choice (D) means to disfigure.

Exercise Four: Vocabulary Review (Part 4)

1. **(C)** *Restricted* means limited. Choice (A) means necessary or essential. Choice (B) means left to choice. Choice (D) means able to be used.

2. **(C)** *Florid* means rosy-colored. Choice (A) means marked with spots. Choice (B) means marked with spots brought out by the sun. Choice (D) means pale.

3. **(A)** *Bruises* are temporary discolorations of the skin caused by an injury. Choice (B) is a break. Choice (C) is a painful injury to a joint. Choice (D) is a deep cut.

4. **(A)** *Dissipated* means spent wastefully. Choice (B) means sent elsewhere. Choice (C) means put in the wrong place or lost. Choice (D) means examined, especially in reference to money and accounts.

5. **(A)** An *exodus* is a departure. Choice (B) is starvation. Choice (C) is a special observation of a holiday or other occasion. Choice (D) is the spread of disease among a large number of people.

6. **(D)** *Adult* means mature. Choice (A) means teen-aged. Choice (B) means youthful or immature. Choice (C) means babyish.

7. **(A)** *Fastidious* means thorough or meticulous. Choice (B) means obedient or servile. Choice (C) means friendly. Choice (D) means talkative or garrulous.

8. **(A)** *Glib* means smooth. Choices (B), (C), and (D) are not accepted meanings of the word *glib*.

9. **(C)** To *notify* means to inform. Choices (A), (B), and (D) are not accepted meanings of the word *notify*.

10. **(B)** To *equivocate* means to mislead by using ambiguous language. Choice (A) means to discuss. Choice (C) means to compel by pressure or threat. Choice (D) means to shout.

11. **(C)** A *rift* is a break, especially in reference to relations. Choice (A) is a complaint. Choice (B) is an agreement or a pact. Choice (D) is a competition or a contest.

12. **(D)** A *tirade* is a long, vehement speech. Choice (A) is a result or a consequence. Choice (B) is a disagreement. Choice (C) is a penalty, especially in reference to a crime or misbehavior.

13. **(A)** A *canyon* is a gorge. Choice (B) is a pasture or a grassland. Choice (C) is a hill with a flat top. Choice (D) is a barren, arid expanse.

14. **(A)** *Dank* means damp or humid. Choices (B), (C), and (D) are not accepted meanings of the word *dank*.

15. **(C)** *Detection* is discovery. Choice (A) is an accumulation. Choice (B) is a duplication or a copy. Choice (D) is a deliberately false statement.

16. **(C)** *Placid* means calm. Choice (A) means warm. Choice (B) means able to be seen through. Choice (D) means shifting.

17. **(D)** To *shun* means to ignore. Choice (A) means to hate. Choice (B) means to injure. Choice (C) means to make ashamed or to dishonor.

18. **(C)** *Brusque* means abrupt. Choice (A) means comical or funny. Choice (B) means unusual. Choice (D) means without contradiction.

19. **(A)** To *plagiarize* means to use as one's own the written work of another. Choice (B) means to distribute. Choice (C) means to steal. Choice (D) means to disfigure.

20. **(B)** To *detach* means to separate. Choices (A), (C), and (D) are not accepted meanings of the word *detach*.

21. **(C)** To *chide* means to tease. Choice (A) means to fascinate. Choice (B) means to follow, usually in reference to high speeds. Choice (D) means to deceive.

22. **(B)** An *increment* is a regular increase, usually in reference to money. Choice (A) is a change. Choice (C) is a general tendency. Choice (D) is a formal request.

23. **(B)** A *slot* is an opening, usually narrow. Choices (A), (C), and (D) are not accepted meanings of the word *slot*.

24. **(A)** *Randomly* means by chance. Choice (B) means by machine. Choice (C) means every year. Choice (D) means as usual.

25. **(A)** To *retrieve* means to recover. Choice (B) means to use something in place of another or to replace. Choice (C) means to hide. Choice (D) means to refuse to notice or to disregard.

26. **(B)** *Wholesome* means healthful. Choice (A) means handy. Choice (C) means prudent or not expensive. Choice (D) means safe.

27. **(D)** To *abdicate* means to give up, in reference to a high office. Choices (A) and (C) mean to use for selfish advantage or profit. Choice (B) means to disregard.

28. **(D)** *Illicit* means unlawful. Choice (A) means more than needed. Choice (B) means ordered, especially in reference to a doctor's order for medication. Choice (C) means lately.

29. **(D)** *Condolences* are expressions of sympathy. Choice (A) is a social association. Choice (B) is a request for someone's participation or presence. Choice (C) is the acknowledgment of someone's achievement or good fortune.

30. **(A)** *Proverbs* are maxims. Choice (B) is a verse. Choice (C) is a sketch. Choice (D) is a written composition, usually including the opinion of the author.

Exercise Five: Vocabulary Review (Two- and Three-Word Verbs)

1. **(D)** Choice (C) means to accompany to the door. Choices (A) and (B) are not two-word verbs.

2. **(B)** Choice (C) means to bring a car to the side of the road. Choices (A) and (D) are not two-word verbs.

3. **(A)** Choice (B) means to regain consciousness or to conclude. Choice (C) means to attack. Choice (D) is not a two-word verb.

4. **(A)** Choice (B) means to telephone. Choices (C) and (D) are not two-word verbs.

5. **(D)** Choice (C) means to assist to one's feet. Choices (A) and (B) are not two-word verbs.

6. **(A)** Choice (B) means to develop. Choices (C) and (D) are not two-word verbs.

7. **(C)** Choice (A) means to refuse. Choice (B) means to deliver or to go to bed. Choice (D) means to ask for help.

8. **(C)** Choices (A), (B), and (D) are not three-word verbs.

9. **(D)** Choices (A), (B), and (C) are not two-word verbs.

10. **(A)** Choice (B) means to be valuable. Choices (C) and (D) are not two-word verbs.

11. **(C)** Choice (A) means to reverse direction or to bend. Choice (B) means to change position. Choice (D) means to disconnect.

12. **(C)** Choice (A) means to ask for assistance. Choice (B) means to hit with a car. Choice (D) means to drive over.

13. **(A)** Choice (B) means to prevent from entering. Choice (C) means to refrain from approaching. Choice (D) means to withhold.

14. **(C)** Choice (B) means to diminish gradually. Choice (D) means to break down resistance. Choice (A) is not a two-word verb.

15. **(C)** Choice (D) means to decrease production. Choices (A) and (B) are not two-word verbs.

16. **(B)** Choices (A), (C), and (D) are not two-word verbs.

17. **(B)** Choice (A) means to continue. Choices (C) and (D) are not two-word verbs.

18. **(D)** Choices (A), (B), and (C) are not three-word verbs.

19. **(A)** Choices (B), (C), and (D) are not three-word verbs.

20. **(A)** Choice (B) means to organize. Choice (C) means to annoy. Choice (D) means to return something to its place.

21. **(A)** Choices (B), (C), and (D) are not three-word verbs.

22. **(B)** Choices (A), (C), and (D) are not three-word verbs.

23. **(D)** Choices (A), (B), and (C) are not two-word verbs.

24. **(C)** Choices (A), (B), and (D) are not two-word verbs.

25. **(B)** Choice (A) means to submit. Choice (C) means to give. Choice (D) means to return.

26. **(D)** Choice (A) means to succeed. Choice (B) means to disclose. Choice (C) means to attack.

27. **(B)** Choices (A), (C), and (D) are not three-word verbs.

28. **(C)** Choice (A) means to write. Choice (B) means to begin. Choice (D) means to postpone or to save.

29. **(D)** Choices (A), (B), and (C) are not two-word verbs.

30. **(C)** Choice (A) means to recover from an illness. Choice (B) means to discontinue a relationship. Choice (D) means to vomit.

Exercise Six: Practice In Reading Indexes And Charts

Passage One

1. **(D)** *Comics* are cartoons. Choices (A), (B), and (C) are not accepted meanings of the word *comics.*

2. **(B)** The Business and Finance section provides a list of the current trading prices of stocks and bonds. It is not customary to find this kind of information in the sections referred to by page number in Choices (A), (C), or (D).

3. **(C)** Obituaries are death notices. It is not customary to find this kind of information in the sections referred to in Choice (A), (B), or (D). Choice (A) contains business news, including the current trading prices of stocks and bonds. Choice (B) contains cartoons and jokes. Choice (D) contains essays and opinions.

4. **(A)** From the references to *classified, editorials,* and *obituaries,* as well as *news,* it must be concluded that the passage is an index for a newspaper. It is not as probable that a similar index would be found in any of the publications referred to in Choice (B), (C), or (D).

Passage Two

1. **(A)** *Rates* are prices. Choices (B), (C), and (D) are not accepted meanings of the word *rates.*

2. **(B)** Choice (B) refers to how much it costs to mail per half-ounce through two ounces for twelve locations, including the Philippines. Choice (A) refers to how much it costs to mail each additional half-ounce in excess of two ounces to the Philippines, not how much it costs to mail a half-ounce letter. Choice (C) refers to how much it costs to mail each additional half-ounce in excess of two ounces to other countries not specifically listed in the chart. Choice (D) refers to how much it costs to mail each half-ounce through two ounces to other countries not specifically listed.

3. **(D)** Since India is not specifically listed in the chart, it would cost $0.31 per half-ounce through two ounces, or $1.24 for the first two ounces, plus $0.26 per half-ounce for each additional ounce, or $2.08 for four additional ounces, for a total of $3.32. Choice (B) refers to the cost of the first two ounces. Choices (A) and (C) cannot be calculated from the chart.

4. **(D)** The rates are listed without the kind of further comment necessary for the purposes referred to in Choices (A), (B), and (C).

Passage Three

1. **(C)** A *glossary* is a dictionary. Choices (A), (B), and (D) are not accepted meanings of the word *glossary*.

2. **(D)** Since we know that Unit Four is about "Writing Reports and Research Papers," we must conclude that the lesson on "Notecards and Outlines" in Unit Four would help the reader learn about outlining research papers. Choice (A) refers to the first page for Unit Two. Choice (B) refers to the page for outlining in Unit Two, "Reading Textbooks," not to the page for outlining in Unit Four, "Writing Reports and Research Papers." Choice (C) refers to the first page for Unit Four, not to the page about outlining.

3. **(A)** Since there are chapters on *lecture notes, reading textbooks, using a dictionary, writing reports and research papers,* and *taking examinations,* we must conclude that the table of contents would be found in a textbook on study skills. Choices (B), (C), and (D) refer to individual chapters, not to the complete book.

4. **(B)** A table of contents is a list of titles of chapters (units) and page numbers. Choice (A) is a list of references to other books and articles used in research. Choice (C) is the first page of the book containing the titles, name of the author, the publisher, and date of publication. Choice (D) is a narrative that summarizes the purpose of the work to follow.

Passage Four

1. **(C)** *Due* means owed. Choices (A), (B), and (D) are not accepted meanings of the word *due.*

2. **(B)** The balance due on May 10 appears in the far right column. Choice (A) refers to the balance due on May 11, not on May 10. Choice (C) refers to the balance due on May 9. Choice (B) refers to the balance due on May 7.

3. **(B)** The charges for May 8 include $30.00 for room, $1.50 for tax, and $0.35 for telephone, or a total of $37.63. Choice (A) refers to the charges for May 10. Choice (C) refers to a number similar to but not the same as the balance due on May 7. Choice (D) refers to the balance due, not the charges, on May 8.

4. **(B)** From the reference to *charges, balance due,* and *room 1006,* it must be concluded that this passage is a hotel bill. Although it would be possible to find dates and columns of numbers in a budget, a train ticket, or a telephone bill, it is not customary to find the combination of references to *charges, balance due,* and *room 1006* on any of the lists referred to in Choices (A), (C), and (D).

Passage Five

1. **(C)** *Features* are special articles. Choices (A), (B), and (D) are not accepted meanings of the word *features.*

2. **(D)** The Sports section provides information and scores for ball games. It is not customary to find this kind of information in the sections referred to by page number in Choices (A), (B), and (C).

3. **(C)** "…low in the mid-60s." Choice (A) refers to a temperature of 60, not the mid-60s. Choice (B) refers to a temperature in the low, not the mid-60s. Choice (D) refers to a temperature in the high, not the mid-60s.

4. **(D)** Choices (A), (B), and (C) are secondary sections that are included in a news magazine.

Exercise Seven: Practice in Reading Instructions

Passage One

1. **(C)** *Infants* are babies. Choices (A), (B), and (D) are not accepted meanings of the word *infants.*

2. **(C)** "…the weaker solutions are fully satisfactory and are preferred…" Choice (A) contradicts the fact that weaker solutions are fully satisfactory. Choice (B) contradicts the fact that ½ percent is used for adults. Choice (D) contradicts the fact that weaker solutions are both satisfactory and preferred.

3. **(A)** From the references to a *solution, relief of nasal congestion, colds* and *hay fever,* it must be concluded that this passage would be found on a bottle of medicine. Choices (B), (C), and (D) are improbable because it is not customary to find specific medical instructions in any of the places listed.

4. **(A)** Choice (C) is secondary information included in the recommendation for dosage. Choices (B) and (D) are not mentioned and may not be concluded from information in the passage.

Passage Two

1. **(A)** *Flammable* means easily burned. Choices (B), (C), and (D) are not accepted meanings of the word *flammable.*

2. **(C)** "Since the propellant is lighter, the weight of the can has been reduced…" Choice (B) contradicts the fact that the weight of the can has been reduced. Choice (D) contradicts the fact that the new can saves you money. Choice (A) is not mentioned and may not be concluded from information in the passage.

3. **(B)** From the references to *hold…without leaving hair stiff or sticky,* it must be concluded that Cleanspray is a hair spray. Choice (A) contradicts the fact that Cleanspray lasts all day. Choices (C) and (D) contradict the fact that you use Cleanspray on hair.

4. **(C)** Each paragraph contains one main point. One of the points, suggestions for using the product, is correct, but the second and third points are not mentioned and may not be concluded from information in the passage. Choices (B) and (D) are true but not complete.

Passage Three

1. **(A)** *Tablets* are pills. Choices (B), (C), and (D) are not accepted meanings of the word *tablets*.

2. **(A)** "KEEP TIGHTLY CLOSED. AVOID EXPOSURE TO LIGHT." Choice (B) contradicts the fact that the directions warn to avoid exposure to light. Choice (C) refers to the warning to consult a physician for children under twelve, not for all people. Choice (D) contradicts the fact that the adult dose is two or three tablets four times daily.

3. **(D)** "...3 tablets four times daily" would be equal to three times four, or twelve tablets every twenty-four hours. The number in Choice (A) refers to the dose per time, not to the total dose for four times daily. The number in Choice (B) refers to the number per day, not to the number of tablets. The number in Choice (C) refers to the minimum, not the maximum dosage.

4. **(B)** "FOR PAIN." The ailments in Choices (A), (C), and (D) are not examples of pain.

Passage Four

1. **(C)** To *contaminate* means to pollute. Choices (A), (B), and (D) are not accepted meanings of the word *contaminate*.

2. **(C)** "Fill contact case one-half full of Comfortact." Choice (A) refers to the number of drops to apply before inserting contact lenses in the eye, not in the case. Choice (B) refers to the number of drops to cover all surfaces. Choice (D) contradicts the fact that one should fill the case one-half full.

3. **(D)** "Wash hands thoroughly before touching lenses. Do not let the tip of the bottle come into contact with any surface which may contaminate the solution." Choice (A) contradicts the fact that one should add a few more drops to cover all surfaces. Choice (B) contradicts the fact that one should wash thoroughly before touching lenses. Choice (C) contradicts the fact that one should not use with soft contact lenses.

4. **(D)** "Comfortact is an all-purpose solution for the care of hard contact lenses. Wets, soaks and cleans." Choices (A) and (C) are true but not complete. The term "soft" in Choice (B) refers to lenses, not to the Comfortact solution.

Passage Five

1. **(A)** A *dosage* is a recommended amount. Choices (B), (C), and (D) are not accepted meanings of the word *dosage*.

2. **(A)** "Consult a physician for use by children under 6..." The number in Choice (B) refers to the number of days one can use the medication before consulting a physician. Choice (C) contradicts the fact that one should consult a physician for instructions for use by children. Choice (D) contradicts the fact that the medication is well-suited for those who should not take aspirin or aspirin-containing products, from which it may be concluded that the medication does not contain aspirin.

3. **(A)** "...2 tablets 4 times daily" would be equal to two times four, or eight tablets per day. Choice (B) refers to the minimum, not the maximum dosage. The number in Choice (B) refers to the number of tablets to be taken each time, not to the total number taken four times per day. Choice (C) is not mentioned and may not be concluded from information in the passage.

4. **(B)** "Especially well-suited for those who should not take aspirin or aspirin-containing products." Choice (A) contradicts the fact that the medication is for those who should not take aspirin. Choice (C) contradicts the fact that the medication is for those who should not take aspirin-containing products. Choice (D) contradicts the fact that the product is well-suited for some people.

Exercise Eight: Practice In Reading Announcements And Advertisements

Passage One

1. **(A)** *Convenient* means close to. Choices (B), (C), and (D) are not accepted meanings of the word *convenient.*

2. **(C)** "Rentals…include heat, air…" Choice (A) contradicts the fact that a 1 year lease is required. Choice (D) contradicts the fact that 1 and 2 bedroom apartments are available. Choice (C) is not mentioned and may not be concluded from information in the passage, although it is not likely that the route would be mentioned in the ad if it were not in service.

3. **(B)** "One pre-school-aged child….Absolutely no pets." Choice (A) contradicts the requirement that the child be pre-school-aged. Choice (C) contradicts the requirement that no pets be allowed. Choice (D) contradicts the requirement that only one child be allowed.

4. **(C)** Choices (A), (B), and (D) are true but are not a complete summary.

Passage Two

1. **(C)** *Accommodations* means rooms. Choices (A), (B), and (D) are not accepted meanings of the word *accommodations.*

2. **(C)** "Visit Nashville, Tennessee, the capital of country music…" Choice (B) is true but not the reason that Nashville is an interesting city. Choices (A) and (D) are not mentioned and may not be concluded from information in the passage. It is the Opry, not the city, that is described as old or "Ole."

3. **(B)** "14-day advanced booking required." Choice (A) refers to a date 1 month, not 14 days, in advance. Choice (C) refers to a date 13, not 14 days, in advance. Choice (D) refers to a date 1 day, not 14 days, in advance.

4. **(C)** Choice (A) refers to the free brochures from Travel and Tours. Choice (D) refers to the location of the company Travel and Tours, not to the location of the bus tour. Choice (D) refers to the name of the travel company.

Passage Three

1. **(B)** *Weekdays* are Monday through Friday. Choices (A), (C), and (D) are not accepted meanings of the word *weekdays*.

2. **(B)** "White w/light blue interior." Choice (A) refers to the color of the interior, not to the color of the car. Choice (D) refers to the name of the owner, Mr. Black. Choice (C) is not mentioned and may not be concluded from information in the passage.

3. **(B)** "$5000 or best offer." Choice (A) contradicts the fact that he will sell to the best offer. Choice (C) contradicts the fact that Mr. Black himself is the original owner. Choice (D) contradicts the fact that $5000 has been set as the asking price.

4. **(A)** A classified ad is an advertisement used to rent, sell, or locate goods or sell services. Choice (B) is an article about a news event. Choice (C) is a statement of opinion by the publisher. Choice (D) is an article on a special topic.

Passage Four

1. **(C)** *Specifications* are requirements. Choices (A), (B), and (D) are not accepted meanings of the word *specifications*.

2. **(A)** "8:00 A.M.–10:00 P.M. Monday–Friday." The number in Choice (B) refers to the time that the service opens in the morning not to the time that it closes in the evening. Choice (C) refers to the time that the service closes on Saturday, not on Wednesday. Choice (D) refers to the time that the service closes on Sunday.

3. **(C)** "$1.25 per page on cotton bond paper." Fifteen times $1.25 equals $18.75. Choice (A) refers to the price of fifteen pages on regular stock, not on cotton bond. Choices (B) and (D) are not mentioned and may not be calculated from information in the passage.

4. **(C)** The passage is an advertisement for a typing service with rates and hours listed. Choices (A) and (B) are true, but they are not the purpose of the announcement. Choice (D) refers to the fact that the service has a new location, but a celebration was not mentioned and may not be concluded from information in the passage.

Passage Five

1. **(B)** A *deadline* is the last day for doing something. Choices (A), (C), and (D) are not accepted meanings of the word *deadline.*

2. **(D)** "...a qualified individual with a degree in industrial engineering and a minimum of five years experience in design of mechanical components." Choice (A) contradicts the fact that the five years experience is in addition to, not instead of a degree in industrial engineering, and contradicts the fact that the experience should be in design of mechanical components, not in nuclear power. Choice (B) is correct, but incomplete. Five years experience is also required. Choice (C) refers to the place where the candidate will be hired, not to the place where he or she has gained experience.

3. **(B)** "Interested candidates should forward resume...to...Box A 304 *Daily News.*" Choice (A) refers to the newspaper where the ad was published, not to the place where the candidate would be employed. Choice (C) refers to the insurance benefits that the candidate would receive, not to the place where the candidate would be employed. Choice (D) contradicts the fact that it is a leading multinational industrial corporation that is seeking a qualified individual.

4. **(C)** An advertisement of a job opportunity is also called a *help wanted* ad. Choice (A) refers to an ad listing items for sale, not to an ad listing a job opportunity. Choice (B) refers to an ad listing items that have been lost or found. Choice (D) refers to an ad listing personal messages.

Exercise Nine: Practice In Reading Academic Information

Passage One

1. **(C)** *Prerequisites* are requirements that must be completed before doing something. Choices (A), (B), and (D) are not accepted meanings of the word *prerequisites.*

2. **(C)** "Computer programming in languages other than Fortran. Major emphasis will be given to PL-1 and Cobol." Choice (A) contradicts the fact that major emphasis will be given to PL-1. Choice (B) contradicts the fact that major emphasis will be given to Cobol. Choice (D) does not refer to the name of a computer language but to an adjective that means *the most.*

3. **(B)** "Fall. Spring." Choices (A), (C), and (D) contradict the fact that the course will be offered both Fall and Spring, or twice every year.

4. **(A)** This is the customary format for a course description in a college catalogue. It is not customary for this format to be used for the purposes in Choices (B), (C), and (D).

Passage Two

1. **(B)** To *drop* means to withdraw from. Choices (A), (C), and (D) are not accepted meanings of the word *drop.*

2. **(C)** "To drop or add a course after the second day of classes…take it [a petition] to the instructor of the course…" Choice (A) refers to the person who must give permission to add a course after the first fifteen days of each quarter. Choice (B) refers to the person who must give permission to add a course on the day of open registration. Choice (D) refers to the person who must be paid, not to the person who must give permission to add a course.

3. **(C)** "…take it [the drop-add petition]…to your academic advisor…" Since students must take petitions to their academic advisors, it must be concluded that they are all assigned one. Choice (A) contradicts the fact that the dean of the college may give permission after the first fifteen days. Choice (B) contradicts the fact that no drops or adds will be permitted after the first fifteen days of each quarter, not semester. Choice (D) contradicts the fact that students must take their petitions from the college office to the registration area in the Student Union.

4. **(D)** "To drop a course on the day of open registration.…To add a course.…To drop or add a course after the second day of classes…" Choice (A) refers to the procedure before dropping and adding courses. Choice (B) refers to one kind of change on a class schedule, not to both dropping and adding courses. Choice (C) is not mentioned and may not be concluded from information in the passage.

Passage Three

1. **(D)** A *specialization* is a major field of study. Choices (A), (B), and (C) are not accepted meanings of the word *specialization.*

2. **(B)** "Candidates…must earn a minimum grade of C or better in each course in the area of specialization." Choices (A), (C), and (D) are grades below a C.

3. **(D)** "Candidates for the bachelor of business administration degree must complete 186 quarter hours of course work…" Since 186 hours is required to graduate, it must be concluded that a student who had completed 170 hours would be in his or her last year, that is, the senior year. Choices (A), (B), and (C) are the first, second, and third years, respectively.

4. **(A)** Choices (B) and (C) are true but are not a complete summary. Choice (D) refers to the fact that business majors must earn a grade of C or better in business courses in their specialization, not in all courses. The average must be C in all courses.

Passage Four

1. **(C)** An *elective* is an alternative among courses. Choices (A), (B), and (D) are not accepted meanings of the word *elective.*

2. **(C)** "110 Graphics I 3 hours." Choice (A) refers to the course number for Chemistry I, Physics I, and Economics I, not for Graphics I. Choice (B) refers to the course number for Calculus I and Chemistry II. Choice (D) refers to the course number for Introduction to Computer Programming.

3. **(D)** Chemistry I, II, and III at 3 hours each or 9 hours, plus Chemistry Laboratory 121 and 122 at 1 hour each or 2 hours, equals 11 total hours. Choice (A) refers to the number of hours for laboratory sessions only, not for classes and laboratory sessions. Choice (B) refers to the number of hours for each class. Choice (C) refers to the total number of hours for the three chemistry classes without the laboratory sessions.

4. **(C)** "CHEMICAL ENGINEERING." Choice (A) contradicts the fact that no grades appear on the report. Choice (B) contradicts the fact that the plan is titled Chemical Engineering. Choice (D) refers to the subtitle, Freshman Year, not to the more important title above it, Chemical Engineering.

Passage Five

1. **(A)** *Unique* means unusual. Choices (B), (C), and (D) are not accepted meanings of the word *unique*.

2. **(D)** "If you are not sure about [the accreditation] of a certain school, don't hesitate to check its reputation with an education officer at the nearest U.S. Embassy." Choice (B) contradicts the fact that the accreditation system is not administered by the government. Choice (C) contradicts the fact that students should make certain that the institution is accredited before registering. Choice (A) is not mentioned and may not be concluded from information in the passage.

3. **(B)** "...a student should make certain that the institution is accredited in order to assure that the school has a recognized standard of...financial support." Choice (A) contradicts the fact that other governments or future employers may not recognize a degree earned from a school that has not received accreditation. Choice (C) contradicts the fact that the government does not administer the accreditation system. Choice (D) contradicts the fact that students should make certain that a school is accredited before registering.

4. **(B)** "Accreditation is a system for setting national standards of quality in education." Choices (A), (C), and (D) are secondary ideas that are used to develop the main idea, "accreditation."

Exercise Ten: Practice In Reading Textbooks

Passage One

1. **(B)** *Briefly* means for a short time. Choices (A), (C), and (D) are not accepted meanings of the word *briefly.*

2. **(C)** "The play [*Beyond the Horizon*] won the Pulitzer Prize for the best play of the year. O'Neill was to be awarded the prize again in 1922, 1928, and 1957." Choice (A) refers to the number of times that O'Neill won the Nobel, not the Pulitzer Prize. Choice (B) refers to the number of times that O'Neill won the Pulitzer Prize in addition to the first time. Choice (D) refers to the total number of times that O'Neill was awarded the Pulitzer and Nobel Prizes.

3. **(C)** "…several themes emerge, including the ambivalence of family relationships, the struggle between the sexes, the conflict between spiritual and material desires, and the vision of modern man as a victim." Choice (A) contradicts the fact that the themes mentioned were controversial. Choice (B) contradicts the fact that most of the characters were portraits of himself and his family. Choice (D) contradicts the fact that O'Neill's plays won so many awards.

4. **(C)** "…his work chronicled his life." Choice (A) contradicts the fact that the first eight lines of the passage describe his life before he began writing. Choice (B) contradicts the fact that the last eighteen lines of the passage describe his work. Choice (D) refers to the fact that his characters were portraits of himself and his family, not to the theme of the passage.

Passage Two

1. **(C)** *Prominent* means important. Choices (A), (B), and (D) are not accepted meanings of the word *prominent.*

2. **(A)** "…as long as the top management maintains the confidence of the board of directors, the directors will not actively intervene to dictate specific policies." Choice (C) contradicts the fact that the directors will not actively intervene. Choice (D) refers to the membership of the board of directors, not to those who formulate policy. Choice (B) is not mentioned and may not be concluded from information in the passage.

3. **(C)** "…customarily some directors are prominent men and women.…Others are usually chosen from among retired executives of the organization." Choice (A) contradicts the fact that some directors are chosen from retired executives of the organization [City Bank]. Choices (B) and (D) contradict the fact that some directors are prominent men and women.

4. **(A)** "Although the composition and role of the board of directors of a company will vary… a few generalizations may be made." Choice (B) refers to the fact that the board of directors and the board of trustees of a college follow the same administrative procedure, not to the main idea in the passage. Choice (C) refers to the fact that the procedure used by the board of directors is similar to the parliamentary system, not to the main idea. Choice (D) refers to the group who must maintain the confidence of the board of directors.

Passage Three

1. **(C)** *Compressed* means reduced. Choices (A), (B), and (D) are not accepted meanings of the word *compressed*.

2. **(C)** "Then, at a moment in time that astronomers refer to as T = O,....Matter formed into galaxies with stars and planets." Choices (A), (B), and (D) refer to an estimate of the time when matter and energy compressed into a ball prior to the explosion that formed the galaxies.

3. **(C)** "As the energy cooled, most of it became matter in the form of protons, neutrons, and electrons." Choice (A) contradicts the fact that energy changed into matter. Choice (B) contradicts the fact that matter is in the form of protons, neutrons, and electrons. Choice (D) contradicts the fact that as energy cooled and became matter, the particles continued to expand.

4. **(B)** Choice (A) contradicts the fact that the Big Bang Model is a popular theory explaining the evolution of the universe. Choices (C) and (D) are secondary ideas used to support the Big Bang theory.

Passage Four

1. **(C)** To *deprive* means to deny. Choices (A), (B), and (D) are not accepted meanings of the word *deprive*.

2. **(B)** "...the animal [rat] learned that it could get food by pressing the bar." Choice (A) refers to the rat's activity before obtaining food. Choice (D) refers to the rat's activity after obtaining food. Choice (C) is not mentioned and may not be concluded from information in the passage.

3. **(C)** "The food stimulus reinforced the bar pressing response." Choice (A) contradicts the fact that behavioral psychologists use many different kinds of equipment. Choice (B) contradicts the fact that behavioral psychologists use (present tense) many different kinds of equipment in operant conditioning experiments. Choice (D) refers to one specific experiment with a hungry rat, not to operant conditioning in general.

4. **(C)** "Although behavioral psychologists use many different kinds of equipment in operant conditioning experiments, one device that is frequently employed is the Skinner Box." Choices (A), (B), and (D) are secondary ideas used to support the main idea, "the Skinner Box."

Passage Five

1. **(A)** A *majority* is the largest number. Choices (B), (C), and (D) are not accepted meanings of the word *majority*.

2. **(C)** "By 1880, large numbers of central and southern Europeans began to find their way to America." Choice (A) refers to the year when most Americans came from England. Choice (B) refers to the year when many Irish, Dutch, German, Swedish, Scottish, and French settlers came to America. Choice (D) refers to the recent years when many Hungarians, Cubans, Lebanese, Syrians, and West Indians have come.

3. **(B)** The account is historical. There is no evidence of the attitudes referred to in Choices (A), (C), and (D).

4. **(A)** Choice (B) contradicts the fact that immigration in the twentieth century is also mentioned. Choice (C) contradicts the fact that Asian, African, and Latin American immigration is also mentioned. Choice (D) refers to the many contributions by immigrants to urban and agricultural development cited to support the main idea, "immigration."

Exercise Eleven: Practice In Reading General Interest Passages

Passage One

1. **(A)** *Regulations* are laws. Choices (B), (C), and (D) are not accepted meanings of the word *regulations.*

2. **(C)** "A change in the federal regulations now requires that every international student admitted to the United States on an F-1 visa be assigned a social security number." Choice (A) contradicts the fact that the number may not be used for off-campus employment purposes. Choice (B) contradicts the fact that if they do not have them [social security numbers] they are asked to depart the country. Choice (D) contradicts the fact that they are granted F-1 visas before they are assigned the social security numbers.

3. **(B)** "Students who wish to work on campus may do so without notifying INS." Choices (A) and (C) contradict the fact that students may not work off campus. Choice (C) contradicts the fact that students may work on campus.

4. **(B)** A notice provides information without subjective commentary. Choice (A) refers to the notice of an occasion with a time, date, and place mentioned. Choice (C) refers to a series of questions. Choice (D) refers to a form with personal and professional information on it.

Passage Two

1. **(C)** *Premises* are property. Choices (A), (B), and (D) are not accepted meanings of the word *premises.*

2. **(C)** "The security deposit shall be refunded...if notice in writing of termination has been given thirty (30) days in advance..." The number in Choice (A) refers to the number of days in advance that written termination, not the keys, must be given. Choice (B) contradicts the fact that the deposit shall be refunded if the premises are undamaged. Choice (D) is not mentioned and may not be concluded from information in the passage.

3. **(A)** "...notice in writing of termination...[must be] given thirty (30) days in advance..." Choice (B) refers to a date two weeks, not thirty days in advance of the move. Choice (C) refers to a date thirty days after, not in advance, of the move. Choice (D) refers to the date of the move.

4. **(A)** A rental agreement, also called a lease, is a legal document. "Your signature on this legal document indicates that you have read and understood its contents..." Choices (B), (C), and (D) are included in sections of the rental agreement.

Passage Three

1. **(D)** A *warranty* is a guarantee. Choices (A), (B), and (C) are not accepted meanings of the word *warranty*.

2. **(C)** "Deliver the product to any one of the authorized service facilities…" Choice (B) refers to the place where questions should be addressed, not to the place where products are repaired or replaced. Choice (D) refers to the company that guarantees the product. Choice (A) is not mentioned and may not be concluded from information in the passage.

3. **(B)** "General Appliance Company guarantees the product to be free from manufacturing defects for one year…provided that damage…has not resulted from accident or misuse." Choice (A) contradicts the fact that the guarantee is for one year (twelve months), not fourteen months. Choice (C) contradicts the fact that the guarantee does not apply to damage from accident. Choice (D) refers to a situation in which no replacement would be necessary.

4. **(D)** "General Appliance Company guarantees the product to be free of manufacturing defects for one year after the original date of purchase." Choice (A) would seem to be true but does not summarize the information in the passage. Choice (B) contradicts the fact that General Appliance will repair or replace the product free of charge, provided that damage has not resulted from accident. Choice (C) is not mentioned and may not be concluded from information in the passage.

Passage Four

1. **(B)** *Samples* are examples. Choices (A), (C), and (D) are not accepted meanings of the word *samples*.

2. **(B)** "On the date that your telephone is to be installed, a responsible person, such as an apartment manager, must be at home to unlock the door for the serviceman." Choice (A) refers to the person in the telephone store who helps customers select a telephone, not to the person who installs it. Choice (C) refers to the person who may unlock an apartment for the serviceman. Choice (D) refers to the person whose name must be given to the sales representative as a reference.

3. **(A)** "A sales representative will be glad to show you samples of the designs and colors [of telephones] available." Choice (B) contradicts the fact that a responsible person, such as an apartment manager, can unlock the door. Choice (C) contradicts the fact that students on scholarship should provide their sponsor's name as a reference. Choice (D) contradicts the fact that the deposit may be paid by Master Charge or Visa.

4. **(C)** The passage provides information without subjective commentary. Choices (A), (B), and (D) would provide more subjective commentary and opinion.

Passage Five

1. **(C)** A *slot* is an opening. Choices (A), (B), and (D) are not accepted meanings of the word *slot*.

2. **(B)** "Remove your card from the slot. The drawer will open with receipt and your cash withdrawal in fifty-dollar packets." Choice (A) refers to what happens after you enter the number. Choice (D) refers to what happens after you enter the amount of withdrawal. Choice (C) is not mentioned and may not be concluded from information in the passage.

3. **(C)** "Enter the amount of withdrawal, either fifty or one hundred dollars....All customers are limited to two withdrawals in one twenty-four hour period." Choice (A) contradicts the fact that the withdrawals are in fifty-dollar packets. Choice (B) contradicts the fact that the identification numbers are six-, not five-digit numbers. Choice (D) contradicts the fact that withdrawals can be made from your City Bank checking or savings accounts.

4. **(B)** "Please use these procedures in order to make a machine withdrawal..." Choice (A) contradicts the fact that the withdrawal must be made from an existing account. Choice (C) contradicts the fact that it is necessary to have a card in order to follow the procedure. Choice (D) contradicts the fact that the procedure is for withdrawals only, not for deposits and withdrawals.

Exercise Twelve: Practice In Reading Sentences

Passage One

1. **(A)** To *afford* means to be able to buy. Choices (B), (C), and (D) are not accepted meanings of the word *afford*.

2. **(B)** "...food production gains...have been consumed by rapid population growth..." Choice (A) contradicts the fact that there have been production gains. Choice (C) contradicts the fact that subsistence food is available but millions of people cannot afford it. Choice (D) is not mentioned and may not be concluded from information in the sentence.

3. **(A)** "...efficient methods of distribution have not been developed to transport food..." Choice (B) contradicts the fact that there have been production gains. Choice (D) contradicts the fact that areas of greatest need are mentioned in the sentence. Choice (C) is not mentioned and may not be concluded from information in the sentence.

4. **(A)** "The most serious problems surrounding the world hunger situation are..." Choices (B), (C), and (D) are secondary ideas used to develop the main idea, "the world hunger situation."

Passage Two

1. **(C)** To *generate* means to produce. Choices (A), (B), and (D) are not accepted meanings of the word *generate*.

2. **(A)** "...by the year 2000, 1 percent of the nation's electricity will be generated from solar cells..." The number in Choice (B) refers to the year, not to solar cells. The number in Choice (D) refers to the cost in dollars, not to solar cells. The number in Choice (C) is not mentioned and may not be concluded from information in the sentence.

3. **(A)** Since the prediction of 1 percent is for the future, it may be concluded that less than 1 percent is available now. Choice (B) contradicts the fact that less than 1 percent is available now. Choice (C) contradicts the fact that the percentage projected for the future is only 1 percent. Choice (D) contradicts the fact that the cost of one billion dollars a year is enormous.

4. **(A)** "According to the Department of Energy..." Choice (C) contradicts the fact that the statement is made by the Department of Energy, not by producers of solar energy. Choice (D) contradicts the fact that the statement is made by the Department of Energy, not by the president's budget committee. Choice (B) contradicts the fact that the passage provides information without subjective commentary or opinion.

Passage Three

1. **(A)** To *claim* means to terminate. Choices (B), (C), and (D) are not accepted meanings of the word *claim.*

2. **(A)** "The second leading cause of death in this country, cancer..." Since cancer is the second leading cause, it must be concluded that there is one condition that ranks above it. Choice (B) refers to the rank of cancer, not the rank above cancer. Choices (C) and (D) are not mentioned and may not be concluded from information in the passage.

3. **(D)** "...over 385,000 Americans [die of cancer] every year." Since 385,000 die every year, 385,000 times 5 or 1,925,000 die every five years. Choice (A) refers to the number who die in one year, not in five years. Choices (B) and (C) are not mentioned and may not be concluded from information in the passage.

4. **(C)** "The second leading cause of death in the country, cancer..." Choices (A) and (B) are secondary ideas that develop the main idea, that cancer is "one of the leading causes of death in the United States." Choice (D) is not mentioned and may not be concluded from information in the sentence.

Passage Four

1. **(B)** *Previous* means past. Choices (A), (C), and (D) are not accepted meanings of the word *previous.*

2. **(C)** "...we should try to attain as great a degree of objectivity as possible..." Choices (A) and (D) contradict the idea of objectivity. Choice (B) also contradicts the idea of objectivity. To *object* means to *disapprove. Objectivity* is *without subjective approval or disapproval.*

3. **(B)** Anthropology is the study of humans. It is usually divided into cultural and physical anthropology. It is not customary to find this kind of information in the books referred to in Choices (A), (C), and (D).

4. **(C)** "The principal of cultural relativism states that..." Choice (A) refers to the fact that patterns of behavior should be understood in terms of the new culture. Choice (B) refers to the fact that new cultures should not be judged on the basis of previous cultural experience. Choice (D) refers to the fact that students of culture should try to attain as great a degree of objectivity as possible. Choices (A), (B), and (D) are secondary ideas that develop the main idea of "cultural relativism."

Passage Five

1. **(B)** To *disrupt* means to disturb. Choices (A), (C), and (D) are not accepted meanings of the word *disrupt*.

2. **(D)** "…the International Year of the Child…[was] part of a continuing effort…to help children…" Choice (A) contradicts the fact that it is a continuing effort. Choice (B) refers to UNESCO, which was formed to help children whose lives had been disrupted by war. Choice (C) contradicts the fact that UNESCO was established thirty years before the International Year of the Child.

3. **(D)** "…UNESCO was formed over thirty years ago…" The dates in Choices (A), (B), and (C) are all less than thirty years ago.

4. **(B)** "UNESCO's activities in connection with the International Year of the Child in 1979 were part of a continuing effort…to help children…" Choice (A) is true but is not a summary of the sentence. Choice (C) is true but is not mentioned as part of the information in the sentence. Choice (D) is not mentioned and may not be concluded from information in the sentence.

Exercise Thirteen: Practice In Reading Restatements

Passives

1. **(D)** Choice (D) is a restatement of the given sentence. Choices (A) and (B) are not the same because in the original sentence the Congress, not the president, is slow. Choice (C) is not the same because in the original sentence the president, not the Congress, was bothered.

2. **(C)** Choice (C) is a restatement of the given sentence. Choice (A) is not the same because in the original sentence they, not the manager, leave. Choice (B) is not the same because in the original sentence they, not the manager, are forced. Choice (D) is not the same because in the original sentence they, not the manager and they, are forced.

3. **(C)** Choice (C) is a restatement of the given sentence. Choice (A) is not the same because in the original sentence Hercules, not Zeus, initiated the games. Choice (B) is not the same because in the original sentence Hercules, not Hercules and Zeus, initiated the games. Choice (D) is not the same because in the original sentence Zeus's son, not Hercules's son, initiated the games.

4. **(C)** Choice (C) is a restatement of the given sentence. Choice (A) is not the same because in the original sentence the bees will reach the borders of the United States, not Africa. Choices (B) and (D) are not the same because in the original sentence the bees will reach the United States ten years from now, not ten years ago.

5. **(D)** Choice (D) is a restatement of the given sentence. Choice (A) is not the same because in the original sentence first-born or only children are expected, not expect, to be successful. Choices (B) and (C) are not the same because in the original sentence the word *studies* refers to research, not school.

Negatives

1. **(D)** Choice (D) is a restatement of the given sentence. *No less an authority* means *a great authority.* Choice (A) is not the same because in the original sentence Kennedy, not someone else, is the authority. Choice (B) is not the same because in the original sentence Kennedy is a recognized authority, not an authority on the University of Virginia. Choice (C) is not the same because in the original sentence Kennedy is an authority.

2. **(B)** Choice (B) is a restatement of the given sentence. *Not illegal* means *legal.* Choice (A) is not the same because in the original sentence American football is similar to European soccer in many respects. Choice (C) is not the same because in the original sentence it is legal to catch the ball and run with it in the American, not European, version of the game. Choice (D) is not the same because in the original sentence it is legal to catch the ball and run with it in American football, not European soccer.

3. **(D)** Choice (D) is a restatement of the given sentence. *Not one* means *none.* Choices (A) and (B) are not the same because in the original sentence not one of the fragments fell. Choice (C) is not the same because in the original sentence Sky Lab did not fall over a densely populated area.

4. **(A)** Choice (A) is a restatement of the given sentence. *Unlikely…without* means *probably…with.* Choices (B) and (C) are not the same because in the original sentence the price, not the level of service, will probably increase. Choice (D) is not the same because in the original sentence the level of service, not the bus system, may not continue.

5. **(B)** Choice (B) is a restatement of the given sentence. *Never…more* means *the most.* Choice (A) is not the same because in the original sentence the tourists thought Cypress Gardens was the most beautiful, not a beautiful, park. Choice (C) is not the same because in the original sentence the tourists saw Cypress Gardens and compared it with other parks. Choice (D) is not the same because in the original sentence the tourists had never seen a park as beautiful as Cypress Gardens.

Chronology

1. **(C)** Choice (C) is a restatement of the given sentence. Choice (A) is not the same because in the original sentence seventy million refers to years, not to the number of dinosaurs. Choice (B) is not the same because in the original sentence dinosaurs became extinct seventy million years ago, man did not appear seventy million years afterward. Choice (D) is not the same because in the original sentence dinosaurs became extinct before, not at the same time, man appeared.

2. **(A)** Choice (A) is a restatement of the given sentence. Choice (B) is not the same because in the original sentence the sodium is added after, not before, the water. Choice (C) is not the same because in the original sentence the water is added to the mixture, not before mixing it. Choice (D) is not the same because in the original sentence the water is added to the mixture before, not with, the sodium solution.

3. **(D)** Choice (D) is a restatement of the given sentence. Choices (A) and (B) are not the same because in the original sentence Henson worked on *Sesame Street* before, not after, he made puppets for the *Muppet Show.* Choice (C) is not the same because in the original sentence other children's programs are not compared with *Sesame Street* and the *Muppet Show.*

4. **(D)** Choice (D) is a restatement of the given sentence. Choice (A) is not the same because in the original sentence one should empty the lint filter after removing clothing from the dryer, not before putting clothing in the dryer. Choice (B) is not the same because in the original sentence one should remove clothing from the dryer, not the lint filter. Choice (C) is not the same because in the original sentence the lint filter should be emptied after, not before, removing clothes from the dryer.

5. **(D)** Choice (D) is a restatement of the given sentence. Choice (A) is not the same because in the original sentence the transfer student should make the appointment with an advisor before, not after, registering. Choice (B) is not the same because in the original sentence transfer students should make an appointment prior to, not in order to, register. Choice (C) is not the same because in the original sentence students are transferring from, not to, other colleges and universities.

Comparatives

1. **(B)** Choice (B) is a restatement of the given sentence. Choices (A) and (C) are not the same because in the original sentence there were double or two times as many whales a few years ago. Choice (D) is not the same because in the original sentence the word *few* refers to years, not to whales.

2. **(D)** Choice (D) is a restatement of the given sentence. Choice (A) is not the same because in the original sentence Macy has fifty acres of floor space and is larger. Choice (B) is not the same because in the original sentence Macy is larger. Choice (C) is not the same because in the original sentence Macy is larger than any other store, not larger than one store.

3. **(D)** Choice (D) is a restatement of the given sentence. Choices (A) and (C) are not the same because in the original sentence the average size is less than one carat, which means that some are larger and some are smaller. Choice (B) is not the same because in the original sentence the diamonds are mined today, not in the past.

4. **(D)** Choice (D) is a restatement of the given sentence. Choice (A) is not the same because in the original sentence the money is cash for the product, not cash to produce it. Choices (B) and (C) are not the same because in the original sentence soybeans, not other products, are more profitable.

5. **(C)** Choice (C) is a restatement of the given sentence. Choice (A) is not the same because in the original sentence supervisors, not employees, have problems. Choice (B) is not the same because in the original sentence explaining, not performing the task, is difficult. Choice (D) is not the same because in the original sentence managers face problems, not employees.

Conditionals

1. **(C)** Choice (C) is a restatement of the given sentence. Choice (A) is not the same because in the original sentence many, not few players, suffered injuries. Choices (B) and (D) are not the same because in the original sentence the Cincinnati Reds would have, but did not, win.

2. **(C)** Choice (C) is a restatement of the given sentence. Choice (A) is not the same because in the original sentence some hardback books are popular. Choice (B) is not the same because in the original sentence when hardback editions are popular, they are published as paperbacks. Choice (D) is not the same because in the original sentence when a hardback book, not both hardback and paperback books, is popular, it is published as a paperback.

3. **(A)** Choice (A) is a restatement of the given sentence. Choice (B) is not the same because in the original sentence the British insisted on heavy taxes and the Colonies rebelled. Choice (C) is not the same because in the original sentence the taxes caused the rebellion but were not imposed so that the rebellion would occur. Choice (D) is not the same because in the original sentence the British insisted on collecting heavy taxes, but not so that the Colonies would rebel and become independent.

4. **(A)** Choice (A) is a restatement of the given sentence. Choices (B) and (C) are not the same because in the original sentence the students could have stayed here if there had been a program but did not stay because there was no program for them. Choice (D) is not the same because in the original sentence State University did not have a program in criminal justice.

5. **(C)** Choice (C) is a restatement of the given sentence. Choice (A) is not the same because in the original sentence the camera was far away. Choice (B) is not the same because in the original sentence it was not a good picture. Choice (D) is not the same because in the original sentence it would have been a good picture, but it was not, because the camera was so far away.

Concessions

1. **(C)** Choice (C) is a restatement of the given sentence. Choices (A) and (D) are not the same because in the original sentence Tecumseh made efforts, but was not able, to unite the Indians. Choice (B) is not the same because in the original sentence Tecumseh was not able to unite the Indians.

2. **(C)** Choice (C) is a restatement of the given sentence. Choice (A) is not the same because in the original sentence you pay a finance charge after, not every, thirty days. Choice (B) is not the same because in the original sentence you have one month to pay the balance, not the finance charge. Choice (D) is not the same because in the original sentence you must pay a finance charge in addition to, not instead of, the balance.

3. **(B)** Choice (B) is a restatement of the given sentence. Choice (A) is not the same because in the original sentence the location would have been ideal, but was not. Choice (C) is not the same because in the original sentence only one nuclear power plant and one location were mentioned. Choice (D) is not the same because in the original sentence the location would have been ideal but was opposed by the people in a nearby town.

4. **(D)** Choice (D) is a restatement of the given sentence. Choices (A) and (B) are not the same because in the original sentence people prefer CD's to savings accounts. Choice (C) is not the same because in the original sentence CD's pay higher interest.

5. **(B)** Choice (B) is a restatement of the given sentence. Choice (A) is not the same because in the original sentence many jokes cannot be translated well. Choice (C) is not the same because in the original sentence some jokes are funny in any language. Choice (D) is not the same because in the original sentence the first language of the translated jokes is not identified.

Other

1. **(A)** Choice (A) is a restatement of the given sentence. Choice (B) is not the same because in the original sentence we were surprised. Choice (C) is not the same because in the original sentence we knew and were surprised. Choice (D) is not the same because in the original sentence we, not people, were surprised.

2. **(A)** Choice (A) is a restatement of the given sentence. Choice (B) is not the same because in the original sentence Chan asked, not should ask, his roommate. Choices (C) and (D) are not the same because in the original sentence Chan, not his roommate, will wear it.

3. **(C)** Choice (C) is a restatement of the given sentence. Choice (A) is not the same because in the original sentence students may use their notes in an open-book examination. Choice (B) is not the same because in the original sentence the word *mind* refers to the phrase *to not mind,* not to students' minds. Choice (D) is not the same because in the original sentence students use their notes to answer questions.

4. **(B)** Choice (B) is a restatement of the given sentence. Choice (A) is not the same because in the original sentence the price decreases when the supply, not the demand, is greater. Choice (C) is not the same because in the original sentence, the greater the demand, the greater the price, not the supply. Choice (D) is not the same because in the original sentence the price falls when the demand is less than the supply.

5. **(B)** Choice (B) is a restatement of the given sentence. Choices (A) and (C) are not the same because in the original sentence the travel agent told us to go camping, not to the beach. Choice (D) is not the same because in the original sentence we were told to go camping, not to a travel agent, because of the hot weather.

Transcript for the Listening Comprehension Practice Exercises

Script for the tapes: This transcript is for all the Listening Comprehension Practice Exercises in Chapter Three. It includes Exercises One to Nineteen. One to Nineteen are available on a cassette tape. (See page 332 for information on ordering cassette tapes.)

Important: Do not read this transcript until after you have finished the practice exercises.

Directions: For each question in Part A, you will hear a short statement. The statements will be spoken just one time. They will not be written out for you, and you must listen carefully to understand what the speaker says.

After you hear a statement, read the four sentences in your test book, marked (A), (B), (C), and (D), and decide which *one* is closest in meaning to the statement you heard. Then, on your answer sheet, find the number of the question and blacken the space that corresponds to the letter of the answer you have chosen so that the letter inside the oval cannot be seen.

EXERCISE ONE: TEENS AND TENS

1. I-90 is one of the busiest interstate highways in the nation.
2. Since your suitcase weighs sixty pounds, you'll have to pay overweight.
3. The International Office has moved to 70 South Speedway.
4. Forty students will receive their Ph. D. degrees in industrial engineering this semester.
5. A one-way ticket to Washington costs eighty dollars.
6. You have fifteen minutes to finish this section of the test.
7. Jane lives in room fourteen on the first floor of Parks Tower.
8. It only costs fifteen cents to call Miami after five o'clock.
9. All of the English classes will meet in room 170 this semester.
10. Turn to page 16 in your textbooks, and do the first fifteen problems.
11. Today's low temperature was thirty degrees.
12. I need eighteen xerox copies before my eight o'clock meeting tomorrow morning.
13. The rate of exchange is thirteen-to-one.
14. A fourteen is a size large in this style.
15. CBS news is on channel thirteen at six o'clock.
16. The answers may be found on page 90 in your textbook.
17. You need an eighteen-cent stamp for this package.
18. Flight forty to Dallas is now boarding at gate two.
19. Fifteen percent of the students who took the examination scored above 450.
20. John will be thirty on November fourteenth.

EXERCISE TWO: COMPUTATIONS

1. At the end of the season, many of these sixty-dollar dresses will be on sale for half price.
2. Dr. Baker got to the corner at 8:40 A.M., missing the bus by five minutes.
3. City College had 520 students in 1960, but since then, the school has doubled its enrollment.
4. Miss Smith always gets to the store a half-hour early in order to check the register before the store opens at ten o'clock.
5. By the time I pay $250 for my rent, I only have half of my salary left.
6. Their flight was scheduled to depart at noon, but the plane was delayed for half an hour.
7. The stadium seats about 50,000 people, but it was half empty for last night's game.
8. Sandy bought a $200 camera for $165.
9. If Jane can type forty words a minute, Judy can probably type eighty.
10. These end tables are on sale for $85 each or $150 for a pair.
11. The class begins at eight o'clock, but Bill is always fifteen minutes late.
12. We expected to sell forty tickets, but we sold twice as many.
13. Since the taxi was late, Dr. Jones didn't get to the airport until eleven o'clock, missing his flight by half an hour.
14. Mr. Black has to leave his house at 8:30 in order to get to work by 9:00.
15. Alice was shortchanged ten dollars when the teller cashed her $300 check.
16. My watch says 9:30, but I always set it ten minutes ahead.
17. This recipe will only serve ten people, and we expect at least twenty.
18. Since the shuttle bus only goes halfway from State University to married student housing, Bob and Carole have to walk half a mile to the bus stop.
19. John was supposed to arrive in time for the noon meal, but he was two hours late.
20. Mary bought a used book for $6, saving about $2.50.

EXERCISE THREE: REFERENCE

1. Jeff's family was happy when he married Nancy.
2. Mr. Johnson wants his nephew to go into business with him because he doesn't have a son of his own.
3. Ann would like us to pick her up at the bus station.
4. Bill bought his wife a suit for their anniversary.
5. I don't remember the last name of Ellen's teacher.
6. Pat refused to accept John's invitation to the party.
7. Nancy made Paul the knit scarf he has on.
8. Tom sent his roommate a card to wish him a happy birthday.
9. Bill's sister was very proud when he graduated.
10. James's mother had already gone to work when he got home.
11. Last night at the party we finally met Mary's Uncle Charles.
12. Bob resented his father's criticizing the plans for his new office building.
13. Mrs. Williams asked her lawyer to draw up a will naming her grandson as the sole beneficiary.
14. Larry took his brother's car to the car wash.
15. Paul wants his wife to go back to school next semester.
16. Mrs. Ayers told Dr. Smith's secretary to cancel her appointment.
17. Alice wants to transfer to the University of Toledo because she has many friends studying there.
18. Professor Baker asked his graduate assistant to give the lecture today.
19. Mary refused to return Bill's telephone call.
20. Sally borrowed her sister's bicycle.

EXERCISE FOUR: NEGATIVES

1. She has hardly any friends.
2. We have no students who are not insured.
3. Business has never been slower.
4. The tour was worth neither the time nor the money.
5. Not many brothers are as nice to their sisters as Tom is.
6. The students had never seen so much snow before!
7. There is no better place to practice driving than the shopping center.
8. Nancy likes nothing better than to sleep late.
9. It's not like Mary to be unfriendly, so she must not have seen you when you waved.
10. The problem was not uncommon for a young man away from home.
11. Professor Ayers speaks neither Arabic nor Farsi.
12. Jane's family hasn't ever met her friend, Bob.
13. There isn't any doubt about it.
14. That copy machine is absolutely useless.
15. Their new apartment was no more comfortable than the first one had been.
16. There is no harder course than English 190.
17. Betty didn't have to work overtime.
18. He has never been unfair with his students.
19. I can't possibly afford a new car right now.
20. John could hardly eat his dessert.

EXERCISE FIVE: COMPARATIVES

1. Traditionally the most successful small business in the United States is the restaurant business.
2. We had more than enough time to get there.
3. When the new students have been here a little longer, I'm sure that they will feel less homesick.
4. Kathy is better looking than her roommate, Ann.
5. The University is farther away than I thought.
6. Bill gets less exercise than he should.
7. Ellen isn't a bit like her husband, Tom.
8. Ann prefers cold weather to hot weather.
9. We haven't lived here as long as the Smiths have.
10. Aspirin is as good as anything for colds and flu.
11. Writing this term paper was a bigger job than I thought it would be.
12. She has been able to learn English more quickly than I had imagined.
13. Some people think that jogging is better for your health, but in my opinion, playing tennis is more fun.
14. Jeff was no more surprised than I was when Tom moved out of the dorm.
15. According to government statistics, the older one is when he gets married, the less likely it is that he'll get a divorce.
16. A steak dinner costs ten dollars at most restaurants, but only three dollars at City Steak House.
17. John studies harder than Bill, but for some reason Bill gets better grades on the exams.
18. Larry's son doesn't look like him at all.
19. Betty prefers living at home with her parents to renting her own apartment.
20. Mrs. Smith hasn't traveled nearly as much as her husband has.

EXERCISE SIX: CONDITIONALS

1. If John had his way, he would spend all of his time playing tennis.
2. Mary could have gotten better grades if she had studied more.
3. The project would have been approved if it hadn't been for the budget.
4. If we had needed to get in touch with them, we could have sent a telegram.
5. If you usually take a size six, you'll need a size seven in this style.
6. If we had arrived on time, we would have gotten good seats.
7. If he had asked her, she would have gone with him.
8. A fur coat like this will last for years if it's cared for properly.
9. Getting up early isn't difficult if you have an alarm clock.
10. We would have had a better class if Mr. Williams had taught it.
11. If she waits much longer to call a cab, she's going to miss the bus.
12. If you are at the corner by six o'clock, I'll pick you up and take you home.
13. Living in another culture isn't difficult if you have the right attitude.
14. If Al keeps studying like he has been, he's going to make himself sick.
15. If you are ready, we can go to the party together.
16. We would have been here sooner if we hadn't gotten lost.
17. Your order will arrive on Saturday if placed by Wednesday.
18. If you want to see the director, he has time this afternoon at two o'clock.
19. John would have helped us if he hadn't had such a bad cold.
20. If you had asked the secretary, she would have told you.

EXERCISE SEVEN: CONCESSIONS (PART 1)

1. Jane usually comes to the ALI to meet her tutor, but Monday she was absent.
2. Thank you for inviting us, but I don't believe that we will be able to make it.
3. The hat isn't mine but the coat is.
4. The State University team usually wins all of its games, but this year it lost two of them.
5. I was going to write you a letter, but I decided to call you instead.
6. Mike was planning to go to graduate school, but he didn't have enough money.
7. Mrs. Baker was told that her illness was incurable, but she never gave up.
8. She doesn't like the dorm, but she does like her roommate.
9. The office is usually closed on Saturdays, but this week the secretary will be there until noon.
10. We ordered an egg salad sandwich, but the waitress brought us tuna fish instead.
11. The doctor isn't in right now, but he should be back shortly.
12. His visa expires in November, but he is eligible to get a three-month extension.
13. Our family ordinarily goes camping on vacation, but this year we're going to take a tour.
14. The food at the cafeteria is usually good, but last night it was awful.
15. There are fifty students scheduled for language lab, but there are only forty-five booths.
16. Anne said that she could babysit any day but Friday.
17. I had just expected my daughter to come, but my son showed up too.
18. Bill wanted to buy some cologne for his wife's birthday, but the store didn't carry the brand she usually uses.
19. Apartments near the University are very expensive, but we decided to rent one anyway, thinking that we would save money on gas.
20. It isn't normally necessary to have an appointment in order to see the foreign student advisor, but during registration it's a good idea to make one.

EXERCISE SEVEN: CONCESSIONS (PART 2)

1. Students in the College of Architecture cannot graduate this semester unless they turn in their final projects by the end of the week.
2. Although the weather is bad, the roads are clear.
3. In spite of the problems, I doubt that Betty and Paul will get a divorce.
4. From his résumé, this candidate appears to be well qualified for the job; even so, I think that we should check with his references.
5. Although you are feeling better, I think that you should still see a doctor.
6. Mr. Brown won't be able to work today, although Miss Smith will be there.
7. Even though she insists that she was not offended, I am afraid she was.
8. Although the rent includes water and gas, electricity costs about twenty dollars extra.
9. Though Ellen can read quite well without her glasses, she needs them to see at a distance.
10. The traffic was very light even though it was rush hour.
11. Contrary to what I had originally thought, the trip turned out to be fun.
12. Since there wasn't any tomato soup on the shelf, I bought beef stew instead.
13. In spite of his injury, James was able to play football in the big game last Saturday.
14. Although my roommate is a very nice person, he's not my best friend.
15. Ellen can't go to the University unless she gets a scholarship.
16. Instead of going back to Florida, you ought to go to California this year.
17. Anna already speaks English very well; even so, she wants to continue studying at the Institute.
18. Since there aren't any tickets left for the concert, let's go to the movies instead of going back home.
19. Although John never means to tell, he just can't keep a secret.
20. Mr. Smith would not stop drinking even though the doctor told him that he must.

EXERCISE EIGHT: HOMOPHONES AND HOMONYMS

1. You can waive your right to appear in court and pay your fine now.
2. This recipe isn't sweet enough because it has too much flour in it.
3. That paper has very fair coverage of the city bus story, don't you think?
4. There were only three males in the litter.
5. Pat went by the window while I was there.
6. We can wait a little more comfortably in the other room.
7. They decided to meet at the cafeteria when they finished taking their test.
8. Doug had to sit in the lounge for three hours before he could board the plane.
9. There were very few students who cited the sources of the quotations.
10. The whole area was unsafe.
11. They took the week off to rest up.
12. In order to lessen the permanent effects of the injury, Mary Anne underwent physical therapy.
13. At night we would sit around the camp fire.
14. His budget has a lot of waste in it.
15. Sue changed jobs so she could spend more time at home.
16. He knows where Dr. Smith's office is.
17. The material was very coarse before it was treated.
18. Let's hear the other side of the argument.
19. He won't desert the rest of us.
20. Don't brake on wet pavement or you may slide into another car.

Directions: In Part B you will hear short conversations between two speakers. At the end of each conversation, a third voice will ask a question about what was said. The question will be spoken just one time. After you hear a conversation and the question about it, read the four possible answers in your test book and decide which one is the best answer to the question you heard. Then, on your answer sheet, find the number of the question and blacken the space that corresponds to the letter of the answer you have chosen.

EXERCISE NINE: CONVERSATIONS/DIRECT INFORMATION

1. Man: Have you started writing your paper for history?
  Woman: Not yet. I'm still writing up my laboratory assignments for chemistry and studying for my midterms in English and French.
  Third Voice: For which class must the woman begin to prepare?

2. Woman: Are you glad that you came to Washington?
  Man: Yes, indeed. I'd considered going to New York or Boston, but I've never regretted my decision.
  Third Voice: Where does the man live?

3. Man: Something is wrong with second gear. It seems to run fine in reverse, and drive, but when I shift it into second, the motor stalls out.
  Woman: I hope that it won't be too difficult to fix.
  Third Voice: Which gear needs to be fixed?

4. Woman: You're always working around the house on Saturday, painting and doing repairs! You must enjoy it.
  Man: Not really. I'd rather relax or go fishing, but Saturday is the only day I have to get anything done. By the time I get home from work during the week, I'm too tired.
  Third Voice: What does the man usually do on Saturdays?

5. Woman: The chocolate cake is very good today.
  Man: No thanks. I'll have apple pie with vanilla ice cream on top.
  Third Voice: What kind of dessert did the man order?

6. Man: The main library is open from eight A.M. until nine P.M. Monday through Friday; noon until six P.M. Saturday and Sunday; and twenty-four hours a day during finals week. This is a recording and will not repeat. If you need further assistance, please stay on the line until an operator answers.
  Woman: Hello. This is the operator. May I help you?
  Third Voice: When is the library open on weekdays?

7. Man: Mr. Black is fluent in Spanish and now he's beginning to study Arabic.
  Woman: He also knows a few words in Japanese and Chinese.
  Third Voice: Which language does Mr. Black speak well?

8. Man: I'm going to the museum Sunday afternoon. There's a new exhibit of Indian art from Arizona and New Mexico. Want to go with me?

Woman: I'd love to, but my best friend is getting married on Sunday and I wouldn't miss it for anything.

Third Voice: Where is the woman going on Sunday afternoon?

9. Man: These silver earrings are only sixteen dollars this week. The gold ones are twenty-four.

Woman: I'll take the silver ones, then; or, on second thought, give me the gold ones. I have a gold necklace that would look very nice with them.

Third Voice: What did the woman decide to buy?

10. Man: It only takes two hours to get to New York, but you'll have a six-hour layover between flights.

Woman: Oh, that's alright. I don't mind having the time in New York. I still have a few things to shop for.

Third Voice: How many hours will the woman be in New York?

11. Man: Are you sure that you brought your purse with you in the first place?

Woman: Yes. I had it when I got in the car. I thought that I might have left it on the car seat, but when I went back it wasn't there. Maybe I put it down on the counter when I checked my coat outside the auditorium.

Third Voice: Where does the woman believe that she has left her purse?

12. Man: Do you have your Christmas shopping done yet?

Woman: Almost. I got a watch for my husband, but I can't seem to find anything for my dad. He would probably like a book or a case for his coin collection.

Third Voice: What did the woman buy her husband for Christmas?

13. Man: I feel obligated to attend the party, but really I'd much rather go with you to the concert.

Woman: I'm sorry that you can't. They will be playing music from the big band era.

Third Voice: Where is the woman going?

14. Man: Which dress do you plan to wear?

Woman: I like the black one, and it fits me better, but it's probably too dressy. I suppose I'll wear the red one.

Third Voice: Why didn't the woman wear the black dress?

15. Woman: John, I'm sorry to be so late. Thank you for waiting.

Man: Oh I didn't mind. I've only been here fifty minutes. You said that you might be as much as an hour late, so I just bought my newspaper and ordered myself a cup of coffee.

Third Voice: How long has the man been waiting?

EXERCISE TEN: CONVERSATIONS/COMPUTATIONS

1. Man: My car gets forty miles per gallon.
   Woman: Really? Mine only gets twenty.
   Third Voice: How does the man's mileage compare with that of the woman?

2. Man: Hello. This is Tom Davis. I have an appointment with Mrs. Jones for nine o'clock this morning, but I'm afraid I'll have to be about fifteen minutes late.
   Woman: That's alright, Mr. Davis. She doesn't have another appointment scheduled until ten o'clock.
   Third Voice: When will Mr. Davis most probably meet with Mrs. Jones?

3. Man: How much are the tickets?
   Woman: They're ten dollars each for the general public, but student tickets are half price.
   Third Voice: How much will the man pay for two general tickets and two student tickets?

4. Man: How much are these sweaters?
   Woman: They're on sale today, sir. Twenty-five dollars each, or two for forty dollars.
   Third Voice: How much does one sweater cost?

5. Man: I'd like to place a station-to-station call to Ann Arbor, please. How much will that be?
   Woman: That's fifty-five cents for the first three minutes, and ten cents for each additional minute.
   Third Voice: How much will the man pay for a ten-minute call?

6. Woman: Excuse me. Do you have the time?
   Man: Yes ma'am. I have 1:15, but my watch is a little bit fast
   Third Voice: What time is it?

7. Woman: That's fifteen dollars, sir.
   Man: I'd like to pay by check. May I make it out for more than that?
   Woman: Certainly. There's a ten-dollar limit over the amount of purchase, though.
   Third Voice: What is the maximum amount for which the man may write his check?

8. Man: Do I have enough postage on this package?
   Woman: Let's see. You already have three fifteen-cent stamps and two twenty-five cent stamps on it. You only need one five-cent stamp.
   Third Voice: What is the total amount of postage required to mail the package?

9. Woman: I thought that these typewriter ribbons cost three dollars.
   Man: They used to, but the price has gone up fifty cents.
   Third Voice: How much do the typewriter ribbons cost now?

10. Woman: Aren't there any direct flights?

      Man: I'm sorry. Your best bet would be a nine A.M. departure on United flight twelve arriving in Chicago at eleven A.M., with a five-hour wait for your connecting flight to Los Angeles.

      Third Voice: What time will the woman leave Chicago?

11. Woman: I like these glasses, but they look like they would be quite expensive.

      Man: They're $15 apiece, or $150 a dozen. Really that's not very expensive for genuine leaded crystal.

      Third Voice: How much does one glass cost?

12. Man: Do you rent rooms by the week? You see, I'm not sure whether I'll stay for a whole month.

      Woman: Yes. The rates are higher though. It's $50 a week, but only $160 a month.

      Third Voice: How much will the man owe if he rents the room for three weeks?

13. Man: We don't have meters here in Washington, because we have zones. This is a two-zone ride, so the fare is $2.45.

      Woman: Here's three dollars. Keep the change.

      Third Voice: How much did the woman give the driver as a tip?

14. Man: Miss Smith, I told Dr. Brown that I would call him in the Houston office at ten o'clock their time. Please find out the time difference for me so that I'll know when to place the call.

      Woman: It's two hours earlier in Houston, sir. I know without looking it up because my sister lives there.

      Third Voice: When should the man place his call to Houston?

15. Woman: Excuse me. I'm trying to get to the Student Union.

      Man: Sure. Just go down here to the corner and turn left. Then go straight for three blocks and turn left at the tower. It's two blocks from there.

      Third Voice: How far must the woman walk to get to the Student Union?

EXERCISE ELEVEN: CONVERSATIONS/PLACE

1. Woman: The special today is baked chicken and dressing.
Man: No thank you. Just bring me a cup of coffee and the check, please.
Third Voice: Where did this conversation most probably take place?

2. Man: Would you please get the phone, Jan? I'm all tied up right now.
Woman: Certainly, sir.
Third Voice: What does the man mean?

3. Woman: Isn't Mary Ellen a beautiful bride?
Man: She is indeed. John looks very happy too, doesn't he? He told me that they'll be going to Florida on their honeymoon.
Third Voice: Where did this conversation most probably take place?

4. Woman: Press twelve, please. *(Pause.)* Thank you.
Man: You're welcome. That's where I'm going too.
Third Voice: Where did this conversation most probably take place?

5. Woman: They'll call the doctoral candidates' names next. Have you found Larry yet?
Man: No. They all look alike with those black robes on.
Third Voice: Where did this conversation most probably take place?

6. Woman: I'd like a dozen glazed doughnuts and a loaf of French bread, please.
Man: Yes, ma'am. That's $1.95 plus 10¢ tax.
Third Voice: Where did this conversation most probably take place?

7. Woman: What was that title again?
Man: *God is an Englishman.* It's a very famous book. I'm sure you must have it.
Third Voice: Where did this conversation most probably take place?

8. Woman: Are these treatments really necessary? They don't seem to help very much.
Man: I'm afraid so, Mrs. Jones. Just be patient and I'm sure you'll see some results soon.
Third Voice: Where did this conversation most probably take place?

9. Woman: We have several kinds of accounts, Mr. Brown. The best interest rate is for the customer club account, but you must maintain a monthly balance of $300.
Man: That will be fine.
Third Voice: Where did this conversation most probably take place?

10. Man: The name is Wilson. We don't have a reservation, but we have time to wait.
Woman: Party of two? It shouldn't be more than ten minutes, Mr. Wilson. We'll call you when we have a table set up.
Third Voice: Where does this conversation most likely take place?

11. Man: Could you please tell me what room Robert Davis is in?

Woman: Yes, he's in the intensive care unit on the fourth floor. I suggest that you check with the nurse's station before going in, though.

Third Voice: Where did this conversation most probably take place?

12. Woman: I just want a wash and set, please.

Man: Fine. Why don't you let me blow dry it this time instead of putting it up in rollers? I think that you would like it that way.

Third Voice: Where did this conversation most probably take place?

13. Man: Good morning, Mary. How are you?

Woman: Oh, fine. I'm just on my way to work, but I thought that I would drop by with the check for my rent.

Third Voice: Where did this conversation most probably take place?

14. Man: You'll be glad to know that no new cavities have shown up on the x-rays, Miss Smith.

Woman: That *is* good news. I'll just have my teeth cleaned then.

Third Voice: Where did this conversation most probably take place?

15. Man: I've forgotten my passbook, but I'd like to make a deposit to my savings account if I may.

Woman: No problem. Just bring this receipt with you the next time you come in, along with your passbook, and we will adjust the balance.

Third Voice: Where did this conversation most probably take place?

EXERCISE TWELVE: CONVERSATIONS/IMPLIED

1. Woman: If I were you, I would take a plane instead of a bus. It will take you forever to get there.
    Man: But flying makes me so nervous.
    Third Voice: What does the man prefer to do?

2. Man: Would you please get the phone, Jan? I'm all tied up right now.
    Woman: Certainly, sir.
    Third Voice: What does the man mean?

3. Man: These gloves are quite a bit cheaper than the leather ones. They are vinyl, but frankly I can't tell much difference.
    Woman: I really like the leather, but I can't pay twenty-six dollars.
    Third Voice: What will the woman probably do?

4. Woman: Do you think that Bob is serious about Sally?
    Man: Well, I know this. I've never seen him go out so often with the same person.
    Third Voice: What conclusion does the man want us to draw from his statement?

5. Woman: Whereas European nations have traditionally employed metric units such as meters and grams, the United States has employed English units such as feet and pounds.
    Man: Both systems are now in use in the U.S., though.
    Third Voice: What are these people most probably discussing?

6. Woman: Jane told me that she was going to quit her job. I'll certainly be sorry to see her go.
    Man: Oh, she always says that! I wouldn't buy her a going-away present if I were you.
    Third Voice: What does the man think about Jane?

7. Man: I wonder what happened to Betty Thompson? I don't see her anywhere.
    Woman: I don't know. She told me that she would be here at the play tonight.
    Third Voice: What do we learn about Betty from this conversation?

8. Man: I can't stand this class!
    Woman: Well, you might as well get used to it. It's required, and you have to take it in order to graduate.
    Third Voice: How does the man feel about the class?

9. Man: I suppose we should look for a bigger house, but I don't see how we can afford one right now.
    Woman: If only we hadn't spent so much money on our vacation this year.
    Third Voice: Will the man and the woman buy a new house?

10. Man: I still haven't received my score on the GMAT test. Maybe I should call to check on it.
    Woman: Don't worry so much. It takes at least six weeks to receive your score.
    Third Voice: What does the woman think that the man should do?

11.

Man:	Your glasses are fine. If you don't like the frames perhaps we could change them.
Woman:	Actually I was thinking of trying some contact lenses, if you think that I would be able to wear them.
Third Voice:	To whom is the woman speaking?

12.

Woman:	How did your interview go?
Man:	I couldn't feel better about it! The questions were very fair, and I seemed to find an answer for all of them.
Third Voice:	What is the man's attitude about the interview?

13.

Man:	Weren't you in class Friday either?
Woman:	No. I had to take my mother to the airport. She went back to New York.
Third Voice:	What do we learn about the two students in this conversation?

14.

Woman:	Maybe we should take Front Street this morning. The radio announcer said that traffic was very heavy on the freeway.
Man:	Well, if he says to take Front Street we should go the other way!
Third Voice:	What is the man's opinion of the radio announcer?

15.

Man:	If you don't have an account here, I can't cash your check. I'm sorry, but that's the way it is.
Woman:	Well, thanks a lot! You're a big help!
Third Voice:	How does the woman feel?

Directions: In this part of the test, you will hear several short mini talks. After each talk or conversation, you will be asked some questions. The talks and questions will be spoken just one time. They will not be written out for you, so you will have to listen carefully to understand what the speaker says.

After you hear a question, read the four possible answers in your test book and decide which one is the best answer to the question you heard. Then, on your answer sheet, find the number of the question and blacken the space that corresponds to the answer you have chosen.

EXERCISE THIRTEEN:
MINI TALKS/OVERHEARD CONVERSATIONS

Mini Talk One

Woman: Good morning.
Man: Good morning. What can I do for you?
Woman: I'd like a ticket to Pittsburgh, please.
Man: Round trip?
Woman: No. One way.
Man: Okay. That'll be twenty-two dollars.
Woman: Twenty-two? Last time I took this bus it was only twenty.
Man: I know. The rates went up this month.
Woman: Just like everything else.
Man: Yeah.
Woman: Does the bus still leave at two-fifteen?
Man: Two-fifteen at gate eleven. You ought to be at the door by two o'clock, though. The driver usually begins loading fifteen minutes before he pulls out.
Woman: Fine.
Man: Do you want to check your suitcases?
Woman: Just two. I'll carry the other one with me.
Man: That's good. We can only check two of them anyway. Give these baggage checks to the driver when you get to Pittsburgh.
Woman: Okay. Thanks a lot.
Man: You're welcome. Have a good trip.

1. Where does this conversation take place?
2. What time does the driver leave?
3. How many suitcases does the woman want to check?
4. What do we know about the woman from the conversation?

Mini Talk Two

Bill: Want to go down to dinner, John? The line is going to close in about half an hour.
John: What time is it?
Bill: Six o'clock. You had better go now if you want to eat. They're serving fish cakes and baked potatoes.
John: I don't think I'll go.
Bill: Oh, come on. Get yourself a big salad if you don't want fish. The dessert will probably be good.
John: No, thanks Bill. I think that I'll keep studying for awhile, and then maybe I'll order a pizza later.
Bill: Suit yourself. Do you have a test or something?
John: Yeah. It's not until Monday but I want to go home this weekend.
Bill: Lucky you. Two days of home cooking.
John: It sure beats the cafeteria at this place.
Bill: True. Well, knock on my door if you decide to get that pizza later.
John: Why? Aren't you going to eat either?
Bill: Sure. But I'll be hungry again by then.

1. What is being served for dinner at the cafeteria?
2. Why is John studying?
3. When will the cafeteria close?
4. What does Bill want John to do?

Mini Talk Three

Man: Will that be cash or charge?
Woman: I want to pay by check if I may.
Man: Certainly. That's cash, then.
Woman: Cash?
Man: Yes. Both money and checks are considered cash. Only credit cards are charge.
Woman: Oh.
Man: Just make the check out to Sears.
Woman: Okay.
Man: And I'll need two pieces of identification. A driver's license or a major credit card like Visa or Master Charge.
Woman: Well, here's my driver's license. I don't have any charge cards, but I do have my student ID card from City College. Will that be alright?
Man: I think so. I need two numbers. Your student number is on the ID, isn't it?
Woman: Yes, it is. Do you need anything else?
Man: Just put your telephone number on the front of the check.
Woman: Okay.
Man: Good. Now let me give you your license, your ID, and your package. And thank you for shopping at Sears.
Woman: Thank *you*.

1. How did the woman pay for the purchase?
2. What is meant by the term cash?
3. What did the woman use as identification?
4. Where was she shopping?

Mini Talk Four

Woman:	I usually advise first-year engineering students to take mathematics, chemistry, and an introductory engineering course the first quarter.
Man:	Oh. That's only three classes.
Woman:	Yes. But I'm sure that you'll be busy. They're all five-hour courses, and you'll have to meet each class every day. The chemistry course has an additional two-hour laboratory.
Man:	So that would be seventeen hours of class a week.
Woman:	That's right.
Man:	Okay. Which mathematics course do you think I should take?
Woman:	Have you taken very much math in high school?
Man:	Four years. I had algebra, geometry, trigonometry . . .
Woman:	Good. Then I suggest that you take the math placement test. It's offered this Friday at nine o'clock in the morning in Tower Auditorium.
Man:	Do I need anything to be admitted? I mean a permission slip?
Woman:	No. Just identification. A driver's license will be fine.
Man:	Do I take a chemistry test too?
Woman:	No. Chemistry 100 is designed for students who have never taken a chemistry course, and Chemistry 200 is for students who have had chemistry in high school.
Man:	I've had two courses.
Woman:	Then you should take Chemistry 200, Orientation to Engineering, and either Mathematics 130 or 135, depending on the results of your placement test. Come back Friday afternoon. I should have your score on the test by then and we can get you registered.

1. How many classes does the woman advise the man to take?
2. What does the man need to be admitted to the examination?
3. When will the man see his advisor again?
4. What do we know about the student?

EXERCISE FOURTEEN:
MINI TALKS/ANNOUNCEMENTS AND ADVERTISEMENTS

Mini Talk One

Are you thinking of writing someone a letter? Call instead. It isn't that expensive, especially when you call during evening, night, or weekend hours. In fact, you can make a ten-minute call anywhere in the Continental United States for just $2.60.

For even greater savings, always dial direct, that is, without an operator's assistance. Rates on direct calls are lower after five o'clock in the evening and lowest after eleven o'clock at night. Collect, credit card, person-to-person, and pay phone calls require the services of an operator, and they cost more than direct calls.

Need to call out of the country? Now calls to many overseas locations may be dialed direct. Check your telephone directory for overseas area codes.

Next time you have good news, or you just want to stay in touch, remember, a phone call means so much more than a letter. This has been a message from Southern Bell Telephone Company.

1. According to this talk, when is a direct dial telephone call cheapest?
2. How much does it cost to make a ten-minute call within the Continental United States?
3. What type of call does NOT require an operator's assistance?
4. What should one do in order to make an overseas call?

Mini Talk Two

Appalachian Airlines will begin passenger service at Charlotte Airport Thursday with morning and afternoon departures daily to Atlanta, and nonstop service to Washington, D.C., with connections in Washington for Cleveland, New York, and Boston.

Tired of being crowded aboard large airplanes? Appalachian Airlines will use comfortable Boeing 737 twin jets with a capacity to seat 106 passengers. There is more room for your underseat luggage, and more room for you.

Most flights will include breakfast and lunch catered by Charlotte's finest restaurants and served by one of Appalachian's courteous flight attendants.

Next time you need to travel, be good to yourself. Fly comfortably. Fly Appalachian Airlines. For reservations or more information, call your travel agent, or call the Appalachian Airlines toll-free number: 800-565-7000. That is 800-565-7000 for reservations to Atlanta, Washington, D.C., Cleveland, New York, or Boston.

1. What is an advantage of taking Appalachian Airlines?
2. Where do passengers get a connecting flight for Cleveland?
3. When do flights leave Charlotte for Atlanta?
4. What is the telephone number for Appalachian Airlines?

Mini Talk Three

The National Highway Traffic Safety Administration estimates that one-half of all fatal traffic accidents involves alcohol. Every year, thousands of passengers and pedestrians are killed because of reckless, irresponsible behavior by a drunk driver.

Ohio law prohibits persons who are under the influence of alcohol to drive. If you do drive while under the influence of alcohol, you can be arrested. If you are convicted of drunk driving, you will be sentenced to at least three days in jail, and your license will be suspended for thirty days. But did you know that the court can sentence you to as much as six months in jail and fine you in the amount of $500 in addition to the mandatory three-day sentence? Think about it the next time you leave a party.

If you drink, don't drive.

This has been a public service announcement by the Ohio Safety Commission.

1. How many accidents resulting in death are caused by drunk driving?
2. What is the minimum required sentence for driving under the influence of alcohol in Ohio?
3. How long may the court require an offender to spend in jail for driving under the influence of alcohol?
4. What is the main idea of this announcement?

Mini Talk Four

Here is your weekend guide to what is going on at the University of Colorado . . . .

And it is a good weekend for basketball. The Colorado Buffaloes will play the Oklahoma Sooners Friday night at Oklahoma, and they will return home to face the Nebraska Cornhuskers Saturday night on the University of Colorado court. The Buffaloes are expected to win both games, fans. Tickets are available from the ticket office at the sports arena.

There are also a few tickets available for the Saturday night concert by Walter Murphy and the Big Apple Band. Most of the tickets are ten dollars, although a very few five-dollar seats are still on sale. To reserve seats, call the Student Union at 666-5771, or stop by the box office.

The University Museum will be open from ten o'clock A.M. until five o'clock P.M. Saturday and Sunday. In addition to the famous rock and mineral collection and the exhibits of early people, there will be a special exhibit of American Indian pottery and sand painting. Admission is free.

And now a report on snow conditions at area ski resorts. Snow Valley is reporting good conditions with six inches of new snow in the last twenty-four hours; Pine Mountain is reporting very good conditions with eight inches of new snow; And the Oak Creek Canyon Resort is reporting very good conditions with nine inches of new snow.

This has been the weekend guide. You are listening to WKID in Boulder, Colorado.

1. What is the name of the University of Colorado basketball team?
2. How can one get a ticket to the Walter Murphy concert?
3. Why is the University Museum famous?
4. What are the general snow conditions at ski resorts?

EXERCISE FIFTEEN: MINI TALKS/NEWS REPORTS

Mini Talk One

The latest diet fad is not really new. It is called the Scarsdale diet and was originally outlined twenty years ago by Dr. Herman Tarnower, a cardiologist and internist from Scarsdale, New York. The diet became popular when people from Scarsdale who had used the diet successfully sent mimeographed copies to their friends in other parts of the country.

Since his book *The Complete Scarsdale Medical Diet* was published last year, he has sold 270,000 copies, and the diet has become a national pastime. In his book Dr. Tarnower claims that a dieter who follows his plan will be able to lose up to twenty pounds in two weeks. He also claims that it is medically safe, and cites twenty years of case histories as proof.

The diet is very simple, but it requires a great deal of discipline. For two weeks at a time the dieter must follow a strict menu that does not provide for any substitutions by the dieter. There is no alcohol, no oil, and no sugar allowed, and raw celery or carrots are the only snacks allowed.

Although the amount of food that the dieter may eat is not limited, most dieters average less than one thousand calories a day. Many complain that their energy levels are low, but most are very satisfied with the results, like Tip O'Neill, the speaker of the United States House of Representatives, who lost forty pounds in four weeks.

1. Why is the weight loss plan called the Scarsdale diet?
2. How much weight can one lose in two weeks on the Scarsdale diet?
3. What is the Scarsdale diet?
4. When was the Scarsdale diet developed?

Mini Talk Two

It is called the Moodymobile, named for its inventor Ralph Moody, a retired stock car driver and mechanic. And it very well could revolutionize the auto industry.

The Moodymobile is a sports car with a diesel engine, and it gets 75 miles per gallon of fuel. Last May, Moody drove it 850 miles from Oak Hill, Florida, to Washington, D.C., in order to testify before the Senate Energy Committee. It took 11.1 gallons of fuel to make the trip.

Before the car can be commercially sold, it must pass a series of environmental tests. And Moody wants to try some modifications to cut down on the noise. But Ford, Chrysler, and General Motors have all expressed interest in buying the rights to the patent.

Moody says that he is filing the names of persons who have written him in hopes of purchasing a Moodymobile. He says that he hopes to market 2,000 of the cars late this year for about $7,000 each.

1. Why is the new diesel car called the Moodymobile?
2. How many miles per gallon of fuel does the Moodymobile get?
3. Why doesn't Ralph Moody sell the Moodymobile?
4. How much will a Moodymobile cost when it is sold?

Mini Talk Three

Nancy Anne Brown was crowned Miss State University in the Centennial Hall auditorium last night after a week-long pageant that included preliminary competitions in the categories of beauty, intelligence, and talent.

A blue-eyed blonde from Los Angeles, California, Miss Brown is 5 feet, 10 inches tall and weighs 120 pounds. She won both the swimming suit and the evening gown competitions to place first in the beauty category. She placed second in the intelligence competition for her extemporaneous responses to questioning by a panel of judges, and third in the talent competition, to give her an overall first place ranking. In the talent competition, Miss Brown sang "I Feel Pretty" from the Broadway musical *West Side Story*.

As Miss State University, Miss Brown received a check for $1,000 and a scholarship award for $2,000. She will represent State University at the Miss University U.S.A. Pageant in Washington, D.C., next May.

If she wins the title in Washington, she will take a one-year leave of absence from her studies at State University in order to devote her time to travel and other responsibilities associated with the title. Miss Brown is a junior majoring in speech and drama. After graduating, she hopes to pursue a career in the theater.

1. How does the new Miss State University look?
2. What place did Nancy Anne Brown receive in the talent competition?
3. How much was the scholarship offered as one of the prizes?
4. What does Miss Brown do at State University?

Mini Talk Four

The cost is going up for just about everything, and college tuition is no exception. According to a nationwide survey published by the College Board's Scholarship Service, tuition at most American universities will be on an average of 9 percent higher this year than last.

The biggest increase will occur at private colleges. Public colleges, heavily subsidized by tax funds, will also increase their tuition, but the increase will be a few percentage points lower than their privately-sponsored neighbors.

As a follow up, the United Press International did their own study at Massachusetts Institute of Technology. At M.I.T., advisors recommended that students have $8,900 available for one year's expenses, including $5,300 for tuition, $2,685 for room and board, $630 for personal expenses, and $285 for books and supplies. Ten years ago the tuition was $2,150. To put that another way, the cost has climbed 150 percent in the last decade.

An additional burden is placed on out-of-state students who must pay extra charges ranging from $200 to $2,000, and foreign students who are not eligible for scholarships at state-funded universities.

On the brighter side, the survey revealed that college graduates are entering the best job market since the middle 1960s. Job offers are up 16 percent from last year, and salaries are good, at least for graduates in technical fields. For example, a recent graduate in petroleum engineering can expect to make as much as $20,000 per year. A student with a liberal arts degree might expect to make about half that salary.

1. What is the average increase in tuition expenses at American universities this year over last?
2. How much did tuition increase at M.I.T. over a ten-year period?
3. According to the reporter, what is a problem for foreign students at state universities?
4. What is the job market like for college graduates?

EXERCISE SIXTEEN: MINI TALKS/WEATHER REPORTS

Mini Talk One

The National Weather Service's three-day outlook calls for temperatures to average a little below seasonal norms throughout most of upstate New York.

There is a frost warning out for tonight with temperatures expected to drop to thirty-five degrees. Tomorrow morning will be chilly under partly cloudy skies, with temperatures in the low forties warming to about sixty degrees by noon.

The cloud cover should lift by the weekend. Again, you can expect those crisp morning temperatures to rise by midday on both Saturday and Sunday. The leaves should be at their most brilliant by then under bright, sunny skies. And it promises to be a beautiful fall weekend.

1. During what season was this weather forecast reported?
2. How do the average temperatures compare with the seasonal norms?
3. What will the weather be like by noon tomorrow?
4. In general terms, what will the weather be for the weekend?

Mini Talk Two

The extended forecast for the Greater Chicago Area calls for more snow today and tomorrow with winds at ten to fifteen miles per hour sweeping in from the lake. Highs are expected in the upper teens and twenties. Lows from zero to ten degrees above zero.

Light snow flurries will continue Friday, clearing by Saturday, with cold but mostly fair weather predicted for Sunday.

Area schools and factories will remain closed today and tomorrow, and residents are asked to restrict travel to emergency only. A group of volunteers is assisting the National Guard in providing essential transportation to those who are out of food supplies or medication. If you have need of emergency transportation, call 875-2000. That is 875-2-0-0-0. Otherwise, stay at home until it clears on Saturday.

1. According to the weatherman, what will tomorrow's low temperature be?
2. What has happened to area schools and factories?
3. What should you do if you need emergency transportation?
4. When is the weather expected to clear?

Mini Talk Three

We interrupt this program to bring you a special weather bulletin. The National Weather Service has issued a tornado watch for the following five counties: Douglas, Johnson, Jefferson, Leavenworth, and Franklin. The watch will be in effect until ten o'clock tonight or until cancellation by the Weather Service.

Remember, a tornado *watch* means that weather conditions are favorable for the formation of a funnel cloud. A tornado *warning* means that a funnel cloud has been sighted. As yet, no tornado warnings have been issued for any of the counties in the area.

1. Until what time will the tornado watch be in effect?
2. Which county was not mentioned as having been included in the tornado watch?
3. What is the definition of a tornado warning?
4. How many counties have been included in the tornado watch?

Mini Talk Four

On the satellite map we can see how the rain and showers in Kansas and Nebraska moved into Illinois and Indiana overnight, crossed Lake Michigan, and dissipated in upstate New York and Canada.

The showers and thunderstorms moved north of us leaving all stations in the Tri-State Area with reports of sunny skies and warm temperatures. Trenton is reporting eighty-five degrees with fair skies. Eighty-seven degrees in Wilmington, and the sun is still shining in New Brunswick with eighty degrees. The current temperature reading here in Philadelphia is eighty-five degrees under sunny skies. The barometric pressure is 30.05 and holding steady. Southwesterly winds at five to ten miles per hour.

For tomorrow, more fair weather with a high expected near ninety degrees, a low of about seventy, and no rain in sight until Thursday or Friday.

1. In general terms, what is the weather like in the Tri-State Area?
2. What is the average temperature for Philadelphia and surrounding cities now?
3. According to the weatherman, what happened to the thundershowers yesterday?
4. When is it likely to rain in Philadelphia?

EXERCISE SEVENTEEN:
MINI TALKS/INFORMATIVE SPEECHES

Mini Talk One

As director of the Office of International Student Affairs, it is one of my more pleasant duties to welcome you on behalf of State University to the annual International Dinner. This year the food that you are enjoying was prepared by students from thirty-five countries. Right now coffee from Brazil and Colombia is being served at the tables, and for those of you who prefer tea, there is a selection of teas from Japan, India, and Ireland at the beverages booth. Please serve yourselves.

In the meantime, I would like to take a few moments to thank some of the people who have worked so hard to make this evening possible, especially Mr. Abdul Al-Husseini, president of the International Student Association; Miss Isabel Ruiz and Mrs. Benne Singh, chairpersons of the food committee; Mr. Sim Lee, chairperson of the program committee; and Mr. and Mrs. George Pappas, chairpersons of the publicity and ticket committee. I am sure that the dinner could not have been such a success without their time and efforts.

And now, as I see, almost everyone has been served, and we will be able to begin our program. First, a fashion show, featuring the typical dress of fifteen countries, followed by a number of traditional songs and dances from around the world.

After the program, may I invite you to stay to dance to disco music compliments of Jim Johnson, here with us from WQAD radio.

1. Who is the speaker?
2. What are the people doing while they are listening to the speaker?
3. What is the main purpose of the talk?
4. After the program, what will the students do?

Mini Talk Two

It is a great honor for me to introduce today's guest lecturer, Dr. C. Henry Taylor, a colleague who is so well known to all of us for his many accomplishments and contributions to the field of architecture and planning that it hardly seems necessary to recount them here. Nevertheless, as customary, I will summarize his long experience as a prelude to his address.

Dr. Taylor received his B.A. degree in urban history at Yale University in 1955. Five years later, he was awarded a masters degree in architecture and a Ph.D. in urban design from Cornell University. Upon graduating, he accepted a teaching position in the Department of Architecture and Fine Arts at Illinois University where he was promoted to chairman of the department in 1969. Last year Dr. Taylor resigned from the University in order to accept a research position with the Department of Housing and Urban Development in Washington as director of planning.

In addition to teaching and research, Dr. Taylor has devoted much time to designing, writing, and lecturing. Some of his most famous buildings are right here in the Chicago area, and include the Twin Towers office building and the Saint Lawrence Seaway Recreation Center. His many articles on functional architecture and urban planning have appeared in scores of journals over the past twenty years, and a half dozen textbooks are to his credit, including one of the books that we use for this seminar, *Trends in Urban Design.*

Today Dr. Taylor will speak to us about federal regulations for urban development, and frankly, I know of no one more qualified to address the subject.

Ladies and gentlemen, please welcome Dr. C. Henry Taylor, scholar, designer, and author.

1. From which university did Dr. Taylor receive his Ph. D.?
2. Where is Dr. Taylor employed now?
3. What is the topic of Dr. Taylor's lecture?
4. How does the speaker feel about Dr. Taylor?

Mini Talk Three

Ladies and gentlemen, in October, 1979, we observed the "Centennial of Light," the one-hundredth anniversary of the electric lamp, without doubt the greatest achievement of America's most celebrated inventor, Thomas Alva Edison. But, you may ask, what does that have to do with the Community Book Club?

Simply this: when I was asked to speak at the Book Club luncheon, I thought about several topics that might be of interest to a group of avid readers, and I considered doing a book review or discussing the life of a well known literary figure. But the one-hundredth anniversary kept recurring in the news, always with reference to Mr. Edison's great love for books and reading. I thought that I would break with tradition today in order to share some anecdotes from the life of a man, who like you, enjoyed reading.

In spite of the fact that Mr. Edison had almost no formal education, spending only three months in school, his mother had taught him to read at quite an early age. Between the ages of nine and twelve, he read such difficult volumes as Humes' *History of England, The Penny Encyclopedia,* Gibson's *Decline and Fall of the Roman Empire,* Muhr's *Dictionary of the Sciences,* and Newton's *Principia.*

As a young man, Mr. Edison decided to read all of the books in the Detroit public library, systematically, shelf by shelf. After finishing the first fifteen feet, he decided to reconsider the task.

A few years later, in Cincinnati, his love for reading almost cost him his life. Having stayed at the library until very late, Mr. Edison started home with a pile of old magazines for which he had paid the large sum of two dollars. Suspecting that he might be a thief, a policeman ordered him to stop. But Mr. Edison was too deaf to hear the order. The policeman shot, and missed.

In addition to the electric light, Thomas Edison is known for inventing the phonograph, microphone, mimeograph, electric storage battery, and photographic film. Whenever he was paid for an invention, he used the money for his two loves—more experiments and more books.

A friend described Edison's life in those busy days. "I went to visit Tom," he said, "and I found him sitting behind a pile of books five feet high which he had ordered from New York, London, and Paris. He studied them night and day, eating at his desk and sleeping in his chair. In six weeks he had read all of the books and had performed more than two thousand experiments using the formulas that he had studied."

1. Who is the audience for this talk?
2. Why did the speaker choose to talk about Thomas Edison?
3. What did Mr. Edison do with the money that he earned from his inventions?
4. Why is October, 1979, an important date?

Mini Talk Four

It is a great privilege for me to be invited to speak at the tenth-year reunion of State University's graduating class.

When you arrived on campus today, after a decade, you were probably impressed by two changes at State: one, the absence of University Tower, the first building constructed on the campus, and an historic landmark for many years; and two, the disappearance of parking lots on main campus.

Two years ago University Tower was inspected and found to be unsafe. In spite of efforts to restore it, it was necessary to level the building. A belltower was constructed on the same site, built for the most part using the good brick that was saved from the original building. The original bells were also preserved.

As for the parking lots, they have been replaced by grass, trees, and pedestrian walkways. Parking is now located in parking garages on the North and West sides of the campus.

Two more subtle changes have occurred within the past decade. One is the creation and expansion of the Division of Continuing Education for the Community, including a Saturday and summer enrichment program for children, and an afternoon and evening special interest program for adults. The other is the addition to the student population of many young people from abroad, especially students from Japan, Latin America, and the Middle East. Most international students are enrolled in the College of Engineering and the College of Business.

And so, State is a different place, but like University Tower, it is built of the same brick. We are still committed to the same age-old ideals of quality education for our citizens, but we have extended our commitment beyond the borders of our state and nation to encompass the citizens and nations of the world.

1. What is the occasion for the man's speech?
2. How is State University the same?
3. Why was University Tower torn down?
4. What is the main idea of the man's talk?

EXERCISE EIGHTEEN: MINI TALKS/ACADEMIC STATEMENTS (PART 1)

Mini Talk One

Yesterday we discussed the problem of rising prices, or, in the economist's terms, inflation. We noted that, during periods of inflation, all prices and incomes do not rise at the same rate. Some incomes rise more slowly than the cost of living, and a few do not rise at all. Other incomes rise more rapidly than the cost of living.

We concluded that persons with fixed incomes, as for example, the elderly who depend upon pensions, and persons with slow-rising incomes as, for example, an employee with a salary agreed to in a long-term contract, will be most seriously affected by inflation. Please recall that while their dollar incomes stay the same, the cost of goods and services rises, and in effect, real income decreases; that is, they are able to purchase less with the same amount of money.

We also talked about the fact that stockholders and persons with business interests and investments would probably benefit most from inflation, since high prices would increase sales receipts, and profits would likely rise faster than the cost of living.

And now, before we begin today's lecture, are there any questions about the term inflation or any of the examples given in our discussion so far?

1. What is the main purpose of the talk?
2. According to the lecture, what is inflation?
3. Who benefits most from inflation?
4. What happens when income rises more slowly than the cost of living?

Mini Talk Two

To review from yesterday's lecture, ecology is the study of organisms in relation to their environment, including the interrelationships of many organisms themselves as well as the relationships of these organisms with the non-organic environment. The total complex of relationships is referred to as the "web of life."

The fundamental components of the environment are plants, animals, minerals, and water. When their relationships do not change much from year to year, we observe a balance of nature. That is, the addition of plants, animals, minerals, and water is equal to that which has been removed. As an example, the minerals taken from the soil are restored, and the plants that die are replaced by similar plants.

Today we will discuss what occurs when the balance of nature is disturbed, either by a geological change such as a change of climate, or a local agitation such as a fire.

After the balance of nature has been disturbed, a period of rehabilitation must occur. The first life to appear is called pioneer flora and fauna. The pioneer life is temporary and soon replaced by other forms of life. In turn, these forms are replaced by others. That is, a series of transitional life forms successively appears, preparing the environment for the forms that will replace them.

Eventually, a new balance is established. The final stage in the relationships of plants and animals in transition tends to be stable for a long time. It is called a "climax association."

For example, after a forest fire, pioneer plants will appear, usually herbs or ground cover. Soon they will be replaced by shrubs. Shrubs will be replaced by the first trees. The first trees will be replaced by other species of trees. And so it goes, until ultimately, a permanent climax flora will establish itself in balance with the fauna, minerals, and water supply.

Interestingly enough, the climax association may not have the same kinds of plants and animals as the association that was prevalent before the fire. What is essential is that the balance of nature permits the association to continue in spite of other organic competition for the area.

1. What is the main topic of today's lecture?
2. Why is the example of a forest fire used?
3. According to the lecturer, why is pioneer life important?
4. What is essential in the identification of a climax association?

Mini Talk Three

In an earlier age, there was a great distinction in the public mind between science and engineering. Whereas the scientist was thought of as an intellectual, motivated by a desire for knowledge and order, the engineer was thought of as a busy, practical person, involved in producing something for which the public was willing to pay. The scientist might discover the laws of nature, but the engineer would be the one to exploit them for use and profit.

Historically, however, the distinction has not been valid. In every century, noted theoretical scholars were deeply involved in the practical application of their own work. For example, in the seventeenth century, Christian Huygens, a Dutch astronomer, mathematician, and physicist who developed theorems on centrifugal force and wave motion also developed the first accurate timepiece. In the eighteenth century, the British mathematician and philosopher Sir Isaac Newton was credited not only with advancing theories of mechanics and optics, but also with inventing the reflecting telescope, a direct application of his theory. In the nineteenth century, the French chemist and bacteriologist Louis Pasteur first proposed theories of disease, and then set about the discovery of vaccines for anthrax and rabies, as well as the process for purification that bears his name to this day.

I propose that the popular detachment of science from engineering has not provided us with a useful model for comparison, and perhaps not even an historically correct one.

1. According to public opinion in the past, how was a scientist different from an engineer?
2. Who was Christian Huygens?
3. Why did the lecturer discuss the work of Huygens, Newton, and Pasteur?
4. What was the lecturer's opinion about science?

Mini Talk Four

Today I want to help you with a study reading method known as SQ3R. The letters stand for five steps in the reading process: Survey, Question, Read, Review, Recite. Each of the steps should be done carefully and in the order mentioned.

In all study reading, a *survey* should be the first step. Survey means to look quickly. In study reading you need to look quickly at titles, words in darker or larger print, words with capital letters, illustrations, and charts. Don't stop to read complete sentences. Just look at the important divisions of the material.

The second step is *question*. Try to form questions based on your survey. Use the question words *who, what, when, where, why,* and *how*.

Now you are ready for the third step. *Read*. You will be rereading the titles and important words that you looked at in the survey. But this time you will read the examples and details as well. Sometimes it is useful to take notes while you read. I have had students who preferred to underline important points, and it seemed to be just as useful as note-taking. What you should do, whether you take notes or underline, is to read actively. Think about what you are reading as a series of ideas, not just a sequence of words.

The fourth step is *review*. Remember the questions that you wrote down before you read the material? You should be able to answer them now. You will notice that some of the questions were treated in more detail in the reading. Concentrate on those. Also review material that you did not consider in your questions.

The last step is *recite*. Try to put the reading into your own words. Summarize it either in writing or orally.

SQ3R—survey, question, read, review, and recite.

1. What do the letters in the SQ3R method represent?
2. What does the word <u>survey</u> mean?
3. What does the lecturer say about <u>reading</u>, step three in the SQ3R method?
4. What is the last step in the SQ3R method?

EXERCISE EIGHTEEN: MINI/TALKS ACADEMIC STATEMENTS (PART 2)

Mini Talk One

Your test on Friday will cover material from both of your textbooks, my lecture notes, and your lab assignments. There will be fifty multiple-choice questions and five short answer essay questions. The multiple-choice will count half of your grade and the essay questions will count half of your grade.

I will tell you right now that there won't be any math problems, but that doesn't mean that you shouldn't review the formulas and know what they are used for.

I wouldn't bother much with the notes from my first lecture since that was an overview of the course, but you'll probably want to look at them when you study for the final.

Oh yes, this test represents twenty-five percent of your total grade for the semester. The lab reports are twenty-five percent, attendance ten, and your final forty.

Any questions?

1. In which class would this announcement occur?
2. What is the purpose of the announcement?
3. On this test, how much will the multiple-choice questions count?
4. What percentage of the total grade will this test count?

Mini Talk Two

Good morning. I trust that you have all read the assignment and that we can proceed with today's lecture. As you know from your text, both heredity and environment play a role in the development of the personality.

In addition, research at the University of Texas at Arlington has shown that the order of one's birth in relationship to brothers and sisters may be a significant factor. Those born first tend to develop personality traits that make them domineering, ambitious, and highly motivated to achieve. And the same is true for only children. In contrast, children born later in the family tend to be more socially adept, likable, talkative individuals.

Also interesting in the research is the fact that a woman with older brothers and a man with older sisters seem to be able to interact more easily with the opposite sex. Having older opposite-sex siblings seems to be important in being able to establish social relationships with members of the opposite sex.

1. What should the students know before they hear this lecture?
2. What is the main subject of this lecture?
3. What personality traits do firstborn children exhibit?
4. Which one of the people listed in question four would probably be the most comfortable interacting with a member of the opposite sex?

Mini Talk Three

The term *parapsychology* was coined by Professor Joseph Rhine of Duke University because he felt that a word was needed to identify the kinds of phenomena that did not fit into the conventional framework of psychology and yet were real in scientific terms. *Para* means *beyond psychology* in Greek. Parapsychology then, deals with those phenomena of the human mind or personality that can't be explained on the basis of ordinary psychology.

Another term that Professor Rhine has given us is *ESP* or *extra sensory perception.* ESP is the means by which parapsychological phenomena occur. With these two terms in mind, let us turn to the topic of today's lecture—the history of parapsychology.

1. Where did this talk probably take place?
2. Who is Professor Rhine?
3. What is parapsychology?
4. What is the topic for today's lecture to be given after these opening comments?

Mini Talk Four

Before you start writing your term papers, I would like to clarify the differences among paraphrasing, quoting, and plagiarizing. All of these activities involve the use of someone else's ideas, but whereas paraphrasing and quoting are legitimate writing strategies, plagiarizing is a serious offense.

In your term papers, I expect you to paraphrase, that is, to summarize someone else's ideas in your own words. I also expect you to quote, that is to copy information from another source and enclose it in quotation marks in your paper.

When you paraphrase and quote, be sure to cite the source of your information. If you do not cite the source, then you are plagiarizing. You are stealing the ideas and using them as your own. If I discover that you have plagiarized on your term paper, you will receive a zero for the paper and an F for the course.

1. What is paraphrasing?
2. What is plagiarizing?
3. What are two legitimate writing strategies?
4. What will happen to a student who plagiarizes on the term paper?

EXERCISE NINETEEN: MINI TALKS/CLASS DISCUSSIONS

Mini Talk One

Smith: Let's talk about the results of your laboratory experiment. Did you have any problems with it?

Bob: Yes, Professor Smith. We did.

Smith: Who's your lab partner, Bob?

Bob: Anne Wilson.

Smith: Well, Anne, can you and Bob go over the procedure for the class?

Anne: Sure. First we put ten grams of crushed limestone in a bottle.

Smith: Anything special about the bottle?

Bob: It was a gas-collecting bottle with a one-hole stopper and bent glass tubing.

Smith: Very good. So you put the limestone in a gas-collecting bottle. Then what?

Anne: Then we poured in ten milligrams of hydrochloric acid, put on the stopper, and collected a bottle of carbon dioxide.

Smith: Right. What was the method of collection?

Anne: Water displacement.

Smith: Good.

Anne: Then, we lit a magnesium ribbon and put it in the bottle of carbon dioxide.

Bob: And carbon deposits began to form on the bottom of the bottle. You see, we didn't have any problem with procedure. . . .

Anne: Well, we had a little problem getting the magnesium ribbon to stay lit until we could get it into the bottle.

Bob: Okay. But we did it. The big problem was that we really didn't understand what happened. Did the magnesium combine with the oxygen in the carbon dioxide?

Smith: You have just answered your own question, Bob. The burning magnesium broke the carbon–oxygen bonds in the carbon dioxide, and then the oxygen combined with the magnesium to produce magnesium oxide.

Anne: And the carbon was freed to deposit itself on the bottle.

Smith: Exactly.

1.   How was gas collected in the bottle during the experiment?
2.   What was deposited on the bottom of the gas bottle?
3.   What caused the deposits?
4.   Why did Bob and Anne have problems with the experiment?

Mini Talk Two

Sally: I'm sorry. I just don't agree with you at all.

Paul: Look. Take the example of an international student applying for university admission. If the student has a 500 on the TOEFL or an 80 on the Michigan Test, most admissions officers will accept the applicant. The student with a 499 or 79 won't be considered. The officer won't even look at transcripts.

Sally: Right. But I think that proves my point, not yours.

Paul: How?

Sally: Well, it's the admissions officer who decides *how* to use the test. The TOEFL and the Michigan are good English proficiency tests, but that's all they are. And English proficiency is necessary for success in an American university, but so are several other factors, including good academic preparation.

Paul: Good academic preparation is more important.

Sally: Maybe. I don't really know. But what I'm trying to explain to you is that admissions officers should use the proficiency test as one of many considerations, and as such, they really shouldn't insist on a rigid cut-off score like 500 or 80.

Ayers: Isn't this the basic disagreement: that Paul thinks the tests are bad in themselves, and Sally believes that the tests are good, but that many people don't use them for their intended purpose.

Paul: I don't agree with having the tests, Professor Ayers, and that's my position.

Sally: But Paul, what would you do to evaluate the English proficiency of a student ten thousand miles away without a standardized test?

Paul: I admit that's a big problem.

Sally: It sure is.

Ayers: Okay, class. For Wednesday, let's consider the problem of evaluation without standardized tests like the TOEFL, the SAT, GMAT, and GRE. Paul says that there ought to be an alternative. Sally doesn't seem to believe that there is an appropriate alternative. Please bring in your ideas and suggestions, and we'll discuss them.

1.   What is Paul's opinion about the TOEFL and the Michigan Test?
2.   What does Sally say about the admissions officers?
3.   What are the SAT, GMAT, and GRE?
4.   Where did this discussion most probably take place?

Mini Talk Three

Tom:	Dr. Anderson, could you please clarify the requirements for this course? Some of us are a little bit confused about the final examination.
Anderson:	Oh? Well, you have two options in this course. You can either take a final examination or you can write a research paper instead.
Tom:	Excuse me, Dr. Anderson. That's the point I need you to clarify. What kind of research paper did you have in mind? A study? A report? A book review, perhaps?
Anderson:	A report. A summary really, based upon current research in the field.
Jane:	How long should the reports be?
Anderson:	Length is really not important. I should think that it would take at least ten pages in order to develop the topic, however.
Jane:	And should we check the topic with you before we begin writing?
Anderson:	You may, if you wish. But the only requirement is that it relate to current trends in United States foreign policy. Are you considering writing a paper, Jane?
Jane:	I'm not sure. I think that I'd like to know a little bit more about the examination.
Anderson:	All right. One hundred multiple-choice questions covering both the lectures and the outside readings.
Tom:	Didn't you say that you would give us one hour for the examination?
Anderson:	Yes, I did.
Tom:	I'm going to do the paper, then.
Jane:	Me too.

1. What are the requirements for Dr. Anderson's course?
2. What kind of research paper has Dr. Anderson assigned?
3. What kind of examination has Dr. Anderson prepared?
4. Based upon the class discussion, which course does Dr. Anderson most probably teach?

Mini Talk Four

Baker: Since so many of you have asked me about how to learn a language, I thought that it might be useful to take some class time today to discuss it. Betty, you speak several languages, don't you?

Betty: Yes, I speak Spanish and French.

Baker: And what helped you most in learning those languages?

Betty: What helped me most. . . . Well, I studied both languages in high school, and I'm still studying Spanish here at the University, but I think that travel has probably been the most help to me. You see, I've been lucky in that I've lived in Europe. Believe me, I didn't speak very well before I moved there.

Bill: You're right, Betty. After studying a language, practice is very useful. When you live in a country where the language is spoken, it's ideal. But, you know, sometimes it's difficult to make friends in a new place, even when the people are very friendly.

Betty: Yes, I know what you mean. Especially if you don't speak the language too well. I had some problems when I first moved to Europe.

Baker: And, of course, some people are shy.

Betty: That's true.

Bill: Professor Baker, whether or not I'm living in a country where the language is spoken, I always go to movies, and whenever I can, I watch TV or listen to the radio in the language I'm trying to learn.

Betty: Me too. And reading is another good way to learn. Books are good, but I think that newspapers and magazines are even better.

Baker: Probably the best way to learn is to combine all of these ideas: traveling, talking with people, going to movies, watching TV, listening to the radio, and reading books, newspapers and magazines. What do you think?

Betty: I agree with that, Professor Baker.

Bill: So do I. But I don't believe that it's possible to take advantage of practice opportunities without some knowledge of the language first.

Betty: Sure. First it's a good idea to study grammar, vocabulary. . . .

Bill: . . . and listening, perhaps even reading.

Betty: Then practice is very, very helpful.

1. What helped Betty most in learning Spanish?
2. What does Bill say about making friends in a new place?
3. How does Bill practice when he is not living in a country where the language is spoken?
4. What is Professor Baker's opinion?

Answer Sheets
for the TOEFL
Practice Exercises

There are now two versions of the TOEFL answer sheet. One is horizontal and the other is vertical. When you take the TOEFL examination, you will receive only one version of the answer sheet.

ANSWER SHEET FOR CHAPTER THREE

EXERCISE ONE: TEENS AND TENS

1 Ⓐ Ⓑ Ⓒ Ⓓ	5 Ⓐ Ⓑ Ⓒ Ⓓ	9 Ⓐ Ⓑ Ⓒ Ⓓ	13 Ⓐ Ⓑ Ⓒ Ⓓ	17 Ⓐ Ⓑ Ⓒ Ⓓ
2 Ⓐ Ⓑ Ⓒ Ⓓ	6 Ⓐ Ⓑ Ⓒ Ⓓ	10 Ⓐ Ⓑ Ⓒ Ⓓ	14 Ⓐ Ⓑ Ⓒ Ⓓ	18 Ⓐ Ⓑ Ⓒ Ⓓ
3 Ⓐ Ⓑ Ⓒ Ⓓ	7 Ⓐ Ⓑ Ⓒ Ⓓ	11 Ⓐ Ⓑ Ⓒ Ⓓ	15 Ⓐ Ⓑ Ⓒ Ⓓ	19 Ⓐ Ⓑ Ⓒ Ⓓ
4 Ⓐ Ⓑ Ⓒ Ⓓ	8 Ⓐ Ⓑ Ⓒ Ⓓ	12 Ⓐ Ⓑ Ⓒ Ⓓ	16 Ⓐ Ⓑ Ⓒ Ⓓ	20 Ⓐ Ⓑ Ⓒ Ⓓ

EXERCISE TWO: COMPUTATIONS

1 Ⓐ Ⓑ Ⓒ Ⓓ	5 Ⓐ Ⓑ Ⓒ Ⓓ	9 Ⓐ Ⓑ Ⓒ Ⓓ	13 Ⓐ Ⓑ Ⓒ Ⓓ	17 Ⓐ Ⓑ Ⓒ Ⓓ
2 Ⓐ Ⓑ Ⓒ Ⓓ	6 Ⓐ Ⓑ Ⓒ Ⓓ	10 Ⓐ Ⓑ Ⓒ Ⓓ	14 Ⓐ Ⓑ Ⓒ Ⓓ	18 Ⓐ Ⓑ Ⓒ Ⓓ
3 Ⓐ Ⓑ Ⓒ Ⓓ	7 Ⓐ Ⓑ Ⓒ Ⓓ	11 Ⓐ Ⓑ Ⓒ Ⓓ	15 Ⓐ Ⓑ Ⓒ Ⓓ	19 Ⓐ Ⓑ Ⓒ Ⓓ
4 Ⓐ Ⓑ Ⓒ Ⓓ	8 Ⓐ Ⓑ Ⓒ Ⓓ	12 Ⓐ Ⓑ Ⓒ Ⓓ	16 Ⓐ Ⓑ Ⓒ Ⓓ	20 Ⓐ Ⓑ Ⓒ Ⓓ

EXERCISE THREE: REFERENCE

1 Ⓐ Ⓑ Ⓒ Ⓓ	5 Ⓐ Ⓑ Ⓒ Ⓓ	9 Ⓐ Ⓑ Ⓒ Ⓓ	13 Ⓐ Ⓑ Ⓒ Ⓓ	17 Ⓐ Ⓑ Ⓒ Ⓓ
2 Ⓐ Ⓑ Ⓒ Ⓓ	6 Ⓐ Ⓑ Ⓒ Ⓓ	10 Ⓐ Ⓑ Ⓒ Ⓓ	14 Ⓐ Ⓑ Ⓒ Ⓓ	18 Ⓐ Ⓑ Ⓒ Ⓓ
3 Ⓐ Ⓑ Ⓒ Ⓓ	7 Ⓐ Ⓑ Ⓒ Ⓓ	11 Ⓐ Ⓑ Ⓒ Ⓓ	15 Ⓐ Ⓑ Ⓒ Ⓓ	19 Ⓐ Ⓑ Ⓒ Ⓓ
4 Ⓐ Ⓑ Ⓒ Ⓓ	8 Ⓐ Ⓑ Ⓒ Ⓓ	12 Ⓐ Ⓑ Ⓒ Ⓓ	16 Ⓐ Ⓑ Ⓒ Ⓓ	20 Ⓐ Ⓑ Ⓒ Ⓓ

EXERCISE FOUR: NEGATIVES

1 Ⓐ Ⓑ Ⓒ Ⓓ	5 Ⓐ Ⓑ Ⓒ Ⓓ	9 Ⓐ Ⓑ Ⓒ Ⓓ	13 Ⓐ Ⓑ Ⓒ Ⓓ	17 Ⓐ Ⓑ Ⓒ Ⓓ
2 Ⓐ Ⓑ Ⓒ Ⓓ	6 Ⓐ Ⓑ Ⓒ Ⓓ	10 Ⓐ Ⓑ Ⓒ Ⓓ	14 Ⓐ Ⓑ Ⓒ Ⓓ	18 Ⓐ Ⓑ Ⓒ Ⓓ
3 Ⓐ Ⓑ Ⓒ Ⓓ	7 Ⓐ Ⓑ Ⓒ Ⓓ	11 Ⓐ Ⓑ Ⓒ Ⓓ	15 Ⓐ Ⓑ Ⓒ Ⓓ	19 Ⓐ Ⓑ Ⓒ Ⓓ
4 Ⓐ Ⓑ Ⓒ Ⓓ	8 Ⓐ Ⓑ Ⓒ Ⓓ	12 Ⓐ Ⓑ Ⓒ Ⓓ	16 Ⓐ Ⓑ Ⓒ Ⓓ	20 Ⓐ Ⓑ Ⓒ Ⓓ

EXERCISE FIVE: COMPARATIVES

1 Ⓐ Ⓑ Ⓒ Ⓓ	5 Ⓐ Ⓑ Ⓒ Ⓓ	9 Ⓐ Ⓑ Ⓒ Ⓓ	13 Ⓐ Ⓑ Ⓒ Ⓓ	17 Ⓐ Ⓑ Ⓒ Ⓓ
2 Ⓐ Ⓑ Ⓒ Ⓓ	6 Ⓐ Ⓑ Ⓒ Ⓓ	10 Ⓐ Ⓑ Ⓒ Ⓓ	14 Ⓐ Ⓑ Ⓒ Ⓓ	18 Ⓐ Ⓑ Ⓒ Ⓓ
3 Ⓐ Ⓑ Ⓒ Ⓓ	7 Ⓐ Ⓑ Ⓒ Ⓓ	11 Ⓐ Ⓑ Ⓒ Ⓓ	15 Ⓐ Ⓑ Ⓒ Ⓓ	19 Ⓐ Ⓑ Ⓒ Ⓓ
4 Ⓐ Ⓑ Ⓒ Ⓓ	8 Ⓐ Ⓑ Ⓒ Ⓓ	12 Ⓐ Ⓑ Ⓒ Ⓓ	16 Ⓐ Ⓑ Ⓒ Ⓓ	20 Ⓐ Ⓑ Ⓒ Ⓓ

EXERCISE SIX: CONDITIONALS

1 Ⓐ Ⓑ Ⓒ Ⓓ	5 Ⓐ Ⓑ Ⓒ Ⓓ	9 Ⓐ Ⓑ Ⓒ Ⓓ	13 Ⓐ Ⓑ Ⓒ Ⓓ	17 Ⓐ Ⓑ Ⓒ Ⓓ
2 Ⓐ Ⓑ Ⓒ Ⓓ	6 Ⓐ Ⓑ Ⓒ Ⓓ	10 Ⓐ Ⓑ Ⓒ Ⓓ	14 Ⓐ Ⓑ Ⓒ Ⓓ	18 Ⓐ Ⓑ Ⓒ Ⓓ
3 Ⓐ Ⓑ Ⓒ Ⓓ	7 Ⓐ Ⓑ Ⓒ Ⓓ	11 Ⓐ Ⓑ Ⓒ Ⓓ	15 Ⓐ Ⓑ Ⓒ Ⓓ	19 Ⓐ Ⓑ Ⓒ Ⓓ
4 Ⓐ Ⓑ Ⓒ Ⓓ	8 Ⓐ Ⓑ Ⓒ Ⓓ	12 Ⓐ Ⓑ Ⓒ Ⓓ	16 Ⓐ Ⓑ Ⓒ Ⓓ	20 Ⓐ Ⓑ Ⓒ Ⓓ

EXERCISE SEVEN: CONCESSIONS (PART 1)

1 Ⓐ Ⓑ Ⓒ Ⓓ	5 Ⓐ Ⓑ Ⓒ Ⓓ	9 Ⓐ Ⓑ Ⓒ Ⓓ	13 Ⓐ Ⓑ Ⓒ Ⓓ	17 Ⓐ Ⓑ Ⓒ Ⓓ
2 Ⓐ Ⓑ Ⓒ Ⓓ	6 Ⓐ Ⓑ Ⓒ Ⓓ	10 Ⓐ Ⓑ Ⓒ Ⓓ	14 Ⓐ Ⓑ Ⓒ Ⓓ	18 Ⓐ Ⓑ Ⓒ Ⓓ
3 Ⓐ Ⓑ Ⓒ Ⓓ	7 Ⓐ Ⓑ Ⓒ Ⓓ	11 Ⓐ Ⓑ Ⓒ Ⓓ	15 Ⓐ Ⓑ Ⓒ Ⓓ	19 Ⓐ Ⓑ Ⓒ Ⓓ
4 Ⓐ Ⓑ Ⓒ Ⓓ	8 Ⓐ Ⓑ Ⓒ Ⓓ	12 Ⓐ Ⓑ Ⓒ Ⓓ	16 Ⓐ Ⓑ Ⓒ Ⓓ	20 Ⓐ Ⓑ Ⓒ Ⓓ

EXERCISE SEVEN: CONCESSIONS (PART 2)

1 Ⓐ Ⓑ Ⓒ Ⓓ	5 Ⓐ Ⓑ Ⓒ Ⓓ	9 Ⓐ Ⓑ Ⓒ Ⓓ	13 Ⓐ Ⓑ Ⓒ Ⓓ	17 Ⓐ Ⓑ Ⓒ Ⓓ
2 Ⓐ Ⓑ Ⓒ Ⓓ	6 Ⓐ Ⓑ Ⓒ Ⓓ	10 Ⓐ Ⓑ Ⓒ Ⓓ	14 Ⓐ Ⓑ Ⓒ Ⓓ	18 Ⓐ Ⓑ Ⓒ Ⓓ
3 Ⓐ Ⓑ Ⓒ Ⓓ	7 Ⓐ Ⓑ Ⓒ Ⓓ	11 Ⓐ Ⓑ Ⓒ Ⓓ	15 Ⓐ Ⓑ Ⓒ Ⓓ	19 Ⓐ Ⓑ Ⓒ Ⓓ
4 Ⓐ Ⓑ Ⓒ Ⓓ	8 Ⓐ Ⓑ Ⓒ Ⓓ	12 Ⓐ Ⓑ Ⓒ Ⓓ	16 Ⓐ Ⓑ Ⓒ Ⓓ	20 Ⓐ Ⓑ Ⓒ Ⓓ

EXERCISE EIGHT: HOMOPHONES AND HOMONYMS

1 Ⓐ Ⓑ Ⓒ Ⓓ	5 Ⓐ Ⓑ Ⓒ Ⓓ	9 Ⓐ Ⓑ Ⓒ Ⓓ	13 Ⓐ Ⓑ Ⓒ Ⓓ	17 Ⓐ Ⓑ Ⓒ Ⓓ
2 Ⓐ Ⓑ Ⓒ Ⓓ	6 Ⓐ Ⓑ Ⓒ Ⓓ	10 Ⓐ Ⓑ Ⓒ Ⓓ	14 Ⓐ Ⓑ Ⓒ Ⓓ	18 Ⓐ Ⓑ Ⓒ Ⓓ
3 Ⓐ Ⓑ Ⓒ Ⓓ	7 Ⓐ Ⓑ Ⓒ Ⓓ	11 Ⓐ Ⓑ Ⓒ Ⓓ	15 Ⓐ Ⓑ Ⓒ Ⓓ	19 Ⓐ Ⓑ Ⓒ Ⓓ
4 Ⓐ Ⓑ Ⓒ Ⓓ	8 Ⓐ Ⓑ Ⓒ Ⓓ	12 Ⓐ Ⓑ Ⓒ Ⓓ	16 Ⓐ Ⓑ Ⓒ Ⓓ	20 Ⓐ Ⓑ Ⓒ Ⓓ

EXERCISE TEN: CONVERSATIONS/COMPUTATIONS

1 Ⓐ Ⓑ Ⓒ Ⓓ	4 Ⓐ Ⓑ Ⓒ Ⓓ	7 Ⓐ Ⓑ Ⓒ Ⓓ	10 Ⓐ Ⓑ Ⓒ Ⓓ	13 Ⓐ Ⓑ Ⓒ Ⓓ
2 Ⓐ Ⓑ Ⓒ Ⓓ	5 Ⓐ Ⓑ Ⓒ Ⓓ	8 Ⓐ Ⓑ Ⓒ Ⓓ	11 Ⓐ Ⓑ Ⓒ Ⓓ	14 Ⓐ Ⓑ Ⓒ Ⓓ
3 Ⓐ Ⓑ Ⓒ Ⓓ	6 Ⓐ Ⓑ Ⓒ Ⓓ	9 Ⓐ Ⓑ Ⓒ Ⓓ	12 Ⓐ Ⓑ Ⓒ Ⓓ	15 Ⓐ Ⓑ Ⓒ Ⓓ

EXERCISE ELEVEN: CONVERSATIONS/PLACE

1 Ⓐ Ⓑ Ⓒ Ⓓ	4 Ⓐ Ⓑ Ⓒ Ⓓ	7 Ⓐ Ⓑ Ⓒ Ⓓ	10 Ⓐ Ⓑ Ⓒ Ⓓ	13 Ⓐ Ⓑ Ⓒ Ⓓ
2 Ⓐ Ⓑ Ⓒ Ⓓ	5 Ⓐ Ⓑ Ⓒ Ⓓ	8 Ⓐ Ⓑ Ⓒ Ⓓ	11 Ⓐ Ⓑ Ⓒ Ⓓ	14 Ⓐ Ⓑ Ⓒ Ⓓ
3 Ⓐ Ⓑ Ⓒ Ⓓ	6 Ⓐ Ⓑ Ⓒ Ⓓ	9 Ⓐ Ⓑ Ⓒ Ⓓ	12 Ⓐ Ⓑ Ⓒ Ⓓ	15 Ⓐ Ⓑ Ⓒ Ⓓ

EXERCISE TWELVE: CONVERSATIONS/IMPLIED

1 Ⓐ Ⓑ Ⓒ Ⓓ	4 Ⓐ Ⓑ Ⓒ Ⓓ	7 Ⓐ Ⓑ Ⓒ Ⓓ	10 Ⓐ Ⓑ Ⓒ Ⓓ	13 Ⓐ Ⓑ Ⓒ Ⓓ
2 Ⓐ Ⓑ Ⓒ Ⓓ	5 Ⓐ Ⓑ Ⓒ Ⓓ	8 Ⓐ Ⓑ Ⓒ Ⓓ	11 Ⓐ Ⓑ Ⓒ Ⓓ	14 Ⓐ Ⓑ Ⓒ Ⓓ
3 Ⓐ Ⓑ Ⓒ Ⓓ	6 Ⓐ Ⓑ Ⓒ Ⓓ	9 Ⓐ Ⓑ Ⓒ Ⓓ	12 Ⓐ Ⓑ Ⓒ Ⓓ	15 Ⓐ Ⓑ Ⓒ Ⓓ

EXERCISE THIRTEEN: MINI TALKS/OVERHEARD CONVERSATIONS

Mini Talk One	Mini Talk Two	Mini Talk Three	Mini Talk Four
1 Ⓐ Ⓑ Ⓒ Ⓓ	1 Ⓐ Ⓑ Ⓒ Ⓓ	1 Ⓐ Ⓑ Ⓒ Ⓓ	1 Ⓐ Ⓑ Ⓒ Ⓓ
2 Ⓐ Ⓑ Ⓒ Ⓓ	2 Ⓐ Ⓑ Ⓒ Ⓓ	2 Ⓐ Ⓑ Ⓒ Ⓓ	2 Ⓐ Ⓑ Ⓒ Ⓓ
3 Ⓐ Ⓑ Ⓒ Ⓓ	3 Ⓐ Ⓑ Ⓒ Ⓓ	3 Ⓐ Ⓑ Ⓒ Ⓓ	3 Ⓐ Ⓑ Ⓒ Ⓓ
4 Ⓐ Ⓑ Ⓒ Ⓓ	4 Ⓐ Ⓑ Ⓒ Ⓓ	4 Ⓐ Ⓑ Ⓒ Ⓓ	4 Ⓐ Ⓑ Ⓒ Ⓓ

EXERCISE FOURTEEN: MINI TALKS/ANNOUNCEMENTS AND ADVERTISEMENTS

Mini Talk One	Mini Talk Two	Mini Talk Three	Mini Talk Four
1 Ⓐ Ⓑ Ⓒ Ⓓ	1 Ⓐ Ⓑ Ⓒ Ⓓ	1 Ⓐ Ⓑ Ⓒ Ⓓ	1 Ⓐ Ⓑ Ⓒ Ⓓ
2 Ⓐ Ⓑ Ⓒ Ⓓ	2 Ⓐ Ⓑ Ⓒ Ⓓ	2 Ⓐ Ⓑ Ⓒ Ⓓ	2 Ⓐ Ⓑ Ⓒ Ⓓ
3 Ⓐ Ⓑ Ⓒ Ⓓ	3 Ⓐ Ⓑ Ⓒ Ⓓ	3 Ⓐ Ⓑ Ⓒ Ⓓ	3 Ⓐ Ⓑ Ⓒ Ⓓ
4 Ⓐ Ⓑ Ⓒ Ⓓ	4 Ⓐ Ⓑ Ⓒ Ⓓ	4 Ⓐ Ⓑ Ⓒ Ⓓ	4 Ⓐ Ⓑ Ⓒ Ⓓ

EXERCISE FIFTEEN:　MINI TALKS/NEWS REPORTS

Mini Talk One	Mini Talk Two	Mini Talk Three	Mini Talk Four
1 Ⓐ Ⓑ Ⓒ Ⓓ	1 Ⓐ Ⓑ Ⓒ Ⓓ	1 Ⓐ Ⓑ Ⓒ Ⓓ	1 Ⓐ Ⓑ Ⓒ Ⓓ
2 Ⓐ Ⓑ Ⓒ Ⓓ	2 Ⓐ Ⓑ Ⓒ Ⓓ	2 Ⓐ Ⓑ Ⓒ Ⓓ	2 Ⓐ Ⓑ Ⓒ Ⓓ
3 Ⓐ Ⓑ Ⓒ Ⓓ	3 Ⓐ Ⓑ Ⓒ Ⓓ	3 Ⓐ Ⓑ Ⓒ Ⓓ	3 Ⓐ Ⓑ Ⓒ Ⓓ
4 Ⓐ Ⓑ Ⓒ Ⓓ	4 Ⓐ Ⓑ Ⓒ Ⓓ	4 Ⓐ Ⓑ Ⓒ Ⓓ	4 Ⓐ Ⓑ Ⓒ Ⓓ

EXERCISE SIXTEEN:　MINI TALKS/WEATHER REPORTS

Mini Talk One	Mini Talk Two	Mini Talk Three	Mini Talk Four
1 Ⓐ Ⓑ Ⓒ Ⓓ	1 Ⓐ Ⓑ Ⓒ Ⓓ	1 Ⓐ Ⓑ Ⓒ Ⓓ	1 Ⓐ Ⓑ Ⓒ Ⓓ
2 Ⓐ Ⓑ Ⓒ Ⓓ	2 Ⓐ Ⓑ Ⓒ Ⓓ	2 Ⓐ Ⓑ Ⓒ Ⓓ	2 Ⓐ Ⓑ Ⓒ Ⓓ
3 Ⓐ Ⓑ Ⓒ Ⓓ	3 Ⓐ Ⓑ Ⓒ Ⓓ	3 Ⓐ Ⓑ Ⓒ Ⓓ	3 Ⓐ Ⓑ Ⓒ Ⓓ
4 Ⓐ Ⓑ Ⓒ Ⓓ	4 Ⓐ Ⓑ Ⓒ Ⓓ	4 Ⓐ Ⓑ Ⓒ Ⓓ	4 Ⓐ Ⓑ Ⓒ Ⓓ

EXERCISE SEVENTEEN:　MINI TALKS/INFORMATIVE SPEECHES

Mini Talk One	Mini Talk Two	Mini Talk Three	Mini Talk Four
1 Ⓐ Ⓑ Ⓒ Ⓓ	1 Ⓐ Ⓑ Ⓒ Ⓓ	1 Ⓐ Ⓑ Ⓒ Ⓓ	1 Ⓐ Ⓑ Ⓒ Ⓓ
2 Ⓐ Ⓑ Ⓒ Ⓓ	2 Ⓐ Ⓑ Ⓒ Ⓓ	2 Ⓐ Ⓑ Ⓒ Ⓓ	2 Ⓐ Ⓑ Ⓒ Ⓓ
3 Ⓐ Ⓑ Ⓒ Ⓓ	3 Ⓐ Ⓑ Ⓒ Ⓓ	3 Ⓐ Ⓑ Ⓒ Ⓓ	3 Ⓐ Ⓑ Ⓒ Ⓓ
4 Ⓐ Ⓑ Ⓒ Ⓓ	4 Ⓐ Ⓑ Ⓒ Ⓓ	4 Ⓐ Ⓑ Ⓒ Ⓓ	4 Ⓐ Ⓑ Ⓒ Ⓓ

EXERCISE EIGHTEEN:　MINI TALKS/ACADEMIC STATEMENTS (PART 1)

Mini Talk One	Mini Talk Two	Mini Talk Three	Mini Talk Four
1 Ⓐ Ⓑ Ⓒ Ⓓ	1 Ⓐ Ⓑ Ⓒ Ⓓ	1 Ⓐ Ⓑ Ⓒ Ⓓ	1 Ⓐ Ⓑ Ⓒ Ⓓ
2 Ⓐ Ⓑ Ⓒ Ⓓ	2 Ⓐ Ⓑ Ⓒ Ⓓ	2 Ⓐ Ⓑ Ⓒ Ⓓ	2 Ⓐ Ⓑ Ⓒ Ⓓ
3 Ⓐ Ⓑ Ⓒ Ⓓ	3 Ⓐ Ⓑ Ⓒ Ⓓ	3 Ⓐ Ⓑ Ⓒ Ⓓ	3 Ⓐ Ⓑ Ⓒ Ⓓ
4 Ⓐ Ⓑ Ⓒ Ⓓ	4 Ⓐ Ⓑ Ⓒ Ⓓ	4 Ⓐ Ⓑ Ⓒ Ⓓ	4 Ⓐ Ⓑ Ⓒ Ⓓ

EXERCISE EIGHTEEN:　MINI TALKS/ACADEMIC STATEMENTS (PART 2)

Mini Talk One	Mini Talk Two	Mini Talk Three	Mini Talk Four
1 Ⓐ Ⓑ Ⓒ Ⓓ	1 Ⓐ Ⓑ Ⓒ Ⓓ	1 Ⓐ Ⓑ Ⓒ Ⓓ	1 Ⓐ Ⓑ Ⓒ Ⓓ
2 Ⓐ Ⓑ Ⓒ Ⓓ	2 Ⓐ Ⓑ Ⓒ Ⓓ	2 Ⓐ Ⓑ Ⓒ Ⓓ	2 Ⓐ Ⓑ Ⓒ Ⓓ
3 Ⓐ Ⓑ Ⓒ Ⓓ	3 Ⓐ Ⓑ Ⓒ Ⓓ	3 Ⓐ Ⓑ Ⓒ Ⓓ	3 Ⓐ Ⓑ Ⓒ Ⓓ
4 Ⓐ Ⓑ Ⓒ Ⓓ	4 Ⓐ Ⓑ Ⓒ Ⓓ	4 Ⓐ Ⓑ Ⓒ Ⓓ	4 Ⓐ Ⓑ Ⓒ Ⓓ

EXERCISE NINETEEN:　MINI TALKS/CLASS DISCUSSIONS

Mini Talk One	Mini Talk Two	Mini Talk Three	Mini Talk Four
1 Ⓐ Ⓑ Ⓒ Ⓓ	1 Ⓐ Ⓑ Ⓒ Ⓓ	1 Ⓐ Ⓑ Ⓒ Ⓓ	1 Ⓐ Ⓑ Ⓒ Ⓓ
2 Ⓐ Ⓑ Ⓒ Ⓓ	2 Ⓐ Ⓑ Ⓒ Ⓓ	2 Ⓐ Ⓑ Ⓒ Ⓓ	2 Ⓐ Ⓑ Ⓒ Ⓓ
3 Ⓐ Ⓑ Ⓒ Ⓓ	3 Ⓐ Ⓑ Ⓒ Ⓓ	3 Ⓐ Ⓑ Ⓒ Ⓓ	3 Ⓐ Ⓑ Ⓒ Ⓓ
4 Ⓐ Ⓑ Ⓒ Ⓓ	4 Ⓐ Ⓑ Ⓒ Ⓓ	4 Ⓐ Ⓑ Ⓒ Ⓓ	4 Ⓐ Ⓑ Ⓒ Ⓓ

ANSWER SHEET FOR CHAPTER FOUR

EXERCISE ONE: PROBLEMS WITH VERBS (PART 1)

1 Ⓐ Ⓑ Ⓒ Ⓓ	4 Ⓐ Ⓑ Ⓒ Ⓓ	7 Ⓐ Ⓑ Ⓒ Ⓓ	10 Ⓐ Ⓑ Ⓒ Ⓓ	13 Ⓐ Ⓑ Ⓒ Ⓓ
2 Ⓐ Ⓑ Ⓒ Ⓓ	5 Ⓐ Ⓑ Ⓒ Ⓓ	8 Ⓐ Ⓑ Ⓒ Ⓓ	11 Ⓐ Ⓑ Ⓒ Ⓓ	14 Ⓐ Ⓑ Ⓒ Ⓓ
3 Ⓐ Ⓑ Ⓒ Ⓓ	6 Ⓐ Ⓑ Ⓒ Ⓓ	9 Ⓐ Ⓑ Ⓒ Ⓓ	12 Ⓐ Ⓑ Ⓒ Ⓓ	15 Ⓐ Ⓑ Ⓒ Ⓓ

EXERCISE TWO: PROBLEMS WITH VERBS (PART 2)

1 Ⓐ Ⓑ Ⓒ Ⓓ	4 Ⓐ Ⓑ Ⓒ Ⓓ	7 Ⓐ Ⓑ Ⓒ Ⓓ	10 Ⓐ Ⓑ Ⓒ Ⓓ	13 Ⓐ Ⓑ Ⓒ Ⓓ
2 Ⓐ Ⓑ Ⓒ Ⓓ	5 Ⓐ Ⓑ Ⓒ Ⓓ	8 Ⓐ Ⓑ Ⓒ Ⓓ	11 Ⓐ Ⓑ Ⓒ Ⓓ	14 Ⓐ Ⓑ Ⓒ Ⓓ
3 Ⓐ Ⓑ Ⓒ Ⓓ	6 Ⓐ Ⓑ Ⓒ Ⓓ	9 Ⓐ Ⓑ Ⓒ Ⓓ	12 Ⓐ Ⓑ Ⓒ Ⓓ	15 Ⓐ Ⓑ Ⓒ Ⓓ

EXERCISE THREE: PROBLEMS WITH VERBS (PART 3)

1 Ⓐ Ⓑ Ⓒ Ⓓ	4 Ⓐ Ⓑ Ⓒ Ⓓ	7 Ⓐ Ⓑ Ⓒ Ⓓ	10 Ⓐ Ⓑ Ⓒ Ⓓ	13 Ⓐ Ⓑ Ⓒ Ⓓ
2 Ⓐ Ⓑ Ⓒ Ⓓ	5 Ⓐ Ⓑ Ⓒ Ⓓ	8 Ⓐ Ⓑ Ⓒ Ⓓ	11 Ⓐ Ⓑ Ⓒ Ⓓ	14 Ⓐ Ⓑ Ⓒ Ⓓ
3 Ⓐ Ⓑ Ⓒ Ⓓ	6 Ⓐ Ⓑ Ⓒ Ⓓ	9 Ⓐ Ⓑ Ⓒ Ⓓ	12 Ⓐ Ⓑ Ⓒ Ⓓ	15 Ⓐ Ⓑ Ⓒ Ⓓ

EXERCISE FOUR: PROBLEMS WITH PRONOUNS

1 Ⓐ Ⓑ Ⓒ Ⓓ	4 Ⓐ Ⓑ Ⓒ Ⓓ	7 Ⓐ Ⓑ Ⓒ Ⓓ	10 Ⓐ Ⓑ Ⓒ Ⓓ	13 Ⓐ Ⓑ Ⓒ Ⓓ
2 Ⓐ Ⓑ Ⓒ Ⓓ	5 Ⓐ Ⓑ Ⓒ Ⓓ	8 Ⓐ Ⓑ Ⓒ Ⓓ	11 Ⓐ Ⓑ Ⓒ Ⓓ	14 Ⓐ Ⓑ Ⓒ Ⓓ
3 Ⓐ Ⓑ Ⓒ Ⓓ	6 Ⓐ Ⓑ Ⓒ Ⓓ	9 Ⓐ Ⓑ Ⓒ Ⓓ	12 Ⓐ Ⓑ Ⓒ Ⓓ	15 Ⓐ Ⓑ Ⓒ Ⓓ

EXERCISE FIVE: PROBLEMS WITH NOUNS

1 Ⓐ Ⓑ Ⓒ Ⓓ	4 Ⓐ Ⓑ Ⓒ Ⓓ	7 Ⓐ Ⓑ Ⓒ Ⓓ	10 Ⓐ Ⓑ Ⓒ Ⓓ	13 Ⓐ Ⓑ Ⓒ Ⓓ
2 Ⓐ Ⓑ Ⓒ Ⓓ	5 Ⓐ Ⓑ Ⓒ Ⓓ	8 Ⓐ Ⓑ Ⓒ Ⓓ	11 Ⓐ Ⓑ Ⓒ Ⓓ	14 Ⓐ Ⓑ Ⓒ Ⓓ
3 Ⓐ Ⓑ Ⓒ Ⓓ	6 Ⓐ Ⓑ Ⓒ Ⓓ	9 Ⓐ Ⓑ Ⓒ Ⓓ	12 Ⓐ Ⓑ Ⓒ Ⓓ	15 Ⓐ Ⓑ Ⓒ Ⓓ

EXERCISE SIX: PROBLEMS WITH MODIFIERS (PART 1)

1 Ⓐ Ⓑ Ⓒ Ⓓ	4 Ⓐ Ⓑ Ⓒ Ⓓ	7 Ⓐ Ⓑ Ⓒ Ⓓ	10 Ⓐ Ⓑ Ⓒ Ⓓ	13 Ⓐ Ⓑ Ⓒ Ⓓ
2 Ⓐ Ⓑ Ⓒ Ⓓ	5 Ⓐ Ⓑ Ⓒ Ⓓ	8 Ⓐ Ⓑ Ⓒ Ⓓ	11 Ⓐ Ⓑ Ⓒ Ⓓ	14 Ⓐ Ⓑ Ⓒ Ⓓ
3 Ⓐ Ⓑ Ⓒ Ⓓ	6 Ⓐ Ⓑ Ⓒ Ⓓ	9 Ⓐ Ⓑ Ⓒ Ⓓ	12 Ⓐ Ⓑ Ⓒ Ⓓ	15 Ⓐ Ⓑ Ⓒ Ⓓ

EXERCISE SEVEN: PROBLEMS WITH MODIFIERS (PART 2)

1 Ⓐ Ⓑ Ⓒ Ⓓ	4 Ⓐ Ⓑ Ⓒ Ⓓ	7 Ⓐ Ⓑ Ⓒ Ⓓ	10 Ⓐ Ⓑ Ⓒ Ⓓ	13 Ⓐ Ⓑ Ⓒ Ⓓ
2 Ⓐ Ⓑ Ⓒ Ⓓ	5 Ⓐ Ⓑ Ⓒ Ⓓ	8 Ⓐ Ⓑ Ⓒ Ⓓ	11 Ⓐ Ⓑ Ⓒ Ⓓ	14 Ⓐ Ⓑ Ⓒ Ⓓ
3 Ⓐ Ⓑ Ⓒ Ⓓ	6 Ⓐ Ⓑ Ⓒ Ⓓ	9 Ⓐ Ⓑ Ⓒ Ⓓ	12 Ⓐ Ⓑ Ⓒ Ⓓ	15 Ⓐ Ⓑ Ⓒ Ⓓ

EXERCISE EIGHT: PROBLEMS WITH COMPARATIVES

1 Ⓐ Ⓑ Ⓒ Ⓓ	4 Ⓐ Ⓑ Ⓒ Ⓓ	7 Ⓐ Ⓑ Ⓒ Ⓓ	10 Ⓐ Ⓑ Ⓒ Ⓓ	13 Ⓐ Ⓑ Ⓒ Ⓓ
2 Ⓐ Ⓑ Ⓒ Ⓓ	5 Ⓐ Ⓑ Ⓒ Ⓓ	8 Ⓐ Ⓑ Ⓒ Ⓓ	11 Ⓐ Ⓑ Ⓒ Ⓓ	14 Ⓐ Ⓑ Ⓒ Ⓓ
3 Ⓐ Ⓑ Ⓒ Ⓓ	6 Ⓐ Ⓑ Ⓒ Ⓓ	9 Ⓐ Ⓑ Ⓒ Ⓓ	12 Ⓐ Ⓑ Ⓒ Ⓓ	15 Ⓐ Ⓑ Ⓒ Ⓓ

EXERCISE NINE: PROBLEMS WITH CONNECTORS

1 Ⓐ Ⓑ Ⓒ Ⓓ 4 Ⓐ Ⓑ Ⓒ Ⓓ 7 Ⓐ Ⓑ Ⓒ Ⓓ 10 Ⓐ Ⓑ Ⓒ Ⓓ 13 Ⓐ Ⓑ Ⓒ Ⓓ
2 Ⓐ Ⓑ Ⓒ Ⓓ 5 Ⓐ Ⓑ Ⓒ Ⓓ 8 Ⓐ Ⓑ Ⓒ Ⓓ 11 Ⓐ Ⓑ Ⓒ Ⓓ 14 Ⓐ Ⓑ Ⓒ Ⓓ
3 Ⓐ Ⓑ Ⓒ Ⓓ 6 Ⓐ Ⓑ Ⓒ Ⓓ 9 Ⓐ Ⓑ Ⓒ Ⓓ 12 Ⓐ Ⓑ Ⓒ Ⓓ 15 Ⓐ Ⓑ Ⓒ Ⓓ

EXERCISE TEN: CUMULATIVE PRACTICE WITH STRUCTURES (PART 1)

1 Ⓐ Ⓑ Ⓒ Ⓓ 4 Ⓐ Ⓑ Ⓒ Ⓓ 7 Ⓐ Ⓑ Ⓒ Ⓓ 10 Ⓐ Ⓑ Ⓒ Ⓓ 13 Ⓐ Ⓑ Ⓒ Ⓓ
2 Ⓐ Ⓑ Ⓒ Ⓓ 5 Ⓐ Ⓑ Ⓒ Ⓓ 8 Ⓐ Ⓑ Ⓒ Ⓓ 11 Ⓐ Ⓑ Ⓒ Ⓓ 14 Ⓐ Ⓑ Ⓒ Ⓓ
3 Ⓐ Ⓑ Ⓒ Ⓓ 6 Ⓐ Ⓑ Ⓒ Ⓓ 9 Ⓐ Ⓑ Ⓒ Ⓓ 12 Ⓐ Ⓑ Ⓒ Ⓓ 15 Ⓐ Ⓑ Ⓒ Ⓓ

EXERCISE ELEVEN: CUMULATIVE PRACTICE WITH STRUCTURES (PART 2)

1 Ⓐ Ⓑ Ⓒ Ⓓ 4 Ⓐ Ⓑ Ⓒ Ⓓ 7 Ⓐ Ⓑ Ⓒ Ⓓ 10 Ⓐ Ⓑ Ⓒ Ⓓ 13 Ⓐ Ⓑ Ⓒ Ⓓ
2 Ⓐ Ⓑ Ⓒ Ⓓ 5 Ⓐ Ⓑ Ⓒ Ⓓ 8 Ⓐ Ⓑ Ⓒ Ⓓ 11 Ⓐ Ⓑ Ⓒ Ⓓ 14 Ⓐ Ⓑ Ⓒ Ⓓ
3 Ⓐ Ⓑ Ⓒ Ⓓ 6 Ⓐ Ⓑ Ⓒ Ⓓ 9 Ⓐ Ⓑ Ⓒ Ⓓ 12 Ⓐ Ⓑ Ⓒ Ⓓ 15 Ⓐ Ⓑ Ⓒ Ⓓ

EXERCISE TWELVE: PROBLEMS WITH POINT OF VIEW

1 Ⓐ Ⓑ Ⓒ Ⓓ 6 Ⓐ Ⓑ Ⓒ Ⓓ 11 Ⓐ Ⓑ Ⓒ Ⓓ 16 Ⓐ Ⓑ Ⓒ Ⓓ 21 Ⓐ Ⓑ Ⓒ Ⓓ
2 Ⓐ Ⓑ Ⓒ Ⓓ 7 Ⓐ Ⓑ Ⓒ Ⓓ 12 Ⓐ Ⓑ Ⓒ Ⓓ 17 Ⓐ Ⓑ Ⓒ Ⓓ 22 Ⓐ Ⓑ Ⓒ Ⓓ
3 Ⓐ Ⓑ Ⓒ Ⓓ 8 Ⓐ Ⓑ Ⓒ Ⓓ 13 Ⓐ Ⓑ Ⓒ Ⓓ 18 Ⓐ Ⓑ Ⓒ Ⓓ 23 Ⓐ Ⓑ Ⓒ Ⓓ
4 Ⓐ Ⓑ Ⓒ Ⓓ 9 Ⓐ Ⓑ Ⓒ Ⓓ 14 Ⓐ Ⓑ Ⓒ Ⓓ 19 Ⓐ Ⓑ Ⓒ Ⓓ 24 Ⓐ Ⓑ Ⓒ Ⓓ
5 Ⓐ Ⓑ Ⓒ Ⓓ 10 Ⓐ Ⓑ Ⓒ Ⓓ 15 Ⓐ Ⓑ Ⓒ Ⓓ 20 Ⓐ Ⓑ Ⓒ Ⓓ 25 Ⓐ Ⓑ Ⓒ Ⓓ

EXERCISE THIRTEEN: PROBLEMS WITH AGREEMENT

1 Ⓐ Ⓑ Ⓒ Ⓓ 6 Ⓐ Ⓑ Ⓒ Ⓓ 11 Ⓐ Ⓑ Ⓒ Ⓓ 16 Ⓐ Ⓑ Ⓒ Ⓓ 21 Ⓐ Ⓑ Ⓒ Ⓓ
2 Ⓐ Ⓑ Ⓒ Ⓓ 7 Ⓐ Ⓑ Ⓒ Ⓓ 12 Ⓐ Ⓑ Ⓒ Ⓓ 17 Ⓐ Ⓑ Ⓒ Ⓓ 22 Ⓐ Ⓑ Ⓒ Ⓓ
3 Ⓐ Ⓑ Ⓒ Ⓓ 8 Ⓐ Ⓑ Ⓒ Ⓓ 13 Ⓐ Ⓑ Ⓒ Ⓓ 18 Ⓐ Ⓑ Ⓒ Ⓓ 23 Ⓐ Ⓑ Ⓒ Ⓓ
4 Ⓐ Ⓑ Ⓒ Ⓓ 9 Ⓐ Ⓑ Ⓒ Ⓓ 14 Ⓐ Ⓑ Ⓒ Ⓓ 19 Ⓐ Ⓑ Ⓒ Ⓓ 24 Ⓐ Ⓑ Ⓒ Ⓓ
5 Ⓐ Ⓑ Ⓒ Ⓓ 10 Ⓐ Ⓑ Ⓒ Ⓓ 15 Ⓐ Ⓑ Ⓒ Ⓓ 20 Ⓐ Ⓑ Ⓒ Ⓓ 25 Ⓐ Ⓑ Ⓒ Ⓓ

EXERCISE FOURTEEN: PROBLEMS WITH INTRODUCTORY VERBAL MODIFIERS

1 Ⓐ Ⓑ Ⓒ Ⓓ 6 Ⓐ Ⓑ Ⓒ Ⓓ 11 Ⓐ Ⓑ Ⓒ Ⓓ 16 Ⓐ Ⓑ Ⓒ Ⓓ 21 Ⓐ Ⓑ Ⓒ Ⓓ
2 Ⓐ Ⓑ Ⓒ Ⓓ 7 Ⓐ Ⓑ Ⓒ Ⓓ 12 Ⓐ Ⓑ Ⓒ Ⓓ 17 Ⓐ Ⓑ Ⓒ Ⓓ 22 Ⓐ Ⓑ Ⓒ Ⓓ
3 Ⓐ Ⓑ Ⓒ Ⓓ 8 Ⓐ Ⓑ Ⓒ Ⓓ 13 Ⓐ Ⓑ Ⓒ Ⓓ 18 Ⓐ Ⓑ Ⓒ Ⓓ 23 Ⓐ Ⓑ Ⓒ Ⓓ
4 Ⓐ Ⓑ Ⓒ Ⓓ 9 Ⓐ Ⓑ Ⓒ Ⓓ 14 Ⓐ Ⓑ Ⓒ Ⓓ 19 Ⓐ Ⓑ Ⓒ Ⓓ 24 Ⓐ Ⓑ Ⓒ Ⓓ
5 Ⓐ Ⓑ Ⓒ Ⓓ 10 Ⓐ Ⓑ Ⓒ Ⓓ 15 Ⓐ Ⓑ Ⓒ Ⓓ 20 Ⓐ Ⓑ Ⓒ Ⓓ 25 Ⓐ Ⓑ Ⓒ Ⓓ

EXERCISE FIFTEEN: PROBLEMS WITH PARALLEL STRUCTURE

1 Ⓐ Ⓑ Ⓒ Ⓓ 6 Ⓐ Ⓑ Ⓒ Ⓓ 11 Ⓐ Ⓑ Ⓒ Ⓓ 16 Ⓐ Ⓑ Ⓒ Ⓓ 21 Ⓐ Ⓑ Ⓒ Ⓓ
2 Ⓐ Ⓑ Ⓒ Ⓓ 7 Ⓐ Ⓑ Ⓒ Ⓓ 12 Ⓐ Ⓑ Ⓒ Ⓓ 17 Ⓐ Ⓑ Ⓒ Ⓓ 22 Ⓐ Ⓑ Ⓒ Ⓓ
3 Ⓐ Ⓑ Ⓒ Ⓓ 8 Ⓐ Ⓑ Ⓒ Ⓓ 13 Ⓐ Ⓑ Ⓒ Ⓓ 18 Ⓐ Ⓑ Ⓒ Ⓓ 23 Ⓐ Ⓑ Ⓒ Ⓓ
4 Ⓐ Ⓑ Ⓒ Ⓓ 9 Ⓐ Ⓑ Ⓒ Ⓓ 14 Ⓐ Ⓑ Ⓒ Ⓓ 19 Ⓐ Ⓑ Ⓒ Ⓓ 24 Ⓐ Ⓑ Ⓒ Ⓓ
5 Ⓐ Ⓑ Ⓒ Ⓓ 10 Ⓐ Ⓑ Ⓒ Ⓓ 15 Ⓐ Ⓑ Ⓒ Ⓓ 20 Ⓐ Ⓑ Ⓒ Ⓓ 25 Ⓐ Ⓑ Ⓒ Ⓓ

EXERCISE SIXTEEN: PROBLEMS WITH REDUNDANCY

1 Ⓐ Ⓑ Ⓒ Ⓓ   6 Ⓐ Ⓑ Ⓒ Ⓓ   11 Ⓐ Ⓑ Ⓒ Ⓓ   16 Ⓐ Ⓑ Ⓒ Ⓓ   21 Ⓐ Ⓑ Ⓒ Ⓓ
2 Ⓐ Ⓑ Ⓒ Ⓓ   7 Ⓐ Ⓑ Ⓒ Ⓓ   12 Ⓐ Ⓑ Ⓒ Ⓓ   17 Ⓐ Ⓑ Ⓒ Ⓓ   22 Ⓐ Ⓑ Ⓒ Ⓓ
3 Ⓐ Ⓑ Ⓒ Ⓓ   8 Ⓐ Ⓑ Ⓒ Ⓓ   13 Ⓐ Ⓑ Ⓒ Ⓓ   18 Ⓐ Ⓑ Ⓒ Ⓓ   23 Ⓐ Ⓑ Ⓒ Ⓓ
4 Ⓐ Ⓑ Ⓒ Ⓓ   9 Ⓐ Ⓑ Ⓒ Ⓓ   14 Ⓐ Ⓑ Ⓒ Ⓓ   19 Ⓐ Ⓑ Ⓒ Ⓓ   24 Ⓐ Ⓑ Ⓒ Ⓓ
5 Ⓐ Ⓑ Ⓒ Ⓓ   10 Ⓐ Ⓑ Ⓒ Ⓓ   15 Ⓐ Ⓑ Ⓒ Ⓓ   20 Ⓐ Ⓑ Ⓒ Ⓓ   25 Ⓐ Ⓑ Ⓒ Ⓓ

EXERCISE SEVENTEEN: PROBLEMS WITH WORD CHOICE

1 Ⓐ Ⓑ Ⓒ Ⓓ   6 Ⓐ Ⓑ Ⓒ Ⓓ   11 Ⓐ Ⓑ Ⓒ Ⓓ   16 Ⓐ Ⓑ Ⓒ Ⓓ   21 Ⓐ Ⓑ Ⓒ Ⓓ
2 Ⓐ Ⓑ Ⓒ Ⓓ   7 Ⓐ Ⓑ Ⓒ Ⓓ   12 Ⓐ Ⓑ Ⓒ Ⓓ   17 Ⓐ Ⓑ Ⓒ Ⓓ   22 Ⓐ Ⓑ Ⓒ Ⓓ
3 Ⓐ Ⓑ Ⓒ Ⓓ   8 Ⓐ Ⓑ Ⓒ Ⓓ   13 Ⓐ Ⓑ Ⓒ Ⓓ   18 Ⓐ Ⓑ Ⓒ Ⓓ   23 Ⓐ Ⓑ Ⓒ Ⓓ
4 Ⓐ Ⓑ Ⓒ Ⓓ   9 Ⓐ Ⓑ Ⓒ Ⓓ   14 Ⓐ Ⓑ Ⓒ Ⓓ   19 Ⓐ Ⓑ Ⓒ Ⓓ   24 Ⓐ Ⓑ Ⓒ Ⓓ
5 Ⓐ Ⓑ Ⓒ Ⓓ   10 Ⓐ Ⓑ Ⓒ Ⓓ   15 Ⓐ Ⓑ Ⓒ Ⓓ   20 Ⓐ Ⓑ Ⓒ Ⓓ   25 Ⓐ Ⓑ Ⓒ Ⓓ

EXERCISE EIGHTEEN: PROBLEMS WITH STRUCTURE

1 Ⓐ Ⓑ Ⓒ Ⓓ   6 Ⓐ Ⓑ Ⓒ Ⓓ   11 Ⓐ Ⓑ Ⓒ Ⓓ   16 Ⓐ Ⓑ Ⓒ Ⓓ   21 Ⓐ Ⓑ Ⓒ Ⓓ
2 Ⓐ Ⓑ Ⓒ Ⓓ   7 Ⓐ Ⓑ Ⓒ Ⓓ   12 Ⓐ Ⓑ Ⓒ Ⓓ   17 Ⓐ Ⓑ Ⓒ Ⓓ   22 Ⓐ Ⓑ Ⓒ Ⓓ
3 Ⓐ Ⓑ Ⓒ Ⓓ   8 Ⓐ Ⓑ Ⓒ Ⓓ   13 Ⓐ Ⓑ Ⓒ Ⓓ   18 Ⓐ Ⓑ Ⓒ Ⓓ   23 Ⓐ Ⓑ Ⓒ Ⓓ
4 Ⓐ Ⓑ Ⓒ Ⓓ   9 Ⓐ Ⓑ Ⓒ Ⓓ   14 Ⓐ Ⓑ Ⓒ Ⓓ   19 Ⓐ Ⓑ Ⓒ Ⓓ   24 Ⓐ Ⓑ Ⓒ Ⓓ
5 Ⓐ Ⓑ Ⓒ Ⓓ   10 Ⓐ Ⓑ Ⓒ Ⓓ   15 Ⓐ Ⓑ Ⓒ Ⓓ   20 Ⓐ Ⓑ Ⓒ Ⓓ   25 Ⓐ Ⓑ Ⓒ Ⓓ

ANSWER SHEET FOR CHAPTER FIVE

EXERCISE ONE: VOCABULARY REVIEW (PART 1)

1 Ⓐ Ⓑ Ⓒ Ⓓ	7 Ⓐ Ⓑ Ⓒ Ⓓ	13 Ⓐ Ⓑ Ⓒ Ⓓ	19 Ⓐ Ⓑ Ⓒ Ⓓ	25 Ⓐ Ⓑ Ⓒ Ⓓ
2 Ⓐ Ⓑ Ⓒ Ⓓ	8 Ⓐ Ⓑ Ⓒ Ⓓ	14 Ⓐ Ⓑ Ⓒ Ⓓ	20 Ⓐ Ⓑ Ⓒ Ⓓ	26 Ⓐ Ⓑ Ⓒ Ⓓ
3 Ⓐ Ⓑ Ⓒ Ⓓ	9 Ⓐ Ⓑ Ⓒ Ⓓ	15 Ⓐ Ⓑ Ⓒ Ⓓ	21 Ⓐ Ⓑ Ⓒ Ⓓ	27 Ⓐ Ⓑ Ⓒ Ⓓ
4 Ⓐ Ⓑ Ⓒ Ⓓ	10 Ⓐ Ⓑ Ⓒ Ⓓ	16 Ⓐ Ⓑ Ⓒ Ⓓ	22 Ⓐ Ⓑ Ⓒ Ⓓ	28 Ⓐ Ⓑ Ⓒ Ⓓ
5 Ⓐ Ⓑ Ⓒ Ⓓ	11 Ⓐ Ⓑ Ⓒ Ⓓ	17 Ⓐ Ⓑ Ⓒ Ⓓ	23 Ⓐ Ⓑ Ⓒ Ⓓ	29 Ⓐ Ⓑ Ⓒ Ⓓ
6 Ⓐ Ⓑ Ⓒ Ⓓ	12 Ⓐ Ⓑ Ⓒ Ⓓ	18 Ⓐ Ⓑ Ⓒ Ⓓ	24 Ⓐ Ⓑ Ⓒ Ⓓ	30 Ⓐ Ⓑ Ⓒ Ⓓ

EXERCISE TWO: VOCABULARY REVIEW (PART 2)

1 Ⓐ Ⓑ Ⓒ Ⓓ	7 Ⓐ Ⓑ Ⓒ Ⓓ	13 Ⓐ Ⓑ Ⓒ Ⓓ	19 Ⓐ Ⓑ Ⓒ Ⓓ	25 Ⓐ Ⓑ Ⓒ Ⓓ
2 Ⓐ Ⓑ Ⓒ Ⓓ	8 Ⓐ Ⓑ Ⓒ Ⓓ	14 Ⓐ Ⓑ Ⓒ Ⓓ	20 Ⓐ Ⓑ Ⓒ Ⓓ	26 Ⓐ Ⓑ Ⓒ Ⓓ
3 Ⓐ Ⓑ Ⓒ Ⓓ	9 Ⓐ Ⓑ Ⓒ Ⓓ	15 Ⓐ Ⓑ Ⓒ Ⓓ	21 Ⓐ Ⓑ Ⓒ Ⓓ	27 Ⓐ Ⓑ Ⓒ Ⓓ
4 Ⓐ Ⓑ Ⓒ Ⓓ	10 Ⓐ Ⓑ Ⓒ Ⓓ	16 Ⓐ Ⓑ Ⓒ Ⓓ	22 Ⓐ Ⓑ Ⓒ Ⓓ	28 Ⓐ Ⓑ Ⓒ Ⓓ
5 Ⓐ Ⓑ Ⓒ Ⓓ	11 Ⓐ Ⓑ Ⓒ Ⓓ	17 Ⓐ Ⓑ Ⓒ Ⓓ	23 Ⓐ Ⓑ Ⓒ Ⓓ	29 Ⓐ Ⓑ Ⓒ Ⓓ
6 Ⓐ Ⓑ Ⓒ Ⓓ	12 Ⓐ Ⓑ Ⓒ Ⓓ	18 Ⓐ Ⓑ Ⓒ Ⓓ	24 Ⓐ Ⓑ Ⓒ Ⓓ	30 Ⓐ Ⓑ Ⓒ Ⓓ

EXERCISE THREE: VOCABULARY REVIEW (PART 3)

1 Ⓐ Ⓑ Ⓒ Ⓓ	7 Ⓐ Ⓑ Ⓒ Ⓓ	13 Ⓐ Ⓑ Ⓒ Ⓓ	19 Ⓐ Ⓑ Ⓒ Ⓓ	25 Ⓐ Ⓑ Ⓒ Ⓓ
2 Ⓐ Ⓑ Ⓒ Ⓓ	8 Ⓐ Ⓑ Ⓒ Ⓓ	14 Ⓐ Ⓑ Ⓒ Ⓓ	20 Ⓐ Ⓑ Ⓒ Ⓓ	26 Ⓐ Ⓑ Ⓒ Ⓓ
3 Ⓐ Ⓑ Ⓒ Ⓓ	9 Ⓐ Ⓑ Ⓒ Ⓓ	15 Ⓐ Ⓑ Ⓒ Ⓓ	21 Ⓐ Ⓑ Ⓒ Ⓓ	27 Ⓐ Ⓑ Ⓒ Ⓓ
4 Ⓐ Ⓑ Ⓒ Ⓓ	10 Ⓐ Ⓑ Ⓒ Ⓓ	16 Ⓐ Ⓑ Ⓒ Ⓓ	22 Ⓐ Ⓑ Ⓒ Ⓓ	28 Ⓐ Ⓑ Ⓒ Ⓓ
5 Ⓐ Ⓑ Ⓒ Ⓓ	11 Ⓐ Ⓑ Ⓒ Ⓓ	17 Ⓐ Ⓑ Ⓒ Ⓓ	23 Ⓐ Ⓑ Ⓒ Ⓓ	29 Ⓐ Ⓑ Ⓒ Ⓓ
6 Ⓐ Ⓑ Ⓒ Ⓓ	12 Ⓐ Ⓑ Ⓒ Ⓓ	18 Ⓐ Ⓑ Ⓒ Ⓓ	24 Ⓐ Ⓑ Ⓒ Ⓓ	30 Ⓐ Ⓑ Ⓒ Ⓓ

EXERCISE FOUR: VOCABULARY REVIEW (PART 4)

1 Ⓐ Ⓑ Ⓒ Ⓓ	7 Ⓐ Ⓑ Ⓒ Ⓓ	13 Ⓐ Ⓑ Ⓒ Ⓓ	19 Ⓐ Ⓑ Ⓒ Ⓓ	25 Ⓐ Ⓑ Ⓒ Ⓓ
2 Ⓐ Ⓑ Ⓒ Ⓓ	8 Ⓐ Ⓑ Ⓒ Ⓓ	14 Ⓐ Ⓑ Ⓒ Ⓓ	20 Ⓐ Ⓑ Ⓒ Ⓓ	26 Ⓐ Ⓑ Ⓒ Ⓓ
3 Ⓐ Ⓑ Ⓒ Ⓓ	9 Ⓐ Ⓑ Ⓒ Ⓓ	15 Ⓐ Ⓑ Ⓒ Ⓓ	21 Ⓐ Ⓑ Ⓒ Ⓓ	27 Ⓐ Ⓑ Ⓒ Ⓓ
4 Ⓐ Ⓑ Ⓒ Ⓓ	10 Ⓐ Ⓑ Ⓒ Ⓓ	16 Ⓐ Ⓑ Ⓒ Ⓓ	22 Ⓐ Ⓑ Ⓒ Ⓓ	28 Ⓐ Ⓑ Ⓒ Ⓓ
5 Ⓐ Ⓑ Ⓒ Ⓓ	11 Ⓐ Ⓑ Ⓒ Ⓓ	17 Ⓐ Ⓑ Ⓒ Ⓓ	23 Ⓐ Ⓑ Ⓒ Ⓓ	29 Ⓐ Ⓑ Ⓒ Ⓓ
6 Ⓐ Ⓑ Ⓒ Ⓓ	12 Ⓐ Ⓑ Ⓒ Ⓓ	18 Ⓐ Ⓑ Ⓒ Ⓓ	24 Ⓐ Ⓑ Ⓒ Ⓓ	30 Ⓐ Ⓑ Ⓒ Ⓓ

EXERCISE FIVE: VOCABULARY REVIEW/TWO- AND THREE-WORD VERBS

1 Ⓐ Ⓑ Ⓒ Ⓓ	7 Ⓐ Ⓑ Ⓒ Ⓓ	13 Ⓐ Ⓑ Ⓒ Ⓓ	19 Ⓐ Ⓑ Ⓒ Ⓓ	25 Ⓐ Ⓑ Ⓒ Ⓓ
2 Ⓐ Ⓑ Ⓒ Ⓓ	8 Ⓐ Ⓑ Ⓒ Ⓓ	14 Ⓐ Ⓑ Ⓒ Ⓓ	20 Ⓐ Ⓑ Ⓒ Ⓓ	26 Ⓐ Ⓑ Ⓒ Ⓓ
3 Ⓐ Ⓑ Ⓒ Ⓓ	9 Ⓐ Ⓑ Ⓒ Ⓓ	15 Ⓐ Ⓑ Ⓒ Ⓓ	21 Ⓐ Ⓑ Ⓒ Ⓓ	27 Ⓐ Ⓑ Ⓒ Ⓓ
4 Ⓐ Ⓑ Ⓒ Ⓓ	10 Ⓐ Ⓑ Ⓒ Ⓓ	16 Ⓐ Ⓑ Ⓒ Ⓓ	22 Ⓐ Ⓑ Ⓒ Ⓓ	28 Ⓐ Ⓑ Ⓒ Ⓓ
5 Ⓐ Ⓑ Ⓒ Ⓓ	11 Ⓐ Ⓑ Ⓒ Ⓓ	17 Ⓐ Ⓑ Ⓒ Ⓓ	23 Ⓐ Ⓑ Ⓒ Ⓓ	29 Ⓐ Ⓑ Ⓒ Ⓓ
6 Ⓐ Ⓑ Ⓒ Ⓓ	12 Ⓐ Ⓑ Ⓒ Ⓓ	18 Ⓐ Ⓑ Ⓒ Ⓓ	24 Ⓐ Ⓑ Ⓒ Ⓓ	30 Ⓐ Ⓑ Ⓒ Ⓓ

EXERCISE SIX: PRACTICE IN READING INDEXES AND CHARTS

Passage One	Passage Two	Passage Three	Passage Four	Passage Five
1 Ⓐ Ⓑ Ⓒ Ⓓ	1 Ⓐ Ⓑ Ⓒ Ⓓ	1 Ⓐ Ⓑ Ⓒ Ⓓ	1 Ⓐ Ⓑ Ⓒ Ⓓ	1 Ⓐ Ⓑ Ⓒ Ⓓ
2 Ⓐ Ⓑ Ⓒ Ⓓ	2 Ⓐ Ⓑ Ⓒ Ⓓ	2 Ⓐ Ⓑ Ⓒ Ⓓ	2 Ⓐ Ⓑ Ⓒ Ⓓ	2 Ⓐ Ⓑ Ⓒ Ⓓ
3 Ⓐ Ⓑ Ⓒ Ⓓ	3 Ⓐ Ⓑ Ⓒ Ⓓ	3 Ⓐ Ⓑ Ⓒ Ⓓ	3 Ⓐ Ⓑ Ⓒ Ⓓ	3 Ⓐ Ⓑ Ⓒ Ⓓ
4 Ⓐ Ⓑ Ⓒ Ⓓ	4 Ⓐ Ⓑ Ⓒ Ⓓ	4 Ⓐ Ⓑ Ⓒ Ⓓ	4 Ⓐ Ⓑ Ⓒ Ⓓ	4 Ⓐ Ⓑ Ⓒ Ⓓ

EXERCISE SEVEN: PRACTICE IN READING INSTRUCTIONS

Passage One	Passage Two	Passage Three	Passage Four	Passage Five
1 Ⓐ Ⓑ Ⓒ Ⓓ	1 Ⓐ Ⓑ Ⓒ Ⓓ	1 Ⓐ Ⓑ Ⓒ Ⓓ	1 Ⓐ Ⓑ Ⓒ Ⓓ	1 Ⓐ Ⓑ Ⓒ Ⓓ
2 Ⓐ Ⓑ Ⓒ Ⓓ	2 Ⓐ Ⓑ Ⓒ Ⓓ	2 Ⓐ Ⓑ Ⓒ Ⓓ	2 Ⓐ Ⓑ Ⓒ Ⓓ	2 Ⓐ Ⓑ Ⓒ Ⓓ
3 Ⓐ Ⓑ Ⓒ Ⓓ	3 Ⓐ Ⓑ Ⓒ Ⓓ	3 Ⓐ Ⓑ Ⓒ Ⓓ	3 Ⓐ Ⓑ Ⓒ Ⓓ	3 Ⓐ Ⓑ Ⓒ Ⓓ
4 Ⓐ Ⓑ Ⓒ Ⓓ	4 Ⓐ Ⓑ Ⓒ Ⓓ	4 Ⓐ Ⓑ Ⓒ Ⓓ	4 Ⓐ Ⓑ Ⓒ Ⓓ	4 Ⓐ Ⓑ Ⓒ Ⓓ

EXERCISE EIGHT: PRACTICE IN READING ANNOUNCEMENTS AND ADVERTISEMENTS

Passage One	Passage Two	Passage Three	Passage Four	Passage Five
1 Ⓐ Ⓑ Ⓒ Ⓓ	1 Ⓐ Ⓑ Ⓒ Ⓓ	1 Ⓐ Ⓑ Ⓒ Ⓓ	1 Ⓐ Ⓑ Ⓒ Ⓓ	1 Ⓐ Ⓑ Ⓒ Ⓓ
2 Ⓐ Ⓑ Ⓒ Ⓓ	2 Ⓐ Ⓑ Ⓒ Ⓓ	2 Ⓐ Ⓑ Ⓒ Ⓓ	2 Ⓐ Ⓑ Ⓒ Ⓓ	2 Ⓐ Ⓑ Ⓒ Ⓓ
3 Ⓐ Ⓑ Ⓒ Ⓓ	3 Ⓐ Ⓑ Ⓒ Ⓓ	3 Ⓐ Ⓑ Ⓒ Ⓓ	3 Ⓐ Ⓑ Ⓒ Ⓓ	3 Ⓐ Ⓑ Ⓒ Ⓓ
4 Ⓐ Ⓑ Ⓒ Ⓓ	4 Ⓐ Ⓑ Ⓒ Ⓓ	4 Ⓐ Ⓑ Ⓒ Ⓓ	4 Ⓐ Ⓑ Ⓒ Ⓓ	4 Ⓐ Ⓑ Ⓒ Ⓓ

EXERCISE NINE: PRACTICE IN READING ACADEMIC INFORMATION

Passage One	Passage Two	Passage Three	Passage Four	Passage Five
1 Ⓐ Ⓑ Ⓒ Ⓓ	1 Ⓐ Ⓑ Ⓒ Ⓓ	1 Ⓐ Ⓑ Ⓒ Ⓓ	1 Ⓐ Ⓑ Ⓒ Ⓓ	1 Ⓐ Ⓑ Ⓒ Ⓓ
2 Ⓐ Ⓑ Ⓒ Ⓓ	2 Ⓐ Ⓑ Ⓒ Ⓓ	2 Ⓐ Ⓑ Ⓒ Ⓓ	2 Ⓐ Ⓑ Ⓒ Ⓓ	2 Ⓐ Ⓑ Ⓒ Ⓓ
3 Ⓐ Ⓑ Ⓒ Ⓓ	3 Ⓐ Ⓑ Ⓒ Ⓓ	3 Ⓐ Ⓑ Ⓒ Ⓓ	3 Ⓐ Ⓑ Ⓒ Ⓓ	3 Ⓐ Ⓑ Ⓒ Ⓓ
4 Ⓐ Ⓑ Ⓒ Ⓓ	4 Ⓐ Ⓑ Ⓒ Ⓓ	4 Ⓐ Ⓑ Ⓒ Ⓓ	4 Ⓐ Ⓑ Ⓒ Ⓓ	4 Ⓐ Ⓑ Ⓒ Ⓓ

EXERCISE TEN: PRACTICE IN READING TEXTBOOKS

Passage One	Passage Two	Passage Three	Passage Four	Passage Five
1 Ⓐ Ⓑ Ⓒ Ⓓ	1 Ⓐ Ⓑ Ⓒ Ⓓ	1 Ⓐ Ⓑ Ⓒ Ⓓ	1 Ⓐ Ⓑ Ⓒ Ⓓ	1 Ⓐ Ⓑ Ⓒ Ⓓ
2 Ⓐ Ⓑ Ⓒ Ⓓ	2 Ⓐ Ⓑ Ⓒ Ⓓ	2 Ⓐ Ⓑ Ⓒ Ⓓ	2 Ⓐ Ⓑ Ⓒ Ⓓ	2 Ⓐ Ⓑ Ⓒ Ⓓ
3 Ⓐ Ⓑ Ⓒ Ⓓ	3 Ⓐ Ⓑ Ⓒ Ⓓ	3 Ⓐ Ⓑ Ⓒ Ⓓ	3 Ⓐ Ⓑ Ⓒ Ⓓ	3 Ⓐ Ⓑ Ⓒ Ⓓ
4 Ⓐ Ⓑ Ⓒ Ⓓ	4 Ⓐ Ⓑ Ⓒ Ⓓ	4 Ⓐ Ⓑ Ⓒ Ⓓ	4 Ⓐ Ⓑ Ⓒ Ⓓ	4 Ⓐ Ⓑ Ⓒ Ⓓ

EXERCISE ELEVEN: PRACTICE IN READING GENERAL INTEREST PASSAGES

Passage One	Passage Two	Passage Three	Passage Four	Passage Five
1 Ⓐ Ⓑ Ⓒ Ⓓ	1 Ⓐ Ⓑ Ⓒ Ⓓ	1 Ⓐ Ⓑ Ⓒ Ⓓ	1 Ⓐ Ⓑ Ⓒ Ⓓ	1 Ⓐ Ⓑ Ⓒ Ⓓ
2 Ⓐ Ⓑ Ⓒ Ⓓ	2 Ⓐ Ⓑ Ⓒ Ⓓ	2 Ⓐ Ⓑ Ⓒ Ⓓ	2 Ⓐ Ⓑ Ⓒ Ⓓ	2 Ⓐ Ⓑ Ⓒ Ⓓ
3 Ⓐ Ⓑ Ⓒ Ⓓ	3 Ⓐ Ⓑ Ⓒ Ⓓ	3 Ⓐ Ⓑ Ⓒ Ⓓ	3 Ⓐ Ⓑ Ⓒ Ⓓ	3 Ⓐ Ⓑ Ⓒ Ⓓ
4 Ⓐ Ⓑ Ⓒ Ⓓ	4 Ⓐ Ⓑ Ⓒ Ⓓ	4 Ⓐ Ⓑ Ⓒ Ⓓ	4 Ⓐ Ⓑ Ⓒ Ⓓ	4 Ⓐ Ⓑ Ⓒ Ⓓ

EXERCISE TWELVE: PRACTICE IN READING SENTENCES

Passage One	Passage Two	Passage Three	Passage Four	Passage Five
1 Ⓐ Ⓑ Ⓒ Ⓓ	1 Ⓐ Ⓑ Ⓒ Ⓓ	1 Ⓐ Ⓑ Ⓒ Ⓓ	1 Ⓐ Ⓑ Ⓒ Ⓓ	1 Ⓐ Ⓑ Ⓒ Ⓓ
2 Ⓐ Ⓑ Ⓒ Ⓓ	2 Ⓐ Ⓑ Ⓒ Ⓓ	2 Ⓐ Ⓑ Ⓒ Ⓓ	2 Ⓐ Ⓑ Ⓒ Ⓓ	2 Ⓐ Ⓑ Ⓒ Ⓓ
3 Ⓐ Ⓑ Ⓒ Ⓓ	3 Ⓐ Ⓑ Ⓒ Ⓓ	3 Ⓐ Ⓑ Ⓒ Ⓓ	3 Ⓐ Ⓑ Ⓒ Ⓓ	3 Ⓐ Ⓑ Ⓒ Ⓓ
4 Ⓐ Ⓑ Ⓒ Ⓓ	4 Ⓐ Ⓑ Ⓒ Ⓓ	4 Ⓐ Ⓑ Ⓒ Ⓓ	4 Ⓐ Ⓑ Ⓒ Ⓓ	4 Ⓐ Ⓑ Ⓒ Ⓓ

EXERCISE THIRTEEN: PRACTICE IN READING RESTATEMENTS

Passives	Negatives	Chronology	Comparatives	Conditionals
1 Ⓐ Ⓑ Ⓒ Ⓓ	1 Ⓐ Ⓑ Ⓒ Ⓓ	1 Ⓐ Ⓑ Ⓒ Ⓓ	1 Ⓐ Ⓑ Ⓒ Ⓓ	1 Ⓐ Ⓑ Ⓒ Ⓓ
2 Ⓐ Ⓑ Ⓒ Ⓓ	2 Ⓐ Ⓑ Ⓒ Ⓓ	2 Ⓐ Ⓑ Ⓒ Ⓓ	2 Ⓐ Ⓑ Ⓒ Ⓓ	2 Ⓐ Ⓑ Ⓒ Ⓓ
3 Ⓐ Ⓑ Ⓒ Ⓓ	3 Ⓐ Ⓑ Ⓒ Ⓓ	3 Ⓐ Ⓑ Ⓒ Ⓓ	3 Ⓐ Ⓑ Ⓒ Ⓓ	3 Ⓐ Ⓑ Ⓒ Ⓓ
4 Ⓐ Ⓑ Ⓒ Ⓓ	4 Ⓐ Ⓑ Ⓒ Ⓓ	4 Ⓐ Ⓑ Ⓒ Ⓓ	4 Ⓐ Ⓑ Ⓒ Ⓓ	4 Ⓐ Ⓑ Ⓒ Ⓓ
5 Ⓐ Ⓑ Ⓒ Ⓓ	5 Ⓐ Ⓑ Ⓒ Ⓓ	5 Ⓐ Ⓑ Ⓒ Ⓓ	5 Ⓐ Ⓑ Ⓒ Ⓓ	5 Ⓐ Ⓑ Ⓒ Ⓓ

Concessions	Other
1 Ⓐ Ⓑ Ⓒ Ⓓ	1 Ⓐ Ⓑ Ⓒ Ⓓ
2 Ⓐ Ⓑ Ⓒ Ⓓ	2 Ⓐ Ⓑ Ⓒ Ⓓ
3 Ⓐ Ⓑ Ⓒ Ⓓ	3 Ⓐ Ⓑ Ⓒ Ⓓ
4 Ⓐ Ⓑ Ⓒ Ⓓ	4 Ⓐ Ⓑ Ⓒ Ⓓ
5 Ⓐ Ⓑ Ⓒ Ⓓ	5 Ⓐ Ⓑ Ⓒ Ⓓ